THE DECLINE OF
THE MEDIEVAL CHURCH

Volume One

The Decline

of the

Medieval Church

Volume One

BY

ALEXANDER CLARENCE FLICK, Ph.D., Litt.D., Ll.D.

NEW YORK
ALFRED A. KNOPF
1930

PRINTED IN GREAT BRITAIN BY
STEPHEN AUSTIN AND SONS, LTD., HERTFORD

CONTENTS

PART I: THE BABYLONIAN CAPTIVITY

v

CONTENTS

PAGE

CONTENTS

PART II : THE GREAT WESTERN SCHISM

CHAPTER VIII : THE GREAT WESTERN SCHISM   249

DECLINE OF THE MEDIEVAL CHURCH

PART I

THE BABYLONIAN CAPTIVITY

CHAPTER I

ATTACK ON THE POLITICAL SUPREMACY OF THE PAPACY

1. *The Medieval Church at close of the Thirteenth Century*

AT the end of the thirteenth century the ecclesiastical empire of Rome was the widest in territorial extent that up to that time had been obtained under any of the Pontiffs. With the exception of southern Spain, the Pope's rule was unquestioned throughout all Central and Western Europe. At the same time plans were being made continually to recapture the places lost in the East.[1] Not only were overtures for unification made with the Armenians, the Russians, and the Greeks; but missionaries were also sent to labour among the Mongols, the Mohammedans, the Persians, and the Chinese. Meanwhile the obligation to wage a holy crusade against all infidels and heretics was ever kept vividly before the imaginations of the Christian princes.

Under the great Pope Innocent III (*d.* 1216) and his sixteen successors in the thirteenth century, upon the accession of Boniface VIII in the year 1294, the Medieval Church had attained the extreme limits of its power. Its dogma had been elaborated and accepted; its canon law had been developed and generally enforced; its hierarchical machinery for governmental purposes had been completed and was in full operation. The complete sway of the papal monarchy over the Church had been universally recognized and the right of the Pope to interfere in the affairs of the European States had been established.[2] With the overthrow of the Hohenstaufen emperors, the Pope stood forth in strong relief as the sole heir and representative of the claim of ancient Rome to universal rule. This universality of papal supremacy was not only ably defended by keen ecclesiastical jurists, by the canon law, by the legislation of numerous councils, and by many historical precedents; but also by the brainiest theologians

---

[1] In 1291, Acre, the last Christian possession in the East, was lost.
[2] Creighton, *History of the Papacy*, i, 25.

of the thirteenth century, such as Albertus Magnus, Duns Scotus, and Thomas Aquinas, who sought to prove that submission to the Roman Pontiff was required of every human being. Thomas Aquinas made the most sweeping statement of the papal theory when he asserted that, under the authority of the New Testament, kings must be subject to the Pope because he had the right to deprive heretical and schismatic rulers of all their authority and to release subjects from their civil obedience. The Angelic Doctor further asserted that Christ had invested the Pope with universal authority over the Church and hence he could not err; consequently it followed that the Church must rule the State, and hence the Church must be controlled by a monarchy sufficiently strong to preserve the unity of faith and to overthrow unbelievers.[1] To enforce these pretensions a veritable papal army, both priestly and monkish, covered Christendom to carry out the Pope's will and to compel obedience to it. Thus the Papacy with the finest organization since the days of Rome, defended by the keenest intellects of the Middle Ages, in possession of a powerful army obedient to every demand, with frightened princes ready to draw the sword for its defence against all enemies, internal or external, and with the credulous and intensely religious masses accepting its claims and prerogatives, was unquestionably the dominant power in European civilization in the thirteenth century.

The fact must be kept clearly in mind that during the thirteenth century the Roman Church consciously perpetuated the Imperial Roman Empire and sought to exercise its prerogatives to the point of monopoly. The theological literature of the day was full of illustrations of the Church as the lord, the soul, and the sun, while the State was the servant, the body, and the moon. As a result the century was replete with conflicts between the papal and secular powers, and, with the fall of the Hohenstaufen house, ended in the triumph of the papal hierarchy. Papal supremacy was well nigh undisputed. The kingdoms of Aragon, Portugal, Sicily, and England were papal fiefs; a Latin Empire had been established at Constantinople; the Armenians bowed to the authority of the Pope; France and Germany were submissive. The Pope, changed from the vicar of Peter to the vicar of

[1] *Opuscula contra errores Graæcorum ; De regimine principium.*

Christ on earth, had become the real Roman Emperor, and held the law and peace of the world in his hand.[1]

Furthermore, to keep the masses of the laity steady in their faith and loyal to the Church, the greatest emphasis was laid on the religious observance of the rites and ceremonies of the Church. The seven sacraments, by this time completely elaborated and ably defended, covered the whole span of human life from the cradle to the grave, while the laity were taught that only through their efficacy could salvation be assured. Transubstantiation, the miraculous mystery of mysteries, whose possession seemed in itself to be a positive guarantee of the truth of Christianity and of the divine nature of the Church, had been accepted as a dogma since the pontificate of Innocent III.[2] Confession to a priest was made obligatory upon all and the power to forgive sins was a mighty weapon in the hands of the sacerdotal class. Indulgences or pardons had come to assume an important rôle by the thirteenth century.[3] The rapid growth in this traffic was due to three important changes: (1) the theory of the treasury of the merits; (2) the development of the institution into the sacrament of penance; and (3) the recognition of a new type of repentance called attribution. Alexander of Hales about 1230 first formulated the theory of the " treasury " and Clement VI confirmed it in 1450. The worship of Mary, the veneration of saints, and the use of relics were developed to a point where they played an important rôle in the religious life of the period.

It must not be forgotten either that, along with its activities in many fields, the Church was deeply interested in soul-saving. The Begging Orders, which originated at the beginning of the thirteenth century, made such a propagandism their business— so much so indeed that the priests complained to the Pope about their encroachments. Preaching by the secular clergy was very common and much of it of a deeply pious character. The wicked were urged to repentance for their evil deeds, and were exhorted to shun the power of the devil over their souls. There existed throughout the Church generally a terrific

[1] Bezold, *Geschichte der deutchen Reformation*, 1.
[2] Hardouin, *Concil.*, viii, 16, 17.
[3] Arnold and Addis, *Catholic Dictionary*, " Indulgences." Thomas Aquinas in *Suppl.* qu. lxxi, a. 10, said that such indulgences were common in his day.

religious fervour—in part a resultant of the crusades and in part a product of the activity of the Begging Orders—which found expression in reputed miracles, in visions and direct divine revelations, in conflicts with the devil, in ecstatic experiences and " stigmatizations ", in flagellations, and other pious excesses, in various types of mysticism, and in many other peculiar phases and manifestations of fanatic piety.

2. *Forces undermining the Papacy*

On the surface of things, and to the short-sighted medieval ecclesiastical opportunist, it looked as if the papal system was everywhere triumphant. But certain forces were already appearing in Western Europe to dispute the lofty and sweeping claims of the Papacy and to weaken the tremendous power wielded by the head of the Roman Church. The causes which were undermining hierarchical authority and pretensions at this time were political, intellectual, economic, and social.

The power of the Medieval Church was due in a large measure to the absence of efficient secular rulers backed up by loyal subjects and an adequate military force. During the period of feudal anarchy the Church easily assumed the functions of the State in maintaining order, in administering justice, in caring for the unfortunate, and in encouraging industry and learning. Nor can anyone gainsay the invaluable service it rendered in these important fields. On the other hand, when the modern national states like France and England began to emerge and felt able to manage their own affairs, to protect their subjects in life and property, and to mete out justice, they attempted to make themselves politically independent of the clergy and the Pope. Educated laymen and civil lawyers became more numerous and gradually replaced the churchmen as counsellors and assistants to royalty. The rise of the national state and the new system of political science on which it rested, together with the able publicists who so successfully defended it, mark a most significant transition from the medieval era to the modern period in the history of Western Europe. This new force not only challenged the validity of the ground taken by Gregory VII and Innocent III in asserting and establishing the supremacy of the Papacy, but it was also largely instrumental in disrupting the feudal system which so generally determined the social, industrial, and political relations of men, and likewise powerfully augmented the hierarchical assumptions of the Roman Church.

In England, more isolated and furthest removed from Continental influences, strivings for national organization began very early. William the Conqueror was not wanting in respect for the Holy See,[1] but when Gregory VII demanded the payment of Peter's pence and homage as a feudal vassal that sovereign replied: " The one claim (Peter's pence) I admit, the other I do not admit, nor am I willing now, inasmuch as I have never promised it, nor do I discover that my predecessors ever did it to your predecessors." [2] Under Henry II much was done to create a strong government and to reform the administration of justice. The Constitutions of Clarendon in 1164[3] revealed a disposition to limit papal jurisdiction by transferring certain cases from the ecclesiastical courts to the king's court ; by restraining appeals to Rome ; by preventing the excommunication of the king's officers ; and by sanctioning the king's appropriation of the revenues of bishoprics and abbeys. Magna Charta in 1215 marks, as Stubbs so well asserts, "the consummation of the work for which unconsciously kings, prelates, and lawyers had been labouring for a century, the summing up of one period of national life and the starting point of another." [4] It was a significant expression of the united barons, speaking for the nation, to assert their national rights against the hostile opposition of both king and Pope.

By the end of the thirteenth century England was a well organized national state. The royal powers were clearly defined, and the rights of the nation plainly outlined. The expression of the nation's will was made through the Model Parliament called in 1295 by Edward I. The policy of national expansion had been inaugurated and already Ireland (1159),[5] Wales (1282), and Scotland (1296),[6] as well as a large part of France, were claimed as fiefs of the English Crown. The outbreak of the Hundred Years War was doing much to arouse

[1] Davis, *England under Normans and Angevins* **54.**
[2] Lee, *Source Book*, 121 ; Gee and Hardy, *Documents*, 57.
[3] Stubbs, *Select Charters*, 135–40 ; Gee and Hardy, *Documents*, 68–70.
[4] Stubbs, *Const. Hist.*, ii, 1.
[5] Cf. Thatcher, " Studies Concerning Adrian IV " in the fourth vol. of *Pub. of Chi. Univ.*, Dec., 1903.
[6] Stevenson, *Documents*, ii, **37.**

a national patriotic spirit, and thus a soul was added to the body of the national state. England, in consequence of these momentous transformations, was in both a position and a mood to resist papal interference in national affairs when Boniface VIII became Pope in 1294. Upon Boniface's attempting to prevent Edward I from assuming the Scottish crown on the ground that it was a papal fief, of remote antiquity,[1] the English Parliament in 1301 promptly retorted that the English king was under no obligation to the Papal See for his temporal acts.[2] " The kings of England neither have been wont to answer, nor ought to answer, touching their rights for the said kingdom, or any other temporal rights, before any judge, ecclesiastical or secular, by the free preëminence of the state of their royal dignity, and of custom irrefragably observed at all times." [3] Edward I is reported to have asserted : " I will defend my right that is known to all the world with all my might." [4] He sent the Pope a long statement of the historical grounds upon which he based his claims to independence.[5] This defiant attitude culminated in that famous letter of remonstrance against Papal oppression in 1397.[6] By this time, says Green, modern England had practically appeared, since the king, lords, commons, courts of justice, language, patriotism, and society itself had " all taken the shape which they still essentially retain ".

The Musselman invasion of Spain was the fundamental agency that affected a fusion of the Celtic, Roman, and Gothic elements into one people, with a common consciousness of right and wrong, a common religion, a common history, and a common aspiration for nationality. The conflict between the Mohammedans and Christians in Spain continued for eight centuries before complete political unity was realized. The first important advance in political unification was made in the thirteenth century, when the small kingdoms were reduced to three, namely, Portugal, Aragon, and Castile, which alone by the close of the century ruled over more than half of Spain. Meanwhile the spirit and consciousness of

[1] Rymer, *Foedera*, ii, 860.
[2] Rymer, *Foedera*, ii, 860 ; Walter of Hemingburgh, *Chron.*, ii, 211.
[3] Walter of Hemingburgh, *Chron.*, ii, 212.
[4] Walsingham, *Annales, Rolls Ser.*, London, quoted in *Dict. of Nat. Biog.* in the article on Edward I.
[5] Rymer, *Foedera*, ii, 863.   [6] Stubbs, *Const. Hist.*, ii, 156.

nationality were growing. The marriage of Ferdinand and Isabella, in 1469, and the conquest of Granada in 1492, completed the process, and Spain took her place among the national states of Europe to play a leading rôle for centuries.[1]

In Italy and Germany the yearnings and at times the positive endeavours to create a true national state never came to full fruition until the nineteenth century. The two powerful factors which prevented such a political development in Italy were the Papacy and the union of Italy with the Holy Roman Empire. In Germany the assumption of the title of Emperor by the kings prevented them from creating a true nation. For three centuries after Otto the Great the German rulers endeavoured to unify Germany and at the same time to dominate Italy and the Papacy. This colossal task proved to be so difficult of attainment that after endless wars and incalculable sacrifices in men and money they lost all. Italy was wrested away from Germany, the Papacy obtained its complete independence, and the German kingdom, instead of developing into a strong monarchy like that of France and England, practically broke up into many small weak states with almost complete independence. The defeat and death of the Hohenstaufen Emperor, Frederick II (1212–50) virtually brought the Medieval Empire to an end. Rudolf of Hapsburg was elected King of Germany, and thereafter few German kings, although they continued to call themselves emperors, regarded it as worth while to go to Rome for Papal coronation. No serious effort was ever again made to reconquer Italy. By the close of the thirteenth century Germany, hopelessly divided into a confused group of small states, had lost her leadership in ecclesiastical matters, was forced to see her prestige pass over to France, and did not regain her ascendency until the Reformation. Italy likewise was broken up into independent states and for centuries was a victim of local wars and foreign conquests.

In France the process of centralizing royal power and of developing a genuine national state began with the Capetian kings. Philip Augustus (1180–1223) greatly extended the royal domain, chiefly at the expense of the English king, strengthened his control over all classes of his subjects, and

---

[1] Burke, *Hist. of Spain*, 2nd ed., Lond., 1900; Watts, *The Christian Recovery of Spain*, N.Y., 1894.

at the same time by tactful concessions he increased his authority over the important towns.   Philip's grandson, the heroic and popular Louis IX (1226–70), improved the government and greatly increased royal power by systemizing justice and taxation and by seeking the advice and assistance of a council made up of the powerful nobles and prelates. This body was divided into three sections : first, the king's council for aid in general matters ; secondly, a chamber of accounts to look after the revenues ; thirdly, the parliament to act as a supreme court with its seat fixed at Paris.   It was left to his grandson, Philip IV, called the Fair (1285–1314), first to play the rôle of an absolute monarch in France.   To begin with he had inherited the best organized and best administered government the country had known up to that time.   He surrounded himself with keen civil lawyers, who had derived their ideas of a monarch's prerogatives from a study of the Roman law and who encouraged Philip to gather up into his own hands the full reins of rule regardless of the privileges of his vassals and the clergy.   Philip IV expelled the clergy from all participation in the administration of the law and made the lawyers supreme in the courts.   They became, in consequence, the stoutest and ablest defenders of French political independence of the Papacy.   Through these wise and efficacious means the decentralizing influences of feudalism were crushed and the foundations for the most powerful monarchy of Europe were laid.

With the development of royalty in France also came a national consciousness, a common language, a common tradition and history, and a common patriotism which made France a strong national state ready to support the king in defending its rights against the pretensions and claims of the Pope.

From this brief survey of the new political forces appearing in Europe in the thirteenth century, it is apparent that from three sources, at least, the assumptions of the Roman Papacy to universal temporal supremacy would not go unquestioned. In the first place the dawning consciousness of nationality among the people of England, France, Spain, and indeed even of Germany and Italy, began to resent the extreme claims of the Pope.   In the second place, powerful monarchs like the kings of England, France, and Spain, and also the weaker rulers in Germany and Italy, supported by their subjects, were ready to assert their political independence of Rome. In the third place many educated lay lawyers, imbued with the fundamentals of the revised Roman law, were prepared to supply the arguments which would overthrow the claims of the head of the Medieval Church to general secular jurisdiction over Western Europe. The opening years of the fourteenth century were to witness a bold attack by these forces upon Papal supremacy, which greatly weakened its control.

The history of the fourteenth century vividly describes the decay of the feudal and hierarchical institutions of the Middle Ages. The concepts of a universal Papacy and Empire, both of which were the products of the Latin attempt at the organization of human society,[1] presented themselves in altered relations, languishing and threatened with ruin. The absolute dominion of the Papacy in the thirteenth century, unable either to compel obedience or to compromise with the new forces of the fourteenth century, was turned with suicidal policy against itself in the Babylonian Captivity, the Great Western Schism, the Reform Councils, and the Reformation. It led to the corruption of the Church in countless abuses ; it aroused the reformatory spirit in Western Christendom ; it encouraged bold thinkers, both orthodox and heretical, to attack the fundamental foundations on which the Papacy rested ; and it challenged the political powers of Western Europe to dispute and to defy the Papal claims to secular supremacy.

The intellectual awakening was seen in the rise of the universities and schools ; in the appearance of a large number of educated laymen who were eager to play a part in the civilization of the day outside of the sphere of the clergy ; in the rejuvenated and intensified scholasticism ; in the revival of art in many fields ; in the increase of the study of Roman law ; and in the new spirit of inquiry noticeable on all sides.[2] These forces were to be largely arrayed against the extreme Papal pretensions and were in consequence undermining Papal authority. The emancipation of culture from the harsh and narrow confines of ecclesiastics transferred it from the cloister

---

[1] Gregorovius, *Rome in the M.A.*, vi, pt. i, 1.
[2] Rashdall, *The Universities of Europe in the Middle Ages ;* Taylor, *The Mediæval Mind*, 2nd ed., ii, ch. 38.

to the court of the prince or knight, or to the burghers of the free towns. The appearance of educated laymen changed the entire literary output. The joyous, worldly side of life was emphasized in place of the ascetic, spiritual view. As a result of this new element, opposition to sacerdotalism and to the Papacy and a pronounced religious indifference appeared.[1] Walter von der Vogelweide (d. 1230) wrote sharp polemics against the Roman Curia's ambitions for worldly power and possessions. Wolfram of Eschenbach (d. 1220), Hartmann von der Aue (d. 1220), Henry of Isernia (d. 1270), and Gottfried von Strassburg (d. 1230?), all revealed the same bent of mind. Dante (d. 1321) came somewhat later, but he displayed the same hostility to Papal desire for secular supremacy.

The day had passed when the Church completely monopolized the intelligence of the peoples of Western Europe. Consequently from the thirteenth century on a more rational spirit began to manifest itself. Roger Bacon (d. 1292) called attention to the possibilities of scientific experimentation. Henry of Gent (d. 1293) dared to criticize the Begging Orders. Niccola Pisano (d. 1280) and Giovanni Pisano (d. 1328) ignored monkish ideals and, as independent laymen, went back to pagan Rome to study sculpture. In painting the first wide-awake laymen were Cimabue (d. 1302) and Giotto (d. 1336), the pioneers and forerunners of the Renaissance, in whose works can be clearly seen the conflict between medieval asceticism and the new age that was gradually dawning.

The Roman Pontiffs of the thirteenth and fourteenth centuries were unfortunately too immersed in their own narrow schemes of self-interest; hence they lost their greatest asset and real strength, namely, the respect, sympathy, obedience, and defence of Europe. They should have stoutly upheld ecclesiastical independence, but instead they them-selves oppressed the clergy and infringed upon their rights. Hence the clergy in countries like France co-operated with the lawyers in developing a revolutionary conception of the liberties of the Gallican Church, which emphasized the freedom of election by chapters, the independence of the patrons of ecclesiastical benefices from papal control or interference, and

---

[1] The troubadours of Southern France, the religious ballads of Northern France, the Christian songs of Spain, the *Song of Roland*, and the minnisingers in Germany. See Anglada, *Les Troubadours*, Paris, 1908.

a denial of Papal taxation without the consent of the French Church and Crown. The Popes ceased to champion civil liberties, had no sympathy with the cause of the people, and consequently were ranked with European princes. In England as a rule the Pope sided with the king, while the clergy were the most stubborn element in opposing royal oppression. In Italy, likewise, the Popes gave no support to the popular party, which in each city was seeking to preserve municipal freedom against foreign aggression and tyrannical princes. The Popes used republican allies in Italy to reduce the power of the Empire, it is true, but when that victory was won they were intolerant of civil liberties and sanctioned the suicidal policy of permitting powerful nobles to suppress republican constitutions and to establish dynasties. In a word, the Papacy had become a great political institution. Its spiritual strength and significance were lost in its worldly ambition and secular importance. Not a saintly monk, but a hard-headed statesman was necessary to its continued supremacy. Consequently, a conflict with the new political forces in Europe was inevitable.[1]

3. *Origin of the quarrel between Boniface VIII and Philip IV*

When the pious but weak and incapable old hermit Pope Celestine V,[2] staggered by the responsibilities of his high office, abdicated the Papal throne in 1294, after four months of feeble rule, to the joy of the cardinals and the sorrow of the people of Rome, he was succeeded by Boniface VIII.

The pontificate of Boniface VIII marks a notable epoch in the history of the Latin Church. On his father's side he was of Spanish origin, but through his mother he represented an ancient family of Roman counts which had given to the Church Innocent IV, Gregory IX, and Alexander IV. Born at Anagni, near Rome, in 1221, he studied civil and canon law in Rome and probably at Paris, received his doctorate, and soon became a recognized expert lawyer.[3] It appears that he served as a canon at Anagni, Todi, Paris, and Rome, and about 1276 he became associated with the Roman Curia and soon rose to prominence. In 1281, at the age of 60, he was made cardinal and represented the Papal See as legate to

---

[1] Creighton, i, 27.
[2] Schulz, *Peter von Murrhone*, Berlin, 1894. A doctor's dissertation.
[3] Finke, *Bonifaz VIII*, 6, disputes the assertion of Bulæus that he studied in Paris.

France and England. His election as Pope occurred at Naples on 24th December, 1294 ; but apparently it was not popular with the Neapolitans, who seem to have had little faith in him.[1] Charles II of Naples accompanied him to Rome, where he was crowned with unusual splendour. The kings of Naples and Hungary walked by his side as, robed in full pontificals and crowned, he rode his white palfrey through the kneeling crowds on his way to the Lateran accompanied by representatives of the Roman nobility.

The inauguration of Boniface VIII looked propitious, but troublous times were ahead. He found the Papacy at the height of its power ; he died leaving it humbled and weak. His ideals were as lofty as those of Hildebrand ; his ambitious pretensions to authority as great as those of Innocent III. He stood confidently on the ground tilled by the former and sowed by the latter, but his harvest was a failure. The causes for the decline of Papal power during his pontificate are quite clear and easily explained.

1. Boniface was an old man on the verge of four-score years when elected.[2] Although still very energetic, keen of intellect, and strong of will, yet he was woefully wanting in common courtesy, human tact, and a compromising spirit. He was overbearing, blunt, implacable, egotistic to an offensive degree, and possessed of a blind, insatiable thirst for power.[3] He was deplorably lacking in wisdom and discernment. Indeed, a more unfortunate choice of Pope at this critical period could not have been made.

2. The times had changed—new forces had appeared in Europe to challenge the claims of the Papacy. These new forces could not be ignored, nor scolded away, nor even frightened into silence by Papal thunders and penalties. They had to be met and either destroyed or compromised with. Boniface, in his blindness, took no account of the new intellectual awakening of Europe. Apparently he was entirely unaware, likewise, of the significant social and industrial stirrings among

---

[1] Finke, 45. For the conflict between the Orsini and Colonna factions in the College of Cardinals, see Huyskens, *Kard. Nap. Orsini,* Marburg, 1902, 28 ff.

[2] Drumann, 4 ; Gregorovius, v, part ii, 596. Finke, 3, makes Boniface fifteen years younger.

[3] He had his inoffensive predecessor imprisoned for the rest of his life. This action may have been justified as a simple measure of prudence, but the alleged barbarous treatment of Celestine, if true, cannot be condoned. It gave his enemies a chance to charge him with murder.

the masses.   He made no allowance for the new spirit of
nationality showing itself in England, France, and elsewhere.
He either stubbornly refused or else was impotent to gauge
correctly the strength of the forces arrayed against him.

3. The open and disgraceful quarrel with Philip IV of
France ended in the mortifying defeat of Boniface personally
and in the weakening of the prestige held by the Papacy since
the period of Gregory VII.   Personal enemies made serious
but in part groundless charges against his character and his
faith.   The French accused him of outright infidelity and even
of denying the immortality of the soul.   Dante, who visited
Rome during his rule, denounced him as " the prince of modern
pharisees ",[1] a usurper " who turned the Vatican hill into a
common sewer of corruption ", and assigned him a place in
the lowest circles of hell.[2]   A contemporary put these words
into the mouth of Celestine V, summing up his whole career :
" He came in like a fox, he ruled like a lion, and he died like
a dog." [3]   He reigned for nine troubled years, but scarcely
achieved a single decisive triumph.   His pontificate marks the
beginning of the decline of the power and glory of the Medieval
Papacy.

The haughty demeanour and senile arrogance of Boniface
is seen in the abject submission of Albrecht, the German
Emperor.   The German envoys were received by the proud
old Pontiff, seated on a throne, with a crown upon his head
and a sword in his hand, as he exclaimed : " I, I am the
Emperor ! " [4]   The servile Albrecht accepted his crown as a
gift and acknowledged that the empire had been transferred
from the Greeks to the Germans by the Pope, and that the
German electors owed the right of election to the Apostolic See.

Boniface incurred the bitter hatred of the proud Colonna
family in Rome by attempting to dictate the disposition of
the family estates.   Failing in that he excommunicated them

---

[1] *Inferno*, xxvii, 85.

[2] *Paradiso*, xxx, 147. Dante further declared that Boniface had shattered
Christendom (*Par*. 71 : 15), and had to do penance among the simoniacs (*Inf*.
19 : 77).   Peter complained that since Boniface held his seat with unrighteousness and had changed his burial city into a cloaca of blood and stinks even
Lucifer did not rejoice (*Par*., 27 : 25).   A wolf was given the leadership of the
lambs (*Par*., 9 : 132).

[3] Muratori, xi, 528.

[4] Boniface is said to have added the second crown to the tiara indicative
of temporal power.   *Cath. Encyc.*, ii, 666.

and peremptorily confiscated their property and gave it to his own nephews. Other instances of his proclivity for interfering are noteworthy. He endeavoured to settle the rival claims of Charles II and James II to Sicily. The Sicilians revolted, however, and chose Frederick, the younger brother of James II, as their ruler. Boniface excommunicated Frederick and put Sicily under interdict, but in the end he lost and was forced to recognize Frederick in 1302. Venice and Genoa rejected the Pope's command to make a truce in 1296, and concluded peace in 1299, without consulting him. Boniface also failed to restore order in Florence and Tuscany. In 1296 he attempted to force France and England to conclude a truce, but both Edward I and Philip IV resented his interference in their affairs. Nor were his efforts to secure a general European peace in order to instigate a crusade against Islam any more successful. Boniface did not comprehend the meaning of these rebuffs.

The Jubilee of 1300, apparently the first celebration of the centenary of the birth of Christ,[1] however, was a conspicuous success.[2] Rome was crowded with pilgrims. Villani, an eye witness, asserts that there was a constant pilgrim population of 200,000 and that 30,000 arrived and left the city daily. The offerings were so generous that two clerics stood night and day by the altar of St. Peter's raking in the coins. But it is ominously significant that no prince or king from north of the Alps went to Rome during the Jubilee. Nevertheless, backed up by the loyalty of devoted hordes of pilgrims from every part of Europe and relying upon his full Papal treasury, Boniface, in his egotistic arrogance, feared no foe.

The predominate event of Boniface's pontificate was his unfortunate and disastrous conflict with France. The immediate cause of the quarrel was the question of taxing Church property by a secular ruler for national defence. Philip IV was waging a war against England and covered at least a part of the cost at the expense of the Church, whose clergy were sorely taxed in 1294 and 1296. The French clergy,

---

[1] Thurston, *The Holy Year of Jubilee*, London, 1900.
[2] The bull authorizing the Jubilee is given in *Mirbt*, Quellen, 147; Thatcher and McNeal, 313; Potthast, 24917; Henderson, *Hist. Docs.*, 349; Friedburg, ii, 1303.

with Papal permission, had often granted large sums to the king, but always for the purpose, real or alleged, of a holy crusade against the enemies of the Church.[1] Consequently some of the French clergy complained to Rome against the authorized levying of taxes for purely secular warfare. Fundamentally the principle involved in the controversy was that of the Medieval Papacy against a modern national state, and that issue was something new. The antagonism between the sweeping claims of the Papacy to universal temporal sovereignty, on the one hand, and the modern doctrine of nationality, which was for the first time defined with a fair degree of clearness in England and France in the thirteenth century, on the other hand, was obvious to both sides.

The fundamental significance of this controversy does not lie in the personal hostility between Philip IV and Boniface VIII ; nor in a conflict between the King of France and the Pope. The vital question involved was the strife for mastery between two essentially different sets of ideas, theories, and principles. One was royal, national, political, modern ; the other was Papal, universal, ecclesiastical, and medieval. So far as the contest was one between temporal and spiritual authority and supremacy, it was not new. The rivalry between the imperial and Papal powers parallels all medieval history and constitutes the major portion of it. But when a national state like France assumed the burden of conflict it marked the dawn of a new era. The Emperor Henry IV, in his struggle with Pope Gregory VII, stood for the political independence of the Empire. Philip IV embodied in his claim the independence of a modern national state. He represented a conscious, unified nation whose rights were clearly understood and ably defended by a body of keen statesmen and publicists, who spoke of the French nation as a new creation and said of the French monarchs : " The kings of the modern French people do not follow in the footsteps of their predecessors." [2] The leaders and thinkers of all Europe saw that this struggle was one between two forces, a universal theocracy and the peoples of Western Europe organized politically on a national basis, and that each one was supported by reason, history, and law. It was just because the fourteenth century

---

[1] For statistics, see Bourgain in *Rev. des quest. hist.*, 1890, xlviii, 62.
[2] Finke, p. lxxxvi.

was to witness the first series of test cases of the clash that it becomes one of the most interesting and most important periods in European history. The questions raised then have occupied the attention of Europe ever since and are not yet definitely settled either in principle or fact.

The roots of this dispute ran back beyond the pontificate of Boniface VIII. As early as 1287 Philip IV ordered that all temporal cases be tried by laymen and thus excluded the clergy from juries and judgeships. This measure was followed the next year by an act cutting the clergy off from the supreme parlement, which was a hard blow on the ecclesiastics. Next, in order to meet the expenses of his war against Edward I of England, which began in 1294, he levied a tax, called the *maltote*, on all persons, thus of course including the clergy,[1] who immediately appealed to the Pope. Meanwhile, Boniface had been elected as head of the Church and sought to bring peace to Christendom by offering his services as arbiter in the Hundred Years War. His offer was rejected, however, by both sovereigns, who peremptorily resented such interference in their dynastic affairs.

The bad feeling engendered in this way was brought to a head when, on 24th February, 1296, Boniface issued his famous bull *Clericis laicus*.[2] The document was written in general terms, but was ordered to be promulgated in France and England with the intention of intimidating Edward I and Philip IV. It affirmed in positive terms the subjection of the state to the Papal See and consequently denied to kings all jurisdiction over both the persons and the property of the priesthood. The bull clearly stated that all taxation of Church property without the Pope's consent was to be resisted by the clergy as illegal. Both clergy and rulers alike, who violated the law, were to suffer the penalty of excommunication. The Pope certainly had precedent on his side. The Lateran Councils of 1179 and 1215 had both enacted similar legislation. Alexander V in 1260 had expressly exempted the clergy from such special taxation, and Nicholas IV in 1291 had emphatically warned Philip IV of France against using ecclesiastical funds for his own schemes without permission.

---

[1] Cf. Christophe, *Histoire de la papauté*, 394–6.
[2] Henderson, 432 ; Thatcher and McNeal, 311 ; Robinson, i, 488.

On 3rd November, 1296, Edward I held a parliament at Bury St Edmunds. The laity made their customary grants to the king. The clergy, however, having in mind the threats of the Papal bull *Clericis laicos*, authorized Archbishop Winchelsey to inform the king that it was impossible for them to grant him anything.[1] Edward ordered them to reconsider the matter and let him know their final decision by 14th January, 1297. On that date he sent proctors to the clergy, who were met in council at St Paul's to decide the question of a subsidy. The proctors first set forth the dangers besetting the kingdom and then declared that unless the clergy granted a sufficient sum for the defence of the country, the king and lords would treat their revenues as might seem good to them. Six days later the obstinate clergy sent a deputation to the king to announce that they found themselves unable to make any grant. In anger the king declared that he would outlaw the whole body of the clergy and take their lay fees into his own hands.[2] The clergy of York under this threat submitted and made a grant. Winchelsey personally refused to yield and sacrificed his lay estates, but wisely advised his clergy to make the best terms they could individually, which they did quickly enough. Thus the English Church yielded to royal force, but did not surrender the principle involved, nor give up their historic rights. The king got the money but won only a partial victory.[3] In this clashing of conflicting powers, the most significant incident was the fact that the laity gave their undivided support to their monarch as their supreme protector.

Philip IV regarded the Papal bull *Clericis laicos* as a favour to his enemy and an insult to himself ; consequently, with the assistance of his able court lawyers, he sought to annul the bull by means of two ordinances. The first act forbade all foreigners entering France and thus excluded the Pope's emissaries. The second measure prohibited the exportation of gold and silver, provisions, arms, and horses from France without the king's written permission. The purpose of the latter decree was clearly two-fold : to injure England and to

---

[1] *Ann. Dunstable*, 405 ; Cotton, *Historia Anglicana*, 314.   [2] Ib., 318.
[3] Under Edward III, on the advice of Wiclif, Parliament repudiated the feudal fee promised by King John, and it was never again paid. Poole, *Wiclif and Movements for Reform*, 5.

cut off all French contributions to the Papal treasury. The
Roman Church drew much of its revenues from France, hence
it was a severe blow to have the numerous Papal collectors
banished.

To a haughty letter from Boniface, threatening punishment,
Philip replied that the king of France had ruled over his
realm before there were any Popes ; that " The Holy Mother
Church . . . is composed not only of clergy but of laity " ;
that Christ himself said : " Render unto Cæsar the things that
are Cæsar's," and hence the Church should heed it ; and
that the clergy were citizens of the State, enjoyed its protection,
and consequently should help to support it. The French
bishops strengthened the king's position by siding with him,
and begged the Pope to recall the bull.[1]

Boniface was a politician with sufficient shrewdness to see
that it would be a great misfortune to lose the goodwill of
France at a time when England was hostile, when the French
clergy were inclined to uphold the king, and when a party in
Rome led by the powerful Colonna family was opposing him.
Hence he tried to explain away the bull *Clericis laicos* by the
bull *Inefabilis amor*, issued on 20th September, 1296.[2] In that
document he told the French monarch that by quarrelling with
the head of the Church he was imperilling his own dynastic
interests. He professed the greatest affection for France
and declared that he did not forbid the clergy from giving
financial support to the State, but only insisted upon exercising
his prerogative of first giving his consent. If the French nation
were really in grave danger, he declared that he would even
order the Church to sell her sacred vessels and crosses to
ensure relief. Step by step Boniface seemed to withdraw from
his early lofty position. In the bull *Romana Mater*, 7th
February, 1297, he authorized the clergy of France to give
voluntary offerings to the king without waiting for formal
Papal consent. On 28th February, at the request of the clergy
themselves, he permitted the tithing of the French clergy for
the Flanders war.[3] To further appease Philip he issued a
fourth bull called *Etsi de statu*, in which he granted thereafter
to the French kings who had reached the age of 20 years the

---

[1] Dupuy, *Diff.*, pr., 13 ; Holtzmann, 24.
[2] Christophe, 98–9; Potthast, No. 24,398, and No. 24,404.
[3] Scholz, *Phillipps des Schönen und Bonifaz VIII*, 5.

right to judge whether or not it was necessary to exact a tribute from the clergy without consulting the Pope.[1] As a further act of reconciliation, on 11th August of this same year he canonized Louis IX, the grandfather of Philip IV.[2] After these proffers of peace, it seems that royal messengers met the Pope and made satisfactory arrangements in reference to the financial questions at issue, and possibly the Pope at that time made a further surrender of 50 per cent of the tithe of one-tenth for crusades.[3] At all events the obnoxious ordinances were withdrawn and the unfortunate rift seemed closed at least for the time being. The principle involved, however, was not settled, and was certain to reappear.

4. Renewal of the Controversy

Philip IV had every reason to congratulate himself upon the temporary adjustment. He had not only secured the much needed cash, but doubtless felt also that he had won a victory for the national state. When Boniface at this juncture again offered to act as umpire between England and France, Philip accepted him as arbiter, not in the capacity of Pope, however, but as a private man.[4] When the decision was published on 30th June, 1298, it was not agreeable to the French king, hence he virtually refused to accept it.[5] It is quite evident that the reconciliation between the ambitious young monarch and the arrogant old Pope was more apparent than real. Still several years passed by without any open hostilities.

In 1301 there appeared a pamphlet, written probably by a keen French lawyer, Pierre Dubois, which clearly revealed the ambitious schemes of the French party. The writer touched on the vital points at issue. He asserted that the Pope should confine his attention to spiritual affairs—to prayers, to preaching, and to the forgiveness of sins. He denied the Pope's right to secular power. On the other hand he cogently defended Philip's political science, encouraged him in his ambitions, and urged him to extend the borders

---

[1] Raynaldus, *Ann.* 1297, No. 50 ; Potthast, No. 24,549.
[2] Duchene, v, 481 ; Potthast, No. 24,557,560 ; Drumann, i, 186.
[3] Holtzmann, 27.   [4] Matt. of Paris.
[5] Gieseler, ii, 240. *The Cath. Encyc.* says it was favourable to Philip. Boniface made the decision in his private capacity, but published it officially as a Papal bull. Cf. Scholz, 10 ; Potthast, No. 24,706,713 ; Holtzmann, 27–8.

of his realm to and beyond Rome.[1] In this treatise Boniface clearly saw the logical limits to which Philip's theories of government might carry him, to the serious jeopardy of Papal prerogatives.

Philip meanwhile, feeling himself victor in the contest, continued his fiscal oppression of the Church to the point where the clergy once more complained to the Pope. In another tract, apparently inspired by the royal will, Pierre Dubois suggested a universal Christian dominion under the headship of France. This new state was to include both the Byzantine and Roman Empires, and with their united strength was to reconquer the Holy Land. Universal peace would thus also be assured to Christendom. The Papacy was to become a purely spiritual patriarchate, its temporalities administered by the French king, who would pay the Pope a fixed salary.[2] Furthermore, since the middle of 1297, Philip had given welcome to the exiled Colonnas, the most bitter foes of Boniface. They spread calumnious charges against the Pope, and urged the calling of a general council to bring about a deposition of the Pontiff.[3] It seems that Boniface sought to offset that influence by calling Philip's brother, Charles Valois, to Italy and by offering him the kingdom of Italy as a bribe.[4]

Early in 1301 Boniface sent the Bishop of Panniers, a bitter foe of Philip, as legate to the king with orders to protest against the continued oppression of the clergy and to urge the use of ecclesiastical tithes solely for the purposes of a crusade. The indiscreet bishop was imprisoned for treason. That was the last straw, and the wrath of the old Pope broke forth. He demanded the immediate liberation of the bishop, and issued the bull *Salvator mundi*, 4th December, withdrawing all privileges granted to the French monarch. This was followed immediately by the famous bull *Ausculta fili* (5th December), in which he stood forth as the mouthpiece of the Medieval Papacy, the true successor of Gregory VII and Innocent III. " God has placed us," he said, " unworthy though we be,

---

[1] *Summaria brevis et compendiosa doctrina felicis expeditionis et abbreviationis guerrorum ac litium regni Francorum*, Scholz, 415.

[2] *De recuperatione terrae sanctae.*

[3] In 1300 William of Nogaret was sent as an agent to Rome to look after the king's interest, and apparently he remained there until 1304. Holtzmann, 30.

[4] Ibid., 37.

over kings and kingdoms in order that we shall root out, destroy, disperse, edify, and plant in His name and by His doctrine. Do not allow yourselves to think that you have no superior and that you are not subject to the head of the ecclesiastical hierarchy. Whoever thinks this is a madman ; whoever supports him in this belief is a heretic." The bull then recited the many grievances against the king ; the use of Church property for secular purposes ; the unwarranted trial of ecclesiastics before civil courts ; the hindrance of episcopal authority ; disrespect for Papal benefices ; and oppression of the clergy.[1] A council of French higher clergy was called, by a third bull, to meet on 4th November, 1302, in Rome to " dispose what is suitable for the correction of abuses and for the reformation of the king and the kingdom ". The king was also invited to be present in person or to send pious persons to represent him.[2]

The bull *Ausculta fili* had nothing new in it, but only expressed the best medieval thought and theory concerning the scope of Papal authority. When it was presented to the king on 10th February, 1302, the Comte d'Artois seized it and cast it into the fire. Philip at once sought to counteract the effect of the bull. He forbade all the French clergy to go to Rome or to send thither any money, and stationed guards on all roads and at all ports to enforce the order.[3] He summoned a national assembly to meet on 10th April, 1302, at Paris, " to advise about the highest interests of the Estates and of the King." A strong appeal was made in the States-General to French patriotism, and to the new sentiment of nationality. The forged bull *Deum time* was read before the Three Estates for its political effect. The Pope was violently denounced by the king's supporters. The king made a personal appeal asking all present to aid him with their counsel. Nobles and burghers offered to shed their blood for their monarch. The third estate, which was here represented for the first time, out of grateful hearts for the honour conferred upon them, declared : " To you, most noble prince, to you, our lord Philip,

---

[1] Dupuy, 606–8 ; Raynaldus, xxiii, 293 sq.

[2] Potthast, No. 25,283.   A false bull *Deum time* was circulated in France as the true bull and did much to arouse national hostility towards Boniface. This enmity was heightened by a forged reply of Philip to Boniface, Holtzmann, 42 ff.

[3] Scholz, 11.

the people of your kingdom present their entreaty and demand that you shall preserve the sovereign freedom of this State, which will not permit you to recognize as your sovereign on earth in your temporal affairs any other than God." [1]   The clergy likewise agreed to write to the Pope in behalf of the monarch and in their letter they begged Boniface to withdraw the call for a council in the interest of prudence and concord.[2] In his reply, Boniface roundly scorned the French ecclesiastics for their cowardice and selfishness, and denounced the use of forged documents to discredit him.

The Roman Council called by the Pontiff met on 30th October, 1302. Notwithstanding the steps taken to prevent the higher clergy in France from attending the council, four archbishops, thirty-five bishops, six abbots, and several doctors of theology obeyed the Papal summons.[3] This number, however, was less than half of the French higher clergy. The king thereupon proceeded to confiscate their goods.[4] The acts of the council have disappeared, but it is known that two bulls were authorized. The one excommunicated whomsoever in anywise ill-treated persons going to or from Rome. The other was the famous *Unam sanctam*,[5] dated 18th November, 1302, and based upon passages from famous medieval theologians like St Bernard, Hugo of St Victor, Thomas Aquinas, and others. It assumed that there is but one true Holy Catholic Church, outside of which there is no salvation ; that there is one God, one faith, one baptism, one Christ, and one Pope, the successor of St Peter. Christ told Peter to feed his sheep—hence those who say that they are not of the flock of Peter and his successors deny Christ as a shepherd. To Peter were given the two swords—hence he who denies the temporal sword to the Pope does not understand the Scriptures. The king wields the temporal sword for the Church, but under the direction of the priest. Since there must be co-operation of members from the lowest to the highest, the spiritual power is above the temporal and should instruct

---

[1] Holtzmann, 42 ff.   [2] Christophe, 406.   [3] Holtzmann, 44.
[4] *Ordinances*, i, 349 ff. ; Boutaric, *Philippe le Bel*, 107, note 1.
[5] Henderson, 435 ; Thatcher and McNeal, 314 ; Schaff, ii, 25, v, 4 ; *Transl. and. Rep.* ; Robinson, i, 346 ; Ogg, 385. See *Cath. Encyc.*, art. on *Unam Sanctam* ; Berchtold, *Die Bulle Unam Sanctam*, Munich, 1887. Since Denifle found a copy of the bull in the Papal archives and printed a facsimile of it all talk about its spuriousness has subsided. *Specimini*, etc.

it and judge it. " Whosoever resists this highest power ordained of God resists God himself. It is altogether necessary to salvation for every human creature to be subject to the Roman Pontiff."

Philip had a refutation of the bull prepared by the Dominican, Jean Quidort.[1] He summarily rejected Boniface as arbiter in the prolonged controversy with England and Flanders. The Papal legate who was sent to threaten Philip with excommunication and interdict and deposition was forced to flee from France in hot haste. A second States-General was called at the urgence of William of Nogaret, and when that body met on 13th June, 1303, a list of twenty-nine grave charges,[2] such as infidelity, loss of the Holy Land, the murder of Celestine V, heresy, simony, gross immorality, magic, and idolatry were made against Boniface, and the king was urged to summon a general council of Christendom to try the Pope. These resolutions were very popular in France, and were quite generally approved throughout the country. Five archbishops and twenty-one bishops sided with the anti-Papal party. The king asserted that in order to protect the Holy See he would co-operate in convening a general council, and royal letters were sent to the princes, bishops, and cardinals of Europe setting forth the king's zeal for a reformed and purified Papacy.[3]

Boniface, experienced and wily, was not to be humiliated without a struggle, hence he called a consistory at Anagni in August, 1303, in which he cleared himself on his solemn oath of the grave charges made against him at Paris. Citations to appear before the Holy See were declared to be valid if merely affixed to the doors of the churches of Rome, while all persons who in any way hindered such citations were pronounced excommunicated. The Archbishop of Nicosia (Cyprus), whose name stood at the head of the schismatical resolutions promulgated in France, was suspended from office. The right to confer degrees in theology and law was taken away from the University of Paris.[4] The right to convene

---

[1] *Tractatis de potestate regia et popoli.* Cf. Goldast, *Monarchia*, ii, 108 sq.

[2] The Colonna furnished the information on which these charges were based. Hefele, vi, 460 ff.

[3] Scholz, 16–17.

[4] The appeal to a general council was confirmed by 700 acts of adhesion from bishops, chapters, monasteries, the orders of friars, and the university of Paris. Poole, *Wiclif*, 8.

a general council was denied to anyone but the legitimate Pope. Finally, it was decided that unless the king repented for his rebellious deeds the Pope would inflict upon him the severest punishments of the Church. By 8th September, a bull for the excommunication and deposition of Philip was ready for promulgation, but events prevented its proclamation.[1]

In the meantime Philip had completed a plot to seize the person of the Pope and either compel him to resign or bring him before a general council, to be held in France, for deposition. As early as April, 1403, William of Nogaret[2] and Sciarra Colonna had been secretly active in Tuscany in raising a band of 2,000 mercenaries. This band, supplemented by Papal enemies in Rome, was taken to Anagni without exciting suspicion among the friends of Boniface, and appeared before the city early on 7th September shouting: " Long live the King of France and Colonna ! " Fellow conspirators in the town opened the gates, and they rushed to the Papal palace threatening " Death to the Pope ". Boniface rejected the humiliating terms offered to him. Thereupon, Sciarra Colonna, sword in hand, broke into the palace, where the elderly Pontiff, clad in his official robes, tiara on his head, seated on the Papal throne, with the cross in one hand and the key of St Peter in the other, awaited the assassins. The defiant Pope was captured and held a prisoner.[3]

On 9th September the burghers of Anagni arose, expelled Nogaret and Colonna, rescued the Pope,[4] and sent him under guard to Rome, where he arrived on 18th September.[5] The Romans celebrated his arrival and victory over his enemies. But the bold spirit was broken ; he gave way to grief and melancholy, and within a month, on 12th October, died.[6]

In the death of Boniface, Philip saw the removal of the greatest obstacle to his ambitious schemes, and the Medieval Church as established under Innocent III came to an end.

Boniface was one of those powerful, many-sided, contradictory characters about whom there was bound to be a divergence of opinion among his contemporaries as well as

---

[1] Potthast, No. 25,283.
[2] See speech of William of Nogaret in the royal council on 12th March, 1303, in Holtzmann, 48 ff.
[3] Holtzmann, 63, 74 ff., 83 ff.   [4] Ib., 77, 98 ff.
[5] Ib., 108.   [6] Ib., 110, 228 ff.

among those who succeeded him. Perhaps the truest estimate of this Pope was made by Giovanni Villani,[1] an eyewitness. He pronounced him the most clever canonist of his time, and the manner in which Boniface conducted his controversies proves the estimate to be correct. Villani further asserted that Boniface was big-hearted, generous, and loved magnificence, but was arrogant, proud, stern in manner, more feared than loved, too worldly-minded for his high office, and too fond of collecting money, both for the Church and for his own family. He was openly guilty of nepotism.[2] He founded the Roman house of Gaetani and, in the ambition to exalt his family, drew down upon himself the deathless and tireless hatred of the Colonna. He could argue as keenly as Innocent III, but was far inferior to him in decisive action.[3] No Pope in the long list held a loftier conception of the Papal sovereignty and perhaps none did more to overthrow it. Boniface was a great judge and legislator, but a failure on the executive side.

5. *Significance and results of the attack on the Papacy*

The fundamental cause of the failure of Boniface was the fact that he was incapable of comprehending the revolutionary changes in political affairs that were sweeping over Europe, and consequently could not readjust his high office and the theories upon which it rested to a corresponding change that was absolutely indispensable to the maintenance of his power. By adopting a conciliatory tone and temper he might have taken advantage of the political distractions of that day. But he could not manage himself, to say nothing of the outer world. Opposition aroused him to anger ; failure lashed him to fury. He flew at the throat of his adversary without weighing the chances of success or defeat. Blinded by his faith in the omnipotence of the Holy See, his whole reign was one continuous blunder. The two-edged sword which in the hands of Innocent III had awed Christendom into silence or obedience was blunted and dulled. He lived and died apparently unconscious of the irreparable injury he had done his own

---

[1] Muratori, xiii, 348 sqq., gives his *Hist. Fiorentine.*
[2] Gregorovius, v, 299, 584 ; Thompson, Usk's *Chronicon.* 259.
[3] For an estimate of Boniface, see Wisemann, *Pope Boniface VIII*, in the *Dublin Review*, 1844 ; Gosselyn, *The Power of the Pope in the M.A.*; Gregorovius, v, 502 ; *Eng. Hist. Rev.*, 1902.

cause, for he had shaken the structure of the Papacy to its very foundations and had incited a revolutionary attack which reduced it every year more nearly to the level of other merely political institutions.

Philip IV was the first French king to appeal from the Pope to a general council of the whole Church as the source of supreme power. That contention was not lost, but continued to live in France and found its logical expression in the Gallican Decrees of 1682. Across the ages Philip IV gave his hand to Louis XIV. The political science of the publicists of 1300 was realized in the seventeenth century. The political theory of Gregory VII and Innocent III received a checkmate —not in the Babylonian Captivity, nor in the Great Schism— but in the minds of the people of Europe. The successor of Peter found it impossible to compel the kingdoms of the earth to acknowledge themselves fiefs of the Holy See. Papal supremacy in temporal affairs was reduced to nothing but a claim—and such it has continued until the present day.[1]

The results of the struggle between Philip IV and Boniface VIII are most significant for the future history of Europe. The king, as a representative of a modern national state, won a noteworthy triumph over the Pope, as a learned and fearless defender of the extreme pretensions of the Medieval Church, which virtually came to an end with his downfall. " The supreme fatherly office of the medieval Pope as the respected head of one family of peoples " had broken down before the new political forces arising in Europe. The medieval Papacy fell with Boniface VIII in fact, though not in theory and name. The determination to make the Papacy the real arbiter among European nations and actually to invest the Pope with the powers of the Emperor perished at the same time. The drama of Canossa had at length been followed by the drama of Anagni.

[1] Lavisse and Rambaud, iii, 313.

CHAPTER II

LITERARY ASSAILANTS AND DEFENDERS OF PAPAL AUTHORITY

6. *Defenders of National State and Empire against Papal Claims*

ONE of the most significant immediate results of this unfortunate controversy between Philip IV and Boniface VIII was the open assault made in the pamphlets of the day upon the claims of the Medieval Papacy, on the one hand, and in defence of the sovereignty of the king of France, on the other. These pamphlets clearly reveal the intellectual change going on in Europe in the fourteenth century, and mark an epoch in both ecclesiastical and political history.

It is a noteworthy fact that for the first time in the history of the Church, educated laymen took the leading part in the discussion. The prelates, princes, and university men of the day constituted the audience, since the rank and file of the people had not yet attained to that degree of intelligence and interest which made them a very important party to the controversy. The general theme of dispute was the Pope's claim to temporal power over the nations of the world. The contestants based their arguments on the Scriptures, Aristotle, reason, canon law, history, and Roman law. The freedom of utterance and the expression of modern ideas of these publicists mark the beginning of a revolution in the thought of Europe. While many of these writers were clerics, all of them were jurists. The principles for which they contended were to become axiomatic in the ages to come. No doubt the victory of Philip over Boniface caused them to speak with an unprecedented boldness.

The most conspicuous defenders of royal prerogatives and of the rights of the national states were: first, the three unknown authors of three important pamphlets: *The Twofold Prerogative*, *The Papal Power*, and *Disputation between a Cleric and a Knight* [1]; next, John of Paris, a learned Dominican

---

[1] For a discussion of authorship and content, see Scholz, *Streitschriften*, 224 sqq.

preacher and teacher, and one of the leading minds of his age [1] ;
then, Peter Flotte, a celebrated lawyer at the court of Philip IV
and his prime-minister [2] ; likewise William Nogaret [3] ; and
finally, Peter Dubois, the most advanced publicist of his
day, original and bold in his thinking, a layman, and a royal
lawyer. [4] Dante, although in accord with these jurists in his
definition of the scope and limitations of Papal power, was a
champion of imperialism rather than of the national state.

The *Twofold Prerogative* [5] sought to prove that the spiritual
and temporal powers were separate and distinct, and that
consequently the Pope had no lordship over secular affairs.
The Levites, it was argued, were forbidden to hold worldly
possessions. Christ refused the office of king. Peter never
laid claim to temporal sovereignty. Both canon law and
Roman law recognized the independence of the civil power.
The King of France received his power from God alone and
therefore had the same rank as the Emperor and recognized
no overlord on earth—not even the Emperor. Both Popes and
Emperors had recognized that independence. Biblical as well
as legal authority proved that both secular and spiritual
powers were from God. The secular power was established
by God both to rule and to punish the body. The Pope had
plenary power only in the spiritual realm. Neither one could
encroach upon the prerogatives of the other. In his temporal
jurisdiction the Pope was limited to his diocese, like any
other bishop, namely, the patrimony of Peter. His secular
sovereignty came solely from being a temporal prince in his
own domain and was not in any way an outgrowth of his Papal
power. The two powers were as distinct and separate as the
East and the West, the soul and the body, earth and heaven.
Should the King of France betray his divine trust and recognize
the Pope as overlord he would expose himself to the death
penalty for treason. [6] It is clear, of course, to a modern mind
that the purpose and no doubt the result of the theory set forth
so convincingly in this tract were to deal a powerful blow at

---

[1] Scholz, 275–333 ; Finke, 170–7.   [2] Scholz, 355–63.
[3] Ib., 363 ; Holtzmann, Wilhelm von Nogaret, Freiburg, 1898.
[4] Scholz, 375–443 ; Poole, 256 ; *Hist. Essays of members of the Owen College*, Manchester, 1902.
[5] *Quaestio in utramqua partem* is given in Goldast, ii, 95, as the work of Aegidius Colonna. Cf. Scholz, 224 sq.
[6] On 23rd Feb., 1302, Philip had his sons take an oath never to recognize anyone but God as overlord.

Papal absolutism and universality and to magnify the authority of the sovereign national state.

The Papal Power [1] asserted that the Pope was not the secular lord of mankind and hence his claim to universal temporal jurisdiction could not be recognized—at least not in France. Nor was he the judge of the world. France had never paid homage to the Pope. To the Pope as *servus servorum* worldly jurisdiction would be an unworthy hindrance. Christ refused all worldly power ; nor did he bestow it upon Peter and his followers. He recognized the claim of Cæsar and paid him tribute. He ministered to the poor and the sick, but assumed no dominion. The Church, therefore, inherited from him spiritual, not worldly power ; the duty of saving men, not judging them. Christ's vicar could not claim for himself what Christ clearly repudiated. The author of this pamphlet gave a unique interpretation to the comparison of the human body to the Church. Christ, he said, was the head ; the king the heart ; the nerves and veins were officers in the Church and State. The soul was not even mentioned. Both Pope and Emperor were significantly omitted in the figure in order to magnify kingly power. Moses was set forth as a type of the secular ruler ; Aaron of the priestly. Each recognized and respected the rights and duties of the other. The gift of Constantine was not denied, but it was asserted that it had nothing whatever to do with France, since France was not a part of the Empire but entirely independent. The tract defended clearly and logically all the prerogatives of the national sovereign state. The old theory of the co-ordination of the Church and State was set aside. The sphere of the Pope as the spiritual father of mankind was strictly defined, and was held up as subordinate to the sphere of the State. Altogether the treatise was a pointed, sane, historical presentation of the claims of the French nation.

The third pamphlet, *The Disputation between a Cleric and a Knight*,[2] was written to substantiate the right of the State

---

[1] *Questio de potestate papae* is printed in Dupuy, 663°83. It is found in manuscript, together with the pamphlet just mentioned, bound up with the works of John of Paris, at Paris. For authorship, see Scholz, 257 ; Poole, *Med. Thought*, 260, attributes it to Pierre Dubois.

[2] *Disputatio inter clericum et militem* is found in Goldast, i, 13 sqq. An English translation attributing the tract to William Occam appeared in London in 1540. Cf. Scholz, 333-53.

D

to tax Church property. It argued that, since the Pope and the Church have nothing to do with laws which govern temporal things, they have no jurisdiction over temporal affairs. Secular matters were held to be subject to laws and not to Papal decretals. The Pope was the exclusive spiritual overlord of the Church. Since Christ said : " My kingdom is not of this world," it was evident that God gave no jurisdiction over worldly matters to the Pope, who merely bore the same relations to all Christendom that each bishop bore to his diocese and had no more supreme political authority over the Christian world than the bishop had in his province. The Old Testament history plainly showed that kings were obeyed by the priests. With these arguments as a foundation, it was contended that the clergy were subjects of a state and consequently were liable to taxation for their possessions.

John of Paris (d. 1306) a graduate of the University of Paris, preacher, theologian, publicist, and Dominican monk, took a decided and influential interest in the national quarrel with Boniface VIII. In June, 1303, he joined 131 other Parisian Dominicans in signing a document demanding a general council, which the university had openly favoured five days before.[1] A monograph on the Lord's Supper produced a charge of heresy against him, and he was forbidden to lecture at the university, to preach, and to hear confessions. He appealed to the Pope, Clement V, for a hearing in order to defend his position, but died in 1306, before it was granted.[2]

John's tract on *The Authority of the King and Pope* [3] appeared about 1302,[4] and maintained a point of view that seems quite modern. He defined the Church as " the body of the faithful ", not " the body of the clergy ". Christ, he asserted, was the real head of the Church. God ruled over the whole world and established both the Pope and the Emperor. The Church had its unity, not in Peter or Linus, but in Christ, who created the two powers, worldly and spiritual. Of one common origin, these powers on earth were independent of each other, and had their separate sphere of activity and influence. By divine arrangement both were monarchially organized.

---

[1] *Chartul. Univ. Paris*, ii, 102.   [2] Ib., 120.
[3] *De potestate regia et popoli* is given in Goldast, ii, 108.
[4] Scholz, 298.

The sovereignty of the French monarch was defended, not only against the Pope, but also against the Emperor. To assert that the Emperor had any authority in France was sheer blasphemy, because the king's will was absolute in France, the source of all law, the source of all justice, the source of all privilege, and the source of all honour. He might change his will, as it seemed to him best, for the welfare of his kingdom and people. All persons within his kingdom, clergy and laity alike, were subject to his will and could depend upon his justice and protection. Church property, like secular property, was subject to his control. It was put into the hands of the spiritual leaders to save souls, to care for the poor and the sick, and to conduct religious services. But if the priests did not fulfil their obligations their property might be taken away from them. The king was duty bound to reserve the right to control church property. He might demand, in return for royal protection given to the clergy, protection money in the form of taxes, for without the king's protection the clergy might be subject to abuse and robbery. The Old Testament was full of examples where the king, under the stress of a national war, seized the goods of the Church to free the people. The welfare of the nation was more important than the interest of any individual church, hence the king was justified in holding to the doctrine that in case of national need he might seize the ecclesiastical possessions. The clergy were State officers and could not escape their political obligations. If they refused to do their duty, the king might deprive them of their privileges. He must see to it that the Church performed its duty in behalf of public welfare, consequently the clergy were subject to his will just as the civil and military officers were, and no one doubted that they were subject to the law of the land. When the radical character of these declarations and principles is taken into account, it is evident that this pamphlet was, for that day, the most revolutionary exposition of the prerogatives of the modern national state.[1]

In the new political, ecclesiastical, and social readjustments that were taking place at the beginning of the fourteenth century, John attempted to define the limits and powers of the ecclesiastical authority. He stoutly maintained that the Church, monarchially organized, had Peter for its head and

[1] Scholz, 352.

that the Pope was his true successor, possessed of God-given primacy. He could punish moral offences, but only with spiritual punishments. He had no right to impose fines, imprisonment, or death. He represented the Church, but was not its lord, because the Church might call him to account for his actions and beliefs. The cardinals might admonish him [1]; the emperor might depose him as did Henry III. The final source of all power in the Church was located in a general representative council, which was above the Pope and could depose him on the ground of insanity, heresy, personal incompetence and abuse of Church property. A general council could be called in case of need without the Pope's consent. The Pope was given absolutely no jurisdiction over the property of the laymen. Christ was no worldly king and gave the Pope no worldly authority. The Pope did not have two swords.[2] No more than Christ did Constantine bestow upon the Pope secular power. The Pope was only the chief servant, the most important member, the representative of the ecclesiastical corporation of the Church, not its absolute master. Sacerdotal power was defined as the spiritual power of the Church, taken over from Christ by the servants of the Church in order to administer the sacraments to the faithful. That power rested in the Church as a whole, and not in the Pope exclusively nor in any single individual. The priests were servants of the Church, and not of the Popes. Church property likewise belonged to the ecclesiastical body, that is to the Church. The Pope and the clergy only administered it for the body corporate. Hence John advocated the election of representatives of each province in the Church to co-operate with the Pope in enacting laws to govern the Church. Thus he advocated the modern idea of democracy in Church government.

Like Aristotle and Thomas Aquinas, John found the origin of the State in the family and not in murder and other acts of violence. His conception was clearly that of the national state. From his point of view the empire had been a supreme power and had ruled the Pope, but it was an

---

[1] This is the first instance of the suggestion of the judicial power of the College of Cardinals acting as representatives of the clergy collectively.

[2] He also demolished the sun and moon theory, which was at least as old as the time of Gregory VII, and had given rise to arithmetical speculations as to the reliable power of Pope and emperor. One asserted the ratio to be 47 : 1 ; another 7744½ : 1. Friedburg, i, 6, n. 4.

outgrown institution no longer necessary for Europe, and if it continued to exist it would have to do so on an equality with the monarchies and not above them. Kingdoms derived their authority direct from God, but natural agencies such as climate, geography, and national characteristics determined their number and size. History furnished indisputable evidence that both Jewish priests and pagan priests were wholly subject to the State. The Pope might instruct the king, not as king, but as a Christian—not in civics, but in faith. On the other hand the royal power cared for not only the corporal welfare of its subjects, but also for their spiritual welfare. The legislator was bound to take into consideration the souls as well as the lives of subjects. The independence of the king from the priest was well established by the records of the past. France was ruled by kings before there were any Christians. Indeed, John asserted that royal power existed 2,000 years before the priestly power began.

Every opportunity was taken by this bold, iconoclastic pamphleteer to laud and defend the national state against both the Empire and the Papacy. He boldly declared that states had existed before the Roman empire came into existence and derived their power independently from God. He believed and predicted that the Empire would be superseded by the national states and declared that such an evolution would be for the progress and betterment of the world. Sovereign power rested first in God, who gave it to all the people, and the people by choice transferred it to kings. Hence it is very amusing to read that Popes usurped power over emperors and kings and even deposed them, whereas in reality the king was the supreme head of his kingdom and in secular matters there was no appeal from his decision, not even to the Pope. On the contrary, indeed, matters of a worldly nature may be appealed from the spiritual courts of the bishops to the king, who was the source of all law and justice.

This tract of John of Paris was the most penetrating analysis and the most pointed criticism of the claims and boundaries of the spiritual power made in the fourteenth century. Indeed it was the first time in the history of the Church that in so energetic a manner and with such thoroughgoing keenness and clearness the real significance of the spiritual power had been established and its extreme claims repudiated. The idea of popular sovereignty in Church and State was also set forth in terms that sound familiar to modern ears, and it led to the development of the theory of conciliar supremacy in the fourteenth and fifteenth centuries. Such intellectual giants as Gerson and Peter d'Ailly took their ideas in large measure from this pioneer publicist.

The bellicose statesman, Pierre Flotte,[1] was in charge of foreign affairs under Philip IV from 1295 to 1302, and managed matters with singular success. He studied law and early went to Philip's court as one of the hungry lawyers looking for a position. After several successful political missions, which he conducted with honour, he became a royal counsellor, and finally prime minister. He was one of the moving spirits in the controversy with Boniface VIII. In all his writings and actions his one fervent purpose was to establish the political supremacy and sovereignty of France. For the realization of that end he relied upon the national consciousness and patriotism of the French people. He was accused, and probably justly, of having written the false bull *Deum time*.[2]

Scholz has practically established the fact that he wrote the tract *Antequam essent clerici*.[3] In it he vindicated the rights and authority of the laity by maintaining that the laity as well as the clergy constituted the Holy Mother Church. He asserted that Christ saved all, brought release from the old law to all, died, and was resurrected for all—and not merely for the priesthood. Hence the clergy and laity constituted one spiritual society. The earthly basis of that society was the national state founded on law. The royal government existed before there were any clergy and like the Church had its own constitution. The secular law applied to both clergy and laity since both were members of the same society. Hence the priests, monks, and bishops were citizens of the State and could be taxed for the welfare of all. True, the clergy had special privileges and liberties, but these were not founded upon that emancipation which had come to all true believers through Christ. The clergy were protected in their rights, persons, and possessions by the State, hence they ought to

---

[1] Renan, *Hist. Litt.*, xxvii, 371 ff.; *La Grand Encyc.*, xvii, 657 ff. Langlois in Lavisse, *Hist. de France*, iii, 2, p. 126; Scholz, 355.
[2] Scholz, 357.   [3] See Dupuy, 21-3; Holtzman, 25.

assist the State gladly in every possible way—by advice, by loyalty, by contributions of money, etc. Those who refused their obligations in these matters were guilty of treason and subject to punishment. This practical statesman argued that the State and its prerogatives were founded on natural law. This pamphleteer clearly saw that the conflict was between a national, popular church under political supervision, on the one hand, and the international universal Church organized under the Papal monarchy, on the other. There are evidences also that Flotte had a vision of the union of the clergy and laity in one great religious society resting on a democratic basis, but it was not advocated as a practical scheme.

William of Nogaret,[1] a teacher of law in the University of Montpellier, and a trusted royal adviser, was the very embodiment of lay interference in spiritual matters. He was an indefatigable writer on political subjects and we have more tracts from his facile pen than from any other contemporary of the period of Philip le Bel.[2] No less than twelve vigorous apologies for the part he took in the assault upon Boniface appeared from his hand.[3] He took the high ground that Boniface was a usurper and not a true, constitutional Pope, hence he could the more readily inveigh against him. To settle the validity of Boniface's claim to the Papacy, he urged the assembling of a general ecclesiastical council. Since the head of the Church alone could summon such a council, Nogaret went to Anagni to bring that about in one way or another.[4] But Boniface could not be induced to call the desired convocation, and his death soon altered the situation. Throughout all his writings Nogaret repeatedly asserted that the French king was the absolute sovereign in all worldly affairs. No one but God was above him. In secular matters he recognized no judge except his own will. Notwithstanding his numerous pamphlets, Nogaret's chief influence consisted in his deeds and oral advice rather than in his writings. It was claimed by his enemies that his father, a citizen of Toulouse, had been condemned as a heretic during the crusade against the Albigensians. If that charge be true, it may account in large

---

[1] Holtzmann, *Wilhelm von Nogaret*, Freiburg, 1898.
[2] See Renan for a list of his writings. *Hist. Litt. de la France*, xxvii, 233.
[3] Holtzmann, 202 sqq.
[4] Scholz, 366 sqq. ; Foquet. *Recueil de historiens des Gaules et de la France*, xx–xxiii ; Richanger, *Annales regis Edwardi primi* (*Rolls Series*), 483–91.

measure for his inveterate hostility towards Boniface VIII. Certain it is that he employed every means at his command to obtain absolution from the Pope for having raised his hand against Boniface, but failed to secure it until 1311, two years before his death.

Of all these publicists the most conspicuous, the most daring, and the most progressive was Peter Dubois (*b.* 1250, *d.* 1312),[1] a layman and an influential lawyer in the court of Philip IV. He may have been a Norman. As a representative in the National Assembly held in Paris in 1302, he acted as the king's spokesman against the Pope. From his trenchant pen went forth a number of treatises [2] in defence of the independent sovereignty of France against both the Emperor and the Pope. He defended the prerogatives of the French monarch with convincing argument and forceful logic.

Dubois took the historical position that the French king was the successor of Charles the Great and consequently had inherited all the power of that great ruler. From that premise he developed the French kingship into a universal lordship over both Europe and the Orient,[3] and asserted that the French ruler had exercised an independent sway for more than a thousand years and therefore preceded all other rulers in his sovereignty.[4] This conception was not the old empire revived under a French emperor, but a United States of Europe under the leadership of the French monarch. He believed that this political organization, co-operating with the Church, could bring about universal peace and all needed social, educational, and religious improvements. Under these conditions, too, a successful crusade to free the Holy Land could be organized.[5] At the same time he was not in favour of an absolute monarch or despotic form of rule, but believed that the king's powers were limited and defined by law.

Dubois's caustic criticisms of the medieval claims of the Papacy and of the lives of the clergy were scarcely equalled in any writings of the pre-reformatory period. His significance

---

[1] Renan, *Hist. Litt.*, xxvii, 471–536; Lavisse, *Hist. de France*, iii, 248ff.; *Hist. Essays of Members of the Owens College*, Manchester, 1902; Poole, *Illustrations of Med. Thought*, 256; Scholz, 374–444.

[2] Cf. Renan, xxvi, 476; Scholz, 385.

[3] Scholz, 385, gives a digest of *Summaria brevis et compendiosa doctrina.* Cf. 395.

[4] Scholz, 387. See de Wailly, *Bibliotheqe de l'Ecole des Chartes*, 2 ser., iii.

[5] Scholz, 396.

will be seen when it is remembered that he lived two centuries before Luther. The foundations of the spiritual supremacy of the Papal power were accepted and defended, but all pretence to temporal jurisdiction was flatly denied. The Pope was recognized as the direct successor of Peter, the appointed moral teacher of mankind, the vicar of Christ, "the light of the world," and his functions were held to be to save souls, to keep peace on earth, to oversee the clergy, and to reform and spiritualize the Church. He denied the legality of the Donation of Constantine as a basis for Papal temporal power and maintained that the only claim the Pope had to secular authority over the patrimony of Peter was his long tenure. He denounced the pretension of the Pope to sovereignty over France as a mortal sin.[1] In the case of international disputes, however, he conceded to the Pope the supreme jurisdiction as the final and decisive court of arbitration.

The Pope and the clergy were accused of worldliness and self-indulgence. Boniface VIII was denounced as a heretic.[2] Prelates were censured for squandering the money of the Church in wars, law-suits, and riotous living. They notoriously neglected their spiritual duties in the care of souls and in inculcating religious truths, and much preferred the worldly atmosphere of princely courts and the study of civil law. The scandalous simony and nepotism of the Roman court were due to shameless avarice. So few of the clergy observed the rule of celibacy that the rule ought to be given up entirely. He argued that Christ conferred the primacy of the Church upon Peter, a married man; that that apostle permitted marriage to all; that the Eastern Church allowed marriage of the clergy; and that celibacy kept many good men out of the service of the Church. He thought that the secularization of all ecclesiastical property would obviate greed and avarice among the clergy.[3] That idea was not a new one, of course, but its application seemed easier, more practicable, and more necessary than ever before.[4] Fixed salaries for all Church officials were urged.[5] A complete reformation of the monasteries was strongly advocated.[6] These innovations were

---

[1] Scholz., 387, 390.
[2] *Deliberatio super agendis a Philippo IV. . . . contra epistolam Bonifacii papæ VIII*, in Dupuy, 44–7.
[3] Scholz. 399.   [4] Ib.   [5] Ib., 402.   [6] Ib., 403.

set forth not solely to purify and strengthen the Church, but to make France the supreme power on earth.

Dubois was a decided progressive who had in his mind a new type of civilization for Europe. His scheme of reformation and advance was not only ecclesiastical, but also political, social, educational, and industrial. He planned for the improvement of both foreign and domestic politics ; for the reorganization of the army ; for the betterment of the courts of justice. He championed the spread of moral and intellectual education as a means of reviving spiritual Christianity. He suggested the codification and unification of law. To win the Orient to Western rule and civilization he suggested the colonization of the Levant ; the study of the Oriental languages in special schools in the West ; and the marriage of Christians with the higher classes of Orientals for the purpose of converting them. The French ruler ought not only to undertake this great work in person, but he ought also to persuade the Pope to call a general council of all prelates, lay princes, and even the Byzantine " usurper " for the purpose of ushering in universal peace and of enforcing these reforms.[1] This council could also create an international arbitration court of six members—three clerical and three secular—to settle all disputes and thus avoid wars.[2]

The progressive platform of Dubois was prophetic and revolutionary. The secularization of Church property ; the abolition of celibacy ; the reduction of the number of cloisters ; the reformation of the whole system of education with the introduction of the study of living languages, natural sciences, and mathematics ; the reorganization of the military system ; the systematizing of law ; the schemes of eastern colonization ; the creation of an international peace society with a court of arbitration ; the organization of a United States of Europe with the king of France as the head—all these propositions sound quite modern and are common enough to us to-day, but they must have seemed new, fantastic, and revolutionary to the men of the Middle Ages. These suggestions were not all new nor were they original,[3] but they were newly stated and were put forth in a very much more practical manner

[1] Scholz, 394.
[2] Ib., 396.
[3] Ib., 376. He thinks that Dubois has been considerably overrated.

than had ever been done before. His style and manner of writing were not scholastic, but indicate that he had outgrown the civilization of his age. This active, practical reformer and seer was popular with the best men of his day, exercised a conspicuous influence on his times, and was much sought after.[1]

Taking these tracts as a whole, it is strikingly evident that they are materially different both in style of expression and in daring ideas from everything that went before in the quarrel between the Church and State. The universities had produced a new method of writing and a new set of convictions in reference to religion and politics. The revival of the study of Roman law was a decisive factor in the radical change that was so noticeable. These defenders of royal prerogatives at the expense of the Papacy were all university men, trained lawyers, and mostly laity, who had replaced the clergy and old nobles as the king's advisers. They supplied the intellectual ideas for Philip IV in his successful conflict with the Pope, gave Europe a new and revolutionary political literature, and paved the way for the radical ground taken by the anti-Papal party which culminated in the decline of Papal power, and the temporary victory of the conciliar theory in the great reform councils of the following century. One can detect three marked periods in the appearance of these pamphlets ; first, those occasioned by the bull *Clericis laicos* ; secondly, those which appeared in 1301–3 ; and, thirdly, those that were written after the death of Boniface VIII.

To this period also belonged Dante (*d.* 1321), whose treatise on government, *De Monarchia*, written about 1311,[2] discussed the relation of the Church and the State—the burning question of the age. He was in no wise connected with the court of Philip IV, although he seems to have been in Paris for a while, and apparently had no sympathy with the ambitions of the French monarch. His treatise dealt directly with the old medieval problem of the relation of the Papacy and the Empire, the rivalry of the Pope and the Emperor.[3] He logically

[1] Dubois was known to Jean du Villet in the sixteenth century, and to Dupuy in the seventeenth, but was then practically forgotten until the latter part of the nineteenth century.
[2] For a discussion of the date, see Henry, *Dante's de Monarchia*, xxxii, sqq.
[3] Flick, *Rise of Med. Church*, 413.

opposed those sweeping claims promulgated in Pope Boniface's famous bull *Unam sanctum*, by arguments founded on reason, history, Aristotle, and the Bible, and stands forth as alternately the jurist, the theologian, and the scholastic metaphysician.

First he established the need of a universal monarch in the interest of peace, liberty, and social welfare. This universal monarchy did not come through the Church, but was created by God and bequeathed to the Roman people. The noblest on earth, Christ himself, recognized the divinely formed Empire when he consented to be born under Augustus and to be crucified under Tiberius. Paul likewise acknowledged imperial sovereignty when he said: "I stand at Cæsar's Judgment Seat, where I ought to be judged." [1]

The position of the Papacy was not ignored, but the Pope was recognized as a governing agency in his subordinate sphere. The passages of Scripture to which the Papal party always appealed were elaborately explained away. The Emperor was to pay due respect to the Pope and give him adequate support and proper protection. The figure of speech of the sun and moon as typical of the relation of the two powers was rejected, since the sun and moon existed before man was created. The two swords were explained as being both spiritual functions. Constantine's Donation to Sylvester was set aside because the emperor had no more legal right to transfer his empire in the west than he had to commit suicide. Nor had the Bishop of Rome any legal right to accept such a gift.[2] The temporal power of the Papacy was given neither by natural law, nor divine ordinance, nor universal consent; on the contrary it was contradicted by Christ himself, who said " My kingdom is not of this world ". But since man has two sides to his nature, the worldly and the spiritual, two guides are needed and were ordained of God, the Pope and the Emperor, each of whom should reverence and assist the other.

Dante probably voiced the sentiment of the age when he declared that Joachim of Fiore (*d.* 1202) with his " Eternal Gospel " was one " endowed with prophetic spirit ". In the Holy Land on Mount Tabor Joachim had received celestial illumination as to his life work. He returned to Italy and became an ardent lay preacher of the absolute necessity of

---

[1] *Acts*, xxv, 10.   [2] *De Monarchia*, iii, 10.

repentance. The ecclesiastical authorities objected to his preaching methods without ordination, so he took the Cistercian habit and was ordained priest in 1168. He was a close Bible student and wrote three works in which he sought to interpret Scriptural prophecy with reference to the history and future of the Church. He thought that he had discovered the " Eternal Gospel ".[1] He declared that the world was to see a new dispensation of universal love based on the message of Christ, when there would be no need for disciplinary institutions, when the Latins and the Greeks would be reunited in a new spiritual kingdom, when the Jews would be converted, and when the " Eternal Gospel " would abide till the end of the world. Among the spiritual Franciscans was organized a sect of Joachimites who soon went far beyond their teacher in declaring that the Catholic Church would fall and that the Bible itself would be replaced by the " Eternal Gospel ". As a result Alexander IV in 1256 had condemned the founder and the followers of the Eternal Gospel,[2] but their ideas lived on through the thirteenth century as the hope of the age in many hearts besides that of Dante.

That Dante's work had a pronounced influence on the thought of his day cannot be doubted, since it was ordered to be burnt by John XXII in 1329, and was put on the Index by the Council of Trent. It deserves mention in this chapter because of its sweeping and violent attack on the claims of the Papacy to temporal power. Aside from that Dante was in complete harmony with the orthodox faith of his age and was a disciple of Thomas Aquinas. He saw the evils and the abuses as all intelligent men did, and he raised his voice in no uncertain terms against them, but there is no trace of doctrinal dissatisfaction, and no suggestion of free inquiry and private judgment.[3] His constant reference to, and his very liberal treatment of, the classical pagan world, however, did much to usher in the Renaissance.[4]

---

[1] Based on the *Apocalypse*, xiv, 6.
[2] Reuter, *Gesch. der religiösen Aufkärung im Mittelalter*, Berlin, 1877; Wicksteed, *The Everlasting Gospel*, in the *Inquirer*, London, 1909; Fournier, *Etudes sur Joachim de Fiore et ses doctrines*, Paris, 1909.
[3] Moore, *Studies*, ii, 65, 66.
[4] Burckhardt-Geiger, *Renaissance*, i, 219.

7. *Papal Apologists*

In this controversy the Papal theory was not without its valiant apologists and defenders, but they were divided into four pronounced parties :—

1. Those who stood forth as champions of the sweeping claims of the medieval Pope as a general proposition, but who were personally hostile to Boniface VIII, or at least not in sympathy with his tactless policy. The leaders of this party were the Colonna of Rome.

2. Those unqualified supporters of Boniface VIII in his adherence to the position taken by Gregory VII and Innocent III and also in his course of action. Chief among the leaders of this party were Augustus Triumphus,[1] James of Viterbo,[2] and Henry of Cremona.[3]

3. The oligarchical party, who sought to change the Papal constitution by placing sovereign power in the college of cardinals. This contention was upheld by the leading members of the college.

4. The conciliar-episcopal party, who defended the supremacy of a general council over the Pope and sought to increase the prerogatives and powers of the bishops. Some of the French higher clergy were the leaders of this group.

A study of the arguments advanced by these four parties shows that they may be reduced to two general factions, namely, the supporters of the Papal theory, and the opponents of the fundamental Papal claims, who sought to locate the sovereignty of the Church in some other ecclesiastical body and not in the State.

The Papal party took up first the origin of papal sovereignty. Easily the foremost leader was Aegidius Colonna (1247–1316), general of the Augustinians, archbishop of Bourges (1295), and a famous theological teacher and writer.[4] He had studied theology under Thomas Aquinas and Bonaventura at Paris, and was well acquainted with the questions involved in the Gallic-Papal controversy. He was a voluminous author, and among his chief writings were *Power of the Supreme Pontiff*, *The Rule of Princes*, and *The Pope's Abdication*. His arguments are clear and pointed. He asserted that the

---

[1] Scholz, 166–89.   [2] Ib., 129 ; Renan, *Hist. Litt.*, xxvi, 45 ff.
[3] Scholz, 152.   [4] Ib., 32–129.

government of the world centred in one ruler, God. An all-powerful, universal hierarchy grew out of the nature of the universe. The prophetic voices of the Old Testament foretold it. The facts of history proved it. Hence in the Church there was one supreme head, the Pope, God's immediate representative. The first priests were Adam, Abel, and Noah.[1] In Old Testament times under the theocracy one person was both king and priest.[2] Jesus Christ created the Church as a universal power for the realization of his plans to save the world and bestowed upon the Pope the two swords not *ad usum* but *ad nutum*. Papal power was given by Christ to Peter ; and so it had gone on unchangeable from Pope to Pope.

As to the nature and extent of Papal power Aegidius held that man may be perfect and may possess spiritual power, but no one could approach the Pope in perfection. He stood above all others, had plenary power to rule all, and all were bound to kiss his feet.[3] He judged all, but could be judged by none. His power extended not only over the bodies of men, but also over their wills and souls. His punishments extended to the soul and every soul was subject to him.[4] Just as the physician prescribed the clothing as well as the food of his patient, so must the Pope rule those who desire spiritual health. He is above all laws, the source of all law, and his rule is universal. He is the source of all justice, the highest judge on earth, and God alone can judge him. In affairs of faith and morals he is infallible. The apostolic chair gave its occupant the most holy position on earth. His power is divine and he may be called potentially the Church, for in him rested the fullness of authority, the entire canons of the Church, and appeals could be made to him in all matters. The whole world was his field of activity and with God alone did he share authority. In his activity he was unlimited and absolute. His power was illimitable, immeasurable, inestimable, and unaccountable.[5] He stood in the same relation to the Church and to all Christians that God did to creation in general. All his subordinate helpers were appointed by him, responsible to him and removable at pleasure by him.

In considering the relation of the Church and the State it

---

[1] Aegidius, *De eccl.*, c. 4, fol. 3–3[1].
[2] Ib., c. 7, fol. 6–7[1].
[3] Ib., c. 2.
[4] Ib., c. 3, fol. 2–3[1].
[5] Ib., c. 12, fol. 56–7[1].

followed inevitably that the ecclesiastical power was superior to the worldly. Proof of the subordination of the secular authority was found in the following: (1) The universal order of things made the spiritual dominate the physical.[1] (2) The choice and appointment of kings by the priest, generally recognized and proved by history, practically established the supremacy of the priest. (3) The tithes which the worldly powers paid to the ecclesiastical was a recognition of the service and obligation due to God and his earthly agents.

If in earlier times the State seemed to be superior, it was true in name only, not in fact or right. The first king was Nimrod, but the first priests were Adam, Abel, and Noah.[2] Just as man has a body and a soul, and needs double nourishment for them, so were there two powers created by God. As the body and soul made a complete unity, so were related the spiritual and worldly powers. In the Old Testament times the two powers were for a while united in one person, but the priestly predominated. The Pope received the two swords from Christ not for the purpose of using them, but in order to possess the authority—not *ad usum*, but *ad nutum*. Princes had the power *ad usum*, but the power *ad nutum* was the higher.[3] The Pope's rule is universal; the king's particular and hence under the universal. The Church set up and took down princes. Like the sun the Pope, in his rule of the Church, held and ordered all within his influence.[4] His field of jurisdiction was the world and over it he could exercise both swords. The example of nature proved that all organs and means of the secular rule must be fashioned in accordance with the will of the ecclesiastical.[5] All States, except those established by priests, were of human origin and due to usurpation and robbery. Still the State is an institution necessary for the Church and should in consequence be controlled by it in order to accomplish its divine purposes. Since the spiritual power established the earthly, it could judge it if it were not good. As the soul controlled the body so the Pope could rule secular matters and had absolute authority in the appointment to all benefices.

The Church had the right to own property. Simple

---

[1] Aegidius, *De eccl.*, c. 5, fol. 3–4[1]. [2] Ib., c. 6, fol. 4–6[1].
[3] Ib., c. 8–9. [4] Ib., c. 2.
[5] Ib., c. 6.

possession did not affect holiness.[1] The Lord did not enjoin
poverty on his Apostles for all time, but only for a special
occasion. In Old Testament times the Levites held whole
cities. Hence the Church had a right to its possessions.[2]
Since the soul ruled the body and since the body ruled its
possessions, so the Pope ruled over soul, body, and possessions.
As the king ruled over bodies and acres, so the Pope ruled
over him. All worldly possessions owed tithes to the Church.
Was not that proof of the dominion of the spiritual power ? [3]

The assertion that both powers were founded with equal
or similar authority was false. The royal power was in reality
only an instrument for and to be used by the spiritual power.
Moses and the judge, Samuel, and Saul were Old Testament
examples demonstrating that relationship. Even if God
created two powers corresponding to the body and soul, the
secular must be subservient to the spiritual, as the body is
ruled by the soul, in order to have a person.[4] Hence the
temporal is subjected to the spiritual control. Hence no man
could have any right of inheritance except through the Church,
and no man could even own a farm or a vineyard except through
the Church, for there is no true justice and no true state of
which Christ is not the founder and by which the Holy Mother
Church is not honoured. The Church had, therefore, universal
lordship over all possessions and the faithful might remain
secure in the consciousness of adequate protection of their
interests.[5] Sin, however, could destroy the right of possession ;
but the Church could reinstate the truly penitent. In short
man had to thank the Church for everything he had and all
the blessings he enjoyed.[6]

Such were the arguments of the boldest and most daring
defenders of the sacred ground on which Boniface VIII stood.

James of Viterbo (*d.* 1308) an Italian Augustinian, and a
prominent teacher at Paris, who occupied the positions of
Bishop of Beneventum (1302) and Archbishop of Naples,
wrote *De regimine christiano*, or *Christian Government*. This
tract was a comprehensive defence of Papal supremacy. It
was dedicated to Boniface VIII as " the holy lord of the kings
of the earth ", and was called forth by the attacks made on
the prerogatives of the Pope. Christ's vicar was both king

---

[1] Aegidius, *De eccl.*, c. 1.   [2] Ib., c. 2–3.   [3] Ib., c. 5.
[4] Ib., c. 5.   [5] Ib., c. 7.   [6] Ib., c. 8.

and priest, and his temporal authority was derived, not from the Donation of Constantine, but from Christ's commission " to bind and to loose ". The Pope was king of kings in both mundane matters and spiritual affairs—the bishop of the earth and supreme law-giver, whom every subject must recognize and obey to insure his salvation. As the source of all law, the Pope could act according to law or against law, just as he chose to do.[1]

Henry of Cremona (d. 1312), an Italian, wrote *De potestate papae*, or *The Power of the Pope*. He was a distinguished canon lawyer, often consulted by Pope Boniface VIII, who sent him with the delegation to take the famous bulls *Salvator mundi* and *Ausculta fili* to Philip the Fair in 1302, and appointed him Bishop of Reggio. He wrote the tract about 1301, and was probably well paid for the work, as were all the defenders of Boniface. His text was Matt. xxvii, 18 : " All power is given unto me." He claimed that the attack on the Pope's temporal jurisdiction was of recent date, and made by certain " sophists " who deserved death for treason. The Pope's authority was based upon the Scriptures, the fathers, canon law, and reason. History proved that God ruled on earth first through Noah, the patriarchs, Melchizedec, and Moses, who were both kings and priests. Moses punished Pharoah. Christ carried both swords, drove out the money-changers, wore the crown of thorns, and had power to judge the world. These same powers were given to Peter and his successors. The State sustains the same relation to the Church as the moon to the sun, and the Emperor has only such power as the Pope confers upon him. Constantine only confirmed powers already possessed by the Pope. The Pope transferred the Empire to Charles the Great, and Innocent IV deposed Frederick II. If at times Popes were abused by rulers, it was no proof of royal superiority. Imperial and royal functions could not be exercised without Papal consecration. When Christ said : " My kingdom is not of this world," he only meant that the world refused to obey him ; and " render unto Cæsar the things that are Cæsar's " implied no obligation on Christ's part to pay tribute to Cæsar.[2]

The oligarchical opposition to Papal absolutism, which

---

[1] Scholz., 129–53 ; Finke, 166–70, 459–71.
[2] Finke, 166–70 ; 459–71 ; Scholz, 152–65.

developed in the college of cardinals, began as early as the time of Gregory VII, when it was asserted that real sovereign power rested not in the Pope but in the college of cardinals, who constituted the true Church of Rome. The Pope, it was held, was simply the executive power to carry out the will of the sovereign college, without whose approval no Papal edict was valid. It professed to have the power likewise to depose the Pope for good cause. Frederick, in his conflict with the Papacy, had done much to encourage that position.[1]

The opposition of the Colonna to Boniface VIII was not without precedent, therefore, and not such an unheard of proposition as it might appear. Jean Le Moine was a writer who stoutly defended the sovereignty of the cardinals against the Pope.[2] He maintained that the Pope and the cardinals together formed the Roman Church. The Pope was the head, the cardinals the body of that supreme organization. Consequently they must work together. The Pope could not abolish the college of cardinals, who constituted the sovereign power. The Pope was supreme, however, and could depose a king or an emperor. He was the ruler of all men and all were subject to him. All nations must give heed to his words and obey his commands—not as slaves, but as freemen. The Pope was not an absolute despot, but only the administrator and dispenser of the highest things. But nevertheless he was constitutionally subject to the cardinals.

The cardinals Jacob and Peter Colonna took the position that Boniface VIII was an illegal Pope—a usurper. They did not appeal from the Pope to a universal council as the highest source of justice, but merely as the best means of getting rid of a false Pontiff. They did not go so far as to advocate the sovereignty of the general council, but viewed it simply as a court to weigh evidence. Theoretically they believed that the Pope was called by God and had his power from God. Hence no assembly of people in a council stood above the Pope. The whole Church was a body ; the Pope was the head of that body, and the source of unity. Papal supremacy was absolute and could not be divided ; it was subject only to the sovereignty of the college of cardinals. That body was under the obligation not only to oppose but to depose a wicked and illegal Pope, because they were both members of the

[1] See Sägmüller, *Kirchenrechts*, 213–137.　　[2] Scholz, 194–8.

universal Church and of the head of that Church. The Church was founded on them and hence together with the Pope they must watch over, guide, and educate the Church. What they sought to establish in the Church was an aristocratic oligarchy of the cardinals as the sovereign power in the Church.[1]

The anti-Papal party accepted all the arguments commonly employed to prove the divine origin of the Church, but they denied that the sovereign power in the Church was in the hands of the Pope. The Pope was only the chief bishop of the Church, possessed of supreme administrative powers, and as such was to be obeyed by clergy and laity alike within the limits of his jurisdiction. The cardinals took the ground that sovereign power was vested in the hands of the college of cardinals. This view reduced the government of the Church to an oligarchy. On the other hand the bishops were prone to take an aristocratic view of Church polity, and to insist that sovereign power was located in the universal council composed of all the higher clergy. Both wings of this party insisted that the secular power was subjected to the ecclesiastical. All organs and means of the worldly rule must be fashioned in accordance with the will of the Church, as amply demonstrated by all nature. The State blessed and aided by the sovereign Church should in return assist the Church in the realization of its lofty purposes and in the defence of its property. This party was not averse to supporting the national state in its conflict with Papal absolutism as a useful ally, while at the same time it repudiated the extreme claims of the publicists who argued for the supremacy of the temporal power over the spiritual authority. The national state might be independent of Papal supremacy in its widest pretensions, but it was subjected to the sovereignty of ecclesiastical authority when constitutionally exercised.

This party might also be called a reform party because it insisted upon a complete reformation of the Church " in head and members " with sweeping vehemence and telling effect, and undoubtedly did much to pave the way for the creation of a powerful reform party in the Church in the next generation.

The most representative spirit of the anti-Papal wing of the ecclesiastical party was William Durand (d. 1331),[2] the

---

[1] Scholz, 198–207.   [2] Ib., 208–23.

Bishop of Mende, appointed to that office while still a youth. He wrote a remarkable work *On General Councils and the Reformation of Church Abuses*.[1] He asserted that the sovereign power in the Church was vested in a general council which had universal oversight over law and order, spiritual and human affairs, the spread of the gospel, and other important matters. The Pope could not change the acts of councils. All power, secular and religious, was from God who established the ecclesiastical hierarchy to rule mankind. All the apostles received power equally and directly from Christ. Peter was only the first among them and not their superior. The commission in Matt. xvi, 19, was intended for all of them and not for Peter alone. The bishops in the Church succeeded to powers of the apostles and consequently had full power over their respective dioceses and must be obeyed. Hence they should take a greater part in Church affairs. A council of bishops should be held twice a year to manage the affairs of the Church. The Pope was merely the bishop of the first see of Christendom. As such, he was God's representative on earth, but he should not attempt to be the prince of the church universal. He should never act without the advice of his cardinals. All of the limitations of the Pope were pointed out and the advisability of restricting him rigidly to his prerogatives was established.

He upheld that set of principles which developed into Gallicanism. He defended the right of the French nation in its quarrel with the extreme claims of Boniface VIII, but at the same time he clung tenaciously to the conviction that the State was subject to the Church organized in a general council, which he thought ought to be convened every ten years.[2]

Durand was probably the first to use the expression of " reformation in head and members ", which came to be so common for two centuries following. He outlined a radical reform programme covering the whole Church and urged the Pope to undertake it and the whole Church to co-operate in it.

This general survey of the literary output occasioned by the Franco-Papal controversy reveals clearly two very important

---

[1] Given in Goldast, ii, 95. [2] Scholz, 214.

facts : first, the fearless, powerful, and radical attacks made upon Papal absolutism by both laymen and ecclesiastics, which were very significant for the ages ahead ; and secondly, the comparatively few and relatively unimportant defenders of the extreme claims of the Papacy. Verily a new day was dawning for the mighty Medieval Church of the time of Innocent III.

8. *Conclusions from a Survey of the Literature*

From the general survey of the literature growing out and resulting from the controversy between the French national state and the Papacy certain significant conclusions may be drawn :—

1. The Middle Ages were dominated by the concept of the unity of the human race and hence the independence of the Church and State seemed well-nigh unthinkable. The Church of the Christians was a God-state—a theocracy—with two powers, or two swords, necessarily related either by subordination or co-ordination according to the view-point taken. The rise of the concept of a sovereign national state led to an open attack on the unity theory and opened a new chapter in estimating political and ecclesiastical powers and relationships. This new organization made a severe assault upon the prerogatives of the Papacy, particularly in reference to the administration of justice, the sacredness of ecclesiastical property, and the independence of the clergy from political jurisdiction.

2. Opposition to the doctrine of absolutism, as advanced by the defenders of the Papacy, was extended even to the very foundations of the spiritual power of the Papacy. The primacy of the Papacy was not wholly broken down. Some denied that Peter was the chief of the apostles, and hence of all Christians ; consequently they repudiated the divine origin of the Papacy. Others asserted that the Papacy rested upon the united apostolic foundation. Still others held that it had a historical development helped on by emperors and councils. These radical ideas were to be much discussed in the following periods and were to win many adherents.

3. Both the importance and the power of the Papacy were greatly reduced. The college of cardinals developed its

own independence and opposed the absolutism of the Pope. The bishops, threatened by both the Pope and the secular rulers with a loss of their prerogatives and privileges, took sides against Papal absolutism. The idea of a parliamentary government of the Church was suggested by Durand and John of Paris. Councils and synods sought to minimize Papal authority. The doctrine of conciliar sovereignty was developed out of the reiterated call for a general council to settle the great problems before Christendom. The questions were raised as to whether the council could be called without the Pope, and whether it could depose the Pope.

4. The laity began to assume a prominence never noticeable before. A secular ruler asserted his superiority to the Pope, and other kings were taking the same position. The Church was defined as composed of both laity and clergy. The general council was to be constituted of both laity and clergy. Laymen began to hold a prominent position in both Church and State never before attained. The clergy from Pope to parish priest were told to attend to their spiritual duties and not meddle in the affairs of the laity. This was all very significant and clearly indicated that the day of priestly dominance in all phases of European civilization was rapidly passing away.

5. The national state appeared as a self-sufficient organization, independent of the Church in its origin and in its purposes. Popular sovereignty was suggested as the basis of the State; although the hereditary monarchy existed everywhere. In England and France little thought was given to the idea of a world empire, as in Germany and Italy. The kings of England and France were sovereign emperors in their own states. The State began to play a new rôle and increased its prerogatives and enlarged its duties at the expense of the Church. The new sphere of governmental activity now included education, social welfare, and even religious matters. Not only were the clergy taxed as subjects, but they were virtually made officers of the State.

6. Many new and revolutionary ideas were struggling for expression and recognition. The literature of the thirteenth century suggested thoughts which were boldly carried to their logical conclusion in the next century by minds like Marsiglio Padua and William Occam, who not only advocated the separation of the Church and State, but urged the democratic

organization of both Church and State. The suggestion of natural law and popular sovereignty awakened a critical spirit and caused the people to think. Many radical tendencies appeared in consequence concerning nobility of birth, slavery, royalty, the right of special privilege, citizenship, the rights of man, and common welfare, which paved the way for the Reformation and the political revolutions of the following centuries. These forces undermined Papal authority and ecclesiasticism, and led to the decline of the Roman hierarchy. Of course, the pretensions and claims of the Roman Church were not surrendered. On the contrary they were asserted with more vehemence than ever, but the Church was impotent to make them good as in the days of Innocent III.

CHAPTER III

THE BABYLONIAN CAPTIVITY

9. *Crisis before the Church at death of Boniface VIII in 1303*

THE death of Boniface VIII in 1303 left the Papacy in a very critical condition. The successful attack upon the Papal claims to temporal supremacy had given both an occasion and an opportunity for an open assault upon the very foundations of the Medieval Church. The Church was confronted by a crisis such as it had never up to this time been called upon to face. Upon the character and personality of the successor of Boniface VIII depended the decline or the ascendency of Papal sovereignty as outlined by Gregory VII and enforced by Innocent III and his successors in the thirteenth century. There had come to the Roman hierarchy a period of fiery trial which was to drag along in its disastrous course for 250 years before the Roman Catholic Church in the sixteenth century was reformed and restored to something like its old power, but with a loss in territory, numbers, and prestige.

The first stage of this crisis was the period from 1305 to 1377, during which, with the exception of three years under Urban V in 1367–70, the head of the Church never once set foot in Rome, the historical capital of the Medieval Church, but remained in France, or in Avignon, on the French border, under the predominate influence of the French monarchy. The disappointed Italians, in anger and jest, denounced this epoch of about seventy years as the Babylonian Captivity or Exile, and referred to the government of the Church as the Avignon Papacy.

The successor of Boniface VIII was Benedict XI, the General of the Dominicans, a cardinal since 1298, and a loyal Italian supporter of the dead Pontiff. Elected Pope in 1303, he died within eight months. He was a mild peacemaker and lacked the wisdom and calm strength so badly needed to confront the perplexities of his position. Instead of taking the weapon from the cold hand of his predecessor to smite the French ruler, he capitulated to that victorious monarch.[1] Punishments and sentences against Philip IV, his lands, cities, and subjects were either modified or recalled.[2] He acknowledged the defeat of the Papacy at the secular hands and signed the death warrant of the political Papacy. To uphold the semblance of Papal authority, Nogaret [3] and Sciarra Colonna, together with their accomplices in the outrage against the haughty old Pontiff at Anagni, were declared excommunicated and summoned to appear before the Papal tribunal.[4] All things considered, however, perhaps a compromising middle course among so many dangers was the safest one to follow, and had he lived longer many of the disastrous results which followed his reign might have been shunted off.[5]

The death of Benedict XI opened up a new opportunity for French statesmen and for the ambitious French king, who was resolved to take advantage of his triumph over Boniface VIII by crowning with the Papal tiara a Pontiff whom he could use for the furtherance of his own plans.

The conclave met in Perugia, and was so torn by rival French and Italian factions that it took nearly eleven months to elect a Pope. Finally, on 5th June, 1305, Bertrand de Got, a Frenchman educated in France, and at the time Archbishop of Bordeaux, was chosen Pope and assumed the name of Clement V. In selecting him for this high office each party thought that a Pope favourable to its interests had been elected. The Italians based their faith on the fact that Clement owed his promotion to Boniface VIII ; that he had attended the Roman council in 1302 against the king's orders ; that he had quarrelled with the king's brother ; and that as the Archbishop of Bordeaux, he was legally the subject and vassal of the king of England.[6] The French cardinals, on the contrary, had direct assurance from the messenger of Philip IV that this candidate had committed himself to French interests. John Villani, a contemporary, asserted that Philip forced

---

[1] Dupuy, *Histoire du différend d'entre le pape Bon. VIII et Phil. le Bel*, Paris, 1665.
[2] Potthast, No. 25,418 ; Holtzmann, 119, 121.
[3] Holtzmann, 121–2 ff. Cf. Muratori, ix, 1,013 : Villani, vii, 80.
[4] Holtzmann, 125.
[5] Funke, *Pope Benedikt XI*, Münster, 1891.
[6] Holtzmann, 131.

Clement to swear to six promises before giving him assurances of election. Five of these promises concerned the total undoing of the acts of Boniface VIII against Philip and the complete recognition of the claims of the French crown. The sixth was a blank promise, the terms of which were to be revealed later.[1] The weight of historical evidence rejects that account now,[2] although it is quite generally held that since Clement certainly owed his election to Philip's influence there must have been some definite understanding between them. In fact, later events clearly indicated some positive arrangement.

The cardinals besought the newly chosen Pontiff to go to Rome for his coronation. He was in France at the time of his election and, to the surprise and consternation of the Italian cardinals, he ordered the college to repair to Lyons, where he was crowned with great pomp in the presence of Philip IV and representatives of the King of England on 14th November, 1305. During the customary public procession a wall fell on the Pope, he was thrown from his horse, the Papal crown was hurled to the ground, and from it the most precious jewel, a rare carbuncle, was lost. This was not the only jewel lost from the Papal crown during the Babylonian Captivity. Other misfortunes occurred. One of the Pope's brothers and ten barons in the Papal retinue lost their lives. The next day another brother was slain in a duel. No wonder the Italians and Germans turned prophets and predicted dire disasters.

For four years Clement V resided at Lyons, Bordeaux, Poitiers, and Toulouse ; and finally, in 1309, he selected as his Papal residence Avignon in Provence, on the border of France, which Philip had turned over to the King of Naples.[3] There Clement lived five years, and was succeeded by six Popes,[4] all French, until 1377, before the Papacy was definitely removed to Rome. Such were the significant beginnings of the Babylonian Exile.

Scarcely ever was a Pope put in a more compromising and humiliating position than Clement V. His subserviency to a

[1] Muratori, xiii, 417 ; cf. Raynaldus, *Ann.*, 1305, 2–4.
[2] Döllinger, *Akad. Vorträge*, iii, 254 ; Hefele, vi, 394–403 ; cf. Archer in *Encyc. Brit.*, xxiii, 164 ; *Cath. Encyc.*, iv, 20.
[3] In 1348, Clement VI paid the Crown of Naples 80,000 gold florins for Avignon. It remained Papal property until annexed to France during the French Revolution.
[4] John XXII, 1316–42 ; Benedict XII, 1334–42 ; Clement VI, 1342–52 ; Innocent VI, 1352-62 ; Urban, 1362–70 ; Gregory XI, 1370-8.

king who had defied and triumphed over the prerogatives of the Papacy was a sorry spectacle. Clement V had a deep love for France, and no doubt his will had been weakened by his sickly condition so that he acceded more readily than otherwise might have been the case to the wishes of the French cardinals and the French monarch. Besides, it must be remembered that Italy was in a state bordering on anarchy, torn by rival factions, and Rome was positively unsafe. These deplorable conditions no doubt had much to do with Clement's " unholy resolve ", as Pastor calls it, to remain away from the old capital.

Philip IV, feeling that Clement was wholly under his thumb,[1] demanded a formal condemnation of his dead foe, Boniface VIII ; his name stricken from the list of Popes as a heretic ; and his ashes scattered to the winds. Clement sought to avert such a disgraceful procedure partly by delay and partly by new favours. Consequently he renewed the absolution granted to the king by Benedict XI ; he strengthened the French party in the Papal court by creating nine French cardinals and by appointing twenty-three French bishops [2] ; he restored the Colonnas to their rank as cardinals ; he gave Philip permission to tithe the Church property for a period of five years ; and he recalled the offensive bulls *Clericis laicos* and *Unam sanctam* so far as they affected and offended France or implied the subjection of the French ruler to the Papal chair not customary before their issue. For a time, in consequence, Philip's ferocity against Boniface was allayed, but he soon returned to his determination to have his old enemy condemned, and now demanded a formal trial of the deceased Pontiff. Clement had to yield at last, and a trial was ordered for 2nd February, 1309, but it was finally transferred to the Council of Vienne held in 1311, in which the faith and good name of Boniface were vindicated.

The implacable monarch was not satisfied. To purchase the postponement of the condemnation of Boniface, Clement V had to pay a humiliating price. He publicly declared that Philip and Nogaret were innocent of all guilt and actuated only by good motives in preferring charges against Boniface.

---

[1] Döllinger, *Akad. Vorträge*, iii, 254.
[2] That gave France a majority in the College of Cardinals. Holtzmann, 132.

He addressed the bull *Rex gloriae* to Philip in 1311, in which it was asserted that the secular kingdom was founded by God ; that France in the new dispensation occupied the place of Israel, the elect people in the old dispensation ; and that Nogaret's actions at Anagni were for the noble purpose of saving the Church. Several other bulls were issued, apparently at the nod of Philip, whenever his conscience began to prick him, recalling all punishments, charges, and censors whatsoever against Philip and France. Further to placate the monarch all of Boniface's decrees were ordered to be effaced from the ecclesiastical records, and these erasures may still be seen in the *Regesta* of Boniface VIII preserved in the Vatican Library.[1] Finally Clement consented to the king's avaricious wish for the destruction of the Templars. On 22nd March, 1312, Clement issued a bull abolishing that Order on the ground of heresy, immorality, and uselessness.[2] In this wise, and only at the cost of these measures, did the Pope save the reputation of his friend Boniface VIII and thus at the same time preserve his own self-respect.

The selection of Clement V as Pope was obviously unfortunate. He bowed to the will of the king of France in nearly every particular except the condemnation of Boniface VIII. He did all he could to build up a French party in the Church by appointing Frenchmen to important positions almost to the total exclusion of other candidates. Nepotism, under his reign, was rampant and he was the chief sinner. Out of nine cardinals created by him, five were his relatives and three of them were only boys. His brother was made Rector of Rome and other kinsmen received Ancona, Ferrara, Spoleto, Venaissin, and other places within his gift.[3]

In money matters Clement was shrewd, greedy, and economical. From Benedict XI he received a fairly large sum. He took pains to levy tribute on churchmen of all grades and collected the incomes of vacant benefices.[4] His yearly income

---

[1] See Tosti *Storia di Bonifazio VIII*, Rome, 1886, ii, 343–4.

[2] Mirbt, *Quellen*, 149 ; Holtzmann, 139 ff.

The Templars had been founded in 1119 to protect pilgrims and to defend the Holy Land. The Order had become rich and useless. Philip coveted its wealth. Hence he had the Grand Master and many Templars arrested in 1397 and thrown into prison. In France the Templars were tried on 127 charges, tortured, burned, condemned, and punished wholesale. Clement V ordered trials in Germany, Italy, Spain, Portugal, England, and Cyprus.

[3] Ehrle, *Nachlass Clemens V (Ar. f. Kirch.)* v, 139.   [4] Haller, 45.

was an average of 225,000 gold florins, while his annual expenses were about 100,000 gold florins.[1] Thus he was able to save about 125,000 gold florins each year. These savings he regarded as his private fortune instead of trust funds for the Church, and consequently he made a will in 1312 disposing of his fortune of 814,000 gold florins. To his nephew, the Viscount of Lomogue, he gave 300,000 for a crusade ; to relatives and servants 314,000 ; to churches and the poor convents the remaining 200,000. In addition a sum of 70,000 had been set aside to be divided between his successor and the cardinals. A loan of 160,000 made to the King of France, and a like sum to the King of England were never repaid.[2] These loans of 320,000 gulden were to be devoted to charity and a crusade when the money was returned.[3] After Clement's death, however, the large sums he had saved and hoarded suddenly disappeared ; consequently his successor, John XXII, brought suit against the dead Pontiff's suspected relatives, and forced the Viscount of Lomogue to return 300,000 gold florins.[4] Villani characterized Clement as " licentious, greedy of money, a simoniac, who sold in his court every benefice for gold ".[5]

Notwithstanding his disgraceful bargains with the King of France, Clement V with increasing arrogance promulgated the principles of universal Papal supremacy. Although these principles were waived in France, they were stoutly defended abroad. He quarrelled with Venice over Ferrara in 1308, and the next year launched against that state a ban and secular forfeiture in terms hitherto unheard of.[6] All princes and bishops were enjoined to despoil and enslave the Venetians found in their dominions. He likewise attempted to force an arbitration between the German Emperor, Henry VII, and King Robert of Sicily as if both of them were his acknowledged vassals.[7]

---

[1] Ehrle, v, 147.
[2] Ib., 126, 135 ; Haller, 46.
[3] Göller, *Päpst. Finanzwesen*, 122.
[4] A few months after Clement's death, the viscount lent the King of France 110,000 florins and the King of England 60,000 florins. In 1322 he paid to John 120,000 florins, and was supposed to use the rest for a crusade. Göller, 122.
[5] *Chronicle*, ix, 59.
[6] Raynaldus, *Ann.*, 1309, No. 6.
[7] Ib., *Ann.*, 1312, No. 44.

10. *Babylonian Captivity continued by successors of Clement V*

When Clement V died on 29th April, 1314, it took the cardinals twenty-seven months to elect a successor.[1] Dante begged them to elect an Italian Pope who would return to Rome.[2] Other Italians voiced that sentiment. The complaint about the long vacancy was bitter and came from all parts of Europe. Finally the new King of France called the conclave of twenty-three cardinals to meet at Lyons, and on 7th August, 1316, Jacques, the Cardinal Bishop of Porto, was elected Pope.[3] One cardinal said : " We have chosen as Pope the worst man who lives on earth." [4] " Small, like Zaccheus," said Ferretus of Vicenza, " with a shrill squeaking voice, stiff, pedantic, uncommonly active and industrious, restless and tireless, ambitious to pose as a theologian, diplomatic, greedy of gain, simple and even austere in his personal habits, broadly cultured, very tenacious of purpose, and dominating by nature "—such was John XXII, the most noteworthy of all the Avignon Pontiffs. He had solemnly promised the Italian cardinals, before election, that he would never mount an ass except to start to Rome but thereafter he absolutely shunned that method of travel. After coronation at Lyons, he took a ship on the Rhône for Avignon, and never again left that city.

John XXII accepted the transfer of the seat of the Papacy to Avignon as an accomplished fact in the interest of France, and in this respect he followed in the footsteps of Clement V. His predecessor had lived in the Dominican monastery as a guest at Avignon, but John XXII set up a magnificent Papal establishment there.[5] Out of eight cardinals appointed at the beginning of his reign, seven were Frenchmen. That act revealed his policy. To make places for his supporters the number of sees in Spain and France was increased. The long-drawn conflict with Emperor Lewis of Bavaria also plainly showed his pro-French predjudices.

[1] The college consisted of 24 members : 8 Italians, 16 French. But the French party was divided into three hostile factions—10 from Gascoyne, 3 from Provence, and 3 from other parts of France. A two-thirds vote is necessary to election.
[2] *Opere minori di Dante,* iii, 510. Firenze, 1857.
[3] Cf. Villani, ix, 81, for a queer explanation of the election of John XXII.
[4] Höfler, *Aus Avignon,* 32.
[5] Faucon, *Mélanges d'archeologie et d'hist.,* ii, 43 ff.

In the conception of the prerogatives of his office John XXII followed Innocent III and Boniface VIII, hence his reign was full of grievous disputes. He was such a determined supporter of the two-sword theory that he heroically wielded the " spiritual sword " to support the temporal sword.[1] He accepted the canonical-legal traditions of his office; he unduly centralized ecclesiastical administration; and he enlarged and partly reorganized the Papal Curia in the interest of greater efficiency. He had studied law as well as theology at Montpellier and Paris, and had taught both canon and civil law at Toulouse and Cahors. His standing as a lawyer was shown by the fact that he was called upon to deliver the legal opinion in favour of the destruction of the Templars, and was attached to the court of Charles II of Naples as chancellor. In ecclesiastical affairs he was likewise very active. He was made bishop in 1300, and was transferred to the see of Avignon in 1310. Two years later he was appointed Cardinal Bishop of Porto by Clement V. Indeed, few Popes of the Middle Ages, before assuming the tiara, had had a wider experience in both political and religious affairs than John XXII. In his new position at Avignon his interest in European affairs was quickened. His vast correspondence and bulls, covering a multitude of subjects, fill 59 volumes of the Vatican archives to-day, and show how closely he followed both the secular and the ecclesiastical movements of his day in all countries, and how everywhere he sought to further the interests of the Church.

John XXII's financial policy was the most conspicuous feature of his reign. In his greed for gold he outdid Clement V. He accepted all the methods of money-raising invented by Clement and devised more. He was the first Pope to organize the granting of grace, temporal or eternal, into a gold-producing source by his reformation of the chancery taxes.[2] He was the first Pope to lay down the principle that no one could have a place without simony.[3] Every position had a price—a bishopric cost 1,000 scudi, another benefice 100 scudi, etc., so that all the clergy were forced by the system to become

---

[1] Sauerland, *Uukunden und Registen,* i, p. xix.
[2] Tangl, *Das Taxenwesen der päpstliche Kanzlei* (Mitteil. des Inst., f. österr. Gesch. XIII, 1–106).
[3] Höfler, *Hus,* 32.

simoniacs. His financial policy was developed into a fine art and will be dealt with later on. It was believed by his contemporaries that he died in 1334, at the age of 85, possessed of fabulous wealth, the richest man in Christendom.[1] Villani reported that he left a fortune of 25,000,000 florins, or $60,000,000 of our currency. Ehrle reduces the amount to $2,000,000,[2] but even this sum for that period was a tribute to John's shrewd and successful financiering. His methods, more vigorously applied by his successors, made the Curia of Avignon generally detested as the chief gold power of the world. He was the innovator of this new regime without justification by precedent or the Papal constitution. Evidently he did not feel it to be his duty to imitate Jesus of Nazareth who knew not where to find a bed on which to rest his head.[3] He wished, like his predecessors, to rule in Christ's name, but differed from them largely in employing money as the best means of enlarging and safeguarding his government of the Church. There were those who even hinted that with his wealth he meant to insure his independence, conquer rebellious Italy, and return in triumph to Rome,[4] as both Pope and Emperor.[5]

John XXII gave a great deal of attention to political matters. In theory he stood firmly by the claims of Boniface VIII. Of course, he owed his elevation to the King of France, and he readily accepted all the obligations that implied. In dealing with France, therefore, he never went beyond giving salutary advice to the reigning sovereign. Haller contends, however, that John did not always meet the royal wishes.[6] But if he exercised little independence in France, elsewhere he arrogantly asserted the political supremacy of the Papacy over all kings and peoples in all affairs.[7] Conditions in Italy and Germany gave him ample opportunity to set forth his claims. He appointed an imperial vicar for Italy and excommunicated Lewis of Bavaria. He settled disputes among rulers and tried to restore peace in England. He published the "Clementines" as the official collection of the Corpus Juris Canonici, and was the author

---

[1] *Galvaneus de la Flamma*, Muratori, xii, 1009. Cf. Haller, 104, 138.
[2] Ehrle, *Die 25 Millionen in Schatz Johann XXII, Archiv.*, 1889, 155–66.
[3] Villani, *Chron.*, ix, 20. [4] Ib., 20. [5] Höfler, *Avig. Päpste*, 32.
[6] Haller, *Papsttum*, 92. [7] Ib., 93.

F

of numerous decretals known as *Extravagantes Johannis XXII*.[1]
He spoke in the same tone of superiority to vassals like Robert
of Naples and Edward II of England.[2] He was not a lover
of peace as Pastor and Losreth would make out.[3]

John XXII was a man of culture for that day, and had a
wide range of interests. He gave generous patronage to
many scholars and artists, and encouraged them to tarry
at his court. He endowed colleges and appreciated the value
of education for clergy and laity alike. He also founded a
large library for that day, at Avignon. He built a magnificent
Papal palace at Avignon, and did much to beautify the city.
But in a genuine reformation of the Papal court and the
clergy at large John took no interest, and apparently felt
no need for it. He was primarily a statesman and a man of
affairs, and consequently did reorganize the Papal Curia and
enlarge it in the interest of greater efficiency.

In suppressing heresy, however, John was very active.
He caused the writings of Peter Olivi and Meister Eckhardt
to be examined, and condemned the former, while he censured
many passages from the latter's works. He took a positive
stand against the Spiritual Franciscans, and not only condemned a formal list of their errors, but also abolished their
separate convents. When they denied his authority, he
summoned sixty-four of them to Avignon. The twenty-five
who refused to obey his commands were turned over to the
Inquisition. Some were burnt alive ; others fled. It is
interesting to note that this very Pope who was so merciless
against the heretics was himself accused of heresy. He posed
as a constructive theologian and was fond of preaching
doctrinal sermons. Before his election to the office of Peter,
he had written a tract asserting that the souls of the blessed
dead do not see God until after the last Judgment. In at least
three sermons after his election he had made similar declarations. For these utterances he was accused by Occam, Cesena,
and others, with holding heretical views concerning the beatific
vision after death. Indeed, Lewis the Bavarian went so far as to

----

[1] Haller, 95.

[2] On one occasion he even ventured to advise Edward II about his food,
clothing, servants, recreations, manners, etc. Ib. 93. Raynaldus, 1317, secs.
45, 46 ; 1318, sec. 28. He spoke in the same style to Philip V of France.
Coulon, No. 60.

[3] Sauerland, iii, p. iv.

write the cardinals demanding a general council for the trial of the Pope. But John felt so confident that his theory was orthodox, that he imprisoned an English Dominican who preached against him and in confidence presented his views to the theologians of the Sorbonne at Paris. They decided against John's interpretation, however, and then Philip VI, who became interested in the controversy, called the Council of Vincennes, but it, too, stood in opposition to John's opinions.[1] Still unconvinced, John summoned a council of his own to meet at Avignon in December, 1333. Meanwhile, his friends apparently convinced him that retraction was the safest way out of the difficulty, for on 3rd January, 1334, he publicly announced that he never meant to teach aught contrary to the Holy Scriptures. Before his death he withdrew his earlier assertions and declared his belief in the contrary doctrine. In 1336 his successor, Benedict XII, issued a bull settling the disputed point in accordance with the view of the Sorbonne theologians.[2]

The third Avignon Pope, a Frenchman of course, was Benedict XII, a simple miller's son who had studied at Paris and received his doctor's degree in theology. He entered the Cistercian Order and became an abbot. By 1310 he was made bishop and in 1327 he was created cardinal. His election as Pope in 1334 on the first ballot, as reported by Villani, was an accident, it seems. He had no wealth, and but little influence that counted, consequently was not seriously considered as a candidate for the Papal office. The necessary two-thirds of the cardinals had voted for him merely to test the mind of the college. But the choice of Benedict was an excellent one, for he was one of the few men of real merit in the conclave. He was a pious, firm, prudent, peaceful, conscientious ecclesiastic, although he knew little of human nature, and was a babe in worldly politics and diplomacy.[3] He was a simple, jovial, joking, kind-hearted Pope,[4] who opposed all pomp and display.

This Pontiff was possessed with the determination to return to Rome and there re-establish the exiled Papacy. A Roman deputation called on him, and had no difficulty in securing

---

[1] Mansi, xxv, 982–4.   [2] Ib., 986.
[3] See Haller, 121, for an interesting characterization of Benedict XII.
[4] *Chron. de Melsa*, iii, 38. For an unfavourable account, see Baluze, i, 241.

an affirmative answer to their appeal. In anticipation of the removal, St. Peter's and the Lateran were repaired. But two powerful influences were brought to bear upon his determination ; first the French king, who of course openly opposed the change ; and secondly, the powerful cardinals who pointed out the practical impossibility of living in faction-rent Rome. Benedict was persuaded not to go to the Eternal City as a consequence, but as a compromise suggested Bologna. In the end, however, he decided to remain at Avignon, and in 1339 began to erect the permanent Papal palace, a grim, fortress-like structure, with thick walls and towers, which still stands as a silent and vacant witness of the destructive folly of the Babylonian Exile. Following the Pope's example, the cardinals built palaces in and near Avignon. These building enterprises made a return to Rome extremely unlikely.

The chief concern of Benedict was a thorough-going reformation of the Church. This desire was the product of his own conscious realization of the wide-spread and deep-seated abuses and corruptions, and of the numerous complaints and demands from all parts of Western Europe for the purging of the Augean stables at Avignon. The city was full of greedy, idle priests pulling wires for promotions and additional benefices. Many and various sorts of questionable practices had come into existence since the days of Innocent III. The following is the comprehensive reformatory programme laid down by this well-meaning leader of Christendom :—

1. All clerics not needed in Avignon were ordered to return to their benefices to perform their spiritual duties. Violators of this law of residence were threatened with summary chastisement.[1]

2. The scandalous " expectancies " granted by his predecessors, which had given rise to the sorry and disgraceful spectacle of six or eight prospective candidates watching with avaricious eyes for every possible vacancy, were all revoked. The qualifications of all applicants for benefices were carefully examined.[2]

3. The unholy practice of conferring benefices *in commendam*, whereby the recipients, often laymen, obtained the income without performing any service, was forbidden.

---

[1] *Cod. Barberin.*, xxxi, 11 f., 152 b.   [2] Baluze I, 210.

4. The appointment of boys to receive canonries in the cathedrals was stopped.

5. The system of " pluralities ", which enabled a favoured person to possess several benefices at once and thus draw an enormous income, was strongly condemned. Benedict granted benefices with such conscientious discrimination that some were left vacant a long time. Hence he was accused by greedy applicants with intentional delay in order to pocket the incomes.

6. A " registry of supplications " was created for the purpose of filing the numerous memorials to the Pope. In this way the custom of countersigning petitions for Papal favours, for which large fees were collected by subordinate officials, was abolished. At the same time the fees for documents issued by the various bureaux were regulated and made uniform.

7. Nepotism was eschewed by the Pope as personally abhorrent. He declared that he would be like Melchizedeck " without father, mother, or genealogy ". During his term of office only one relative was appointed to an office, and he was a worthy man urged upon the Pope by the cardinals.

8. As an upright, scholarly monk himself, Benedict was keen for monastic reforms, and endeavoured to revive the pristine monastic spiritual fervour as well as devotion to study. But he only incurred the ill-will of the monks, who had no desire to be reformed. One of them wrote the following famous couplet :—

" Nero he was—to laymen death ; a viper to a monk !
He never told the truth and constantly was drunk."

When the Pope died, in 1341, another monk wrote : " Nobody cried much for him."

9. He revised the list of Papal officers of his predecessors.[1]

This scheme of reformation was admirable, considering the circumstances, and does much credit to the motives and intentions of Benedict XII. For the Church it was most unfortunate that this worthy leader did not live a generation longer, because he might have done much to ward off the evil days ahead.

[1] Haller, *Papsttum*, **154** ff. An inventory of the Papal archives, catalogued according to country, province, and diocese, was made in **1336**. The sources of income of the Papal *camera* was also specified. Schäfer, *Röm. Quartalschr.*, 1909, vol. 23, p. 63.

At the same time heresy was combated wherever it appeared. The bishops were urged to search for its traces and root it out. The Inquisition was generously employed for that purpose in southern Europe, and Edward III was requested to use it in England and Ireland.[1]

Benedict was imbued with lofty ideals of Papal prerogative, and fought the anti-Papal doctrines and theories of the French political scentists. Following the ambition of Innocent III for world riule, he manifested a deep interest in the Greek and Armenian churches and sought to unite them with Rome. Though he was determined to act independently of the French monarch, yet by one means or another that ruler usually had his own way. Benedict wanted peace with Lewis of Bavaria, but Philip VI circumvented it. In vain the Pope tried to prevent war between England and France. Reformer, foe of heresy, builder of the Avignon castle, ally of France, and enemy of Germany against his own will,[2] Benedict made many and bitter enemies. Among the numerous hostile writings of that day the diatribes of Petrarch probably had the most influence.

There could not be a sharper contrast between two Popes than between Benedict XII and his successor Clement VI, who was elected in 1342, at the age of 51, and ruled the Church for a decade. He was a Benedictine monk, a loyal French-man, like the other Avignon Pontiffs educated at Paris, and later a professor of theology. His official promotion was rapid ; from abbot of his Order he was soon made bishop ; then archbishop in 1335 ; and finally cardinal in 1338. For some time he filled the responsible position of chancellor to the French king. Thus he was accustomed to the society of aristocratic prelates of noble origin, and moved in the circle of princes and monarchs.[3]

Clement VI held aloft the traditional claims of the Papacy and, when opportunity afforded, did not hesitate to enforce them. He asserted in 1344 that it was his prerogative to dispose of fiefs and benefices all over Christendom, and consequently he scattered favours with a prodigal hand.[4] In the old quarrel with Lewis the Bavarian he asserted the Papal right to pass

---

[1] Lea, *Hist. of Inq.*, i, 354 ; ii, 151, 301, 431 ; iii, 123, 159, 459.
[2] Benedict is reported to have said that if he had two hearts he would give one of them to the French king. Loserth, *Stud. zur. Kirchenpol.*, 20.
[3] Haller, 123. [4] Baluze I, 263, 284.

on the validity of all laws, and when the German princes disputed this pretension, he excommunicated the Emperor, deposed him, and had the electors choose Charles IV in 1346. To a Castilian prince he gave the Canary Islands in 1344 on the promise of the payment of tribute. He attempted, likewise, although unsuccessfully, to extend Papal jurisdiction by bringing the Greek and Armenian churches under Roman rule.

Shortly after his election a deputation, of which Rienzi and Petrarch were members, begged him eloquently to return to Rome, and conferred upon him as " Knight Roger " the senatorial dignity of the Eternal City. Clement was affable, and granted Rome the permission to hold a jubilee every fifty years, but he refused to go back. In fact, he was ardently attached to France and, it may be added, to his French relatives body and soul. Most of the twenty-five cardinals he created were Frenchmen, and twelve were his own kinsmen— one a brother and another a nephew. With no thought of restoring the Papacy in Rome, he purchased Avignon from Joanna of Naples at a cost of 80,000 florins and a release of the fair recipient from the charge of having murdered her first husband, together with a permission to marry a second. As a result of this conspicuous pro-French policy, Clement naturally had but little influence outside of France.

In studying the records which reveal the personality and purposes of Clement and his court, one thinks more of a temporal prince and courtiers, like those who surrounded Louis XIV, than of the successor of the lowly Nazarene and his followers. Indeed, Clement had both the manners and the defects of a great lord—traits which no doubt he inherited from the French nobility to which by birth he belonged. A gallant, gay, generous Frenchman, he forgave and forgot like a truly royal personage. In morals he was easy and most accommodating. He was a lover of good cheer, ease, comfort, horses and high living[1]; hence his court was renowned not alone for sumptuous banquets and brilliant receptions, to which ladies were freely admitted, but likewise for drinking carousals and loose morals.[2] Loving splendour and culture, his generous hand patronized letters and the fine arts. The great Papal palace was enlarged, and painters, architects, and poets

[1] Pastor, i, 76 ; Haller, i, 123.
[2] Villani, iii, 39 ; *Fontes rer Aust.*, iv, 227 ; *Chron. de Melsa*, iii, 89 ; Baluze I, 311.

thronged its halls. This prodigal liberality soon used up all
the funds amassed by the economical John XXII and saved
by the parsimonious Benedict XII. As a result, fresh taxes
were imposed, benefices were " reserved ", favours of all
sorts were sold, and the questionable methods of raising
money which Benedict had sought to abolish were revived.
At the death of Benedict XII and the accession of Clement,
all the world seemed to flock to Avignon for favours and
lucrative places.[1] Even the pleasure-loving immoral Petrarch
denounced Avignon as the sink-hole of Christendom, and said :
" Whatever you read of the gates of hell will apply to this
place." [2]

Clement cared naught personally for reforms, and gave
but little heed to the many complaints that poured in upon
him. Peter of Aragon urged him to send home to their
ecclesiastical duties the indolent horde of clergy living at his
court and begged him not to appoint any more foreigners to
the benefices in the kingdom of Aragon. But he was too
indulgent by nature to suppress the disorders surging about
him. He was a good theologian and an eloquent preacher,
like John XXII, but his sermons were of a very formal type,
entirely lacking in spiritual fire and conviction. He was not
deficient in personal courage, as is shown by the protection
he gave to the Jews during the Black Death in 1348–9, which
spread all over Europe with unspeakable suffering and fatality.[3]
In Avignon alone nine cardinals, seventy prelates, and half
of the population died. On the advice of his physicians,
Clement stayed within doors and kept large fires lighted.
Popular report charged the Jews with having brought the
plague from the East and in consequence massacres broke
forth in many cities. The Jews in large numbers fled to
Avignon, where Clement not only protected them but issued
two bulls to Christendom in which he declared the Jews to
be innocent of the charge against them and sought to suppress
the massacres. Another illustration of this Pope's sense of
justice ought to be cited. During the ravages of the dread

---

[1] Sauerland, i, xix.
[2] Compare the words of St. Birgitta, *Revelations*, vi, 63.
[3] Gasquet, *Black Death* ; Knighton, *Chronicon* Rolls Series, ii, 58–65 ;
Rogers, *Six Centuries of Work and Wages* ; Rogers, *England before and after
the Black Death ; Fortnightly Review*, viii, 190 sqq. ; Jessopp, *Coming of the
Friars.*

disease, the begging friars showed such devotion and self-sacrifice that large bequests were left to them. The secular clergy became very jealous, and demanded of Clement the suppression of the Mendicant Orders. It was reported that the Pope defended the monks with generous eloquence in these words : " Suppose the friars were to stop preaching : what would you preach ? Humility ? You, the proudest of all sorts of men ! Poverty ? You, who are so greedy that all the benefices on earth are not enough for you ! Chastity ? I am silent. God alone knows how your bodies are pampered. The friars well deserve any benefits they may have received from legacies. It is a fit reward of their courage and their zeal, and you are opposing them not from principle, but out of sheer envy." [1]

The college of cardinals entered into conclave at Avignon in 1352 to elect the fifth Pope of the Exile. Before proceeding to ballot a rule was adopted limiting the college to twenty members and stipulating on oath that the new Pope should divide his power and revenues with the cardinals. Innocent VI was then chosen and one of his first acts was to declare the agreement illegal and null because it limited the divinely appointed Papal power. He had conditioned his obligation with these words : " in so far as it is not contrary to Church law."

Innocent was a professor of law at Toulouse, and rose to the highest judicial rank. In 1338 he was made bishop ; four years later he became cardinal ; and in 1352 he was filling the office of grand penitentiary. He was a man of force, learning, and good morals. He patronized the arts and education.[2] He knew how to rule and he administered his high office with tact and wisdom. He favoured his family, as was natural, but appointed only competent representatives to office. His relations with the French court were friendly, but he was very much more independent than any of his four predecessors. When Avignon was attacked by French freebooters in 1357, he made a stubborn resistance, but in the end was forced to purchase his freedom at an enormous cost.

After Benedict XII, Innocent VI accomplished most in

---

[1] Locke, 67.

[2] Renan, *Hist. Litt.*, xxix, 21, refutes the charge that Innocent VI was an enemy of learning. Cf. Pastor, i, 94.

the way of reformation. He ordered the numerous ecclesiastics who flocked to Avignon for jobs and sinecures back to their benefices under penalty of excommunication. Some of the appointments of incompetents made by his predecessor were recalled. Numerous reservations were abolished,[1] and pluralities were disapproved. Luxury and fast living were banished from the Papal court, and the cardinals were advised to reform their lives. Judges were given a fixed salary in the interest of honesty and justice. All these reforms were, to be sure, very commendable, but by no means obliterated the many abuses that had crept into the Church.

Innocent VI had the eye and brain of a statesman, as well as of an able churchman. He stood on the ground tilled by Innocent III, and was much more discreet in managing his crops than Boniface VIII. In Italy the Papal States, under petty princes, were in open hostility to Papal authority. Innocent was determined to crush the revolt. To that end he sent Cardinal Albornoz in 1353 with plenty of gold and unlimited power to subdue Rome, and with him went Rienzi to quiet the people. Rome was taken and Rienzi again seized the reins of rule as senator. His victory was short-lived, however, for on 8th October, 1354, a popular uprising resulted in his death. But Albornoz with the mailed fist, a judicious use of gold, and diplomatic tact, restored Papal authority.

The attitude of this Pope towards the German empire was friendly and peaceable. He gave hearty approval to the coronation of Charles IV at Rome, since it would strengthen the Papal influence there, but the German king was required to give a solemn pledge that he would leave Rome on the very day of the ceremony, which occurred on Easter Sunday, 1355, when the imperial crown was placed on the king's head by a cardinal representing the Pope. Charles IV kept his promise, and returned at once to Germany to issue in 1356 the famous Golden Bull [2] in which the Pope's name was not even mentioned. The Pope, as a matter of course, protested because that constitutional document silently passed over the Papal claim of the right to confirm the election of German kings and to administer the empire in case of a vacancy, but the bull stood, never-

---

[1] Lux, *Reserv.*, 41.
[2] The Golden Bull is found in Henderson, 220 ; Thatcher and McNeal, 283 ; Ogg, 409.

theless, as the fundamental law regulating imperial elections. When Charles a little later proposed the reformation of the German clergy without consulting the Pope, Innocent again objected, but finally submitted in the interest of peace.

In other parts of Europe Innocent was equally active. He sought to end the war between France and England, and at length, in 1360, succeeded in arranging the Peace of Bretigny. His endeavours to reconcile Castile and Aragon proved to be fruitless, however, and the severe censures he laid upon Peter I of Castile, who had poisoned his wife, produced results of little consequence. Towards the end of his life he thought of a crusade and planned for a union of the oriental Christian Churches with Rome. His death in 1362 put an end to these high hopes. Nearly all historians regard Innocent VI as a sincere, conscientious, and capable ruler who laboured untiringly for the welfare of the Church. He never carried out his intention of going to Rome, but he paved the way for Urban V.[1]

The sixth Avignon Pope was Urban V, the son of a French knight, who early entered the Benedictine order, and in it rose to the rank of abbot. He was a university trained man, took his doctorate in law with high honour, and then taught canon law and the Holy Scriptures in Montpellier and Avignon.[2] On various important occasions he was used as a Papal legate by Innocent VI and indeed was returning from such a mission to Naples when he was chosen Pope in 1362.[3] He was not a cardinal, nor had he even been elevated to the rank of bishop.

Of the seven Avignon Pontiffs, Urban V was the purest in character, and the most spiritual.[4] He was the first Avignon Pope to visit Rome, and was the last occupant of Peter's chair to organize an actual crusade. Firmly convinced that the most pressing problem before him was the reformation of the clergy, he laboured hard and successfully to purify his own court ; to suppress simony and pluralism in the Church ; and to abolish immorality on the part of the clergy. Idle monks were set to work and absentee prelates were sent to their benefices, while new positions were given only to worthy

---

[1] Martène-Durand, *Thesaur.*, ii, 946, gives the letter to Charles IV announcing his intention to visit Rome.
[2] Christophe, *Papsttum in vierzehnten Jahrh.*, ii, 253.
[3] Froissart, i, c. 151.
[4] In 1870 he was canonized by Pius IX.

candidates.[1] He enforced the rule of holding provincial councils, so long neglected to the detriment of the local churches. He put a stop to the disgraceful practices of the advocates and procurators of the Papal court and made justice accessible to the poor and rich alike. He gave his personal attention to all Papal affairs, held his consistories punctually, kept strict order in his court, dispatched all business promptly, and put down all kinds of graft, fraud, and oppression.[2] He was free from all taint of nepotism, and even persuaded his father to give up a pension granted to him by the King of France. Although of a yielding disposition, yet whenever he believed the rights and interests of the Church were concerned, he was fearless and aggressive, so much so in fact, that he astonished all who knew him.[3] At the same time, he took the most vigorous measures against all heretical teachers.[4] He spent the vast sums which came into the papal treasury, not on vice and luxury, but in rebuilding Roman churches and in founding colleges. These worthy deeds were approved on all sides. Europe was for once at peace and nearly every court sent ambassadors to Avignon to extend congratulations to the new head of the Church.[5]

The greatest single event of Urban V's career was his return to Rome. The Eternal City had seen no Pope within her walls for more than sixty years. At Florence, Urban had declared that he was willing to die to see the Pope back in Rome. Petrarch at the time an old man, joined other patriotic Italians in urging Urban as he had implored other Pontiffs, to return to the historical capital of the Church. He severely rebuked the Avignon curia for its vices and lack of spirituality, and urged Urban not to hide himself in an obscure corner of the earth, but to return to Rome, which had been the centre of the whole world for so many centuries. He compared deserted and bleeding Rome with fat and fair Avignon, rolling in immorality and luxury, and asked Urban " whether at the day of judgment he would rather rise among the famous sinners of Avignon than with Peter and Paul, Stephen and Lawrence " in the Christian capital. The Romans also added their customary

---

[1] Christophe II, 266–9 ; Magnan, *Urb. V*, 147 ; Haller, *Papstthum*, 156.
[2] Schwab, 18.   [3] Pastor, i, 99.
[4] Raynaldus, *Ann.*, 1363 ; No. 27 ; 1365, No. 17 ; 1368, No. 16 ; 1369, No. 12, 13 ; 1370, No. 16.
[5] Christophe II, 256.

beseeching request. The Emperor Charles IV visited Avignon and offered to escort the Pope to Rome. Yielding to these influences, and actuated by the worthiest motives, Urban finally in 1366 announced his determination to remove the seat of the Papacy back to the Eternal City. Naturally the French king and all the cardinals except the three Italians, vehemently opposed the transfer, but in vain. Orders were sent to Rome for the restoration of the dilapidated buildings and churches.[1]

In April, 1367, Urban V quitted Avignon for the earlier home of his spiritual predecessors. On 19th May, a fleet of sixty vessels, contributed by Genoa, Venice, Pisa, and Naples, escorted the head of the Church from Marseilles first to Genoa, and then to Corneto, where he landed on 4th June. There envoys from Rome met him, and turned over to him the keys of the castle fortress of St Angelo, the emblem of sovereign power over the city of Rome. Thanks were offered to God, and mass celebrated on an improvized altar. The Pope then travelled slowly by land to his ecclesiastical home, and everywhere the people showed due respect and submission.[2] On 30th October, mass was celebrated at the high altar of St Peter's—the first since the death of Boniface VIII. The Romans received the Holy Father with fervent outbursts of loyalty and affection. Urban chose as his place of residence the Vatican, in preference to the Lateran. The Papal palace had been completely restored—roofs, floors, doors, walls, and walks all had to be renewed at a cost of about $15,000. The Papal expenses, as shown by the account books still preserved, from 27th April, 1367, to November, 1368, amounted to about $40,000.[3]

During the Babylonian Exile the proud old city of Rome had become almost a deserted ruin. The noble families had deserted the city, and even the priests had forsaken it. The population had dwindled to 17,000.[4] Public and religious

[1] Theiner, *Cod. dipl.*, ii, 430 ; *Arch. della Soc. Rom.*, vi, 13, 14 ; Adinolfi, i, 130.

[2] Raynaldus, 1370, n. 19 ; Froissart, ix, 49–51.

[3] Kisch, *Rückkehrs*, p. ix, xxx, 190–95.

[4] Döllinger, *The Church and the Churches*, 353. See Gregorovius, vi, 438, for a slightly higher estimate.

Part of his court remained in Avignon to manage affairs there. An inventory was made of all properties and documents, and copies were made of all official records, so that they could be taken to Rome. Schäfer, *Röm., Quartalichr.*, 1909, vol. 23, p. 65.

buildings, as well as private palaces, had fallen into a state
of decay. The Lateran had been burned in 1360 ; St. Paul's
was a ruin ; other sacred edifices were in sad need of repair.
Rubbish and disease-breeding pools of stagnant water filled
the streets. The beauty and ancient grandeur of Rome had
disappeared, and the city was a vast museum of Christian
and pagan antiquities. It is small wonder that Petrarch
compared the restoration of the Papacy to the return of Israel
from Egypt.

Urban's first concern was the restoration of the sacred
edifices. For repairs he gave 2,000 florins to the Lateran
and 5,000 florins to St Paul's. Quickly Rome began to revive
as the social, political and religious centre of Europe. The
clergy flocked to the city from all lands and the aristocratic
nobles returned to their palaces and estates, while the common
people began to pour in from the other Italian towns. Soon
Rome was privileged to welcome as its guests Joanna, the
Queen of Naples ; the King of Cyprus ; Emperor Charles IV ;
and the Byzantine Emperor, who came in 1360 to exchange
the possibility of union with the Roman church for material
assistance against the aggressive Turks. The old days of
Rome's greatness and power seemed about to be revived.

But Urban was keenly disappointed in everything and could
not measure up to his great opportunity. He was a man of
the best intentions, but of small ability, and was unable to
cope with the serious problems confronting him. His strong
right arm, Cardinal Albornoz, who had subdued Rome and
Italy with a harsh policy, was dead. The Italian states were
unsettled and troublesome. Perugia broke out in rebellion
and had to be put under the ban in 1369. The French
cardinals ever kept before the Pope's mind the striking
difference between cool, quiet, restful Avignon and foul,
decayed, barbarous, riotous Rome until his weak will gave
way to their petty grumbling and he decided to return
to guilt-laden Babylon. The prayers of the Romans, the
warnings of Petrarch, the dire prediction of his death by
St Birgitta and the calamity prophesied by Pedro of Aragon
were unavailing to turn him from his fatal decision.[1] On
5th September, 1370, he set sail from Corneto for Marseilles
and on 24th September he re-entered Avignon, but only to

[1] Pastor, i, 96–7.

die a little less than two months later on 19th December, 1370. When Petrarch heard the tidings he wrote : " Unhappy man, who might have died before the altar of Saint Peter and in his own habitation ! " [1]

The last Avignon Pope was Gregory XI, the son of a French count, and the nephew of Clement VI, who had lavished benefices upon him and in 1348 had made him cardinal at the early age of eighteen. As a young cardinal he attended the university of Perugia, where he made himself proficient in theology and canon law. Seemingly he was not spoiled by his social and ecclesiastical connections, but on the contrary won an enviable reputation for his learning and piety, his humility and purity of heart, as well as for his elegant manners and charming address. In 1370, at the early age of 35, he was elevated to the Papal throne at Avignon. His greatest fault was the one not unnatural for that age and of which most of his predecessors were guilty, namely, nepotism.[2] He seemed bent, likewise, upon strengthening the French party in the Church, as is shown by his creation of eighteen French cardinals and by his appointment of Frenchmen to Church offices in Italy. The latter policy, particularly, was a grave mistake, because it resulted in the uprising of the spirit of Italian nationality against the French Papacy.

Such a Pope, so long associated with both the best and the worst in the Church, with his keen eyes wide open to all faults as well as virtues of his age, had an excellent opportunity to comprehend the needs of the great organization committed to his guidance. As a pious scholar he believed that heresy threatened both the unity of the ecclesiastical organization and the purity of its doctrines, and therefore it must be suppressed at all hazards. Hence he issued no less than five bulls against Wiclif and the Lollards, and used strong methods in dealing with heretics elsewhere.[3] He also realized the need of a pure-minded, spiritual priesthood and consequently attempted to reform the clergy. In 1372 he sent home the idle priests at Avignon and in 1375 forbade the customary presents for appointments.[4] He sought to correct flagrant

[1] Robinson, *Petrarch*, 65.   [2] Scholz, 5.
[3] Lea, i, 356, 530 ; ii, 153, 176, 188, 294, 388, 442 ; iii, 454, 612.
[4] Haller, *Papsttum*, 157 ; Mirbt, *La politique pontificale et la retour du Saint Siege à Rome en* 1376 (1899), p. 10, 11 ; Denifle, *Désolation*, ii, 610.

evils like reservations, but found it to be necessary to compromise with the evil.[1] He gave his hearty approval to such orders as the Spanish Hermits of St Jerome. Like those before him he, too, sought to bring about a union of the Greek and Roman Churches and talked of a crusade as a means to that end.

No doubt more would have been accomplished by this active Pontiff to purify the clergy and to remove the rampant scandals in the Church, had not his health been poor and had not secular affairs so fully occupied his time. The old feud between France and England had broken out afresh and he strove in vain to bring about a reconciliation. He pacified Castile, Aragon, Sicily and Naples. But by far the most serious problem before him was the lawless and rebellious state of northern and central Italy, which threatened the Papacy with the permanent loss of the Papal States and even the election of an anti-pope. In Milan the all-powerful and truculent tyrant, Duke Bernabo, was again in open revolt. Gregory put him under the ban, but the self-confident duke forced the French Papal legates to eat the parchment bull and heaped insults upon them and their master. In 1372 the Pope declared war upon him and sent the forces of the Queen of Naples, the King of Hungary, and that English soldier of fortune, John Hawkwood, against him. Bernabo was brought to his knees and had to sue for peace, following which a truce was agreed upon in 1374. The next year, however, Florence joined Bernabo against the Pope and stirred up the Papal States to open revolt. A red flag with " Liberty " on it was unfurled and the overthrow of the priesthood itself was proclaimed. A league of 80 cities was formed to abolish the Pope's temporal power. Genoa and Pisa followed the example of Florence. The Papal Cities were called upon to throw off the yoke of tyranny and recover their old rights. " What Italian," asked Florence, " can endure the sight of so many noble cities serving the barbarians appointed by the Pope to devour the goods of Italy ? "[2] The appeal struck a popular, patriotic chord and consequently the Papal Cities of Bologna, Perugia, Narni, Viterbo, and Ferrara raised the banner of rebellion in 1375, and indeed the rebellion bade fair

[1] Lux, 45.
[2] Mirbt, *Rétour*, 48 ; Gregorovius, vi, 466 sqq.

to spread over the whole Papal patrimony.   Rome and Ancona alone remained loyal to the Pope.   The flame of discontent was intensified when the Pope sent 10,000 Breton mercenaries, under the leadership of that iron-hearted cardinal, Robert of Geneva, to crush the uprising.   Gregory then resorted to the thunderbolts of his office, and they accomplished more than the foreign hirelings.   An interdict hurled against the Florentines in 1376 excommunicating them and outlawing them and their possessions in very harsh terms—permitting the inhabitants to be seized as slaves and the city plundered —brought them to their senses and forced them to sue for peace.[1]   Genoa and Pisa were humbled by similar maledictions.

This conflict with the stubborn and rebellious states of Italy was carried on for five years before the Pope was absolutely convinced that the only remedy that would bring peace and save Italy to the Papacy was the removal of the government of the Church from Avignon to Rome.   This, undoubtedly, was Gregory's fundamental motive in deciding to make the transfer,[2] but other causes were also at work. Froissart says that Gregory had declared before his election, that, if the high honour of leading the Church should come to him, he would locate his Papal seat nowhere but in Rome.[3] The usual Roman delegation went to Avignon in 1374 to plead for the restoration of Rome as the ecclesiastical capital, and even threatened secession.   He promised the committee to return to Rome.[4]   The last words of Petrarch, who died in 1374, rang with patriotic earnestness as he urged the head of the Church to leave Avignon, " the sewer of the earth."   The Scandinavian saint, Birgitta, who went to Rome in the jubilee year 1350, busied herself to restore Rome once more as the spiritual and imperial centre of the world.   She turned seer and pretended to have divine relations.   When Urban V announced his decision to quit Rome in 1370, she had predicted for him a speedy death.   And her words came to pass.   She warned Gregory that death would also smite him if he did not return to the true capital of the Christian world.   But her own end came in 1373 before she saw her wish fulfilled.

---

[1] Baluz i, 435 ; Gieseler, iii, 62 (Smith rev.), gives the bull.
[2] Kirsch, p. xvii ; Mirbt, p. viii, 7 sq. ; Scholz, 4 ; Pastor, i, 110.
[3] *Chronicles*, ix, 46.
[4] Scholz, 5.

G

Catherine of Siena, a wonderful woman for that age or for any age, wrote letter after letter to her " sweet Christ on earth ", as she called Gregory, and urged him to break away from his exile to which she charged all the evils afflicting Christendom. " Be a true successor of Gregory the Great," she wrote him. " Do not bind yourself to your parents, or to your friends. Do not be held by the compulsion of your surroundings. Aid will come from God. Listen only to God, who calls you to hold and possess the seat of the glorious shepherd, St Peter, whose vicar you are." [1] She told him that the fear of bodily harm in Italy ought to be scorned by a servant of God.[2] In 1376 Catherine went to Avignon as a commissioner to sue for peace in behalf of Florence and declared that she found the false capital of Christendom a stench of infernal vices, not a paradise of heavenly virtues.[3] Her unselfish appeals confirmed Gregory in a decision already made.[4]

As early as 1374 Gregory wrote to the emperor, Charles IV, that it was his fixed intention to transfer the Papacy to the Eternal City,[5] and asked him to safeguard him on the journey.[6] Orders were given for the preparation of the Vatican for the Papal household. But the journey was delayed by the Italian revolt, by the protests of the King of France and the cardinals, and by the entreaties of his father, mother, and four sisters. Notwithstanding the appeals of such influential personages, Gregory's determination could not be shaken, and on 13th September, 1376, he left Avignon accompanied by a large court and all his cardinals, except six who were left in Avignon to conduct affairs there. He took ship at Marseilles on 2nd October for Corneto, where he arrived on 6th December after a stormy passage. The fleet consisted of 22 ships furnished by Joanna of Naples, Peter IV of Aragon, the Knights of St John, the Italian cities,[7] and a number of galleys and boats hired by the Pope himself. A strong force of mercenaries were taken along as a protection on sea and land and

---

[1] Scudder, *Letters of St Catherine*, 132 sq.; Gardner, *St Catherine*, 158, 176, etc.
[2] Scudder, 182 sqq.　　　　[3] Mirbt, *Quellen*, 154.
[4] Mirbt, 101 ; Pastor, i, 110.
[5] See Mirbt, 52, concerning Gregory's alleged early vow.
[6] Kirsch, *Rückkehr*, p. xviii, 171 ff. ; Mirbt, 36, 112.
[7] Kirsch, xviii, asserts that these ships were also hired.

particularly to guard the Pope in Rome. The expenses of this peaceful Armada were kept in a very business-like manner and may be seen to-day carefully tabulated in the ledgers preserved in Avignon and the Vatican. The first entries were for wines and the sums were very large. Indeed the expense of the journey was so heavy that the Pope was forced to borrow 30,000 gold florins from the King of Navarre to supplement the large sums in the Papal treasury. The total cost of the entire expedition appears to have been about $300,000 in our coinage.[1] After tarrying at Corneto for more than a month, in order to make arrangements concerning the future government of Rome, Gregory left on 13th January for Ostia, sailed up the Tiber, and made his entry into Rome on 17th January, 1377, amidst rejoicing throngs. At last the Babylonian Exile had come to an end, and the part played by Gregory XI in bringing it about has immortalized his name.

The conclusion of the unnatural residence of the Papacy at Avignon was a turning point in the history of the Church as well as in that of Rome. Still the return did not bring the peace anticipated. Italy was still seething with hostilities. The Florentines were continually stirring up sedition in Rome.[2] The notorious massacre of Cesena, ordered by Cardinal Robert of Geneva and executed by the brutal Bretons, embittered the Italians still more against the Pope. Gregory found no rest in Rome amidst the anarchy and turmoil and was forced to remove to Anagni towards the end of May, 1377. The commotion was gradually quelled, however, and the Pope's authority was once more acknowledged by an increasing number of Italian commonwealths as a result of his sincere peace efforts. In consequence on 7th November, he returned to Rome, only to die within five months at the age of 47 on 27th March, 1378, while a peace congress was in session at Saranza. The expectations, which he had hoped his personal presence in Rome would bring about, were not realized. In fact he was so disappointed in the results of his transfer of Papal power to Rome and so weary of Italian politics with its interminable squabbles, that it is highly probable that nothing but death prevented his return to Avignon. He admonished his cardinals in his last breath not to give ear to

[1] Kirsch, p. xviii, 171 ff. ; Mirbt, 36, 112 sq.
[2] Pastor, i, 111.

foolish prophesies as he had done.[1] France never gave the Church another Pope.

11. *Character of the Papacy During this Period*

The seven Popes associated with the Babylonian Exile were men of a very high average degree of intelligence and ability. Clement VI, Urban V, and Gregory XI were of noble birth ; the others were of humble origin and won their promotion to the highest office in the Church on merit. All of these Pontiffs were university-trained in civil and canon law and at least four of them taught the subject. Three of them were monks of marked ability and rose to the rank of abbot. All but one, Urban V, had experience as bishops ; and all but two, Clement V and Urban V, served in the college of cardinals. With the exception of Clement V they were all men of good repute, as human character was judged in that day, and most of them would stand the test of present-day standards. All of them except John XXII and Clement VI could be called spiritual-minded. The business acumen and administrative fitness of these French Popes were quite remarkable because they proved themselves to be experts in raising funds and fairly wise and economical in spending it. While they all, as was natural, favoured France yet, omitting Clement V, it can be said that these ecclesiastical heads were less dependent upon the will of the French sovereign than is now commonly believed.[2] Urban V and Gregory XI, against the will of the French monarch, both removed the seat of the Papacy to Rome. Certain it is that these Church rulers did not surrender, either in theory or practice, at least so far as nations other than France were concerned, the loftiest claims to temporal power. Not even Boniface VIII stated these pretensions more positively than did John XXII. Indeed the idea of the Papacy, which had been expressed in this period, was incapable of further extension, and on the surface of things the papal victory seemed to be absolute. Nor were these Pontiffs blind to the corruptions and abuses of the day, as is commonly charged against them, but on the contrary the majority were eager for reformation, and did attempt to correct many of the most flagrant evils.

[1] See Pastor, i, 116.
[2] Haller, *Papsttum*, 24.

John XXII and Clement VI alone were notoriously indifferent to the remedying of the serious ills of the Church.

The subserviency of the Avignon Popes to the French court was not so pronounced as their constant endeavour to strengthen the French party in the Church. Clement V, weak-willed and sickly, stands forth more conspicuously than any of the others as the servile tool of the powerful and ambitious Philip IV, who had just won a significant victory in the spectacular controversy with Boniface VIII.[1] But even Clement V did not readily give way at every point. On the contrary he fenced and parried and finally succeeded in at least contravening Philip's determination to vilify the memory of his Papal antagonist. The Popes who succeeded Clement V obeyed the wishes of the French monarchs only so far as such demands served the interests of the French party in the Roman Church.

Just as it seems very clear now that the Avignon Pontiffs were not so completely under the thumb of the French monarch as has been generally believed, so does it appear to be true likewise that the Avignon residence did not lessen the influence of the Papacy in Europe nearly as much as has been asserted. The Babylonian Captivity proved that the Papacy was not tied to Rome in bondage. It showed that the Church of God was more important than the Eternal City. The material prosperity of the Avignon régime gave the Papal court a lustre and influence that it had never possessed before. The whole period was one of extraordinary freedom of thought and action. Gayet has proved that, between 1100 and 1304, Popes had been exiled from Rome 122 years, thus showing that long periods of absence were not unknown, although none of them lasted as long as the Captivity.[2]

Haller maintains that the French church in the fourteenth century was more completely subject to the Papal authority than the Church of any other land.[3] After its freedom had been lost the Gallic Church began to speak of its freedom.[4] The name " Papal age " was given to the period.[5]

During the Avignon period, although the papal court was so predominantly French, nevertheless it still preserved its

[1] Haller. [2] Le grand schisme, Berlin, 1889.
[3] Ibid., Papsttum, 24, 205. [4] Ib., 206.
[5] Hist. de l'église gallicaine, xiii, ii ; Religieux de St. Denis, i, 694.

international character [1] and one might have found representatives of all peoples in Western Europe there.   There is indisputable evidence in the records of a comparatively large German contingent.   One street was named " German Street ".   Under John XXII there was a group of German soldiers stationed at Avignon, mostly from the Rhine section.   The list of renters shows the names of 19 German priests, three of whom were curial officers, 5 hand artisans, 4 innkeepers, 9 merchants and 1 *comes palatinus*.   In the list of receipts and expenditures appear many other German-sounding names.[2] It was as natural that these French Popes should rule the universal Church from France and in behalf of French ecclesiastics as that Italian Pontiffs should do the same from Rome.   Few Popes of the Middle Ages were able to free themselves entirely from family and national prejudices and give the whole Church a strictly impersonal rule.   Consequently at Avignon the government of the Church became overwhelmingly French.   The college of cardinals and the Papal curia were predominantly French.   Most of the officers and legates appointed by the Popes to act in the various European countries were French.   This unhistorical and unwarranted gallicization of the medieval Church was one of the most unfortunate results of the Avignon Exile.   It led to a storm of protests, denunciations, and exaggerated charges.   It likewise furnished an excuse for the discontented, the heretical, and the rebellious elements in the Church to assert themselves.

12. *General results of the Babylonian Captivity*

Ultimately the Babylonian Captivity set in motion certain forces and ideas which resulted in the decline of the power of the Medieval Church, but one of the immediate results was the increase and centralization of Papal power.   During that epoch the doctrine was developed that the Bishop of Rome was the one universal bishop in whom all spiritual and ecclesiastical powers were summed up.   All other members of the hiearchy were simply delegates selected by him for purposes of administration.   Hence the Pope was an absolute monarch over a kingdom, which was called spiritual, but which in reality was as thoroughly material as France, Spain,

---

[1] Souchon, i, 1, asserts that the Papal curia lost its international character.
[2] Schäfer, *Röm. Quartalschr.*, 1904, vol. xviii, p. 162 ff.

or England. It must be remembered that the term spiritual was used in a unique sense in the Middle Ages. Men were spiritual if they had taken orders or the monastic vow. Lands and buildings were also spiritual if they belonged to the Church. The Papal monarchy was peculiar in this sense that it was scattered all over Europe as a part of every kingdom and principality and city of Western Europe. The Pope's subjects, the clergy, were found everywhere, but owed no allegiance to secular rulers. They were outside of the sphere of secular law and taxation and were subject to ecclesiastical law only. This situation led inevitably to all sorts of complications.

The Papal court at Avignon had the same sort of machinery in courts, constables and prisons for civil and criminal jurisdiction that the royal courts of Europe possessed. In a city of 50,000 people such as Avignon was, with a constant stream of strangers of all characters constantly coming and going to all parts of Europe, together with the pretensions of the Pope to civil jurisdiction all over Christendom, the Papal court was confronted by the necessity of deciding many civil and criminal cases. Consequently the Papal camera as well as the *auditor camera* found it necessary to pass judgment on both criminal and civil cases. The office of *marcellus justitiae* began in the thirteenth century. Cases such as the forgery of bulls, letters, documents and seals ; counterfeiting money ; murder, theft, and other crimes were tried in the Papal law-courts.[1] The vice-chancellor was given the same civic and criminal jurisdiction as the auditor, although the supreme power of the *camerar* was protected and safeguarded.[2]

The financial system, the vast wealth in lands and buildings, the well-organized and powerful Papal court, the admirable administrative machinery, and the army of comparatively loyal officials at the command of the head of the Church all combined to form a power such as the world has seldom seen. Avignon was literally the capital of the western portion of Europe. The man who resided there and called himself the Bishop of Rome was still the most powerful monarch of the Old World, and represented the only great world power of his day.[3]

---

[1] Schäfer, *Röm. Quartalschr.*, 1905, vol. xix, 190 ff.
[2] Göller, *Papst Johann XXIII und König Sigismund im Sommer* 1410, *Röm. Quartalschr.*, 1903, vol. xvii, 190 ; ib., 1902, vol. 416.
[3] Haller, 143.

CHAPTER IV

THE AVIGNON FINANCIAL SYSTEM

I. INCOME

SINCE the time of the crusades a great economic revolution had been slowly transforming the civilization of Western Europe—first in Italy, then France, Germany and other countries. The system of barter was gradually displaced by the employment of silver and gold money as a medium of exchange in business. The Medieval Church profited greatly by this significant transition from natural products to a gold basis as a measure of values. The Avignon period conspicuously marked the last stages of that evolution, and the Papal curia through its network of international relationships became the greatest financial power in Europe and the world.

13. *The theory of temporal sovereignty materialized the Papacy*

The two fundamental characteristics of the Avignon Papacy were : first, the centralization of authority, and, secondly, the development of finance into an efficient science.[1] The theory of the temporal sovereignty of the Pope, expanded to its utmost limits and put into practice so far as was possible in the thirteenth and fourteenth centuries, had the disastrous result of secularizing the office of Peter and of surrounding it with a worldly court at Avignon. The consequent decrease in the spiritual power of the Church was one of the most serious results of the age. The Roman Church ministered to the spiritual wants of the millions under its jurisdiction, and upon that service was based its rightful claim to the financial support, which had been paid for centuries without serious protest. But it required an immense sum of money to support the worldly Papal establishment at Avignon in luxury and extravagant ease ; to satisfy the greed of thousands of hungry officials, great and small ; to wage wars for political advantage ; to organize holy crusades ; and to manage the multitudinous affairs of a powerful organization that covered

[1] Haller, 125.

all Central and Western Europe. The needs of the Papal hierarchy of that day were somewhat similar to those of a great modern nation like Russia. Consequently the financial policy of the Avignon Pontiffs not only employed the old practices and methods of raising funds, but also invented new and unprecedented devices, which resulted in gross excesses and in an unscrupulous traffic in both spiritual benefits and ecclesiastical offices. Every spiritual favour exacted a fee and every appointment to office required the payment of a bonus. John XXII, in particular, developed a magnificently organized system for the taxation of Christendom and made the raising of money the chief business of the Papal office. The machinery devised under his shrewd management for collecting revenues was more intricate and more efficient than the treasury department of any secular power of the age. His extraordinary aptitude for high finance was as pronounced as that of Gregory VII and Innocent III in elaborating the constitutional and doctrinal foundations of the Medieval Papacy.[1] Under his genius for business and through his clever manipulations, the Church was so commercialized that it did not fully recover from the dire effects for two centuries. The old sin of simony, against which the best men in the Church had fought more or less successfully for hundreds of years, was practically legalized. Every service the Church had to give, every privilege it had within its power to confer, and every possible appointment to position high or low, were exploited in one way or another by the Papal curia.

14. *The Standard Revenues of the Papal Court*

The Popes had been accustomed to receive their revenues from the following sources: (1) the Papal States in Italy; (2) tithes levied on the whole church or a part of it for worthy purposes like crusades; (3) Peter's pence; (4) fixed tributes paid by states held as fiefs of the Papal chair; (5) free-will offerings and voluntary gifts; (6) special fees for visitations, dispensations, absolutions, and indulgences; and (7) appointments to benefices. But the income from these established sources no longer sufficed to meet the actual needs, much less the avaricious demands, of the huge Avignon Papal court. The removal of the seat of the Papacy from Rome to Avignon

---

[1] See Haller, 102 ; Tangl, 40.

threw the Papal States into such a surly state of rebellion that they refused to pay their monetary obligations except under force. The strife and turmoil in the rest of Italy ; the quarrel of Lewis the Bavarian, prolonged for years ; the stubbornness of Edward III of England, and his parliament ; and the wide-spread opposition elsewhere in Europe to the Avignon régime, resulted in diminishing the legitimate sources of Papal income to an alarming degree. The special tithes for certain pious undertakings payable to the Papal treasury, and even the customary tithes for the support of the clergy and for charity, had come to be regarded as a burdensome tax and were collected with much difficulty. Hence with the embarrassing decrease in the Papal income, the Avignon Pontiffs were confronted by the very perplexing problem of devising new sources of revenue to run the great ecclesiastical machine. The system instituted proved to be very effective in raising the necessary funds. Although it was denounced as revolutionary and illegal by those hostile to the Avignon Papacy, the Popes themselves and their advisors took the greatest pains to base it upon practices, methods, precedents, and the canon law of preceding centuries.

15. *The Right of Papal Taxation*

To the supreme right of the Pope to appoint to office in the Church was added the sovereign power to tax the clergy. For centuries the head of the Church had levied taxes on the clergy and the property of the Church for crusades and other holy purposes. For centuries ecclesiastical benefices had been sold by Popes who at least honestly thought that they were acting legally.[1] For centuries fees had been collected for all kinds of privileges and services. Thus every office, every service, and every favour came to have a current market value in gold on which a conservative financial system could be constructed. Consequently during the Babylonian Exile these old practices were made the basis of financial calculations superior to anything the Church had ever known and far more efficient than any system found in the secular courts of Europe, for the purpose of (1) supporting the extensive and expensive Papal court ; (2) replacing the rich revenues drawn from the

---

[1] Cf. Woker, *Das kirchlichle Finanzwesen der Päpste*, Nördlingen, 1878. Introd., 2.

Papal States, which were either very uncertain or purposely withheld ; and (3) making up for the offerings of European countries other than France, which during the Exile were given in smaller amounts and with less frequency.

16. *Organization of the Papal Court into Four Departments*

If the Avignon Pontiffs were more independent of the French monarchs than is commonly acknowledged, at the same time it must be stated that they were more dependent upon the Papal Curia, predominantly French, of course, than is generally believed. Hordes of wily, tactful, hungry sycophants, candidates, and officials swarmed around and in the Papal palace day and night. Nothing but a saintly giant could have withstood their intrigues and greedy demands. It was this grasping, conscienceless, all-powerful body of clerics in the curia, who blocked every endeavour to introduce reformation, who grew fat and worldly on the income of the Church, who made the hierarchy little more than a mighty secular power, and who put every spiritual service of the Church on a financial basis. The chief departments of the Papal government taken collectively constituted the Curia, or Papal court. The most important departments were the following : (1) the *Cancellaria*, which administered affairs pertaining to the Popes and the cardinals ; (2) the *Dataria*, which had to do with absolutions, dispensations, etc. ; (3) the *Camera*, which supervised the finances ; and (4) the *Rota*, which was the supreme court of justice.

The Avignon Popes proceeded upon the theory and constitutional principle that in the Papal office was vested the universal right of appointment. This was the logical outcome of the centralization of ecclesiastical administration in the hands of the Roman Curia during the thirteenth century. Thus gradually ecclesiastical benefices, both large and small, became more and more " collated ", that is, granted directly by the Pope. In 1265 Clement IV issued a bull which laid down the fundamental rule that the Pope, as the absolute head of the Church, might dispense all the dignities, offices and benefices in the Christian Empire.[1] That decision clearly violated the old right of election.[2] The Avignon Pontiffs

---

[1] Friedberg, ii, 102 ; Lux, 5.
[2] Haller, 107. Urban IV withdrew the right of electing church officers from the Ghibelline cities in upper Italy. Martin IV reserved all bishoprics

accepted the theory and during their period of rule a regular election by a chapter was the exception.   Kings and princes even joined hands with the Pope in violating the established rights of electors in the Church.   The canon lawyers of the day, such as Augustinus Triumphus, defended this prerogative of the head of the Church.[1]   The system of appointments also included reservations, expectations, and provisions—hence there was scarcely a benefice in Western Christendom that was not subject to the Pope's pleasure.   Eager to strengthen the French party in the Latin church, the Avignon Pontiffs, even the best of them like Gregory XI, named French candidates to office, not only in France but also in England, Denmark, Germany, Spain, and Italy.   The spiritual and administrative qualifications of the appointees were not carefully considered— influence and income alone determined the election.   The poor were   shut   out   regardless   of   their   fitness.   Consequently Frenchmen fairly swarmed over Europe as the possessors of the most lucrative ecclesiastical offices.   The chronicles of the day teem with instances of these Papal appointments in various parts of Christendom and also with numerous protests against Papal usurpations and with complaints about the unfitness of the appointees.   Papal patronage included cardinalships and offices of the higher clergy like archbishoprics, bishoprics, and abbeys ;   lower offices of the clergy like canonries, and the enormous body of departmental heads, secretaries, clerks, lawyers, janitors, and helpers of all sorts connected with the Papal court.   In the course of time these offices all came to have a fixed monetary value and consequently were graded and disposed of according to their desirability.   Indeed the system   of   extraordinary   " collation ",   or   power   of   Papal appointment, came to mean in actual practice little more than the open buying and selling of offices—the grossest sort of simony, against which every good man in the Church—Pope, priest, bishop and layman—had raised a loud voice.

17. *Sources of Papal Income: The Papal States*

During the Avignon epoch the Popes derived their income for the support of their large court and for the numerous

---

in Sicily. Boniface VIII reserved all churches in France. Ibid., 37. He appointed from 20 to 47 annually. From 1295 to 1301 only one out of sixteen vacancies was filled by election. Ibid., 38.

[1] Quoted in Gieseler, ii, 123.

enterprises they were continually undertaking partly from old, established sources and partly from new devices and practices, which may be set down categorically as follows :

The Papal States, commonly called the Patrimony of Peter, were subject to taxes such as any European sovereign might levy on the subjects of his realm and, therefore, theoretically, paid large revenues to the Papal treasury, but the sums actually paid during this period were very uncertain. The cities played the most important rôle in the Papal States. At the head of the secular government of the city stood the *podesta* and the captain of the people appointed for one year ; then came the big council composed of the burghers, which was the real ruling body ; and finally under the council was the congregation of the citizens. The rural districts were divided up into great estates over which feudal lords ruled somewhat like the *podesta* of the city and frequently sub-infeudated their holdings. A rector appointed directly by the Pope was the political head of the Papal States and subordinate to him were local rectors in the cities and country, also named by the Pope, with councils of advisors. These local rectors, acting directly in the name of the Pope, policed the provinces, meted out justice, commanded the Papal troops, and collected the Papal revenues. Their position was one of great trust, but they were not bound to official residence. A treasurer and a vice-treasurer were appointed by the *camerar* and Papal treasurer for each province, but were subject to the orders of the rectors and, in their name, received the customs, taxes and rents. Their books were kept in a very business-like manner in duplicate, one set being sent to the camera at Avignon. The records show that receipts were received from (1) procurations raised by the rector from castles and cities ; (2) *tallia militum*, or an army tax ; (3) *focatiscumor*, a house and hearth tax ; (4) *passagium*, or road tax ; (5) confiscations ; (6) duties ; (7) *census* or feudal dues ; (8) fines, and various other minor sources. The treasurers paid all salaries and were responsible to the curia for an accurate record of all receipts and expenditures. Payments were often made in kind as well as money. Papal legates were frequently sent out to see that everything was done in an honest and orderly manner.

On the whole the Papal States seem to have been well

governed for that day, although the system did not always
work in an ideal manner.[1] Angered by the Pope's desertion
of Rome, the local authorities for the most part refused to
pay their customary obligations unless forced to do so by some
strong, efficient representative of the head of the Church.[2]
Under John XXII the whole territory was in open rebellion
because he sent only Frenchmen, many of them his own
relatives, to hold the offices and to receive the rich benefices.
These greedy and worldly officials robbed the people in order
to send gold to Avignon. They squeezed 200,000 florins out
of Bologna, and like sums from Perugia and Romagna. Under
the able ruler, Cardinal Albornoz, the Papal States were brought
once more into proper submission and forced to make regular
contributions.[3] Up to the present time the documents are
lacking from which an accurate account can be made of the
total income from the Papal States during this entire period.
For a portion of the period the receipts were as follows: Tuscany,
1320–33, 8,063 florins; Spoleto, 1318–33, 34,759 florins;
Romagna, 1325–6, 6,000 florins and the same for other
years; Ferrara, 1319, 4,000 florins, and 1329, 2,000 florins;
Ancona, 1317–27, 14,316 florins; Campagna, 1323–6,
3,588 florins; Benevento, 1319–26, 7,000 florins, 1332,
3,653 florins, and 1333, 2,855 florins. And even these sums
were mixed up with the tithes. In one year 2,000 pounds were
collected in fines. The ravages of war also tended to greatly
reduce the revenues which in normal times would have been
collected. From the sources available it may be safely said
that the Papal revenues from the Papal States at this time
were comparatively insignificant. Furthermore, since the
time of Nicholas IV (1289), the cardinals claimed and received
one-half of the total income from this source, but the amount
was so small that little quarrelling ensued over the division.[4]
Only two per cent of the income of John XXII was derived
from this source [5] and it is very likely that the other Avignon
Pontiffs received but little more. Indeed it is very probable
that more money was spent on the Papal States during the
Exile than was received in the way of income. The curtailment of these funds forced the Papacy to look elsewhere for

[1] Eitel, *Der Kirchenstaat unter Klemens V*, gives an excellent picture of
the conditions in the Papal States of that day. See Gottlob, 99.
[2] Tangl, *Taxenw.*, 20.   [3] Scholz, *Die Rückkehr*, 4.
[4] Göller, *Einnahmen*, 66*, 70*.   [5] Schäfer, *Ausgaben*, 37*.

the necessary means with which to administer the affairs of the Church.

The county of Venaissin, another direct possession of the Pope, was also managed by a local treasurer, who sent his reports to Avignon several times a year, but the income was likewise very small.[1]

18. *Peter's Pence*

Peter's Pence was a very irregular source of income at this time.[2] In theory all Christians were expected to pay it in return for the protection given them by the Church of Rome, but in practice it was collected only from the countries of northern Europe—England, Ireland, Norway, Sweden, Prussia, and Poland.[3] Although Gregory VII attempted to collect it from France and Spain, yet it seems that those two countries, together with Italy, were free from it. During this period England stands out most conspicuously in the records connected with this tax. Edward II in 1316 agreed to pay the twenty-four years' deficit of 24,000 marks and Edward III assumed a like obligation of 30,000 marks.[4] Impatient at the non-payment, John XXII sent a legate to England to hurry up the remittance and apparently with some success. But in 1343 that country refused to pay the tax and in 1366 defiantly withheld it because of the Pope's hostility to the statute *praemunire*. Again in 1379 Urban VI sought to secure the arrears by sending special nuncios to England, but with what result is not clear.[5] The Scandinavian countries paid a moderate sum with considerable regularity. Other states, cities, nobles, bishops, and private individuals, who were under some sort of vassalage to Rome, contributed sums of various amounts. Altogether, however, Peter's Pence did not bring a very large amount into the papal treasury.[6]

19. *Feudal Tributes*

Feudal tribute, or *census*, was collected from such states as acknowledged a feudal vassalage to the Pope—like Naples,

[1] Göller, 70*.

[2] Baumgarten, cxxvi ; Fabre, 129 ; Jenssen, *Der Peterspfennig*, Heidelberg, 1908.

[3] *Cath. Encyc.*, art. *Annates*, by Kirsch.

[4] Haller, 135 ; Raynaldus, *Ann.*, 1317, No. 49.   [5] Bliss, iv, 257.

[6] The tax was fairly regularly paid by England until abolished by Henry VIII.

Sicily, Sardinia, Corsica, England, and Spain. Single estates and castles held as Papal fiefs paid the *census*, although the amounts were not large—often as small as one gold florin. Cloisters, churches, and religious institutions directly under the protection of the Pope, or the states of the Church, paid a special feudal tax.[1] The tribute money was paid directly to the Pope or to his official collectors, and some payments were regular while others were very irregular. One of the earliest conspicuous instances of feudal tribute was the promise of King John of England to pay the Pope 1,000 marks sterling annually over and above Peter's Pence, but the payment was not made regularly. Boniface VIII complained that eleven years remained unpaid, and Clement V and John XXII experienced difficulty in making collections. John XXII forced the English monarch to pay 4,000 gold gulden in 1317, and a like sum was paid to the cardinals in 1320. An additional 1,000 marks were secured in 1330 and three years later 6,000 gold gulden were sent to Avignon.[2] About that time it seems that the delinquent payments were remitted, or at least partially cancelled, in consideration of a promise to pay 5,000 marks annually for the future.[3] The case of Naples was typical as a tribute state of the Pope. In 1307 Charles II still owed the Pope in delinquent payments the enormous sum of 93,340 ounces of gold.[4] Although King Robert paid in 1316 25,000 florins ; in 1317, 20,000 florins ; and in 1319, 25,000 florins, yet in 1323 he still owed 85,000 gold florins.[5] Further payments were made between 1325 and 1330, but the sums sent to the Pope fell so far short of the stipulated annual tribute that in 1330 the total amount still due was 444,263 gold florins, or only 22,463 florins less than the sum owed in 1307. It was then agreed that the regular annual *census* should be 8,000 ounces of gold, or 40,000 florins, and to this yearly payment should be added an additional 40,000 florins to apply on the debt. For some years the promised 80,000 florins were paid, so that when John XXII died in 1334 about

---

[1] Göller, 56*, 65* ; Blumenscock, *Der päpstliche Schutz in Mittelalter, Innsbruck*, 1890 ; Fabre, *Etude sur le Libre censum de l'eglise Romaine*, Paris, 1892.
[2] Bliss, iv, 494 ; Göller, 65. Of the 1,000 marks, 700 were for England and 300 for Ireland.
[3] Bliss, iv, 494.   [4] Kirsch, 32.
[5] Göller, 29 ; Schultz, *Quellen* ii, 209.

half of the old indebtedness had been met. Nevertheless the amount still due the Pope from Naples in 1350 was 88,852 ounces of gold.[1] Sicily's annual *census* of 3,000 ounces of gold, or $15,000, was compromised by King Frederick (d. 1250) for an annual payment of 7,500 florins. In 1272 the Pope received 8,000 ounces of gold from Sicily, but divided it with his cardinals, and in 1304 3,000 ounces of gold were sent to Avignon. No doubt similar contributions were made during the following years.[2] In 1297 the King of Aragon agreed to pay an annual tribute of 2,000 marks for Sardinia and Corsica on Peter and Paul's festival, but the sum was collected with great difficulty.[3] In 1325 1,000 marks were sent to the Pope and the remainder appears to have been remitted.[4] Another interesting type of tribute was the toll levied in the name of the Pope by the Archbishop of Cologne in 1306 on all persons passing up and down the Rhine River at Bonn and Anderach.[5] The total amount received from this source during the Avignon period must have been relatively large, but no accurate estimate can be made. Some idea can be formed of the sums paid, however, from the fact that for the period of John XXII's pontificate 523,850 gold florins were received for the *census* and visitations—the largest amount, 61,800 florins in 1330–1, and the smallest, 2,500 florins, in 1318–19.[6] If an average should be struck between these two extremes and multiplied by seventy years the total amount would be 2,150,500 florins.

20. *Appointments*

The *servitium commune* was a tax, which patriarchs, archbishops, bishops, abbots, canons, and officials in the Papal court, who owed their appointment or promotion to the curia, were bound to pay to the apostolic camera and the cardinals, provided their benefices yielded a yearly income above 100 gold florins. Bishoprics and abbeys with an annual income under 100 florins were not required to pay this tax.[7] The *servitium commune* may be regarded as a general term used

---

[1] Kirsch, 32 ; Schaff, v, pt. i, 788.
[2] Kirsch, *Finanzverwaltung*, 3 ; Rückkehr, xv, xli, for the valuation of coins.
[3] Ib., 34 ; Baumgarten, cli.
[4] A Spanish mark was equal to four gold gulden and somewhat less than an English mark.
[5] Gottlob, 196.   [6] Göller, 21.105.   [7] Göller, 20*–21*.

H

to include fees for service and information, the pallium money, free-will offerings, etc. A fixed list of the earnings of the various benefices was made by the camera and on this basis the appointees to office paid from one-third to 40 per cent of one-year's income.[1] The letter of confirmation was withheld from the " electus " until the tax was paid, which was usually done when the candidate visited Rome, although payments were not infrequently made through a commercial house.[2] The recipients of these offices were required to sign an " obligation ", or note, according to an established form, agreeing to pay the fees and tax charged against the position, and when the " obligation " was met a regular receipt was given. A complete record of these " obligations " issued during the Avignon was kept. Although regular tax registers were made up during this period,[3] in some instances the *servitium* was recorded in the ledger with this explanation, " not taxed on account of poverty," and in other cases it was decreased by Papal permission or by composition with the camera. Urban V, for example, reduced the *servitia communia* in most of the French dioceses 50 per cent, while Gregory XI applied the favour to all of them.[4] Indeed the tax was raised as well as lowered, as the value of the benefice changed. Thus in 1326 the see of Breslau was decreased from 4,000 to 1,785 florins,[5] while in 1420 Mainz and Treves were increased to 10,000 florins each.[6] When the incumbent died without having paid the tax in full, the deficit was charged to his successor. Thus in 1370 the Archbishop Frederick Scarweden promised Urban V 123,000 gulden, which included the *servitia* for his four predecessors as well as his own, but Urban VI finally let him off with a payment of 30,000 gulden. It was customary for the higher clergy to borrow large sums of money to meet these taxes,[7] but extensions of time for payment were common.[8] Censures for non-payment were frequent.[9] In 1328 John XXII in public audience announced that since the *servitia* had not been paid, excommunication, suspension or interdict had fallen on 1 patriarch, 5 archbishops,

---

[1] Göller, 21* ; Gottlob, 120 ; Kirsch, *Finanzverwaltung* ; Baumgarten, xcvii.

[2] Gottlob, 130.   [3] Woker, 70–1.   [4] Gottlob, 191.

[5] Kirsch, 8.   [6] Baumgarten, cvi ; Schulte, 97 ; Woker, 11.

[7] Gottlob, 136.   [8] Göller, 43*.

[9] Ibid., 46* ; Schäfer, *Röm. Quartalschr.*, 1908, vol. xxii, 47.

30 bishops and 46 abbots. From 1365 to 1368 7 archbishops, 49 bishops, 125 abbots and some minor officials were excommunicated for the non-payment of their obligations.[1] The Archbishop Frederick Scarweden, who had failed to meet the promised tax, was suspended, excommunicated as a perjurer in 1375, and the next year declared " irregular " by a Papal nuncio, but later compromised and was reinstated.

The *servitia communia* constituted the largest source of income for the Avignon Pontiffs and bore heavily on the higher clergy. John IV appointed abbot-elect of St. Albans (1302–08) by the king went to Rome in 1302 to secure his letter of confirmation. He left an itemized account of his expenses at the Papal court. To the Pope he gave for a private visit 3,000 florins or 1,250 marks, and for *communi visitation* another 1,008 marks. To members of the Papal curia—priests, cardinal nephews of the Pope, lawyers, masters, procurators, advocates, and notaries—and for bulls, the correction of letters, the execution of documents and various fees and a ring—he paid the sum of 326 marks. Hence the total cost of his trip at Rome was 2,585 marks, or about 10,340 gold guldens.[2] In 1304 the Archbishop of Magdeburg paid 5,000 florins, and in 1309 the Bishop of Münster 9,000. Abbot William of Autun in 1316 promised John XXII 1,500 florins for his confirmation tax.[3] Another abbot-elect went to Avignon with six of his monks and congratulated himself that he got off with a payment of only 3,600 florins. After three months of bargaining the Abbot-elect of Canterbury paid 148 pounds sterling for his office. The Bishop of Bamberg in 1335 left Avignon either because he could not or would not pay the tax.[4] A Papal confirmation for the young Archbishop Walram of Cologne in 1332 cost his brother 40,000 gulden, of which 30,000 went for *servitia*.[5] Archbishop Frederick Scarweden promised 120,000 gulden, but finally compromised for one-fourth that sum. According to the tax register formed by the curia in the fourteenth century, the following

[1] Haller, 133–53 ; Baumgarten, 215–24 ; Müller, 12, 46–7 ; Friedberg, 326 ; Wasserschleben, 100–1.

[2] In 1326 a mark was worth 5 gold gulden and one gold gulden of that time is worth 10 marks to-day. Hence in present monetary values the abbot's visit and consecration in Rome cost him 103,340 marks, or about $25,835.

[3] Kirsch, 77–8 ; Gottlob, 162.   [4] Göller, 69.

[5] Gottlob, 191 ; Sauerland, xliii.

servitia were levied : Winchester 12,000 florins ; Cologne, Salzburg, Mainz, Aquileja, Narbonne, and Canterbury, 10,000 florins ; Lüttich, 7,200 florins ; Trier, Treves, and Ely, 7,000 florins ; Exeter, Passau, and Metz, 6,000 florins ; Gressen, Tournoy, and Lincoln, 5,000 florins ; Utrecht, 4,600 florins ; Verdun, 4,400 florins ; Breslau, Friesing, and Reims, 4,000 florins ; Olmutz, 3,500 florins ; Bamberg, Münster, Basel, and Milan, 3,000 florins ; Prague, 2,800 florins ; Magdeburg, Strassburg, and Constance, 2,500 florins ; Wurzburg, 2,400 florins ; Litten and Trient, 2,000 florins ; Regensburg, 1,400 florins ; Lausanne and Worms, 1,200 florins ; Augsburg, Eichstädt, and the abbey of Corvey, 800 florins ; Geneva, 600 florins ; Paderborn and Halberstadt, 100 florins.[1]

Archbishop Gerlach of Mainz was appointed and consecrated at Avignon. He took the oath of fealty to John XXII against Lewis of Bavaria and promised 10,985 florins *servitia* from himself and his predecessors.[2] From the year 1316 to 1326, a period of ten years, the total number of " obligations " recorded was 669, from which was derived in *servitia communia* the enormous sum of 897,545 gold florins, ranging in amounts from 25 to 12,000 florins. The largest amount promised was 168,105 florins in 1317. Some conception of the number of these lucrative appointments made by the Avignon Popes may be had from the fact that John XXII during his 18 years of rule named 175 candidates in the single diocese of Utrecht, and Benedict XII during his pontificate of 8 years selected 11 more.[3] For the entire Church, therefore, the total number must have run into the thousands. The French and the Italians were the worst scavengers for offices in the Church and far outnumbered all others at the Papal court. The sums actually collected, however, from the " obligations " fell far short of the face value. For instance, during the pontificate of John XXII of 18 years only 561,501 gold florins were received, or an annual average of 31,194 florins.[4] The largest sum really paid was 52,710 florins in 1317, and the smallest was 5,910 in 1318.[5] The highest amounts received from

---

[1] Stovely, *The Roman Horseleech*, London, 1769 ; Sauerland, xlii ; Schulte, *Gesch. des Mit. A. Handels*, i, 232–3 ; Müntz, *L'argent et le luxe à la cour pontificale*, in *Rev. d. histor.*, vol. 66 ; Gottlob, *Päpstl. Darlehensschulden des 13ten Jahr.*, in *Hist. Jahrb.*, xx, 665.

[2] Sauerland, xxxiii ; iii, 542 ; ii, 1598.   [3] Gottlob, 136.

[4] Göller, 105–238, gives all the important items.   [5] Ibid.

single individuals were 2,000, 2,500, and 3,000 florins ; many payments of 500 and 1,000 florins were made ; and a very large number of sums between 5 and 50 florins were recorded.[1] From these figures it may be seen that the *servitium commune* was about three times more lucrative to the Papal court than any other single source of income. The total amount paid from 1334 to 1378, was 1,097,957 gold florins,[2] or nearly 25,000 florins annually. The *servitia communia* were divided equally between the Pope and the college of cardinals, each receiving half.[3]

Little is known from the sources about the origin of the *servitium*. Apparently it was in use long before it came to be regarded as a source of income by the Pope. It is probable that it was an old practice among the bishops and German kings taken over by the head of the Church. Certain it is that German rulers had enjoyed not only the *spolia*, but had also demanded the first year's income of bishops and abbots.[4] The first instance of the *servitium* being paid was in 1248.[5] Under Alexander IV (d. 1261) this tax must have been developed into something like a system, because the records of his reign show that the higher prelates were required to pay large sums to the Pope and the cardinals for their appointments.[6] Under his successors Urban IV and Clement IV the camera's registers contained many letters about the *servitia*. Hence it may be concluded that the voluntary fee for episcopal consecration in Rome of the earlier days had gradually developed into comparatively fixed, obligatory taxes by the middle of the thirteenth century. Under Boniface VIII there were but few instances of the payment of the *servitium*.[7] Clement V levied fees on all the higher clergy, whether they were consecrated in Rome or not.[8] Up to the time of John XXII the old custom of paying one-third of the total income of the first year by all persons appointed to benefices

---

[1] Göller, 105–238.
[2] Ibid., 46*. Gottlob, 191, contends that the *servitia communia* during the later years of the Exile must have averaged 90,000 florins annually, but this sum must have been based on the " obligations " and not on actual receipts.
[3] The cardinals had claimed a division on this basis as early as the time of Gregory IX.
[4] Mon. Ger., Const. II, 69.   [5] Haller, 89.
[6] Göller, 32*, gives a list of the appointments under Alexander IV.
[7] Ibid., 38*.   [8] Gieseler, § 103, note 25.

yielding an annual revenue of more than 100 gulden was commonly observed, but it was left to that Pontiff to develop the *servitium* into a definite and regular tax with the addition of ecclesiastical punishment for refusal to pay.[1] However, no Papal constitution is extant dealing with the *servitium*. Upon visiting Avignon to receive the pallium, metropolitans, primates, and archbishops were required to pay large fees for that honour as well as the *servitium*. Benedict XII (d. 1342) connected the *servitium* with visitations as a permanent source of income in lieu of the *census* and Peter's Pence.[2] Thus the Mainz pallium cost 26,000 gulden and the *servitium* amounted to 4,000 more.[3] Wimpfeling complained about the excessive cost of the pallium, because, whereas the earlier cost was only 10,000 gulden, in his day the *servitium* alone cost that amount. John XXII regularly required the pallium tax, together with the *servitium*, and by the end of the fifteenth century the sums demanded had become so exhorbitant that there was a loud outcry against the evil.[4]

In addition to the fixed tax, *servitium commune*, the recipients of benefices with an income above 100 florins usually found themselves subject to additional tips and fees at the Papal court called *servitia minuta*. These payments were required to straighten out curial officialism, to avoid delays, to expedite registration, to pay notarial charges, to insure the influence of cardinals and other high officials, and to expedite confirmation and consecration. For instance, the Abbot-elect of St. Albans had to spend three months at the Papal court in 1302 in cutting red-tape before he secured from the Pope his letter of confirmation, which cost him in tips and gifts 1,308 florins in addition to the 9,032 florins he paid " the lord Pope and cardinals ". Abbot William of Autun in 1316 agreed to pay John XXII's officials 170 florins in addition to the confirmation tax of 1,500 florins.[5] The consecration fees were very different from the *servitia minuta*, although Gottlob in his discussion makes no distinction.[6] They were received not for the appointment but for the consecration of

---

[1] Göller, 43* ; Kruger, ii, 173. Gottlob puts the minimum income at 200 gold gulden, and says that those who paid the tax were appointed in the Papal consistory.

[2] Göller, 22*.   [3] Ib., n. 2 and 3.

[4] Ib., 27*.   [5] Kirsch, 73–7 ; Gottlob, 126.

[6] Göller, 47*, 50*.

a bishop, or the blessing of an abbot, and were mentioned as
early as the twelfth century. Innocent III decreed that the
horse and mantle of a newly consecrated bishop should not
be appropriated by the court attendants, but that he should
instead pay them a *gratiarum*, or tip, in money. Later Popes
continued that practice.[1] In the fourteenth century the
camera received one-third of the consecration fee, the camerar
one-third, and the servants the remaining third.[2] The first
clear evidence of the payment of the *servitia minuta* was under
Alexander IV (1254) when the Archbishop of Mainz promised
1,000 marks in silver to the camera of the Pope and 50 marks
" pro familia pape ". Under Gregory X (1271) the payment
of this tax had become a fixed practice and was divided into
eight parts—one for the vice-chancellor, one to be shared
between the auditor and corrector, and the remaining six
parts for the six notaries. Under Boniface VIII the chaplains
and the cardinals' " families " received portions, and after
1299 the *cubincularii* and *ostiarii* received a share also. Under
Benedict XI (1303) the chancery and camera received two
special fees of their own. Clement V (1304–14) divided the
servitia minuta into five classes. One share fell to the lords
cardinals; and the other four portions went to the " familiaribus
et officialibus " of the Pope and the Roman Church—one part
to the camerar and his clerks ; a second to the chancery—
the vice-chancellor, notaries, auditor, and corrector ; a third
to the chaplains and the " little family " of the Pope ; and the
fourth to the *domicelli, cursores, cubincularii,* and *ostiarii*.
Under John XXII these fees in 1326 amounted to 1,743 florins ;
1327, 4,195 florins; and in 1327 2,948 florins, and were divided
as in the time of Clement V. The *servitia minuta* thus came
to be a fixed tax and amounted to from one-fourteenth to one-
twentieth, or from 5 to 7 per cent of the *servitia communia*.[3]
The practice of giving secret tips must have developed into a
serious abuse in the Papal court, since Clement V issued an
order abolishing the evil, although without much effect, for
these voluntary gifts continued throughout the entire Avignon
period.[1] Indeed to avoid the legal charge of simony, both forms
of the *servitium* were given the appearance of voluntary gifts.

---

[1] Göller, **51*** ; Gottlob, 159.
[2] Göller, **51*** ; Haller, *Quell. u. Forsch*, i, 37.
[3] Gottlob, *Die Servitienlaxe*, 101 ; Kirsch, 12.

Although they were not generally regarded as simoniacal, yet the practice was so far from ideal that it was denounced as an evil by the best men in the Church down to the Reformation.[2] One of the most serious charges made was that this tax defeated the intent of many ecclesiastical foundations by diverting money, that should have been expended locally, to the Papal court.[3]

The *servitia*, it must be remembered, were very different from the *annates*. The *annates* were customary fees paid by the lower clergy, or the holders of small benefices, and began in the provinces. The *servitia* were special fees of distinctly curial growth. Strange to say, they began as a reform, but soon lost that character in the fourteenth century and became a flagrant evil. They originated as a voluntary fee or tip and then developed into a fixed tax, which had to be paid for certain favours. The fundamental abuse was the excessive amount of the tax, which led to charges of simony. The moral results of the system were the worst features. The history of the *servitia* is the history of the moral degeneration of the Papal court, and higher clergy. These taxes also played an important economic and industrial rôle. When the reform councils sought to abolish the *annates* and the *servitia* it was found to be extremely difficult, because it involved both a complete change in the government and law of the Church and a reorganization of the Papal court ; and that was too big an undertaking. Not the curia alone but all the higher foundations of the bishoprics and abbeys were involved.[4]

21. *Annates and Media Fructus*

The *annates* [5] or *fructus primi anni*, were paid by the appointees to the smaller benefices with an annual income below 100 florins and above 6 marks silver, or about 24 florins.[6] This payment was first called *annua gratia*, then *annualia*, and finally *annates*. It grew out of the fee or tax paid to the bishop by

---

[1] Göller, 52*.　　　　[2] Göller, 46*.　　　　[3] Ibid., 30*.

[4] Gottlob, *Die Servitientaxe im 13ten Jahrhundert*, Stuttgart, 1903.

[5] This term did not come into general usage until the fifteenth century, after which it included all monies collected for the " collation ", or granting of benefices. See Kirsch, *Annaten*, Paderborn, 1908.

[6] Sauerland, i, xlv, estimates 6 silver marks at 30 gulden, or florins.

those ordained to ecclesiastical office. From the eleventh to the fourteenth century there was a gradual development in the payment of the *annates*. In the twelfth century the appointee to a benefice had to pay to the bishop the first year's income for local uses, such as the repair of church buildings. By the thirteenth century arose the practice of appropriating the income of one year from vacant benefices in many cathedral and collegiate churches, for the bishop or some other ecclesiastical officer.[1] About the same time the Popes permitted certain prelates and princes to extract the *annates* from the entrants of vacant benefices. For example, the Archbishop of Canterbury in 1245 was permitted to use the *annates* for a period of seven years to pay off the debts on the cathedral church. Before the fourteenth century there was no uniformity in the amount paid, or in the thoroughness with which the *annates* were collected.[2]

A distinct development occurred when the *annates* came to be paid directly into the Papal treasury—a change which took place under the Avignon Popes Clement V in 1306 reserved for the Papal treasury a year's revenue from all benefices in England and Scotland at that time vacant, or to be vacant within three years.[3] It was John XXII, however, called in the fifteenth century the " father of *annates* ", who by the bull of 1317 made a sweeping reservation for the Papacy of the first year's income of all vacant benefices with an annual income over six silver marks for the following three years.[4] He also systematized the collection of *annates* all over Christendom and sent out his own official collectors to gather in this tax on pain of Papal censures. At the same time he gave the King of France the privilege of collecting *annates* for his own use for a period of four years.[5] The system was completed by John XXII, when on 13th August, 1327, he promulgated the principle of collecting the *medii fructus*, that is, the income of all vacant benefices so long as they remained vacant.[6] The

[1] Bird, *Handbook to the Public Records*, 100, 106 ; Kirsch, xiv.
[2] Göller, 80*–6*.
[3] Ibid., 85*-6*, says that Clement V was the first Pope to demand *annates* in England.
[4] Ibid., 87* ; Haller, 101, explains how John XXII built on the plans of Clement V.
[5] Haller, 102 ; Coulon, No. 26, 27.
[6] Göller, 113* ; Sauerland, xlv, says that half of the first year's income was paid ; Gottlob, 194.

appropriation of the income of the vacant Archbishopric of Gran in Hungary was the first conspicuous example of the application of this new ruling. Soon the stipends of all vacant benefices were paid into the Papal treasury.[1] The better Avignon Pontiffs sought to repudiate this wholesale practice, while those less scrupulous, on one pretext or another, refused to fill vacancies in order to reap the benefits of this source of revenue.

Clement VI stopped the practice of collecting *medii fructus*, although he renewed the *annates* every two years. Benedict XII again legalized the *medii fructus* and applied the rule to all *apud sedum apostolicum* vacancies, thus realizing an enormous source of income from this practice.[2] He allowed places to remain vacant during his entire pontificate, so that at one time 330 vacant benefices were reported and of course the incomes went into his treasury.[3] Although very little was heard of these abuses under Benedict XII, still his successor Innocent, in his zeal for reformation, felt called upon to abolish all reservations.[4] Urban V and Gregory XI, in sharp contrast to the two preceding Popes, required all appointees to vacant benefices to pay the *annates* and also made it a practice to withhold the filling of livings in order to secure the entire incomes.[5] By a series of four shifts made by Gregory XI in one year, 1374, he was able to collect *annates* four different times from new incumbents. Apparently there were considerable log-rolling and promotions for the sole purpose of collecting monetary contributions. In the archbishopric of Mainz alone the *annates* amounted to 175,000 florins,[6] while the smaller benefices of France paid 697,000 florins in *annates*.[7] The archbishopric of Rouen was taxed 12,000 florins, the see of Grenoble 300, the abbey of St. Denis 6,000, and St. Cyprian of Poitiers 33.[8] Benefices *apud sedem apostolicum* in six French provinces yielded 1,478 gold florins ; two others 18,000 agn. gold ; another 1,000 florins ; and eight more large sums. In 1333-4 the receipts from English benefices were 95,240 gold florins. The collectors and nuncios of Sicily sent in 6,000 gold florins ; and Norway, Sweden, and Dacia contributed 7,000 more.

[1] Lindsay, 13.   [2] Haller, 129–30.
[3] Ibid., 130 ; *Galv. de la Flamma*, Muratori, xii, 1009.   [4] Lux, 41.
[5] Haller, 130.   [6] Woker, 27.
[7] Ibid.   [8] Lindsay, 13.

The incomes from all vacant benefices were very carefully kept in the Papal archives.[1] This evil practice continued and became more flagrant until the time of the Council of Constance, when the flood of complaints compelled that body to attempt a reformation.

Thus the *annates*, which were levied by different Popes for a short period of two, three, and four years as sort of a special emergency tax,[2] developed under the Avignon Pontiffs into a permanent tax, collectable from every person appointed to a vacant benefice with an income between 24 and 100 florins. In France all parishes were rated as having an income of 30 florins. While the law called for the collection of the entire first year's income, as a rule only 50 per cent was taken by the Pope. To the *annates* was added the *medii fructus*, which brought the whole income of all vacant benefices into the Papal hands so long as they remained unfilled. When one considers the large number of vacancies occurring over Latin Christendom continually, some realization can be formed of the Papal income derived from this revenue. This tax went directly into the Papal treasury and was not divided with the cardinals.[3] It was collected partly by local collectors and partly directly by the curia. Regular registers were kept in a very business-like manner, with lists of all benefices paying the *annates*, with the various amounts due, together with other details. At this distance it is almost impossible to secure a true idea of the elaborateness and complexity of this system and of the machinery necessary to manage it.[4]

The receipts for *annates* under John XXII for the years 1317–34 were recorded in the account books of his day. In 1317 all Europe was divided into provinces and collectors were appointed to collect the *annates*. France, Germany, and Italy were divided each into seven provinces with two, four, and six collectors respectively. Spain had two provinces and five collectors. England had one province and one collector. Hungary and Portugal had one province each with two collectors. Scandinavia, Poland, and Bohemia and Cyprus each constituted one province and had one collector. Collectors were to make allowance for the tithes. Sub-collectors were also appointed. Authority was given collectors to hold

---

[1] Göller, 384, 387.   [2] Haller, 180.

[3] Kirsch, *Annaten*, x.   [4] Ibid., xlviii. Sources given.

Church censures over the heads of delinquents, but there was to be no seizure of books, pictures, and furniture needed for church service. Payments were to be made semi-annually and all scandals in connection with collections were to be avoided. The new recipients of benefices were held responsible for the back payments. Should a given benefice become vacant twice in one year, the *annates* were collectable but once. Of course the *annates* did not apply to archbishoprics, bishoprics, and abbeys, since they paid their obligations in another form,[1] namely the *servitia*.[2]

In many instances the *annates* were paid directly to the curia. Kings likewise were induced to make collections because they possessed special machinery to force payments. In 1316 Philip the Fair was given the privilege of collecting the *annates* in French Navarre and in the Dukedom of Burgundy for four years.[3] The assistance of the King of England was secured by giving him 50 per cent of the collections.[4] The King of Hungary in 1331 was granted one-third of the *annates* for a period of three years.[5] It can readily be seen that from this source enormous sums were raised by the Avignon pontiffs. In 1329 John XXII gave the Archbishop of Cologne 25 per cent for collecting the *annates* and *medii fructus*. He also levied the *annates* on Cologne for an additional three years, and Clement VI levied them for two years, but little was collected.[6] It is not very difficult to understand why these taxes were hated and denounced by the clergy with small incomes on whom they were levied.

The *annates* aroused considerable opposition on the part of the clergy. In one way or another they attempted to evade payments. From 1344 to 1348 the Papal collectors in Cologne, Utrecht, Lüttich raised 2,713 pounds " *turnosen* ", but only 86 pounds came from rich Cologne.[7] Clement VI in his first year granted only 19 benefices, whose possessors were bound to pay the *annates*. The collectors of Trier got very little money during the first four years of the rule of Clement VI.[8] In the last seven years of Clement's reign only five clergy paid their promised *annates*. In 1355 the collector, Gerardus de Arbento, wrote, " When four years ago I went to Lotharingia,

[1] Göller, 87*-96*.　　　　　[2] Ibid., xlv.
[3] Samoran-Mallat, 24 ; Coulon, No. 23, 27, 29 ; Haller, 102.
[4] Bliss, ii, 138 ; Haller, 117.　　[5] Göller, 96*.　　[6] Sauerland, xlvi.
[7] Sauerland, xlvi : Kirsch, *Päpst. Kollekt.*, 262, 272.　　[8] Kirsch, 190–4.

in order to collect the *annates*, I came to the city of Trier and there appointed as sub-collector a man who was too indifferent. When he wished to collect the *annates* after my departure, he was shamefully mistreated in such a manner that he wrote me that he would busy himself no more with the business of collecting *annates*, for he would probably have been drowned, had he not given up the effort. When I had travelled through a few of those districts, I saw that the aforesaid collector had spoken the truth. Then I appointed the Metz ' Princier Fulco Bertrand ', a powerful and well-established gentleman in that community, as sub-collector in both Trier and Metz, hoping with his aid to collect the *annates*. He had many judgments made against all Trier benefice holders, who had not arranged to pay, and sent a messenger to carry summonses throughout the district. As he travelled through the region, he was set upon and all processes in his possession were seized and torn up, and in order that he might not bring more, his hands were cut off. Later on the ' Princier ' drew up new summonses and sent them out ; again they were destroyed and the bearers were strangled. Thereupon I went to the curia and told about the condition of affairs to the Papal officers. It was then decreed that the provisions bull for that district should be withheld, or sent to the sub-collector at Metz to be withheld by him, until they paid, or the citizens should stand responsible for the payments. That decree was not carried out, however. Later in the year 1354, the Arcbishop of Trier was named collector for his diocese. At the command of the camera officials, I sent him the Papal appointments and a list of the benefices obligated for *annates*, together with the documents on the tithes. He answered me that he did not dare to put the measures into operation." [1]

The number of benefices in the Church, of one sort or another, high and low, must have run up into the hundreds of thousands. In the Rhineland alone the benefices of all kinds numbered 8,000 from the little provostships and the archdeaconate to the countless canons for non-priests and canonical scholars, as well as the worldly offices and lay benefices, of which the church of St Mary in Cologne had nineteen. There were many endowed houses with parish chapels. A goodly number of these benefices were transferable, that is marketable,

[1] Kirsch, 195 ; Sauerland, xlvii–viii.

to another person.   After the twelfth century Popes gave individuals the right to sublet benefices.[1]   The bishop controlled a large number of the appointments to these minor benefices and of course augmented his income by resorting to all the practices of the Pope in connection with the larger benefices.   The official holders of benefices also developed the practice of turning all the duties of the office over to a vicar as early as the twelfth century and it was a common practice in the Avignon period.   In fact, it was done so much that the *vicarius perpetuus* developed.[2]   The Pope appointed only nine per cent of the benefices in the Rhine Valley.[3]   In the diocese of Strasburg alone there were 8,000 priests in 1300.   The chapters of that region, and no doubt elsewhere, were mostly monopolized by men of noble birth.   For instance out of 44 canons all were nobles except one *Freiherr*, and even he had a " von " in his name.   From 1300 to 1400 the chapter of St Thomas had 115 canons, of whom 59 were patricians, 17 non-patricians, 9 knights, and 31 foreigners.   Out of the 73 canons connected with the chapter of St Peter, 47 were patricians, 13 non-patricians, and 13 foreigners.   Half of the prebends and chaplains in Strasburg received an income under 11 pounds, or about \$37·50, and the income of others was as low as 2 pounds, or \$8·50, but of course they also had gifts of food, supplies, etc.   The cloisters had an income of from 30 to 80 pounds above gifts and contributions.[4]

Between 1304 and 1377 Germany paid to the Church in one form or another the sum of 281,000 gold florins, or a sum equal in present values to \$2,750,000.[5]   One cannot say what proportion of this sum came from the *annates*, but it must have been a very large percentage.   No doubt similar sums were collected from Italy, Spain, and England, and a very much larger sum from France, so that the total sum realized from *annates* ran into millions of dollars.

[1] Haller, *Papst.*, i, 28 ff.
[2] Schäfer, *Röm. Quartalschr*, 1904, vol. 18, p. 131, 137 : Herzog, *Realencycl.* " Regalie u. Patronat."
[3] Schäfer, ibid., 140.
[4] Kothe, *Kirchliche Zustände Strassburgs in vierzehnten Jahr.*, Breslau, 1902, 38, 39, 50, 51.
[5] Kirsch, *Die Päpst. Kollectorien in Deutschl.*

22. *Reservations*

Through the system of reservations, which grew out of the exaggerated usurpation of the right of appointment and taxation, the Popes augmented their income : (1) by increasing their opportunities to collect the *servitia* and the *annates*, and (2) by appropriating the entire income of benefices during the period of reservation.   At the close of the twelfth century it had become customary, in case clerics died while in Rome, for the Pope to fill the vacancies so occasioned.   Innocent IV, the first Pontiff to exercise the right of election on a large scale, in 1248, filled 17 out of the 20 places in the cathedral of Constance.   Clement IV in 1265, converted the practice into an ecclesiastical law, known as the constitution " Licet ", which reserved all " *ecclesiae, dignitates, personatus et officia* " vacated by the death of holders " *apud sedem apostolicam* ".[1] He (Clement) forbade all customary elections in England in 1265, and reserved for himself the right to fill offices until his commands were obeyed.   On the pretext of unwarranted disturbances, he likewise reserved all benefices in Sicily. Urban IV withdrew the right of election from the Ghibelline cities of Lombardy.   Martin IV and Honorius IV applied the rule to all cathedral appointments in Sicily and Aragon, and the latter Pope in 1286 extended the law to include cases where the clergy resigned their benefices into the Pope's hands,[2] and monopolized every appointment to the Latin Church in the East.[3]   Boniface VIII in 1295 widened the law so as to include all benefices whose holders died within two days' journey of the Curia, wherever they might be located.[4] To offset the claims of Philip IV of France he reserved all appointments to " cathedral and regular churches " in France, as well as the four Oriental patriarchates.[5]   Of the sixteen sees vacant in France between 1295 and 1301, only one was filled in the regular manner by election.[5]   Benedict XI recalled the constitution of Boniface VIII.[6]

This practice of making reservations, which had been gradually growing more common for over a century, was eagerly seized upon by the Avignon Popes and exploited to the limit.   In 1306 Clement V in his constitution *Etsi in*

---

[1] Potthast, 19, 526.   [2] Lux, 16.
[3] Haller, 37.   [4] Lux, 13, 19.
[5] Göller, 33* ; Haller, 33 ; Lux, 17.   [6] Göller, 33*.

temporalium withheld the incomes of all vacancies and appropriated them himself.[1] He reserved not only the benefices of dead bishops, who had been consecrated at the curia, but also all those vacated by resignation, translation, and permutation.[2] John XXII explained to his chancery in 1316 that his appointive power extended to practically every important office in the Church and incorporated this principle in the law *Ex debito*.[3] He forbade prelates holding more than two benefices and reserved the remainder for himself. In 1319 he applied his rule to all places in the Papal States,[4] and in 1322 he punished the disloyal bishops in upper Italy by reserving the sees of Aquileja, Ravenna, Milan, Genoa, and Pisa.[5] He made similar reservations in the German dioceses of Metz, Taul, Verdun (1329), and Cologne (1339). Murimuth complained that John reserved all the good livings in England.[6] Single benefices over Christendom were repeatedly reserved and of course in all these instances the revenues went into the Papal treasury. In 1327 the rule was applied to all offices whose incumbents had been named by the Pope.[7] In France at first the clergy gave hearty approval to this policy, because they believed that it would make them more independent and protect them against the State, but the approval was of short duration.[8]

The other Avignon Pontiffs accepted the system of reservations and profited by it.[9] Benedict XII trod in the foot steps of John XXII in issuing a constitution called *Ad regimen* concerning ecclesiastical benefices, in which he recognized the regulations of John as legal and binding, accepted all previous constitutions, and widened their sweep. All benefices vacated for any reason by cardinals, members of the curia, and prelates of any rank, were declared reserved.[10] The laws *Ex debito* and *Ad regimen* were the two foundation stones of the legalization of reservations and were adhered to by later Papal rulers.[11]

[1] Haller, 61.   [2] Lux, 20.
[3] *Flores. Historiarum (Rolls Series)*, 3 vols., London, 1890, iii, 175 ; Lux, 51 ; Haller, 107, 110 ; Wharton, i, 563 ; Stubbs, iii, 323 ; Göller, 94*.
[4] Haller, 109 ; *Bullar. Taurin.*, iv, 287.
[5] Lux, 28 ; Haller, 107 ; Raynaldus, 1322, No. 4.
[6] Merimuth, 175.   [7] Kirsch, *Annaten*, xvi ; Haller, 96.
[8] *Flores Histor.*, iii, 175 ; Haller, 113. The council of Vienne sanctioned the Papal policy. Coulon, No. 792.
[9] Lux, 47–107, gives many of the documents proving this fact.
[10] Haller, 126 ; *Röm. Quartalschr.*, viii, 169.
[11] *Regulae Cancellariae*, 15, 18, 28, 29, 113, 124, 162, 181.

Benedict XII even went so far as to reserve single churches and benefices during the life-time of the possessor—a practice that was so reprehensible that Clement VI and Innocent VI released a portion of such reservations.[1] Urban V definitely took away from bishops and cloisters the right of election,[2] and Gregory XI confirmed the act.[3] The commentaries on the Papal rules in chancery of which, after the time of Urban V, the reservations formed a part, differentiated between *reservationes speciales*, which were individual benefices, and *reservationes generales*, which were very complex and included an entire class of benefices. After the time of Urban V it was customary to accept as valid all reservations of predecessors, whether special or general.[4]

The following records will give some idea of the sweeping operation of this system. In England between the years 1317 and 1334, eighteen important benefices, and no doubt many smaller ones, were reserved.[5] In 1337 the see of Dunkeld in Scotland had a disputed election. The Pope annulled the election and appointed a bishop of his own choice, but declared the see reserved to his own use for the two succeeding bishops' terms at least.[6] In France in 1324, the *annates* were reserved for one year in the provinces of Aix, Arles, and Embrun ; and the action was repeated the next year in Aix, and in 1326 and 1334 in Embrun. In 1329 and again in 1334, reservations were made for one year in Switzerland. Similar action was taken in Cologne for three years, but later recalled, and in Spain for three years. Reservations were made in 1323 in Cyprus for three years ; in Poland in 1325 for one year ; in Scandinavia in 1326 for two years ; and in Italy in 1323 and 1325 for one year, in 1327 for two years, then repeated every two years until 1333, when they were made in southern Italy for one year.[7] Thus it will be observed that the system was extended to all kinds of benefices all over Europe until it would be difficult to say what ecclesiastical preferments escaped the Papal net. In the town library of Trier is an old manuscript of the Rule of the Roman Chancery on which is

---

[1] Haller, 126. [2] Ibid., 127.
[3] *Regulae Cancellariae*, 15, 17, 28.
[4] Haller, 127. [5] Stubbs, iii, 322.
[6] Coulon, Nos. 100, 101, 103, 107, 123, 170, 432, 733, 941, 1,145 ; *Mon. Hung.*, i, 502.
[7] Göller, 98*.

I

sketched the head of a Pope with the words " *Reservamus omnia* " coming from his mouth. This announcement of the Papal monopoly of all benefices was typical of two facts ; first, that more power than ever had been centralized in the hands of the Pope ; and, secondly, that wide-spread discontent was brewing in Christendom. The immediate result of the practice was to bind all patrons to the chair of Peter and thus strengthen Papal prerogatives, but, on the other hand, the chronicles of the various European countries were full of protests against reservations. Opposition came also from bishops, abbots, and other ecclesiastical officials, who viewed reservations as nothing but confiscations and a suspension of the democratic right of chapters to elect their own bishops. The secular rulers likewise regarded the system with hostility, because it invaded their rights, and consequently sought to limit its effectiveness by special bargains or concordats with the Pope, or by enacting retaliatory laws like *praemunire* in England.[1] The evil grew rapidly during the Babylonian Exile and the Great Schism, and was one of the causes that brought on the great reform councils of Pisa, Constance, and Basel.

The moneys received from reservations must have been a large sum. To insure collection Europe was divided up into provinces and collectors were appointed to gather in the revenues. For instance, France, as the best field for exploitation, was cut up into thirteen provinces with twenty-three collectors to reap the papal harvest. Narbonne, and Toulouse were particularly well combed. Spain and Germany were in like manner invaded by these Papal representatives to augment the Papal income.[2] While the records are not clear on the point, it is more than likely that the collectors of *annates* and reservations were the same officials. The variations in the number of provinces created and officials named may have been occasioned by the reorganization of the machinery under different pontiffs.

23. *Provisions*

Provisions formed another means of raising funds and grew out of the theory of reservation. A provision originally meant a promotion. Afterwards it came to signify that the Pope had the right to supersede by his own appointment an election

---

[1] See source-books on English history ; *Source Book*, No. 93.
[2] Göller, 96*.

made in the ordinary way.[1] By this means Popes could cause all benefices not filled by their nominees to be vacated, and thus all benefices in the Church were brought under their patronage. The Avignon pontiffs made scandalous use of this method of raising funds. In the first year of his reign, Clement V made 20 provisions, and in the seventh year seven more, in England alone, while John XXII in his first year made 200 provisions, in his second year 87, and in his eighteenth year 64, in that same country. The number of provisions was much larger for France and very considerable for other lands. In all, the provisions during the Babylonian residence must have numbered thousands.[2]

In opposition to this attempt to monopolize all lucrative benefices, England in 1351 passed the Statue of *Provisors*,[3] which was supplemented by the acts of 1353, 1364, and 1389.

During the Avignon period thousands flocked to the Papal court in order to obtain an expectation or a provision. In the Vatican library 22 huge folio volumes contain nothing but petitions and letters asking for places.[4] Many of these men were university graduates, but they were not in the majority. About the only way the Pope could accommodate the multitude of hungry office seekers was by a sort of rotation of office, and here the system of provisions worked in splendidly. Consequently there was a wholesale confiscation of ecclesiastical offices, and a general distribution, which of course brought the gold to the Papal treasury.[5]

In Strasburg from 1324 to 1330 there were 41 provisions in connection with three churches. From 1300 to 1400, 140 new benefices were created in that one city, and even that record is not complete. The münster had over thirty altars and chapels and from one to three benefices were connected with each one.[6] The benefices were as low as 2, 3, 4, and 5 pounds, hence it was not at all surprising that the holders desired to hold a number of them.[7] In Cologne and Trier in the first year of the rule of Clement VI, twenty-six Papal provisions were made.[8]

---

[1] Bliss, *Calendar*, ii.   [2] Haller, 112.
[3] Lee, *Source Book*, No. 92.
[4] Sauerland, lvii.   [5] Ibid.
[6] Kothe, *Kirchliche Zustände Strassburgs im vierzehnten Jahrh.*, Breslau, 1902.
[7] Ibid.   [8] Schäfer, *Rom. Quartalschr.*, 1904, vol. 18, p. 138.

24. *The spolia*

The *spolia* was another source of income and was closely connected with reservations. The conflict of the Pope against the imperial right of *spolia* was settled in the Pope's favour with the victory over Frederick II and afterwards over Otto IV and Philip of Swabia.[1] Claim was then made to the property of a prelate dying at Rome without having made a will. In 1246 Matthew of Paris stated that the Pope took the property of three prelates who died intestate. Urban IV followed that precedent and it became the general practice.[2] Collectors in Spain, France, Germany, and Italy appropriated such property, and Nicholas III in 1278 enforced the rule in England. Boniface VIII forbade under penalty of suspension the division of dead clerics' property among the canons or monks. John XXII took many such properties for which he officially recorded the proper receipts, and Urban V formally reserved all such estates left by bishops, abbots, deans, provosts, priors, and rectors, and the order was repeated by Gregory XI and Clement VII. There was no special rule for members of the curia dying intestate. John of Bremen died intestate at Avignon and left about 8,000 gulden, which were at once reserved by John XXII. France paid most of this kind of wealth during the Avignon period, but much was collected elsewhere. The rule was likewise extended so as to apply to deposed prelates.[3] Clement VI was the first to collect delinquent *spolia* out of the estates of bishops and abbots. When the Archbishop of Trier died, the Pope ordered the Archbishop of Cologne and his general vicar to make out a double inventory of the deceased prelate's estate so that the *spolia* could be turned over to the curia.[4]

25. *Expectations*

Expectations constituted another lucrative source of income. These were anticipatory grants of ecclesiastical benefices, not vacant at the time, but which would become vacant upon the death of the holders. This was an old practice, which had been prohibited in the Third Lateran Council of

---

[1] Tangl, *Die Vita Bennonis und das Reglien- und Spolienrecht*, N. Archiv., xxiii, 77.

[2] Kirsch, xv.   [3] Göller, 106*–112*.

[4] Sauerland, iii, 817.

1179, but without effect. In 1248 there were fourteen "expectants" for the twenty places connected with the cathedral of Constance. Indeed it was customary to appoint a number of "expectants" for a single office so that chances were sold down to the tenth degree. The whole system was a species of ecclesiastical gambling, in which each "expectant" took a risk on the life of the holder of a benefice and on the lives of other "expectants" ahead of him. Naturally the value of the tenth expectation was very small, while that of the first might be of great value, particularly if the holder of the benefice in question was a very old or a sickly man. Alexander IV in 1255 sought to curb the evil by reducing the number of "expectants" to four for each office. Matters were made worse, however, by giving to universities, Papal legates, princes, and others the privilege of appointing "expectants" on certain conditions which redounded to the benefit of the Papacy.

The Avignon Popes were not slow in taking advantage of this opportunity for raising funds. No Pontiff was so free in granting expectancies as John XXII,[1] but Clement VI developed the system to its highest point. In Cologne and Trier, in one year, ninety-two benefices were disposed of and sixty-six expectancies were sold.[2] Princes, counts, cardinals, and bishops were all busy begging expectancies for their friends and subordinates. Expectancies were so numerous that many had to wait years, while others died before realizing anything. Those marked by the chancery " *Gratis pro deo* " were usually given preference. The system resulted in many expensive law suits, which often lasted so long that both litigants died, and caused much bitter feeling. The protests against expectancies came from the clergy and laity alike, but without avail, and the big business in these gambling risks continued almost unchecked throughout the entire Avignon period.[3]

26. *Visitation Fees*

Visitation fees brought considerable sums to the Papal curia and, like the *census* and *servitium commune*, were divided

[1] *Galv. de la Flamma*, Muratori, xii, 1009 ; Murimuth, 25.
[2] Cf. Schäfer, *Röm. Quartal schr.*, 1904, vol. 18, 140. Three went to the cardinals ; eight to the clergy of the King of Bohemia ; five at the request of Archbishop Walram, etc.
[3] Expectancies were not abolished until the Council of Trent.

equally between the Pope and the college of cardinals. Theoretically the Pope visited the bishops of Christendom and the bishops and archdeacons in turn visited the parish priests to supervise the temporal and spiritual welfare of the Church. The expenses and food supplies required for such visits were provided by the different communities visited. One of the duties of all the bishops of the Roman Church was to visit periodically the tombs of Peter and Paul at Rome, at which customary visits fees were expected to be paid to the Pope. By the twelfth century regular visits by the higher clergy to Rome at stated periods had been established and the next century appointees to office took an oath to visit Rome as a sign of honour to the Holy Chair and for the purpose of binding them loyally to the Pope.[1]   Hence after the time of Alexander IV (1264) visits to Rome were held to be compulsory—yearly for those living south of the Alps ; bi-annually for those residing beyond the Alps ; and every three or five years for those stationed beyond the seas.   During the Avignon period the visitation fees were regarded as an obligatory tax whether the Papal court was visited or not. After 1350, by paying a procuration tax, the visitation obliga-tion could be met by sending a representation to the Papal court, which was almost equivalent to securing a dispensation. Consequently the actual number of visitations became surprisingly small, because it always meant the payment of money and besides it was much more economical to buy a permission to remain away. Many of the prelates took advantage of the opportunity to compromise with the Pope's requisition on some favourable monetary basis.

Procurations were simply charges, commuted to money payments, which bishops were authorized to make for their personal expenses while on tours of inspection and visitation throughout their dioceses. Gregory IX and Innocent III had permitted bishops on their visitations to make moderate demands, not of money, but of victuals. Boniface VIII extended to all the higher clergy, who had the right of visitation, the permission to receive money procuration, but only one each day. Benedict IX issued a bull *Vos electiones* in which he set down the method of collecting the tax and the amount of it. Out of the local procuration the bishop was supposed

---

[1] Kirsch, *Finanzverw*, 22 ; Baumgarten, cxxi-cxxii.

to save enough to pay his visitation fee to the Pope. John XXII was the real creator of the system, as a regular tax payable by the whole Church through the bishops to the Pope. Whenever the Pope visited a bishop, he collected the procuration. For instance the Abbott of St. Mauer-Fossat said that when the Pope visited there in 1274 the Church paid him a procuration. And Boniface VIII sent two cardinals to France and England as legates to receive the procurations. They appropriated a part for themselves and sent the rest to the Pope. John's theory was that all churches should pay the Pope the procuration just the same as if the Pope had actually visited all of them. He ruled that all churches that were visited were required to pay a procuration tax not to exceed 100 big turnoses and that sum could be collected in the Pope's name. Indeed it was even held that the Pope could reserve procurations and Urban V (1362) made such a general reservation.[1] Thus the Pope began by demanding a share of the procuration and ended by claiming the whole amount.[2]

Some idea of the sums paid for visitations fees may be had from the following figures. The Archbishop of York paid 1,200 florins every three years, whether Rome was visited or not. Every two years the Archbishop of Canterbury paid 1,500 florins; the Archbishop of Tours 400 pounds; the Archbishop of Rheims 500 pounds; and the Archbishop of Rouen 1,000 pounds.[3] In 1301 the Archbishop of Armagh paid 250 florins and fifty years later back payments for the interval were demanded, presumably because no officer from that diocese had been to Rome to pay the tax. In another instance 16,400 florins were demanded of five prelates for back visitation money.[4] It is reasonable to suppose that similar amounts were collected from all over Christendom. The total amount received during the pontificate of John XXII for the *census* and visitations was 523,850 gold florins,[5] but the latter tax was relatively small.[6] Nevertheless many bitter complaints were registered against this system during the fourteenth century.[7]

[1] Göller, 74*–9*; Haller, *Papsttum*, 131.   [2] Lindsey, 13.
[3] Baumgarten, xcxi; Kirsch, *Finanzverw*, 22. The pounds mentioned were Tournois, of which eight equalled five gold florins.
[4] Deprez, No. 180–4.
[5] Göller, 21–105.   [6] Ibid., 56.   [7] Haller, 131.

27. *Special Fees*

Special fees were collected from both laymen and prelates for all kinds of favours, such as commutations, remissions, privileges, dispensations, absolutions and indulgences. There was a regular list of prices for favours granted by the Pope and curia. John XXII in a bull dated 1331 explained that these charges were made not for the grace imparted but merely for the labour of writing the documents.[1] The cost, however, was out of all proportion to the small secretarial work involved.

Dispensations were granted to priests born out of wedlock, to prelates wishing to absent themselves from their livings, to persons wishing ordination before the canonical age, to clergy who said mass in interdicted places and collected a florin for absolutions,[2] to relatives wishing to marry, and for other similar infractions of Church law.[3]

Benefices were united to meet the personal wishes of those who were willing to pay for the privilege, and benefices were also divided to create more places to be disposed of. By commendation more than one place was bestowed upon one individual. The English prelate Wykeman (1324–1404) drew 60,000 pounds from twelve big livings in 1361.[4] Walter of London held eleven different livings under this system of pluralities.[5] The unity of the diocese was broken up by exemptions, absolutions, and reservations, and this resulted in insecurity in ecclesiastical and legal practices. Henry of Diesenhofer, the Papal chaplain, had three livings without any dispensation and this custom apparently became a common thing.[6] Cloisters, hospitals, monastic orders, and universities, as well as the clergy, both high and low, were by these favours bound to and made dependent upon the Papacy. Everywhere the earlier power and independence of the bishops were broken down. Bishoprics, cloisters, and individual churches were given dispensations for unjust gains in trade.[7]

Special indulgences were granted for particular cases and the price, like the fees of physicians and lawyers to-day, depended upon the station of the recipient and the value of

---

[1] Tangl, 21.
[2] Woker, 77, quotes John Winterthur in 1345.
[3] Tangl, 74.   [4] *Dict. of Nat. Biog.*
[5] Bliss, ii, 521.   [6] Haller, 112.
[7] See Luther's *Address to the German Nobility* ; Lindsay, 14.

the favour. Queen Joanna of Sicily paid $150 for the privilege of taking the oath to the Archbishop of Naples as the Pope's representative. The bull readmitting Margaret of Maultasch and her husband, Lewis of Brandenburg, the son of Lewis the Bavarian, to the sacraments of the Church cost the princess $600. For $45 the King of Cyprus secured permission for his subjects to trade with the Egyptians.[1] There was a graduated scale of prices for Papal letters permitting the laity to choose their confessors outside of their regular parishes.

In theory the Pope could change either canon law or divine law. The canon law could be set aside at will, but divine law could be changed only when warranted by an excellent reason. Of course the Pope was the sole judge of the validity of the reason. Consequently these special privileges covered the whole range of human affairs and a little money could buy a permit for nearly everything. Thus the political, ecclesiastical, educational, social, and industrial institutions were regulated to a considerable degree by these special Papal privileges. The following list will give an idea of the sweeping operation of this system of fees for particular permits :

A. POLITICAL	Groschen.
To a prince to exercise the right of coinage	500
To a king to carry his sword on Christmas day	150
To a ruler to collect tithes for two years	100
To a litigant to transfer his case to another court	60
To a king to legitimize his illegitimate children	60
To a city to change its wax seal from green to red	50
To a ruler extending the right to collect tithes another year	20

B. ECCLESIASTICAL	
To a city for freedom from the penalties of an interdict	60
To a sick nun granting a permit to go home	60
To a converted Jew giving permission to visit his parents	40
To a cloister freed from episcopal excommunication	40
To hold an unlimited number of benefices	36
To hold four benefices	21
To hold three benefices	16
To free a cloister from the provincial bishop	30
To free a bishop from the archbishop	30
To free a parish church from a bishop	20
To permit a noble to receive the sacrament in an interdicted place	30 [3]
To divide a dead man and put him in two graves	30
To permit nuns to have two maids	20
To permit the choice of a special confessor	20
To permit monks to build a bell tower	16
To permit a pilgrimage to the Holy Land	16
To secure freedom from fasting	10
To obtain immunity from excommunication	6

[1] Kirsch, *Kollektorien*, xxvi ; see Woker, 94.
[2] A groschen = about two cents.
[3] A yearly tax of two florins was sometimes substituted. Woker, 89 sqq.

C. Educational   *Groschen.*

To permit a city to establish a school   30
To permit the addition of a second school   30
To permit the transfer of a school   50
To permit a layman to hear university lectures on law and physics   12

D. Social and Industrial

To permit a city to erect a hospital (John XXII)   .   .   .   100
To receive stolen goods to the value of 1,000 gr.   .   .   .   50
To trade with the infidel Mohammedans, for each ship   .   .   50 [1]
To trade with heretical lands   8
To permit common people to marry relatives of the second degree   50
To permit common people to marry relatives of the third degree   20
To permit common people to marry relatives of the fourth degree   16
To permit nobles to marry relatives of the second degree   .   100
To permit nobles to marry relatives of the third degree   .   .   30
To permit nobles to marry relatives of the fourth degree   .   20

The theory upon which was based the right to grant permissions and special privileges of all sorts was that the Pope possessed the power by virtue of his office to change the canon law at will, but he could change the divine law only in case of an unquestionably valid reason.[2]

There were special taxes for alienation, for the union of benefices, for the creation of new orders and congregations, for promotions, for personal honours and favours, for baccalaureate and doctor's degrees, for wills, and almost innumerable other concessions and privileges.[3]

28. *Tithes*

The system of tithes was exploited to the limit during the Babylonian Captivity for the purpose of replenishing the Papal treasury. Theoretically tithes were established by Divine Law and had been paid for the support of the Church from the earliest days of Christianity.[4] In the sixth century Popes and councils urged the perpetual claim of tithes. The capitularies of Charles the Great applied the tithes to the maintenance of the bishop, the clergy, the poor, and the fabric of the Church.[5] The clear intent of the canon law of the Church was to make the tithes the exclusive patrimony of the parochial and labouring clergy, but as time passed this

---

[1] John XXII tried to force the Venetians to pay for the privilege of trading with the Mohammedans, and Benedict XII forced them to pay 9,900 florins yearly.

[2] Woker, 160, gives, " Das Buch der Taxen der Apostolischen Kanzlei und der Pönitentiarie " of 1520.

[3] Gottlob, 193–4.

[4] Selden, *History of Tithes*, 1618.

[5] Milman, Book XIV, ch. 1.

simple, universal tax came to be subject to all sorts of irregularities and suffered the fate of other Church property. It was appropriated by the higher clergy; it was alienated or seized by force or fraud by laymen and cloisters; it was turned over to absentee holders of benefices; and it was pounced upon by the Popes as a legitimate source of revenue. Just as the law of the Church permitted the clergy to demand from the laity one-tenth, not only of all produce of the land, but also all other products such as cattle, poultry, bees and even fish, so the Popes came to claim the right to collect tithes from the clergy for the purpose of pious enterprises involving the welfare of Christendom, such as the suppression of revolt in the Papal States, the crushing of heresy, the expulsion of unbelievers from Christian lands like Spain, and the recovery of sacred places like the Holy Land. No one questioned the absolutely legal right of Popes to tax the property of the Church for these undertakings by levying tenths and twentieths.[1] Thus all Christendom was held responsible for Papal tithes, which might be proclaimed as a general tax on all Christian countries, or as a special tax on particular lands.

The tithes were collected by the Popes originally to finance crusades, and Innocent III was the first pontiff to tax the whole Church for this purpose. Boniface VIII and Clement V both applied the principle of tithing to single countries. John XXII proclaimed more tithes than any pontiff had done before his day and was unprecedentedly successful in collecting them. In all instances the principle of a crusade of some sort was given as the occasion for the tithe. Out of the old practice of levying tithes for the local diocese grew the theory that everywhere the property of the Church was under obligation to pay some kind of a Papal tax, hence the doctrine was promulgated that a Papal demand of a tenth, or a twentieth, of all ecclesiastical incomes was a legitimate request.

The method of levying and collecting a tithe was very simple. The authorization of a council was first secured if convenient, and then the Pope issued a proclamation of the tithe. This proclamation was sent to the archbishop, who in turn sent copies to his suffragan bishops, and they notified the collectors and sub-collectors. Then the collection

[1] Gottlob, 190.

began.   It seems that the division of Christendom into
provinces, in order to systematize the work of gathering in
Papal revenues, and the machinery devised for that work,
were utilized to collect the tithes.[1]   The clergy paid their tithe
as a rule twice a year, usually on church festivals.   Monks
as well as priests were subject to the tithes, although the
Knights of St. John were ordinarily free, and the Begging
Orders were always exempt.   Of course, payments were made
in local money, and the funds collected were sent on to the
Pope accompanied with very business-like accounts of the
receipts.   An effort was made to supervise carefully the whole
system.   Since considerable difficulty was experienced in
collecting the tithes through the Papal collectorial agencies,
the Popes frequently found it to be highly advantageous to
make regular agreements with princes and bishops to share
the tithes with them.[2]   This practice led to a great deal of
bargaining between the Popes and the secular rulers.[3]   The
kings employed the royal collectors to force the payment of
tithes and as a rule retained from one-third to one-half as
compensation, although there are instances where three-
fourths or even the entire amount was permitted to be taken.
When the Pope and the king united and worked in harmony,
popular and clerical opposition was useless—the money had
to be paid.   The Kings of Spain were permitted again and
again to levy tithes for their unceasing war against the Moors.[4]
In France tithes were granted to the king in 1306 for two years,
in 1316 for four years, in 1317 for one year, in 1326 for two years,
and in 1333 for six years.[5]   In England the king was granted
a portion of the tithe in 1317, one year's tithe in 1319, 75 per
cent of two years' tithe in 1324, and 50 per cent of the four
years' tithe still due in 1330.[6]   In Hungary the tithes and
annates were divided with the ruler.[7]   The monarch of Sweden
in 1326 received half of the tithes ; the King of Castile got
a portion of the tithes ; and the Duke of Austria was given
all the tithes.[8]

---

[1] Henning, *Die Päpst. Zehnten aus Deutschland*, Halle, 1909.   Germany
had seven provinces.

[2] Haller, *Papsttum*, 45, note 2.   [3] Ibid., 119.

[4] Woker, 47–8.   [5] Thomassni, i, c. 44, § 3.

[6] *Flores Histor.*, iii, 182 ; Bliss, *Calendar*, ii, 138, 414, 416, 442, 449 ;
Wilkins, ii, 464 ; Haller, 117 ; Göller, 98*.

[7] *Mon. Hung.*, i, 553.

[8] Haller, 117 ; Göller, 98*, 99*.

To crush the Italian rebellion and to recover the patrimony of Peter, Pope Innocent VI levied a tax of one-tenth for three years on Germany, and in 1336 Urban V extended it to all Christendom.[1] When Urban V returned to Rome he sought to pay the expenses of the journey by means of this tithe.[2] Gregory XI in 1375 called on the archbishops of Canterbury and York to collect 60,000 florins for the purpose of defending the Apostolic See.[3] By combining with kings money was raised repeatedly to wage war against the Pope's private enemies.[4]

Perhaps the most typical tithe levied for a crusade was that of Vienne in 1312. The Council of Vienne authorized the collection of this tithe for the recovery of the Holy Land. Pope Clement V then issued a bull on 1st December, 1313, ordering the tithe to be collected twice a year from 1st October, 1313, to 8th April 1319. The knights of St John and the Teutonic Knights were exempt from the tax on the ground that they would pay their tithes with the sword. Notwithstanding the excellent system of Papal collectors, this tithe was collected with considerable difficulty. Upon the shoulders of John XXII fell the duty of raising this money. He sent his own collectors to Germany and paid them at the rate of $7.50 per day. The Bishop of Regensburg made a small payment in 1319, and Magdeburg, the Rhineland and Metz contributed small sums, so that in 1326 John complained that " little or nothing " had been collected in that country.[5] The records show that in all Germany a total of 2,000 marks was collected.[6] In Poland and the East the project was so unsuccessful that by 1335 from 400 paying benefices only 635 marks had been collected by the Papal agents and 375 marks by local collectors, making a total of only 1,010 marks for that region.[7] Up to 1331 nothing had been paid in Hungary, so the king in 1332 was given one-third of all outstanding tithes to expedite the collections. Similar inducements were offered other monarchs. Thus in Spain in 1323 the King of Aragon was given 150,000 liber Borchinon to collect the six years' tithes, and the next year King James was allowed to

---

[1] Kirsch, *Kollektorien*, xx, xxi.   [2] Woker, 48.
[3] Cardinal's benefices in England were exempt from this tithe.
[4] Woker, 47–8.   [5] Hennig, 15–21.
[6] Ibid., 22.   [7] Ibid., 21.

collect a two years' tithe.[1] In 1330 the King of Aragon was granted another two years' tithe. King Alfonso of Castile received a four years' tithe in 1328 and a similar tithe in 1331. In 1328 the Pope gave King Robert of Naples the right to raise tithes for three years. In 1326 the ruler of Sweden was permitted to keep one-half of all the delinquent Vienne tithe to crush heathenish outbreaks.[2] Duke Leopold of Austria in 1326 was granted a three year remnant of the same tithe. In 1324 the monarch of England was urged to pay 25 per cent of back tithes and in 1330 50 per cent. In 1329 the King of Scotland was authorized to collect a new tithe for three years, and the same year a new tithe for two years was laid on the island of Cyprus. In 1321 practically all of Italy was under a three years' tithe, but it was suspended for Naples in 1326. In 1331 a new two years' tithe was levied on the Papal States and in 1333 it was prolonged another year. In 1329 Portugal was urged to pay the outstanding tithe for three years. The Vienne tithe raised in France was turned over to the king for a crusade, but was used instead for the wars in Flanders. Philip the Long demanded that John XXII release him from the obligation of restoring the money and his request was granted.[3] These examples are by no means exhaustive, but are ample to show what a complex and lucrative business the collection of tithes was.

Opposition to the collection of Papal tithes was widespread and very pronounced and supplied the fundamental excuse for the bargains struck between the Popes and rulers by which both profited at the expense of the clergy. An Englishman complained that the Church was despoiled between the Pope and the king like an ox or an ass.[4] Another English chronicler said of Clement V: " In Vienne he called a council and proclaimed tithes for a crusade, but he did nothing for the Holy Land. He bestowed the tithes upon kings and plundered the churches and the poor ".[5] The Magdeburg Schöppen-chronicle asserted of John XXII: " He sent legates into all lands and proclaimed a crusade to the Holy Sepulchre and then began to raise money. As a result very much gold went to the Papal court. That money sent to the Pope was given

---

[1] Gottlob, 98*–102*.   [2] Haller, 117.
[3] Samoran-Mallat, 14; Göller, 98*.
[4] *Flores Histor.*, iii, 182.   [5] Haller, 67–8.

to his stomach and to his friends—a shameful transaction ".[1]
When in 1329 John XXII declared another six years' tithe on
the city of Cologne for the purpose of suppressing ecclesiastical
rebels and waging a holy crusade, he put three local prelates
in charge of collecting the desired fund. So much hostility
was encountered, however, that he was forced to withdraw
the bull.[2] Indeed, Germany, and particularly Cologne and
Mainz, was in a state of chronic rebellion against the payment
of tithes to the Avignon Pontiffs. The tithes were hated
by the clergy quite as generally and quite as deeply as the
annates, hence all sorts of obstacles were invented to increase
the difficulties of the collectors.[3] When John XXII proclaimed
a general six years' tithe in 1333, no attention was paid to it
in Germany, although in France and England, where the rulers
were given a large share for co-operation, considerable sums
were raised. Philip VI collected the enormous sum of
2,800,000 gulden. The rulers of both these countries
appropriated the tithes for waging the Hundred Years' War.[4]
Dissatisfaction was so great that the successor of John XXII,
Benedict XII, in 1336 recalled the tithe and ordered the
clergy to return the moneys paid in.[5] In 1347 the Pope
was still collecting tithes levied by Boniface VIII. The tithe
demanded of the German clergy by Innocent VI in 1359
was refused and in 1366 the Archbishop of Gressen with his
suffragan bishops protested against a tithe proposed to be levied
on them for three years by Urban V. The clergy of Mainz
in 1372 united to resist a tithe levied by Gregory XI and in
1375 the Archbishops of Mainz, Treves, and Cologne refused
to pay the tithe to the Pope.[6] This deep-rooted opposition
developed in the face of Papal threats of excommunication
and deposition of bishops who delayed or refused to collect
the tithes.[7]

The simple Cistercian monk, Benedict XII (1334–42)
spared the pocket-book of Christendom and not even the
wily French king could squeeze a tithe out of him. But the
worldly epicure, Clement VI, in whom Pastor says the " exile
of Avignon culminated ", and who boasted : " My predecessors

---

[1] Hennig, 23.   [2] Ibid., 21.   [3] Sauerland, 1.
[4] Haller, 137, 138 ; Hennig, 23 ; *Chron. d. deutsch Städte*, ix, 582.
[5] Gottlob, 98*–102*.   [6] Detmar, *Chronic.*, i, 301.
[7] Woker, 50–1.

did not know how to be Pope," [1] resumed the traffic in tithes. Under him in 1343 was levied the first " Turkish tithe "— a term that replaced the ordinary crusade tithe and was intended to operate more realistically on the fears of Christendom. In ten years he gave the French king ten tithes amounting to 717,000 gulden and to the relatives of the king an additional 103,500 gulden.[2] This change in the name of the tithe was a very shrewd move, since the eyes of Europe were centred on the danger of an invasion of the Ottoman Turks into Central Europe. Such a tithe was levied on Germany for three years and the bishops were appointed as collectors with orders to preach war against all enemies of the Christian faith.[3] Not much money was raised, however, so Papal collectors were sent into Germany and the tithe was changed into a *subsidium contra Turcos* payable by both laity and clergy, but the Pope received from his special agents nothing but complaints.[4] Rulers and bishops alike opposed the tax and little in the way of funds was realized. The Archbishop of Trier raised some money, but never sent it to the Pope, and Poland paid 6,000 marks in silver.[5]

Innocent VI declared a tithe *contra Turcos* in 1353, but little is known concerning it and probably it amounted to nothing.[6] In 1355 a tithe was proclaimed for the re-conquest of the Papal States. France and England were at war at the time, hence refused to pay, so the burden fell upon Germany. The tithe was levied on six German provinces for three years and the archbishops and bishops were ordered to collect it at Easter and on All Saints Day. There was a storm of opposition, such as had not been seen since the Council of Wurzburg in 1287. The clergy of Cologne took the lead, and were joined by the clergy of Trier, in a written protest in September, 1355. They said that they were not in a condition to pay the tithe, because the strife between the Pope and Emperor Lewis had impoverished the German Church. The churches were destroyed ; spirituality was at a low ebb ; priests were so impoverished that they scarcely had enough

---

[1] Baluze, i, 311.   [2] Hennig, 24 ; Haller, 134.
[3] *Mon. Boh.*, i, No. 249; *Vat. Akt.*, No. 2209, 2230 ; Hennig, 25 ; Kirsch, 183.
[4] Kirsch, 183 ; *Mon. Boh.*, i, No. 711, 740.
[5] *Mon. Pol.*, i, 481 ; Kirsch, 384 ; Rhein, iv, No. 93, 94, 96.
[6] Hennig, 26, 27.

to live on ; and the pest had destroyed the sources of income of the clergy. For a long time the imperial churches had borne heavy Papal taxes, although the revenues from benefices had decreased from 400 marks silver to 40, and hence the clergy were not able to meet the demands. If forced to pay the tax, they would not have enough to live on and would be forced to resort to begging and thus bring the Church into disrepute. Already the laity were full of hate for the clergy and the secular princes were feared, particularly by the priests. The civil authorities would prevent money leaving their territories. That condition made it impossible for the clergy to pay the tithes.[1]

Innocent VI declared the protest to be " frivolous ", sharply commanded the tithe to be paid, and asserted that the Pope as the representative of Christ possessed the same powers God had given to Moses.[2] Charles IV was begged to assist in raising the money and was disposed to do so. Diplomatic collectors were sent to Germany to persuade the clergy and nobility to change their attitude. The poor clergy were excused from paying the tithe, and the tax was modified to make payments easier. Many letters were written to the German prelates in which were dire threats of ecclesiastical punishment. The Metz Reichstag sought to compromise matters by granting a subsidy in 1356, but it was not satisfactory. The Pope persisted, and sent new representatives to carry on the work. So little was collected, however, that in 1357 the Pope changed the tithe to a two years' subsidy to be paid out of procurations and visitations. The constitution of 1336 had authorized an archbishop to collect in visitation money for each day from 220 to 320 great turnose silver ; a bishop from 150 to 220 ; an abbot from 80 to 100 ; an archdeacon 50 ; and an archpriest 10. The clergy, who received these fees, were to pay the subsidy, and collectors were appointed. The clergy of Salzburg refused to pay till 1358. The Bishop of Passau was excommunicated. Innocent dangled reforms before the Germans to induce them to pay the tithes.[3] But it was of no use ; the opposition was more pronounced than ever. Collectors were imprisoned and a general conflict ensued. Those dioceses that refused to pay

[1] Hennig, 28–9.   [2] Ibid., 29.
[3] Raynaldus, *Ann.*, 1359, No. 11.

K

were put under the ban. Under Papal pressure Kirsch says that \$200,000 was paid, but up to 1370 the susbidy was still being collected. Metz paid the Papal collector 115,000 marks, but he turned over to the camera only 70,000 marks.[1]

Urban V, one of the best and at the same time one of the weakest, of the Avignon Popes, in 1364 levied the last tithe for a crusade to recover the Holy Land, at the suggestion of Peter I of Cyprus. King John of France was appointed to lead it, and was granted a tithe for six years, while the Emperor Charles IV, Lewis I of Hungary, and the Dukes of Bavaria and Austria were urged to co-operate. On 1st April, 1364, a tithe for six years was declared. But John broke his oath, and the other leaders haughtily refused to lend assistance, so the whole crusade fizzled out with the exception of a small force which was defeated in Egypt.[2] The Turkish and Tartar tithes from that time on succeeded the Holy Land tithes.

Gregory XI, hard pressed for funds to carry on war against the Visconti of Milan, proclaimed a new tax in Germany for one year and appointed the bishops to collect it. Although the Pope told the clergy that the tithe must be given precedence over all other payments, still the German clergy once more rebelled. The churches of Cologne were put under the ban and the clergy complained to the Pope in a most interesting and significant memorial :

" The great pest, which has brought death and desolation to the land ; the numerous bad harvests and wars ; the general clipping of the money, which has resulted chiefly through the sending of this money to Avignon ; and other misfortunes, have brought us to such a bitter state of need, that we cannot pay the tax. On account of the harsh Papal invasion of our land, we clerics have sunk to a state of the greatest poverty. We are put on a plane with slaves and Jews, and hated in a horrible manner. The laity clamour for our blood and rob us of property and liberty. The Holy Chair and the Papal name, which formerly stood here in honour and reverence, are so despised that as a result the catholic for the most part has come into a shaky condition, since the laity see how the clergy high and low have been oppressed by the Apostolic Chair and its various methods of taxation for so long a time hated. The laity despise the Roman Church, because it,

---

[1] Hennig, 29–34.   [2] Ib., 36 ; Samoran-Mallat, 18.

contrary to the earlier custom, almost never sends out a preacher, or a reformer of vicious lives, but pompous, self-seeking, sly, money-getters. Things have gone so far in many places, that only the name of Christian remains. Now in order to avoid this danger and to prevent the tithe completely failing, we bind ourselves by an oath not to pay the tithe and to help each other in case an attack is made on us in consequence. In case one of us is brought to trial by the Pope for non-payment, we will all stand by him. If any one pays the tax, or even enters into a compromise concerning the payment, so will he receive, as a punishment for perjury, which will operate *ipso facto*, the loss of all his benefices and incomes in the city and diocese of Cologne. He will become infamous (*infamis*) and will never be able to recover his honour." [1] This example was followed in Bonn, Xanten, Soest, Mainz, and was generally approved throughout Germany. Nevertheless Papal pressure was so strong that 50,000 gulden were collected, the largest amount any Pope received in tithes from Germany during the fourteenth century. [2]

Subsidies in times of dire need, especially to crush rebellion against Papal authority in Italy, were demanded of the clergy. It was called *subsidium charitativum*. [3] Next to the tithes and the *census* the subsidies formed the chief income of the Papal Curia in the thirteenth century and was a large portion of the income of the Avignon period. Bishops as well as Popes used this means of raising funds because the canon law gave them the right, in case of great necessity, to resort to that practice. This method of replenishing an empty Papal treasury lasted until the Reformation. In Constance in 1491 a bull ordered all prelates to pay five per cent of their income to their bishop. During the Avignon period collectors were used by the Popes to secure subsidies. In 1318 moneys " pro subsidio " began to appear in the Papal account books. In 1322 the cardinals gave a subsidy of from 200 to 2,000 gold gulden each, or a total of 12,000 gulden. Between 1322 and 1330 Cardinal Peter of Palestrina turned over to the Pope many sums. Under John XXII the French bishops made frequent gifts to crush heresy and to suppress rebellion. Between 1324 and 1333 over 300,000 gold gulden were raised in this manner in France alone. After 1324–5 substantial sums in the form

---

[1] Hennig, 37–8. [2] Ib., 38–41. [3] Kirsch, p. xxii.

of subsidies were collected in Portugal and Spain. Very little was paid in this form in Germany because of the political quarrel with the Papacy, yet the Bishop of Strassburg contributed 4,000 gulden.[1] The Cluniac and Cistercian monks made up a big purse and gave it to the Pope, but the German chapters refused to contribute. There seems to be no record of such gifts from England. These grants always had the appearance of voluntary gifts, but there was generally more or less pressure behind them.[2]

Subsidies were commonly denounced as a system of extortion. With all other expenses to be met, the demand for a subsidy looked like a heavy and unjust burden.[3]

The Papal account books are not clear as to just how much was collected from tithes during the Avignon period, but the total amount was less than that secured from *annates*.[4] Judging from the remarkable diligence and elaborate machinery employed by Popes and kings to collect the tithes, one may conclude that a relatively large sum of money from this source found its way into the Papal treasury. If to the tithes were added the subsidies, the receipts would have constituted a comparatively huge amount for that day.

29. *Presents*

Presents ought also to be reckoned as a part of the Papal income. Visitors to the Papal court complained of the incessant demands on every side for gifts.[5] These presents were made to the Pope at any time in person or by will, but were most numerous in jubilee years. The presentation of 4,000 florins to the Pope by the Bishop of Strassburg in 1330 and 3,000 florins by the Bishop of Toul in 1331 are typical specimens of the moneys derived from this source.[6] Presents were also given for some pious enterprise like a crusade when the Pope winked at irregularities like pluralism.[7] The account books have many items of gifts and legacies from one gold gulden up. The librarian of Ferrara left the Pope by will 240 gulden. In 1327 the cardinals gave John 5,000 gulden which were used in the Italian wars. Cardinal Peter of Columpua bequeathed

---

[1] Kirsch, p. xxiii.   [2] Göller, 103*–15*.   [3] Sauerland, p. L.
[4] Göller, 99*, 385, 396–437. The " Book of Tithes " is printed in a summary, but it is very difficult to ascertain the total amount.
[5] Woker, 54 sqq.   [6] Kirsch, *Kollektorien*, xxiii.
[7] Kirsch, *Annalen*, xix.

the Pope 12,000 gulden saved from his tithes and benefices. Bishop John of Dol left him 3,000 gulden. Besides the Pope repeatedly thanked the higher clergy for big gifts not recorded in the account books and which probably went into his private purse—such as 3,000 gulden by Archbishop William of Paris, 4,000 from Bishop Jacob of St Andrews, and 6,000 gulden by Bishop Robert of Salisbury.[1]

30. *Tax on Bulls*

The tax levied on bulls also brought in considerable sums. After Clement V a regular tax was collected. Under John XXII the largest annual sum taken in was 6,400 golden florins; under Benedict XII 2,000 yearly; and under Clement VI 10,000 annually.[2] So well was this tax regulated that John XXII found nothing to improve. From 1299 on the tax was paid to the camera every Saturday, but under Clement V every Sunday. John XXII organized the first "bull" department and placed two Cistercians over it as *bullatores*. The income from this source varied with the character of the Popes. Thus Pope Benedict XII was stingy with his bulls, while Clement VI was very lavish.[3] The cardinals had no share of this income.

31. *Fines*

Irregular receipts came likewise from fines, restitutions, releases from vows, redemptions, and other miscellaneous sources. Fines were paid for disobedience; for violation of ecclesiastical laws; for failing to pay the *servitia*; and for numerous other causes. Money was also paid to escape the punishment of the interdict. These fines were called *condemnationes*. Restitutions were paid as conscience money, *pro secreta restitutione*, mostly for property taken illegally. The sums paid were both large and small, and were received by the Papal penitentiaries. Often the restitution was made in a will, *in articulo mortis*. Persons who had taken vows to take the cross, to make pilgrimages, or to perform some other religious act were permitted to redeem their obligation by money payments. John used this money to fight the Lombards, and other Pontiffs used it to erect churches. The technical

---

[1] Göller, 115*.   [2] Krüger, ii, 173.   [3] Göller, 71*–3*.

term was *redemptiones vatorum*. A person who secured a benefice in an illegal manner, or who was not of age, or who was not consecrated, or who held too many benefices, usually bought a dispensation or compromised for a definite sum, probably one year's income. This was called *fructus indebite percepti*. There were many such instances, particularly in Germany. The income of the bishopric of Avignon was taken at times by the Pope. Seal fees for the camera court ; the sale of the privilege of doing the Papal banking ; the burial insurance of the *cubicularii* ; the sale of remnants of cloth, provisions, cattle, houses, and many similar transactions went into the Papal treasury.[1]

32. *Sale of places in the Papal Court*

The practice of selling places in the Papal court was quite a lucrative source of income. These places had fixed incomes and consequently came to be sold at a definite price. The purchase was supposed to carry with it a life-long tenure. The positions were graded according to monetary value into first, second, and third classes. The following list will give an idea of the proportion between the annual income and the price at which the place sold :—

Office.	Annual income. $	Sold for. $
The *Magister plumbi*	1,375	13,750
A door-keeper	750	6,500
A Papal secretary, who did no writing	500	6,250
A notary in the *Rota*	500	2,500
A collector of lead	325	3,250
A secretary of the " Brevan "	300	3,000
A janissary	300	2,700
A Papal messenger	225	2,000

The janissaries, or Papal guards, numbered 100, hence their offices alone brought into the Papal purse $275,000.[2] All the offices of the various grades were sold for the enormous, sum of 158,000 scudi.[3] There was apparently little or no secrecy about these transactions. The lists seem to have been public property and no more disgrace was attached to a sale of an ecclesiastical office than there is to the sale of a share of stock or a bond to-day. Many of the offices were purely honorary without any real duties to perform. As

[1] Göller, 117*–22*.   [2] Woker, 2–4.
[3] A scudi was worth approximately one dollar (96 cents).

a rule the price of the position covered the income for the first
ten years : after that the salary was clear.   In case of promotion
it seems that the lower places were retained with full income.[1]
The purchasers often found it difficult to pay the entire
purchase price in advance and at the same time assume all
the risk of living long enough to make the investment profitable.
Hence companies were organized to advance up to 50 per cent
of the purchase price and as compensation took 12 per cent
of the income.   In case of the death of the purchaser the whole
transaction came to an end and the office reverted to the
Pope.   So there was no difficulty in selling offices.   Hence
the Pope, when hard pressed for funds, created new offices
to be sold.[2]   Under Clement VI there were 100,000 place-
hunters in Avignon.   Benedict XII took eight days to consider
the requests of the cardinals for patronage.[3]   Before 1471
there were 650 offices for sale in Rome with an income of 100,000
scudi.[4]   Sixtus IV created 13 more offices and Innocent VIII
added 300 with an average value of 200 pounds gold.   Alexander VI appointed 80 secretaries of briefs, who paid 750
scudi each for their places.   Leo X brought the number up to
2,150 and obtained an additional 900,000 gold gulden.   Paul III
created 600 offices, Paul IV 300, and Pius IV 535.   Sixtus V
created 260 knightships and sold them for 130,000 scudi,
and raised the prices of many of the old places.   Thus the
Master of the Treasury, whose office was sold for 15,000 scudi,
was advanced to 72,000 scudi.   Through these changes and
the creation of new offices this Pontiff was able to realize
an income of 1,500,000 scudi.[5]   Moroni gives the following
list of Papal officers :   48 offices of the first class ;   588 offices
of the second class ;   and 2,559 offices of the third class, and
says that these numbers lasted until the French Revolution.[6]

33. *Financial Machinery*

The apostolic camera was the supreme financial organ of
the Roman Church.   It supervised all financial matters
of the Church and in consequence touched every department
of ecclesiastical life.   It represented the Pope and the cardinals,

---

[1] Woker, 5.   [2] Ib.
[3] Haller, 141 ; Cf. Wharton, *Anglia*, i, 765.
[4] Ranke, *Hist. of the Popes*, i, 307 (Bohn).   [5] Woker, 6.
[6] Schäffer, 883–94, gives a list of officers of the Papal court mentioned
in the accounts kept during the pontificate of John XXII.

and in times of vacancy it even exercised Papal authority. It also controlled the business of the Papal States. It signified the victory of the monarchial principle in church government.[1]

The *camerarius* was the head of the camera, a house prelate of the Pope, and the most important officer in the Papal court. He was a member of the consistory. He was chosen by the Pope, took an oath of loyalty and faithfulness to him, and served as his chief financial adviser. On the death of the Pope he took the keys of the Papal palace and guarded the Papal treasures. He arranged for conclaves. He wore a special badge of office, had his own escort, and a whole corps of assistants, who took an oath of loyalty to him. He possessed appointive power for certain offices and could even issue certain bulls. He supervised the auditors, granted passes and permits, and had jurisdiction over the whole income of the Church. The office grew out of the archdeaconate of olden times. Then the *arcorius* paid salaries, alms, and other items. The office of *camerar* appeared first under Gregory VIII. The *camerar* was not necessarily a cardinal until the time of Eugenius IV (1432), but after him a cardinal held the office. His powers were increased by Urban VI, Boniface IX, Gregory XII, Martin V, and Innocent VIII.[2] The Pope had a secret *camerar* for his private account.

The *thesaurar*, or treasurer, first appeared in 1262 as a paymaster, or sort of a vice-camerar. He guarded the funds and kept the books. He had his own seal and paid out moneys on order and received moneys. Later he was called treasurer-general. All collectors, rectors and provincial treasurers were under him. He was appointed by the Pope, or the *camerar*.[3]

A *camerarius gabellarum* was named to take special charge of that tax called the gabell. Under the *gabellieri* were the *dohonerii*.[4]

General collectors had to be clergy of episcopal rank. In 1371 Gregory XI even sent the Patriarch John of Alexandria to Germany, Hungary, and Bohemia on a daily salary of 15 gold gulden.[5] The collectors were in turn assisted by sub-collectors. The various Papal collectors scattered over Europe made regular reports to the Papal treasurer and these reports

---

[1] Gottlob, *Aus der Camera Apostolica des* 15 *Jahrhundert*, Innsbruck, 1889.
[2] Ib., 78–83.   [3] Ib., 95–6,   [4] Ib., 103.   [5] Ib., 104–9.

were recorded in the official financial records,[1] which constitute the basis for an estimate of the receipts of the curia during the Babylonian Captivity.

Regular receipts, such as would be given by any modern government, were made out and given to debtors who paid their obligations. These receipts were issued by both the Pope and the *camerar*, and copies were carefully recorded in the official records.[2]

The greedy Clement V received from his predecessor a fairly large sum of money, and succeeded in collecting during his nine years of rule an income of an annual average of 225,000 gold florins.[3] Since through economy he was able to reduce his yearly expenses to 100,000 gold florins, he was able to save about 125,000 gold florins each year. Consequently in January, 1313, the Papal treasury held 987,000 gulden and the Kings of France and England had been lent 320,000 gulden.[4] The will of this pontiff revealed the fact that during the summer of 1313 he had disposed of 814,000 gulden—300,000 for a crusade, 314,000 to relatives and servants, and 200,000 in gifts to the poor, to churches and to cloisters for the salvation of his soul. In addition he set aside 70,000 gulden to be divided between his successor, John XXII, and the cardinals.[5] The relatives of Clement V and the monarchs of England and France prevented an immediate investigation of the deceased Pontiff's finances, but it was begun in 1318 and lasted two years, when John XXII approved of the bequest of the 200,000 gulden and forced a restitution of the 300,000 given to relatives.[6] There is no documentary proof, however, that Clement V left to his favourites, as rumour reported, the enormous sum of 3,000,000 gulden.[7] The yearly income of the Papacy under this ecclesiastical ruler approximated $565,000.

---

[1] Göller, 638.
[2] Ibid., 607–631, gives receipts from the camera; 631–8, receipts from the Popes.
[3] Ehrle, v, 147. Göller, 122*, gives 1,300,000 gulden as the amount paid into the Papal treasury under Clement V.
[4] Göller, 122* ; Ehrle, v, 126, 135 ; Haller, 46.
[5] Ehrle, v, 1 sqq.
[6] Ibid., 114.
[7] Ibid., 116 ; Göller, 123*.

34. *Total Annual Income*

Since the records for the 18 years of the reign of John XXII are the most complete, the receipts of his pontificate may be set forth as typical of the income of the Avignon Papacy. Upon the accession of John XXII he received the 70,000 gulden bequeathed to him by Clement V,[1] and he promptly divided that sum with the cardinals as was stipulated by his predecessor. That left him scarcely enough to pay Papal expenses for one month. The enforced restitution of Viscomte Bertrand of Lomogue was not made until 1322, when 150,000 gulden were turned over to John and a like amount was to be used for a crusade.[2] Hence John had to busy himself in raising funds. He appointed Camerar Gasbertus and Treasurer Guido Radulphi to take general supervision of finances. His books were carefully kept by them and show that his total income was over 4,500,000 gulden.[3] That is only the book account, however. In addition to the amounts recorded, large sums were paid in by collectors, merchants and others, and used for papal needs without being entered in the records. Thus in 1321-4 the legate Bertrand de Poyet had the sum of 61,896 gulden from tithes, vacant benefices, etc., and it was never paid in to the Papal treasurer. Again, the 150,000 gulden paid by Viscomte Lomogue were not recorded. But John may have felt justified in taking such sums himself since he paid out of his own purse 440,000 gulden and thus prevented a deficit.[4]

John's treasurer, Gasbertus, received from Benedict XII's treasurer a receipt for 524,456 florins.[5] On 4th December, 1334, John ratified the official acts of his *camerar*, Gasbertus, and released him from all further responsibility, and on 7th April, 1335, Benedict XII gave him a receipt for all the moneys received and spent during the Papal vacancy.[6] The night before John died he left to his curial servants and officials all *annates* due from benefices, together with all back debts for that tax. He recalled all reservations of ecclesiastical benefices. He endowed the churches of Avignon with benefices and left 100 marks for a bell for St Agricola. To Cardinal

---

[1] Göller, 1.   [2] Ehrle, 116; Göller, 123*.
[3] Göller, 124*, 4–18.   [4] Ib., 125*.
[5] Ib., 125*. Benedict XII gave a second receipt in 1336. Ib., 129*.
[6] Ibid., 20, 21.

Nicolinus he gave 10,000 gulden ; to his brother Peter he gave 72,000 gulden, with which to purchase property ; and out of his own personal purse he granted 10,000 gulden to secure the release of Count John of Armagnoc. There seems to be no evidence that at that time he presented other relatives with large sums of money.[1] The sum of 25,000,000 florins estimated to have been left by John, according to Villani, is completely disproved by the account books. Nevertheless, it was true that his nephew Peter di Via had to refund a sum of money, 329 gold and silver rings with valuable stones, and 1,928 volumes of books.[2]

That John had a personal account and treasury is also established by the records.[3] Into it went his own private fortune, the numerous large gifts, and the income from his own benefices. Every sum not in the account books went into the private fund. He drew on that fund for the Italian wars and for the extermination of heresy. From 1321 to 1327 John spent 1,627,809 gulden for war—and even more was spent in later years. Besides, funds were used for the King of Armenia, the Patriarch of Jerusalem, missionaries, and various charities.[4] In John's private treasure room was found after his death 100,000 gulden,[5] which Benedict XII gave to his cardinals. Sägmüller estimated that John left in his secret account and uncoined gold and silver 775,000 gold gulden, and articles of value to the amount of 41,000 gulden, or a total of 816,000 gold gulden. Ehrle made an estimate of 700,000 gold gulden. Göller accepts Sägmüller's figures as being substantially correct.[6] Among the sums that went into John's private treasury were : the 35,000 gulden received by John from Clement V [7] because it was not entered in the regular account of the Papal treasurer ; and gifts such as the 3,000 gulden sent to the Pope by Archbishop William of Paris, 4,000 gulden from the Bishop of Strassburg, 4,000

---

[1] Göller, 126*-8*.   [2] Ib., 131*.   [3] Ib., 132*.
[4] Ib., 133*.
[5] The private funds of John at the time of his death consisted of :—
42,052 gold florins.
9,600 regales auri.
1,376 agni auri.
1,300 Parisien auri.
33 denarri auri
2,414 dupl. auri.
Göller, 129*.
[6] Ib., 130*.   [7] Ib., 2.

gulden from Bishop Jacob of St Andrews, 6,000 gulden from Bishop Robert of Salisbury, and other contributions. The income from his own private benefices was included. In 1331 John gave the Bishop of Schleswig a receipt for 2,000 gulden and the Bishop of Siguenza a receipt for 1,000 *duplas auri*, and there were many other similar instances of which there is no record in the public accounts.[1] The Book of Receipts *a domino vostro papa*, or the private account, shows that for the six years from 1323 to 1329 John appropriated for his private use something over 436,640 gold florins, mostly in the year 1326.[2]   John's private account is given by Göller as 1,164,363 gold florins.[3]   After Benedict XI it became customary for the Popes to keep two separate accounts (1) the private fortune brought by the Pope to the Papacy, and (2) all he received from his predecessor and all taken during his pontificate.[4]

Under the head of " de diversis ", or miscellanies, the income of John XXII was considerably augmented each year.   In 1316–17 the receipts from that source amounted to 34,000 gold florins and ranged from one florin, left by the will of the Dean of Lingonen, to 17,000 florins given by the cardinals.   There are no entries for 1328 and 1331, but in other years the receipts ranged from 2,000 florins to 20,095 florins ; so that the total amount taken under John must have been quite a bit over 170,000 florins.[5]   From 16th April, 1334, to the day of John's death almost 4,000 gold florins were recorded under this head.[6]

If the sum of 4,500,000 gulden be accepted as the total income of John for his entire pontificate,[7] then the annual

[1] Göller, 135*.

[2] Ib., 569.

[3] Ib., *Röm. Quartalschr.*, 1902, vol. 16, pp. 181–2.

[4] Göller, 131*.

[5] Ib., 284–384.   The summary of the account books " de diversis " is given on pages 438–569.

[6] Ib., 593.

[7] John's total income included the following sums :—

3,645,657 gold florins.
272,259 agn. auri.
78,628 regal. auri.
3,237 ducat. auri.
149,425 dupl. auri.
3,975 Parisien. auri.

For values see Göller, 125*, note 1.

income for the 18 years would be 250,000 gulden or approximately $625,000, as shown by the official financial records. Since many contributions, particularly gifts, were not included in the public accounts, his total actual income must have been considerably more than $625,000.

The total income of Benedict XII for his rule of seven years from 1335 to 1342 was 1,195,000 gold florins, which made an average annually of 165,000 florins, or $403,000.[1] If he was not so skilled in raising money as John, at the same time he was less lavish in spending it, hence he left a surplus at the time of his death twice the size of John's. The entire receipts for the eleven years' rule of Clement VI from 1342 to 1352 were 1,979,000 florins, which made an annual average of 188,500 florins, or $470,000.[2] Innocent VI during his pontificate from 1353 till 1362 enjoyed the exceptionally large annual income of 254,000 florins, or $635,000.[3]

If the average annual income of Clement V be accepted as $565,000, that of John XXII as $625,000,[4] and that of Innocent VI as $635,000, it may be fair to assume that for the entire period of the Babylonian Exile the yearly receipts of the Papal treasury must have approximated $500,000. By way of comparison it may be stated that the total revenues of the King of France, Philip the Fair, in 1301 amounted to 267,900 pounds.[5] The amount of smaller fees received by members of the Papal Curia—the secretaries, notaries, doorkeepers, and a host of minor officials known as " familiars " [6]— probably totalled in the aggregate $100,000.

The cardinals received as their share of the income of the Church a sum collectively as large as that of the Pope, or about $500,000 a year. To them went as a rule fifty per cent of the income of the Papal States, the feudal dues, *servitia*, visitation fees, and the large sums paid by the highest ecclesiastics for letters of confirmations.[7] For example, between 1316 and 1323 the total annual sum realized from letters of confirmation was over $200,000, hence $100,000 from that source alone went into the pockets of the cardinals yearly.[8] In 1372 Gregory XI received in feudal dues $90,000

[1] Göller, 15*, 12.　　　　[2] Ibid., 17*, 18.
[3] Ibid., 18*, 25.　　　　[4] Ehrle, v, 147.
[5] Göttlob, 133.　　　　[6] Cf. Tangl, 64–7 ; Göller, 46.
[7] Baumgarten, cxx.　　　　[8] Ibid.

and half of that amount went to the cardinals.[1]   It was also customary for Popes in their wills and upon election to make gifts to the cardinals, which were divided equally among them regardless of time of service or social rank.   Thus Benedict XI bestowed upon the cardinals 46,000 gold gulden ; Clement V, 24,000 ; John XXII about 100,000 ; Benedict XII, 100,000 ; Clement VI, 108,000 ; Innocent VI, 75,000 ; Urban V, 40,000 ; Clement VII, 42,000 ; Benedict XIII, 84,000.   These sums made a grand total of 619,000 gold gulden, or about $1,547,500 for the period.[2]   The *servitia* during the last year of the pontificate of Clement VI amounted to 52,787 gulden, hence the share of each one of the twenty cardinals was more than 2,500 gulden or about $6,250.   Besides, the cardinals also held many fat benefices from which they drew revenues.   Thus the cardinal priest Guido received from Clement VI benefices with an annual return of 4,000 gulden, or $10,000.   In addition they received many gifts from private individuals and collected numerous fees for various services.[3]   It seems quite probable that the income of the cardinals in the fourteenth century was larger than that of the present day.

35. *Papal Loans*

Assuming that the Popes of this epoch received about $500,000 yearly, that the cardinals had a similar income, and that the fees of the minor officials averaged $100,000, the total income for the entire papal court must have been approximately $1,100,000 a year, or between seventy and eighty million dollars for the entire period—an enormous sum for that day and unequalled by any secular ruler of the period.   But even that large revenue was not always sufficient to meet the numerous expenses of the Papal household and an army of officials, to say nothing of international diplomacy, and Papal wars.   Hence Popes frequently borrowed money from cardinals, bankers and princes.   Urban V secured $75,000 from his cardinals.   Gregory X borrowed a like sum from the King of Navarre and $150,000 from the Duke of Anjou on one occasion and $100,000 on another.[4]   These loans suggest the inadequacy or uncertainty of the Papal

[1] Kirsch, *Rückkehr*, xv.
[2] Schäfer, *Röm. Quartalschr.*, 1908, vol. 22, 36–47.
[3] Sauerland, I, lii–iii.   [4] Haller, 134.

revenues and also reveal the fact that kings and princes received a considerable share of the funds of the Church.[1]

When there was no such a thing as systematic book-keeping in any secular state in Europe, and absolutely no such thing as a public budget showing receipts and expenditures, the Papacy had a thorough modern and sharp official control of all finances. It is not a matter of surprise, therefore, that the Papal financial system, established on such a scientific basis, surpassed all private and national systems in Europe, exercised a predominant influence in the money markets of the period, and became a great international social, political, and economic power, which indelibly influenced the civilization of the world of that day. Unfortunately the Papacy, after having won a decided victory over the Empire, became a victim to French terrorism in the Babylonian Captivity. The effort made by the Papacy to regain its independence ended in the unfortunate Schism.[2]

---

[1] Haller, 135.

[2] Gottlob, 178–9. In the Empire it was not until the time of Maximilian that a good system of imperial accounts was introduced. Ib., 181.

CHAPTER V

The Avignon Financial System

II. Expenditure

36. *Method of Book-keeping*

THE whole financial system of the Papacy during the period of the Avignon residence was kept in a very businesslike manner. Competent Papal secretaries and book-keepers kept accurate records in registers, or ledgers, of all receipts and expenditures.[1] These archives remained at Avignon until the seventeenth century, when they were transferred to the Vatican library at Rome. An inventory was made of them first in 1594, when it was discovered that there were two sets of archives known as the upper and lower archives. In the upper archives were the acts and ordinances of individual Popes, the records of provincial governments, reports of collectors, tithe registers, minutes of trials, etc.[2] After the transfer to Rome a second inventory was made in 1671, when they were put in about the same order as found to-day. During the nineteenth century they were newly arranged and catalogued.[3] It appears that two copies or sets of books were kept each year for both receipts and expenditures. One set was "official", the other was used for reference. The expense account was divided into fifteen sections corresponding apparently with the departments of the Papal household: namely, kitchen, bakery, cellar, barn, building, seals, washing, alms, etc. The entries are given for monthly and bi-monthly expenses. In these manuscripts expenditures

---

[1] Kirsch, *Kollektorien*, lxvi, gives an excellent specimen of the method of book-keeping of incoming funds. Schäfer, *Die Ausgaben der Apostolischen Kammer unter Johann XXII, Nebst den Jahresbilanzen von* 1316–75, Paderborn, 1911, in vol. ii of *Vatikanische Quel. zur Gesch. d. Päpst. Hof- u. Finanzverwaltung* 1316–78, published by the Görrer Gesellschaft., vol. i, is Göller, *Die Einnahmen der Apostolischen Kammer unter Johann XXII*, Paderborn, 1910. Dr. Florian Watzel plans to cover the financial systems of previous Pontiffs in the studies of the Austr.-Leo-Gesellschaft. See Schäfer, 12*.

[2] Schäfer, *Die Ausgaben der Apostolischen Kammer unter Johann XXII*. Paderborn, 1911.

[3] *Archiv. Vatic.*, Index, 145, 146.

take three times more room than receipts. Yearly balances were made, but obviously the years ended differently under the various Pontiffs.[1]

37. *Historical Significance of Financial Records of the Period*

These historical sources shed much light upon the Avignon period, and clearly show that Avignon was the financial centre of Europe and regulated the value of exchange. Italian banking houses established branches in that city and acted as intermediaries between the Popes and their debtors, and sometimes collected funds and transmitted them to Avignon.[2] No state of Europe had developed such a perfect financial machine. Competent agents were sent to all parts of Europe. Collectors and sub-collectors were found in every diocese to gather in the *annates*, tithes, and other moneys.[3] The officers of the financial machine were paid definite salaries [4] and sent regular reports to the central office at Avignon. Experts estimated the values of the different coins in use and reduced them to the most widely current standard, namely, the gold florin.[5]

38. *Total Annual Expenses of the Avignon Popes*

The annual cost of the Papal household of Clement V was 100,000 gulden, and his pontificate was so economical that he was able to leave behind him in the Papal treasury about 1,000,000 gulden in savings.[6]

The total expenses of John XXII from 1316 to 1334 was 4,191,446 Florentine gold gulden. The yearly expenditures ranged from 72,083 gulden in 1332 to 528,857 gulden in 1325 and the average amount spent annually for the eighteen years was 233,000 gulden. This does not include 16,368 gulden paid by John between his election and coronation, nor certain

---

[1] Schäfer, 13*.

[2] Kirsch, *Kollektorien*, lxxi, gives an excellent chapter on the current value of various coins.

[3] Ib., xxx, ff. gives a fine description of the system of collectors.

[4] Ib., vii, xlix. Documents of collectors cover over 400 pages. John XXII allowed collectors five gold florins a day, or about $7·50 in our money.

[5] Ib., lxxviii, *Rückkehr*, xli ; Gottlob, 133, 174 ; Baumagrten, ccxl. A gold florin was generally estimated to be equivalent to $2.50 in U.S. money to-day. Schäfer, pp. 38*–151*, gives the values of the various coins in use. A table of coins in Florentine values is given on page 898.

[6] Ehrle, v, 746 ; Baumgarten, *Camera*, 244 ; Haller, 133.

L

presents of gold rings, precious stones, and other gifts mentioned in the accounts. The total income of this Pontiff was 4,100,000, or an annual average of 228,000 gulden. Hence John would have left a deficit of over 90,000 gulden had not he received 150,000 gulden from his predecessor, and had he not paid out of his own pocket 445,000 gulden. His finances were managed so skilfully that in 1334, the year of his death, there was a surplus of 499,000 gulden notwithstanding the costly wars waged in Italy.[1]

The total expenses of Benedict XII from 1335 to 1341 and three months in 1342 was 728,683 gulden, or an annual average expenditure of 116,575 gulden, which was under one half as much as that of John. Nor did the disbursements of any single year approximate John's within 117,000 gulden. Benedict's receipts amounted to 1,195,000 gulden, or an average annual income of 164,827 gulden. In consequence he had a surplus in the Papal treasury every year which amounted at the time of his death to 468,484 gulden, although only 367,000 gulden were found in the chest and no satisfactory explanation of the difference of over 100,000 gulden has ever been made. The accounts clearly show that Benedict was much more economical than John in the management of the Papacy, and at the same time was not so skilful in collecting funds. Had he been as lavish as John he would have left a large deficit and had he been as skilful in collecting funds his surplus would have been doubled.[2] If the surplus of John's reign of 499,000 gulden be added to the 468,000 gulden left by Benedict the Papacy was in a flourishing financial condition in 1342.[3]

The total outlay from 1342 to 1352 under Clement VI was 1,667,852 gulden, or an annual average of 159,000 gulden, which was 62 per cent higher than under Benedict. At the same time the receipts amounted to 1,978,977 gulden, or a yearly average of 188,500 gulden, which was 22,000 gulden more than under his predecessor. This left a comfortable margin for surplus which amounted in all to 311,115 gulden. During four years there was a deficit of small sums, but the surplus of seven years wiped out the deficits and left a good sized margin. Nothing further is heard of the large sum in the treasury at the beginning of Clement's pontificate.[4]

[1] Schäfer, 13*, 14*, 8 ff.   [2] Ib., 15*, 12 ff.   [3] Ib., 16*.   [4] Ib., 17*, 18 ff.

Innocent VI spent during his pontificate of nine years the sum of 2,122,728 gulden, or a yearly average of about 236,000 gulden. That was the highest average of the four Popes and 16,000 gulden more than under John. This extra expense was due, apparently, to the Italian wars waged under Cardinal Albernoz. The largest expenditure was 346,750 gulden in the year 1355. During two years there was a deficit. The annual income was 253,600 gulden and the surplus averaged for the entire pontificate 18,715 gulden. In 1360 the Papal treasury was forced to borrow 35,000 gulden from the cardinals to meet pressing obligations.[1]

John, Clement, and Innocent all appear to have had private banking accounts, probably of personal funds, which were used for papal purposes in case of an emergency.[2]

For two months after the death of Innocent the Papal chair was vacant. During that time the expenses amounted to 27,000 gulden, while the receipts were only 8,000 gulden, leaving a deficit of 19,000 gulden.[3]

Under Urban V and Gregory XI it became increasingly more difficult to raise money for current expenses. The superior financial system of John seems not to have been faithfully followed and no doubt as European criticism of the Avignon Papacy increased the customary payments were withheld.

Both pontificates closed as a result with deficits. The books were not kept with as much care either, and hence it is rather difficult to make out totals and draw averages. The monthly expenses for the first year of the reign of Urban V were 20,800 gulden or 249,600 gulden for the year. The total for the second year was 195,600 gulden. When he went to Rome in 1367–8 the expenses at Avignon fell to about 51,000 gulden, but still there was a deficit of 8,500 gulden. The expenses of the first year were increased by the gift of 2,000 gulden to each cardinal and by the use of 40,000 gulden " in sui creatione ".[4] Urban V borrowed from his cardinals the sum of 30,000 gulden. Gregory XI at his election bestowed upon each of his cardinals the sum of 3,000 gulden as presents. In 1372 he began a costly war against the Visconti in Lombardy, and hence the expenses increased until in 1374 and 1375 they

---

[1] Schäfer, 18*, 25 ff.   [2] Ib.
[3] Ib., 19*.   [4] Ib., 19*, 35 ff.

reached the enormous annual sum of 500,000 gulden.[1] In 1371–2 the expenses were also very high because of the many costly presents to his relatives, cardinals, princes, nobles, etc.[2] Hence he was continually pressed for funds and had to borrow from the Kings of Navarre and France, the Duke of Anjou, and the Emperor Henry IV. The annual deficits were large, and when the Papacy finally returned to Rome the Papal treasury was heavily in debt.[3]

The Papal household accounts were kept with such surprising faithfulness and accuracy of detail that one may ascertain not only the exact cost of the various departments of the Papal household minutely, but also much of interest and significance concerning the personality, economics, and administration of the pontifical court. The different departments were remarkably well organized. The whole system of book-keeping would compare very favourably, in principle and purpose at least, with the system of one of our gigantic business corporations of to-day. At the head of the entire Papal court was the *camerar*, or sort of a grand chamberlain, who supervised all the departments. A *thesaurar*, or chief Papal treasurer, took charge of all finances. John XXII held one treasurer responsible for a faithful record of all receipts and expenditures, and Innocent VI followed his example, but other Pontiffs divided this work among two or more treasurers. From 1305 to 1432 there were eight *camerarii pape*[4] and from 1305 to 1389 there were sixteen *thesaurarii pape*.[5]

39. *Departmental Expenses of John XXII*

A description of the expenses of the various departments of the Papal household under John XXII will suffice to give an approximately accurate picture of the entire Avignon period. The accounts were kept under the following sixteen departmental heads—a practice which was probably borrowed from his predecessors and which his successors apparently used without change.

1. The kitchen heads the list of departments. A superintendent of court cooking[6] had general charge of purchasing

---

[1] Theiner, *Cod. d.plom. S. Sedis*, ii, No. 561, p. 556.
[2] Baluze, i, 442.   [3] Schäfer, 19*, 41 ff.
[4] Ib., 4–6.   [5] Ib., 6–7.
[6] *Coquine administratores emptores magistri.*

provisions and the preparation of food, while a court cook, *coqui pape*, and a large force of kitchen helpers; *coquine servientes*, did the work. Day-books were kept showing all expenditures for the provisions used with tables of weekly expenses for meat, fish (which was a large item), and miscellanies. The prices of single items were given. For example, in 1320 a sheep cost 16 s. vien. and a chicken 1 s. vien. Neither firewood nor salaries were counted in this department.

The total cost for eighteen years was 83,426 gulden, or a annual average of 4,635 gulden. The first year 5,359 gulden were spent. For the years from 1322 to 1326 the average cost was high because soldiers were kept at the court. The highest annual cost was 7,195 gulden in 1324–5 and the lowest was 3,005 in 1327–8. The kitchen expenses of John constituted only two per cent of the whole household expenditures. The average yearly cost of this department under Benedict XII was 2,487 gulden, or somewhat more than half of the cost under John. On the other hand, the yearly average under Clement VI was 15,880 gulden, or eight per cent of his entire household expenses. That was three times the amount spent by John and six times the amount spent by Benedict. Clement's coronation feast alone cost 15,000 gulden. These differences are an excellent index of the character of these Pontiffs.[1]

2. The bakery was in charge of two *pantorii* and a staff of assistants. They had a special clerk or secretary to keep accounts. Not only bread but vegetables, salt, cheese, fruit, and table cutlery were accounted for in this department. The total expenditures for John's rule was 6,752 gulden, or an average of 385 gulden for each year. This department consumed ·16 per cent of the entire household expenses. The highest sum was spent in 1323–4 and amounted to 496 gulden, while the smallest sum was 309 gulden in 1329–30.[2]

3. The cellar was managed by officers known as *buticularii*, who were also assigned a clerk to keep accounts. John employed three or four *buticularii*, while later Popes had but two. They had charge of the wines in the Papal cellar and on the table, and also purchased the general supplies of fruit,

[1] Schäfer, 21*, 47–123.
[2] Ib., 22*, 123–32. The word bakery is not a very good translation of the term *pantoria*, which covered more articles than bakestuffs.

such as apples, pears, grapes, figs, oranges, and nuts. These officials might be laymen but were usually clergy. The total amount charged to this department under John was 14,239 gulden, or ·35 per cent, or a yearly average of 822 gulden. The highest sum spent was 1,216 gulden in 1324–5, and the lowest 341 in 1427–8. The records show that during the last third of his pontificate John was more economical in this department.[1]

4. The stable of John had in it from 20 to 30 horses and mules, and was in the charge of two or three head officials, or marstalls, whose names are all preserved in the records, The office was very old and it appears that originally there were a white and a black marstall named after the colour of the horses. They kept the stables in order and clean, and superintended all purchases. A clerk kept the accounts and the books are still preserved. Salaries were not included. Items showing the purchase of horses, wagons, harness, horse-blankets, oats, hay, straw, etc., and expenditures for black-smithing, lights, etc., are given. Wax candles were purchased on 1st December and 25th June, to be burned in honour of St Eligius, a saint of horses.[2] Special agents were sent out frequently to purchase large quantities of oats and hay, although the church grounds of Avignon supplied most of these articles. Straw was particularly cheap. The total cost of this department for eighteen years was 12,931 gulden, or ·33 per cent, or an annual average of 720 gulden. The highest expenditure was 1,450 gulden in 1317, owing to the high cost of oats, and the lowest 414 in 1321.[3]

5. The clothing department was both expensive and important. In the early days practically all curial officials received their clothing from the Pope. That involved not only the purchase of enormous quantities of cloth, but also the employment of a large force of tailors to make up the various garments. John XXII inaugurated a change by paying clothing money twice a year to a majority of the members of the court. Thus every *poenitentiarius* received 8 florins, every *palafrenarius* 2 florins, every *serviens armorum* 5 florins, the *magister palatii* 12 florins, the *magister curie* 12 florins, etc. Other officials like the *magistri hostiarii milites*, the *scutiferi domicelli*, the secret *camerar*, etc., still received

[1] Schäfer, 23*, 132–64.   [2] Ib., 165.   [3] Ib., 164–94.

their clothing from the Pope. Clement VI put all officials on a money basis and later Popes followed that practice.[1] When that was done these payments were included under the department of salaries.

John also made many presents of fine clothes to the cardinals, and to his lady friends.[2] His own wardrobe was extensive and very expensive. His court was famous for fine clothes and elegant manners. Indeed it is not easy to-day to imagine the gaudy display of expensive materials and striking colours of the Papal court on a great festal day.

The cloth and other materials required to meet the varied needs of the Papal court cost a large sum and entailed the exercise of much care in buying and in manufacturing. The Pope in person or through his *camerar* bought the materials. A certain favoured few merchants, whose names are preserved. did a thriving and lucrative business. Special agents were sent over Europe to make purchases. Heavy cloth, fine furs, wash goods, boots, etc. for John XXII were selected by his *physicus*, or body physician, and a special Papal tailor, *sartor pape*, made them up on an annual salary of 20 gulden. A court furrier, or *furrerius pape*, fashioned the furs. Certain *milites* and *domicelli scutiferi* were named to guard the wardrobe. In the record are almost countless instances where the old clothes were given to the poor.

The total cost of this department under John was 141,167 gulden, or 3·35 per cent, or a yearly average of 7,842 gulden. There were no fluctuations from year to year, but a gradual increase from 3,100 to 12,500 gulden. The cost of wine went down as the cost of clothes went up.[3]

6. The art and decoration department included a very wide range of subjects, such as : (*a*) costly wall decorations of gold, silver, brocade, silk, etc. ; (*b*) many fine pictures and woven tapestries from Paris, North France, Flanders, England, and once from Germany ; (*c*) rugs of every kind and bleached linen for curtains ; (*d*) expensive tables and other household articles for the Pope, in silver, gold, and ivory ; (*e*) altar necessities and furnishings such as crucifixes, reliquaries of various sorts, sacred images, golden goblets and tabernacles,

---

[1] The *cambrerii* seem to have continued to receive clothing from the Pope.

[2] Schäfer, 196.   [3] Ib., 194–241, 25*.

altar cloths, candelabras, ampullae, portable altars, episcopal chairs, and other articles for the chapel of the Papal palace and for other chapels and churches in Avignon and the surrounding territory; (*f*) parchments, costly book bindings for the Gospels, Missals, legends of the Saints; Ordinaries, and book catalogues; ecclesiastical garments like stoles, mitres, and the pallium; (*g*) costly precious and semi-precious stones and pearls for the Pope, his intimate friends, and relatives. The golden rose given annually to some person as a mark of Papal favour [1] was also included under this head.

This account was kept from 1316 to 1331 in the hand of Reciis Corboli, the Papal court merchant (*mercator curie Romane*). In 1332 another *mercator* took his place. The names of a few goldsmiths are given but no artists are mentioned by name.[2]

The total expenditures in this department were 7,123 gulden, or ·17 per cent, or an annual average of 431 gulden—not a large sum considering the costly character of many of the articles. The most expensive year was 1317, when 1,846 gulden were spent, and the least expensive year was 1322, when only 92 gulden were used.[3]

7. The Papal library was of sufficient importance to warrant a separate department. The various entries are very valuable for a history of the origin of the Papal library in Avignon. Numerous hand-written books were purchased and many manuscripts were copied for the Papal collection. Moneys were paid out not only for books, but also for copying, illuminating, book-binding, and parchment. The works written or copied under John included such subjects as canon law, theology, natural science, mathematics, Church history, politics, medicine, and military science.[4] The names of the librarians are given [5] and apparently they had rather wide discretionary power, although it seems that the *camerar* and even the Pope spoiled many a good book bargain by direct interference. The total amount spent was not large,

[1] Schäfer, 241. See Muntz, "Les roses d'or pontificales" in *Rev. de l'art chretian*, 5th ser., vol. xii (1901), pp.1–11.
[2] Ib., 241. See Faucon, *Les Arts à la cour d'Avignon sous Clement V et Jean XXII*, pp. 45, 101, 103.
[3] Schäfer, 26*, 241–60.
[4] The titles of these books are given in the records.
[5] Schäfer, 361.

however, and amounted to 6,650 gulden, or ·16 per cent, or an
annual average of only 370 gulden. Even these expenditures
show some interest in cultural things. The most money was
spent in 1316, namely, 742 gulden, while only 19 gulden were
used in 1328. Benedict XII used ·22 per cent of his entire
appropriations, or a yearly expenditure of 323 gulden, in this
department. Clement VI's accounts show ·13 per cent, or
210 gulden yearly.[1]

8. The building department's accounts were connected
mostly with three places, namely, Avignon, Chateau Neuf
Calcernier, and Pont de Sorgues. One can follow the rebuilding
and widening of these structures in the records, but the
entries were not itemized for the different palaces.[2] Many of
the appropriations in this department were for non-Papal buildings such as cloisters and churches in and around Avignon.
Ordinarily such items as these were put under department
No. 15, "pro elemosina." Other items like goldsmithing should
have gone under No. 6 and the purchase of kitchen wares
under No. 1. A superintendent of buildings, called *Administrator operum*, or *Operarius pape*, had general supervision of
all construction and repair work,[3] but it seems that there was
also an overseer for Chateau Neuf and for Pont de Sorgues.
All of these superintendents were clergy of one rank or another.[4]
The names of the two bell-casters were given. The painter
appeared as Petrus Massonerii. The wages of the various
workmen were carefully recorded. The total cost for this
department was 122,065 gulden, or 2·9 per cent. of the whole
amount, or 6,800 yearly. The highest sum was 21,975 gulden
in 1319–20, and the lowest was 195 gulden in 1329–30, when
the Italian wars were being waged.[5]

Not only are the records for the various Papal buildings
at Avignon quite complete and perfectly preserved, but the
documents give a description of three buildings in addition
to those mentioned above ; the Papal Castrum Novarum near
Avignon with a special keeper ; Castrum Biturrite with a
particular guardian ; and S. Laurentius du Arboris, a home of
the Bishop of Avignon with its own keeper. Under Clement VI

[1] See Ehrle, *Historia bibliothecae Romanorum Pontificum*, Rome, 1890.
Schäfer, 260–73. Hilgers, *Die päpstl. Bibliothek in Avignon*, 1900. p. 39 ff.
[2] See Ehrle, *Hist. bib. Rom. pontif.*, 587–700, for cost of the Avignon palaces.
[3] The names are given, ib., 274.
[4] Ib., 275.   [5] Ib., 274–315.

(1342–52) Villa Nova near Avignon was built as a Papal summer residence. It was located on the right side of the Rhone river in French territory and of course had a custodian. A special *manualia* was devoted to the expenses of that building.[1]

9. The department of Papal bulls and letters was in charge of a *bullator*, who supervised the sealing of Papal letters, bulls, charters, and other official documents. In the twelfth century the office was presided over by one *bullator*, but the next century two were appointed, and that number was continued until the Schism, except during the years 1338–42, when there were three. The Pope named the *bullatores*, and had them take an oath of office.[2] They were mostly members of a monastic order—almost invariably the lay brothers of the Cistercian order. On at least one occasion, however, Papal masters of horse and gardeners were elevated to the sealing office, apparently because they were "illiterati" and could neither read nor write and hence it was believed in the curia that they could neither falsify nor misuse the Papal seals.[3] Under Clement V these officials received a daily salary of 8 great turnosen and under John 7 little turnosen, which in the latter case would make an annual salary of 200 gold gulden. To that income were added the fees for sealing, which were most numerous under Gregory XI. The ordinary fee was one large turnose for each seal. Since the number of official documents was extraordinarily large, the receipts for fees alone must have been very large. Leo X established a fixed fee of from one great turnose to three or more ducats. This office also shared in the small tips of the papal court. The sealing office occupied a rented office in the parish of S. Simphorian at Avignon, and the Camera paid the rent of 30 sh. vien. or 1·36 gold gulden. The *bullatores* lived rent free in the same building from 1316 to 1350, when they took a neighbouring house. The department had rather large endowments, because legacies were left to it by well-to-do people, perhaps for charitable purposes. The *bullatores* were always paid off on Sunday for the previous week, but under Benedict XII pay-days were at longer intervals and on a week day.[4]

---

[1] Schäfer, 276.   [2] Ib., 315.
[3] Ib.   [4] Ib., 316.

The salaries and emoluments of the *bullatores* were not included under this department, but only the necessary expenses of carrying out the official work and for materials like lead, hempen cords, silken cords, wax, stearin, parchment, etc. The making and repair of iron stamps for the bulls were also charged up to this account. In exceptional cases under Innocent VI and Urban V lead for bulls was taken out of the storehouse in the great tower of the Papal palace at Avignon. Under John XXII the purchase of much paper and parchment was made through the office of seals, but it was done on order of the Camera. At the same time under this Pontiff supplies for this office were charged up to the library account, No. 7.[1]

The total expenditures for this department were the smallest of any in the Papal court and amounted to only 4,597 gulden, or ·12 per cent, or an annual outlay of 255 gulden. Benedict XII spent only a total of 583 gulden, or an annual average of 83 gulden, while Clement VI's average was 220 gulden yearly.[2]

10. The department of unusual services and military expenditures had no special organized office force. Innocent VI named this department *Pro Guerra*. This account seems to have been kept for the purpose of enabling the Pope and *camerar* to make a comparison with the treasurer's account. Officials of other departments presented monthly or weekly bills to this department. In the first year of John's reign there was a big expense for the care of prominent prisoners, for punishing counterfeiting money and bulls, for heresy, and for political crimes.[3] In later years the payments were made mostly for defence and military purposes, for weapons of all sorts such as ballistæ, catapults, crossbows, armour, helmets, lances, shields, swords, and for fortifications at Avignon and at the Papal castles of Chateau Neuf and Castrum Novarum. During the Lombard war and the Emperor Ludwig's journey to Rome, the military funds were very large. This account also included the travelling funds of ambassadors, collectors, legates, intermediaries, spies, etc., for the numerous political missions. In 1330 when the Count of Holland took an army of 8,000 soldiers to Spain to fight the unbelievers,

---

[1] Schäfer, 316.   [2] Ib., 315–34.
[3] Ib., 335 ; cf. Christophe., i, 4.

he went by way of Avignon probably for the purpose of soliciting funds, but John sent them home.[1]

The total amount expended in this department was 120,159 gulden, or 2·8 per cent, or a yearly average of 6,675 gulden. There was no expenditure for 1321, while 35,000 gulden were spent in 1325 and 28,500 gulden in 1323.[2]

11. The department of extraordinary expenses was the most voluminous and included a large number of miscellanies which should have been entered under other departments. No special officers supervised the department and apparently it was controlled immediately by the *camerar*, or the Pope, or some other departmental official. The entries are usually general and not in detail. Schäfer has attempted to organize these accounts under eight heads as follows :—

(*a*) Wax, candles, and torches used in the Papal palace and also given away as presents and for decoration. The traffic in wax was a big business at Avignon and it was usually supplied by privileged merchants. Under Benedict XII a special wax office was created with an annual salary of 100 gulden.[3]

(*b*) Provisions and household goods made up a large item. A Papal *cursor* provided for the camera. The body physician of the Pope supplied all fine drinks, medicines, foods, expensive sugars, and spices, as well as clothing and furnishings for the Pope. A special custodian was in charge of the Papal hospital. Large quantities of household furniture bought from favoured merchants was recorded in this department. The cost of painting the Papal palaces was entered here, and especially the summer palace at Pont de Sorgues. Likewise purchases for the general kitchen were recorded.

(*c*) Messenger service used a lot of money. Papal letters were carried by *cursores*, and *nuntii* were continually going hither and thither for the Pope and the court on all sorts of missions. This was one of the most important divisions.

(*d*) Military affairs required the largest expenditure of funds, and the entries are for enormous sums. The largest amounts were sent to Cardinal Legate Bertrand, the nephew of the Pope, to whom John gave chief command of the Italian war after the end of 1319.

---

[1] Schäfer, 367.   [2] Ib., 335–81.
[3] Ib., 382.

(e) The care and transportation of prisoners took no small sum of money. In 1320 these accounts were recorded under a separate department.

(f) Presents not for the general welfare of the Church or for charity were entered in these accounts. They went mostly to John's nephews, other relatives, and royal visitors.

(g) Exceptional cases of charity were put under this department.

(h) Many items which should have gone under departments like kitchen, cellar, clothing, etc., were for some reason not quite clear transferred to this account.

The total expenditure under John was 2,672,408 gold florins, or 63·7 per cent of all monies spent in the Papal household, or an annual expenditure of 148,470 florins. The largest sum spent was 438,627 florins in 1325 during the Italian wars, and the least was 1,790 florins in 1318. In 1317 26,877 florins were used for the purchase of the castle of Valesianum.[1]

12. The department of regular salaries of members of the Papal court gives an illuminating picture of the size and activity of the Pope's household. Golletti gave the first public list of the curial officers in 1278.[2] Haller first supplied a similar list with salaries and provisions of Papal officials for 1305.[3] Clement V began to transform food into money payments, and the salaries of most of his officials are now known.[4] But John XXII was the first Pontiff to systematize salaries and make a fixed list.[5] All lists show that the basis of salaries was daily wages plus food and quarters. Under John the names of the officers were recorded when the first payment was made but after that only the offices were recorded, such as *scutiferi, servientes, armorum, penitentiarii, clerici, intrinseci,* etc. The documents give the salaries of all officials paid directly by the camera.

Gollitti's list for 1278 gives the *camerar's* salary as 12 viande just like the chancery. Haller's list for 1305 does not mention his salary, but in 1307 he received 21 viande, which was three

---

[1] Schäfer, 31–2*, 381–554.
[2] *Memorie de tre antiche chiese di Pieti* (1765), p. 173 ff.
[3] *Zwei Aufzeichnungen über die Beamten der Kurie im 13 und 14 Jahrhundert.* In *Quellen und Forschungen d. Preuss. Hist. Inst.* in Rome, i (1898).
[4] Given in the Appendix to *Regestum Clementis papae V*, published by the Benedictines.
[5] Schäfer, 545.

times more than the vice-chancellor received. John's lists do not give the *camerar's* salary, nor that of the treasurer and the three or four clerks of the camera. Schäfer thinks that the *camerar* received at least as much as the chancellor.[1] Many subordinate officers were not paid by the camera directly, but by the department officials who had money for such special needs. Such assistants were the *servitores* in the kitchen, the *voileti* and *saumaterii* in the stable, the *elemosinarii et servitores* and *familiares elemosine* in the alms department, etc. Perhaps the countless writers and clerks in the chancery, of whose salary nothing is said, in addition to their emoluments and writing fees, received daily compensation from the salary of the vice-chancellor.[2]

Officers sent on mission had their departure and return recorded by the Papal notary. Lists for 1361–7 and 1372 are preserved showing the departure and arrival of curial officers. Their salaries began on the day of departure, and Sundays and holidays were paid for.[3]

The camera always paid salaries at the end of fixed periods of work. Pay-days were not uniform under John. During his first year payments were made weekly ; in his second and third years pay-day came every four weeks (not monthly) ; in his fourth year and thereafter, the members of the court received their wages every eight weeks (not bi-monthly). Under John, pay-day always came on Saturday, and so it remained throughout the Avignon period.

In addition to regular wages and food, members of the Papal court also received other moneys, perquisites, and benefits as follows [4] :

(*a*) The *servitia minuta*, or minor fees, were paid out of the central treasury and distributed according to some regular system.[5]

(*b*) Clothing money was paid twice a year for summer and winter out of the regular treasury. Thus the *magister sacri palatii* received 12 florins twice a year ; the penitentiary 8 florins ; *servientes armorum* 5 florins ; *palafrenare* 2 florins ;

---

[1] Schäfer, 546.   [2] Ib., 545.
[3] Also recorded under departments 10 and 11.
[4] Schäfer, 10*.
[5] Haller, *Servitia Minuta* ; Karlsson, *Mitt. d. Inst. f. Österr. Gesch.*, 81, 582 ; Gottlob, *Die Servitientaxr im 13. Jahrh.* ; *Gött. Gel. Anz.*, 1903, No. 1 . An officer's share depended upon the total amount paid out.

and others similar amounts. Under John his immediate followers like the *hostiarii milites* and the *scutiferi domicilli* still received their uniforms from the camera, although later they too were put on the money basis.

(c) At Christmas and Easter, by an ancient arrangement, the so-called presbyterium was given out of the papal camera to the curial cardinals in the form of victuals and a little spending money. At Christmas the *camerar* and vice-chancellor each received a hog for himself and his officers—and one was even given to the *servientes armorum*, but at Easter a sheep was given.[1] Upon the occasion of the annual coronation feast the *scriptores cancellarie* received a rooster as a present.

(d) The chancellor received in 1307 in addition to his salary of 18 viande 15 *prebende equorum*. Haller and Golletti both show that in the time of Clement V he received 12 viande and 7 *prebende equorum* and 4s. *provisinorum* and 1 *ferrum* (a tip for a horse-shoe). That made a daily compensation of 47 tur. gross. for the Avignon period.

(e) The curial officers from the *camerar* down likewise held one or more benefices from which they drew the income. As a rule the *camerar* had an archbishopric or at least a bishopric. Minor officials owned small benefices usually at a distance from Avignon.[2]

This whole system of salaries and perquisites was organized before the time of John and under him took place only a few minor changes and additions. The salaries of the thirteenth century remained about the same in the fourteenth, and there was little variation throughout the Babylonian Captivity. After John's rule a catalogue of the salaries of the curial officers was given under a special heading called *Vadis ordinaria familiarium pape*.[3]

The total amount paid out for salaries during the eighteen years of John's pontificate was 533,611 gulden, or 12·7 per cent of the total expenditures, or 29,645 gulden yearly. That there were no extremes in this department is shown by the fact that the annual expenditures range from 20,167 gulden in 1328 to 38,424 gulden in 1333. During the Lombard wars

---

[1] Schäfer, 546.

[2] Peter de Nogareto received a bishopric, hence no longer drew a salary from the Papal camera. Ib., 10*. The Papal officials were often much better off than royal courtiers in France and England.

[3] Schäfer, 548.

the annual appropriations ran low because money was scarce. From 29th January, 1317, to 13th August, 1317, there were 46 pay-days, on which a total amount of 12,350 gulden was paid out, or an average of 334 gulden every two weeks, or 167 gulden weekly, which seems a small sum for so large a force. From 24th September, 1317, to 29th July, 1318, the total was 30,074 gulden or 2,506 every four weeks, or 627 gulden weekly.[1] The salaries ranged all the way up to 20,000 florins.[2] Salaries were also paid under departments number 10 and 11.

13. The department of rents paid for Papal officials at Avignon shows the mode of living in that city.[3] Originally court officials had free quarters provided by the apostolic camera.[4] In 1306 the following officers had homes furnished for them: *camerarius, clerici, camere, marescallus, justitii, milites, domicelli, cancellarius, sivi notarius, auditor contradictorum, corector, bullatores, supracoci, coci, scriptor, coquine, panatorii, scriptor panatorie, buticularii, scriptor buticularie, marescalli marestalle, elemosinarii cum familia sua, servientes armorum, cursores, penitentiarii, porterii exteriores, abreviatores camere, correctorii*.[5] But many of these officials like the *servientes* and *cursores* began to receive money compensation instead of a free living. Under John XXII such money was paid to military persons, the penitentiary, curriers, gatekeepers, and kitchen helpers. Officials who lived in the Papal palaces of course received no rent money. Fixed sums were paid during the entire Avignon period according to the status of the official. Thus thirteen *apost. penitentiarii* were paid 10 s. tur. p. monthly by the camera; another received 10 s. tur. p. monthly for two rooms, a medium-sized kitchen, *curtem* and *latrinas*; another had only 7 s. tur. p. monthly; and another was paid 40 s. 2 d. tur. p. yearly.[6]

A catalogue of 1322 contained a list of all the houses in Avignon rented to curial officers, with the rent price, the condition of the property, name of the renter, and owner. Whole houses were rented for one purpose or another.[7] The

[1] Schäfer, 562.   [2] Ib., 32*, 544–602.
[3] See Baumgarten, *Aus Kanzlei und Kammer*, 47–86.
[4] Haller, 544.   [5] The same list is found for 1278.
[6] Haller, *Quellen und Forschungen*, i, 27–8 ; Göller, *Päpstliche Poeniten-tiarie* i, pt. 2, p. 172 ff.
[7] Schäfer, 607.

alms superintendant, the keeper of the seal, the Papal jailor, the *scola theologie*, the master of horse, the cellarer, and the head cook lived in separate rented houses for which the camera paid the rent, which varied greatly and was paid at irregular times. The cardinals and their courts had their own separate establishments and a few other officials had their own homes and paid their own rents.

A special officer was chosen from among the *domicelli* to superintend the cleaning of the quarters, and to furnish supplies. He divided beds, mattresses, pillows, quilts, towels, and other supplies among a long list of officials. He likewise supplied clothing to certain classes entitled to them. The Papal furrier usually held this position.

Numerous were the quarrels between the tenants and the landlords, hence Nicholas III ordered that a committee of one man from his court and one burgher should appraise houses at their rental value, and that rate was final. In the Avignon period a committee of three members, the *assignatores domorum*, composed of the Papal chaplain, a knight, and a burgher, was appointed to settle disputes. For the appraisal of a house the renter had to pay a tax to the committee. In the case of unusual quarrels a special committee was appointed to adjust the difficulty.[1] Numerous were the complaints, likewise, that the rents exceeded the rental money allowed by the camera.[2]

Since the rents were not paid with any regularity, no annual estimates were made. The total amount expended was 10,370 gulden, or ·24 per cent, or an annual average of 575 gulden.[3]

14. The department of Papal property dealt with the purchase of ground and buildings at Avignon, Pont de Sorgues, Chateau Neuf Calcernier, Castrum Novarum, and later Villa Neuve ; with the enlarging, repair, and fortification of the palaces at these places ; and with the acquisition of smaller houses, estates, castles, and fiefs. Considerable sums were spent for remodelling papal edifices for military purposes. The income derived in kind or money for property sublet was also entered in this account. No special officer had charge of this department. The various expenses were met directly by the *camerar* or treasurer, and totalled 20,483 gulden or ·4 per cent. The outlay was very irregular. No

---

[1] Schäfer, 618. [3] Ib., n. 2. [4] Ib., 33*, 603–20.

entries were made for 1320 and 1324-9, and other years the annual expenditure varied from 46 to 6,391 gulden.[1]

15. The department of customary and extraordinary charity is one of the most significant in the Papal court. Most of the departments were such as would naturally belong to any great establishment of that day and therefore were to be expected in the Papal court. But this department shows to what extent the mediaeval Church was conscious of its obligations to public welfare—to the poor, to the sick, to the unfortunate, to the aged.

This department was exceptionally well organized. At its head stood the superintendent of alms called *administrator et dispensator elemosine papie* or *administrator domus elemosine pinhote*. The position was one of unusual responsibility and great trust, hence the Pope always personally appointed him. Innocent VI in a bull of 1356 provided for the appointment of a new head of the alms office and explained all his duties.[2] This office was filled without exception by the secular clergy and was usually in possession of a canon. The names of the incumbents were given.[3] The superintendent of alms made out weekly accounts for the department.

The Popes also had private almoners who at times served as superintendents of alms. Their names have likewise been preserved.[4]

Under the superintendent of alms was a sub-overseer known as the *elemosinare* who had general charge of the almshouse, or poorhouse. That office was monopolized by the Cistercian monks who were frequently promoted to *bullatores*.[5] They took the oath of office from the *camerar*.

The *servitores* completed the official staff and performed the various menial duties of the department. Only in exceptional cases were their names recorded.[6] They appear to have been clerics and received a salary of three great turn. monthly.

The whole *familia elemosina* apparently lived together and had a common kitchen and a common table.

The almshouse[7] was presided over by two *elemosinare* and their ten assistants, who did the work and lived nearby

[1] Schäfer, 34*, 620-37.   [2] *Archiv. Vatic. Instr. Misc.*, 1356-7, ch. 10.
[3] Schäfer, 639.   [4] Ib., 640.
[5] Baumgarten, *Aus Kanzlei und Kammer*, 45.   [6] Schäfer, 639-40.
[7] The almshouse is spoken of as *pankota, pinkota,* and *pinquota* and meant literally breadhouse.

in a house for which a rent of 6 s. 8 d. vien. was paid monthly. The *elemosinare* lives in another rented house. Great stores of bread and wine were kept in the almshouse. The poor and the pensioners who lived in the almshouse were well cared for and were supplied with a simple table. Needy pilgrims and the sick were also provided for in the almshouse, where about 25 inmates could be regularly accommodated.

Another building devoted to charitable work was the *Domus elemosine*, a big building rented from one Peter Christofori at a monthly rent of three gold gulden. From this building were given to the needy clothing, cloth, shoes, and other necessities.

Under later Popes the almshouse and *elemosine* seem to have been combined into one house.

To secure adequate supplies of cloth, grain, leather, wine, and other supplies the superintendent and the *elemosinare* often took journeys into the country, sometimes in company with other Papal officers like curriers, legates, and guards.

In addition to the regular contributions to charity, many special cases were brought to the department by other officers. Particular contributions were given on the first of each month to the hospitals of Avignon and on from 10 to 15 of the holidays similar gifts were given varying from two pounds small tur. up. Many payments were also made to cloisters and individual members of monastic orders. Regular gifts of money went to the Dominican Minorites, Carmelites, and Augustinians in Avignon, and to the nuns of S. Clares, S. Lorenz, S. Veran, and S. Catherine, the four nuns' orders in Avignon. These contributions were usually made on the forty festival days of each year. In addition to money, clothing, bedding, ecclesiastical furnishings, religious ornaments, and even buildings were occasionally given away. Dowries were also supplied to poor girls.[1]

The sums recorded in this department amounted to 301,186 gulden, or 7·16 per cent, or a yearly average of 16,732 gulden. The sums ranged from 11,312 gulden during the Italian wars to 25,270 gulden.[2]

---

[1] Schäfer, 641.

[2] Ib., 35*, 637–814 ; cf. Kasimir Heyn, *Rom. Quart. Schr.*, vi (1892), p. 209 ff. ; Mallat, *Revue d'histoire eccles.* 1904, p. 3 ; Schäfer, *Monatsblätter f. Kath. Religionsunterricht* (1904), p. 198 ff.

16. The moneys recorded in the *Liber de Diversis* [1] seem to have been for the private purposes of the Pope. There was no regularity about these outlays and there are only seven entries, all however for comparatively large sums. These payments were made for political purposes, as presents, and for debts. To King Robert of Naples was paid 62,000 gulden, and to Philip and Charles of Valois 5,000 gulden. To the kingdom of Armenia was charged 2,000 gulden. A large tract of land for Peter de Ozia, the nephew of John, cost 61,000 gulden. The cardinals received 18,000 gulden and 2,000 gulden went into the Pope's private purse for purposes not stated. The appropriation for presents amounted to 14,800 gulden. The total aggregate in this department was 164,800 gulden or 3·98 per cent of the total disbursements under John. [2]

One of the most interesting items in this department is the appropriation of funds for needy women whose names are given and for poor girls as marriage dowries. For instance, in 1325 on 3rd February, the sum of 100 florins was given to 20 girls " pro subsidio matrimoniorum contractorum " ; 9th February, 60 florins to 15 women ; 12th February, 221 florins to 82 women ; 15th February, 150 florins to 30 women ; 25th February, 35 florins to 7 women. A total of 966 florins was granted " pro puellis maritandis ". [3] A dowry was granted as a special favour to the family of Castrum Novum. [4]

Other miscellaneous items were such as the 100 florins paid to send a missionary to the Armenians. [5] The canonization of S. Louis cost 277 florins and the canonization of S. Thomas Aquinas cost 151 florins. [6] The cost of making a Tartar boy a Minorite monk was borne by the Papacy and charged up to charity. [7]

Of the entire sum spent by the Papal treasury 63·7 per cent was for war—a sad and suggestive commentary on the ecclesiastical activities of that day. That left but 36·3 per cent for meeting the various needs of the Papal court. Of this 36·3 per cent, 12·7 per cent was appropriated for the payment of salaries ; 7·16 per cent was given away in charities, a relatively small amount which was probably supplemented

[1] Göller, *Die Einnahmen der Apostol. Kammer unter Johann XXII*, 12.
[2] Schäfer, 36*, 814–820.
[3] Ib., 730.   [4] Ib., 694, 706–8, 719.
[5] Ib., 787.   [6] Ib., 709.   [7] Ib., 657.

by the employment of private means ; 3˙35 per cent was used in the purchase of clothing ; 2˙9 went for buildings ; 2˙5 was spent to supply the table with food and drink ; ˙4 per cent was devoted to repairs ; ˙33 per cent furnished the stables ; ˙24 covered the rents ; ˙17 per cent was spent for art ; ˙16 per cent was contributed to the library ; ˙12 per cent supplied the seals ; and special demands consumed the remainder.[1]

40. *Chaplains and other Court Officials*

The Papal chaplains formed quite a little group in the Avignon curia. Nicholas III at Rome in 1278 had 25 chaplains. John XXII had from 16 to 19 chaplains, from 11 to 17 presbyters and 1 or 2 *clerici intrinseci*. Benedict XII had 16 chaplains, 13 clerics, and 1 *clericus capella*. Clement VI had the same number of chaplains and clerics, and 3 *clerici capellae*. Innocent VI had 28 chaplains, from 8 to 11 clerics, and 4 *clerici capellae*. Urban had three kinds of chaplains in addition to the honourable chaplains. The third class was also called *centores* and received a weekly salary of 2 gulden. The first class received a weekly allowance of 4 gulden. On coronation day and Christmas presents were bestowed upon them. The Christmas presents, altogether, amounted to $25. They were also fed at the court and on Christmas, Easter, and Whit-Sunday they had the honour of dining with the Pope. John paid his chaplains during his first two years of rule weekly on Sunday ; his third and fourth years monthly ; and thereafter bi-monthly, but Sunday was always pay-day. Other Avignon Pontiffs followed the practice set by John. Under Clement V the chaplains said mass in the Papal household. Under Urban V acolytes, *cubicularii papae*, and even a theological professor of the Papal academy were added to the Papal clerical force. The famous reform preacher Konrad of Wakthausen was honorary chaplain, and under Clement VI, Urban V, Gregory XI, and Clement VII 70 such appointments were made.[2] Clement VII had his own private confessor, and also his own organist.[3]

---

[1] Schäfer, 35*.
[2] Schäfer, *Röm. Quartalsch*, 1907, vol. 21, p. 97–104.
[3] Ib., 1904, vol. 18, pp. 337, 339.

Göller gives a list of the curial officials found in the financial accounts. He makes 44 different classes, and puts from one to fifty officers under each heading. His list in all probability was far from complete.[1]

The admirably kept financial records of the Avignon period enable one to realize what a great business and trade centre Avignon was during the period of Papal residence. Money changers and bankers were numerous. Intermediaries between the Apostolic Chamber and the debtors lived in a section called the " exchange ", which was the best part of the city. Crowds of traders of all sorts brought to Avignon such things as were needed by the great Papal court and the numerous visitors—grains, wines, fish, and meats, cloths, leather, gold, and silver articles, rich stuffs, tapestries, laces, and numerous other articles.[2]

41. *The cost of various commodities*

The task of supplying food, clothing, and drink for the Papal court in the fourteenth century was no small problem. There seems to have been a great fluctuation in the prices of various articles. For instance, in 1316, a last of wheat cost 35 shillings Viennese, in 1329, 76 ; a last of oats in 1316 cost 22 denare Viennese, in 1329, 48 ; a quintal of firewood cost in 1316, 11 little turnosen, in 1328 the same ; and other articles differed in like manner. This seems to show that prices had doubled, but the difference was due to the fact that Viennese money exchange had doubled. In reality, in 1328–9, these supplies cost less than in 1316. In the fourteenth century the standard of weights changed three times : (1) Viennese ; (2) Florentine ; and (3) Cologne. A last of wheat was 250 litres, or 180 kilograms, but it was retailed in little lasts of 200 litres, or 145 kilograms. A little last would bake 600 loaves of 8 ounces, but after the time of Urban V loaves of 6 ounces were baked. Bread was usually made of two-thirds of wheat, and one-third barley or rye. Under John XXII from 4,000 to 9,000 lasts of wheat were purchased yearly, depending upon the harvest of the Church lands. In 1346 under Clement VI 22,000 lasts were bought, or 39,600 double centner. The price averaged from 1·8 to 2 florins per last, or about $2·50 per double centner. 1347–8 was a dear year when the price of a

[1] Göller, 775.   See the price list given in Woker, 11.

double centner went up to $7·50. In the fourteenth century, however, money had four times the purchasing power it has to-day, so that wheat to-day costs 50 per cent less than then. Wine was bought in bulk in large or small barrels, and was measured by 100 litres. Often the grapes were purchased and wine made from them. John XXII made 250 lasts of wine and bought 200 more yearly. The average cost for wine from southern France was from three-fourths to four-fifths of a gold gulden, or from $1·88 to $2 ; consequently a litre would cost about two cents, or only half a cent in our money to-day. The Burgundian wine was dearer and a litre cost from five to six cents—due in part to the higher cost of transportation. Bread was also bought from the Avignon bakers or from those of the surrounding towns directly by the camera, or by their commissioners, or through merchants. Countless poor and needy were fed and clothed at the Papal court and this consumed enormous supplies.

A fat ox cost $27·50, an ordinary ox $5 to $20. Calves cost from $5 to $7·50. Sheep brought from $1·65 to $2·50, and goats and kids from $0·85 to $1. Hares varied with the scarcity and cost from $0·20 to $0·75. Salt beef and pork was bought by the centner, which was equal to 70 pounds to-day and cost from $3·75 to $5, wholesale, and from $5 to $10 retail. A pound of meat cost ordinarily from seven to ten cents. Hogs varied in cost from $1·25 to $9·50 each. The price of fish fluctuated with the supply of the market. In 1320 175 pounds of fish cost $87·50, or fifty cents a pound ; six sturgeon cost $50 ; 325 small sea-fish cost $47·50, while one small sea-fish cost fifteen cents in our money ; two large eels cost $2·50, but 100 small eels cost only $5. In 1321 2,000 herring cost $11·25 and one small herring half a cent. On the whole, therefore, fish was no cheaper than to-day. Ten chickens cost from $1·65 to $2·10. Pheasants and geese were very expensive in Avignon—pheasants cost $2·50 each and a goose $1·90. Ten doves could be purchased for $1·25. In May, 1323, 6,200 eggs were bought for $35, or over five cents apiece. In the Papal court an ox was killed every day except on the fast-days ; from 25 to 40 sheep were used monthly ; an average of one hog a week was eaten and it was

---

[1] Schäfer, *Lebensmittelpreise und Arbeitslöhne an der Päpstlichen Kurie im 14. Jahrhundert.* In *Römische Quartalschrift*, 1911, vol. 25, p. 226* ff.

customary to kill a large number and preserve them for the winter months; fish was consumed in great quantities in Lent and on fast-days; from 200 to 400 chickens were needed each month; and large quantities of eggs were devoured.

Sugar came from the Orient and was very expensive. It was purchased in centners of 70 pounds each at from $50 to $75 or from $0·75 to $1 per pound. Thus it was fifty times dearer than it is to-day. Wood and charcoal was used for heat and cooking and were bought by bundles, bags, baskets, or lasts. From 15,000 to 25,000 centners of charcoal were used annually. In 1328–9 36,000 centners were burned at a cost of ten cents per centner. Twenty baskets of charcoal cost $2·50 or one basket fifteen cents. Tallow and wax candles were used for lighting. One quintal of wax equal to 70 pounds cost $30, or over forty cents a pound. From 22 to 125 quintals were purchased at one time and then made up into candles at the Papal court.

Rents were very much cheaper than to-day. Two rooms with a kitchen and a stall cost but $1 per month; one room with a kitchen only $0·55 a month; two rooms with a kitchen and a cellar cost $1·90 a month; a large two-storey house cost $3·75 a month; and a seven room house with a stable cost $6·90 a month. It cost from $2,500 to $25,000 to build a village church.[1]

Wages and salaries varied greatly according to the kind of work done, but the average was not much lower than to-day when the purchasing power of money is taken into account. There was little change throughout the fourteenth century. In 1320 a day labourer received up to $175 yearly and food was included, and an assistant labourer received up to $75 and keep. A mason or carpenter received from $0·28 to $1·67 per day; a painter from $0·63 to $0·75 per day; an ordinary helper about $0·28 a day; and a plasterer about $0·85. A gardener earned about $0·30 a day and a woman received about $0·45 a day. All these wages seem to include food, and were very high as compared with the yearly income of $75 received by an ordinary canon or vicar. It does not seem to be true, so far as Avignon is concerned, that the wages were increased after the pest year of 1348.

There were no salaries in the modern sense at the Papal

[1] Schäfer, *Röm. Quartalschr.*, 1904, vol. 18, pp. 163–5.

court. All salaries were reckoned on the basis of day labour and Sundays were always counted in. The whole industrial system of that period was based on the daily wage. Deductions were made for absence. The palace guards, who were not knights, received annually $275 ; those who were knights received $450 ; while the officers of the guards received $660. The marshal of the Papal court was paid $3,125, but had to pay all his subordinates out of that sum. A curial judge for criminal cases was paid $200 annually, but a judge of civil cases received $250. A general auditor's salary was $250 yearly. The *avocatus fisci* received a like amount. The body physician of the Pope had $450 a year. The twenty-five members of the gendarmerie were each paid $125 yearly. All these officers were laymen. The salaries of the offices held by the clergy were somewhat higher. The Papal chaplains, who numbered from 20 to 30, the auditors of the chancery, the correctors, and the *bullatores* all received $500 annually. The 12 to 18 penitentiaries received each $675 yearly. The kitchen officials, the cellar officials, the master baker, the master builder, and the master of horse all drew $275 a year. These salaries taken as a whole were not high, but it must be remembered that they were supplemented by tips and fees and by benefices. All things considered the Papal officials were about as well off as the officials of the kings of France and England in the fourteenth century. Taking salary, cost of foods, and the price of rents into account one could live more cheaply at that time than to-day and save up a larger margin. Life was simpler and all the ordinary needs were fewer.[1]

[1] Schäfer, *Lebensmittelpreis*, etc.

CHAPTER VI

General Results of the Babylonian Captivity

42. *General Character of the Papal Financial System*

THE Avignon Papacy can be summed up in two words : centralization and finance. A tremendous attack had been made upon the Papacy. Hence the Pope sought to strengthen his power in internal ecclesiastical affairs, which resulted in an unprecedented centralization. The curia took pains to interest itself in the smallest ecclesiastical trivialities all over Christendom and to have all cases settled in Avignon. To carry out these schemes money was absolutely necessary. Consequently the small and uncertain income from the Papal States no longer sufficed. The clergy were expected to collect the necessary funds and hence arose the *servitia*, Peter's Pence, the *census*, tithes, subsidies, reservations, *annates*, *spolia*, taxes, loans, gifts, and all sorts of fees. The political universality was behind the financial universality of the Papacy and it was the evident intention to carry both to the limit. It was the shrewd brain of John XXII that outlined and put into execution the most consummate financial plan yet devised.

It was an easy thing to set up the absolute supremacy of the Pope as the primary supervisor of the whole Church, but the practical supervision of the thousands of questions coming up for decision every day was a most difficult problem. No one man could do it, hence a personal supervision of the countless persons and offices was absolutely out of the question. Many petitions had to be heard, thousands of appointments had to be made, and the whole vast machinery of the Church had to be kept in motion. Consequently the Pope was forced to have an army of helpers at Avignon and throughout the Church. It was largely a result of these conditions that gave rise to so many abuses and evils ; that made Avignon swarm with place-hunters high and low with all sorts of requests ; that developed so much red tape and so many formalities ;

and that produced the profession of go-betweens and intriguers, at a time when the spiritual character of the Church depended upon the appointment of good men to office. As a result of the wonderfully complicated system, the Pope was practically powerless and was forced to trust to his numerous subordinates. Complications, delays, disappointments, injustice, and all kinds of abuses were inevitable. Reformation was well-nigh impossible even if attempted by a worthy Pope. It is no wonder that offices were sold as so much merchandise. Money had to be found to run the hierarchical machine and to satisfy the hordes of hungry officials. No sense of personal responsi- bility existed. Benefice, not office, was the supreme thought on all sides. The Church had changed from a community of faithful believers to a community of politicians. The Church was in grave danger of becoming a secular institution, a mighty business organization. What was needed was not reform of the curia, but a return to a noble, clean, religious organization. To do that the system had to be abolished. That was the cry that came from the far-seeing reformers all over Christendom.

Pluralism was all too common and resulted in the most serious neglect of ecclesiastical obligations. Little thought was given to pastoral duties and spiritual care of the laity. At best incompetent vicars were named merely to meet the legal demands, and the evil of absenteeism was denounced from one end of Europe to the other.[1]

The Third Lateran Council, the eleventh universal council, held in 1179, sought to abolish pluralism by prohibiting the accumulation of dignities and parish benefices in the hands of one person.[2] The Fourth Lateran Council, or the twelvth œcumenical council, in 1215, complained that the decree had not been observed and forbade the clergy holding more than one benefice without Papal dispensation. Heavy ecclesiastical penalties were threatened against violators of the law. The holder of a benefice, who took a second without permission, should *ipso facto* be deprived of the first, and should he persist in attempting to hold both he should lose both. The collator who received a second benefice should within three months bestow the first upon another person ; should

---

[1] Sauerland, *Urkunden*, etc., i, pp. xvii–xviii.
[2] Mansi, xxii, 213 ff. ; Hefele, v, 711 ; ch. 13.

he fail to do so within the given limit, he should lose the right of collation and his benefice would revert to the papal chair. He who illegally retained his first benefice after receiving a second was bound to restore all income from the beginning of the illegality. The law applied alike to appointive and elective benefices. The Pope reserved the right, however, to grant a dispensation in the case of worthy and learned persons.[1] Sixty years later the second council of Lyons again sought to prevent the accumulation of benefices in the hands of one person by still more stringent legislation. No one was to receive a benefice who was not eligible by adequate knowledge and good morals, and 25 years of age. Benefices granted to persons under 25 were null and void. Recipients of benefices were bound to obtain consecration and enter upon residence within one year otherwise the appointment *ipso facto* became invalid. Bishops were ordered to enforce the law strictly and thus eliminate the abuses. Of course the Pope could grant dispensations, and the bishop could for good cause dispense with residence for a parish priest, providing such favours did not injure church services or the worship of God.[2]

Notwithstanding these stringent measures the evil of pluralism not only did not cease but increased. Hence John XXII on 19th November, 1317, issued the constitution *Execrabilis*, which renewed the old law that he who received a second benefice should at once surrender the first ; forbade the holding of two or more separate benefices without dispensation ; ordered all benefices except the last one to be given up within a month ; limited Papal dispensation to two benefices selected voluntarily ; fixed as penalties for violating this order the loss of all beneficies, ecclesiastical infamy, and deprivation of the right to receive benefices and consecration ; and decreed that all benefices vacated by this constitution should revert to the Pope.[3] John's motive apparently was not so much to correct these evils as to get as many benefices as possible in his own hands. Pluralism and absenteeism were not suppressed simply because the Pope and the curia did not enforce the law, or granted so many dispensations that it

---

[1] Hefele, v, 872 ff. ; Sauerland, 1, lx, ch. 29.
[2] Sauerland, 1, lxi, chs. 13, 18.
[3] Ib., 1, lxi.

was practically invalidated.   In instances where the violator of the edict was deprived of his benefices and debarred from future privileges, he went to Avignon, where through the influence of powerful friends or the liberal use of money, he secured absolution and was reinstated.[1]   In case he had neither friends of power, nor money, he was pretty certain to be denounced to the curia by some cleric covetous of his place, who applied for the place and began to pull wires to get it. Consequently all sorts of schemes were concocted, or resorted to, to hold places and to secure them.   The entire business was very lucrative for the Papal court, greatly multiplied Papal provisions and reservations, and increased the curial bureaucracy.[2]

The efficient work of the collegiate chapters was greatly diminished by the non-residence of the canons in the fourteenth century, when the simple canonicates were viewed as sinecures by prelates who held as many as half a dozen or more.   To lessen the evils of absenteeism some of the chapters voted to pay " presence money " to those who attended the services and performed the duties of the offices.   In some cases absentee canons received but half of the income of those in residence ; and in another instance the resident canons received 89 gulden while the absent canons received but 30 gulden. In this way it was necessary of course that the absentees should have several benefices in order to be assured of a competence.   These absentees were commonly the younger sons of the nobility and oftimes the sons of bishops.[3]   It is not a matter of surprise, therefore, to find that ecclesiastical laws were ignored and violated over and over again to the great injury of church services and spiritual helpfulness.[4]

Clement VI recognized the constitution *Execrabilis* as a profitable source of Papal income, whether it was enforced or violated.   To the tax for reinstatement was given the pious name of *Subsidium contra Turcos*.   One of the worst evils of the period was the fact that many parishes were in the hands of residents or absentees who were not even consecrated as priests,[5] notwithstanding specific laws to prevent it.   The Third Lateran Council had decreed that all

---

[1] Sauerland, lxiv.   [2] Ib., lxv.   [3] Ib., lxii–iii.
[4] Ib., 1, lxiii.   [5] Ib., lxvi.

prelates appointed to benefices must be consecrated within
a year,[1] and other councils repeated the rule. Under Clement VI
there were many such violations of law. The holders of
parishes remained for years at the court of the bishop or the
local prince, without consecration. Papal dispensations
permitted many such infractions of the imperative need of
the Church to the utter neglect of soul-care in the parishes.
As a compromise vicars were often appointed, but these vicars
were mostly cheap incompetent men who sought only to squeeze
the most money out of the parishes. Nicholas of Gymnich,
a boy of 7, was given a parish of Siehenborn by its patron. To
perform the clerical duties he sent a vicar who promised to
pay the boy 25 gulden yearly. At the age of 15 he took another
parish from a layman with an income of 30 gulden, and
appointed a vicar to take charge. Eleven years later he
received a third parish from a lay patron at 100 gulden income.
The Bohemian King John finally gave him a fourth benefice,
a canonship at Prague with an income of 100 gulden, which
he enjoyed eight years. At the age of 34 he was in the service
of John's son, Charles IV, who sent him to Avignon as an
ambassador, where he took advantage of his opportunity to
have the Pope legalize all his benefices. Of course he had to
pay the " Subsidy for the Turkish " war. He was given a
dispensation for non-residence, and in one way or another
succeeded in postponing consecration and in fact was never
consecrated. In addition to the regular incomes from his
benefices, he received from his vicars gifts, and fees for the
sacraments, masses, burials, and other religious services. Many
rich parishes were ruled for years by hard greedy vicars.[2]

Concubinage of the clergy, so common that " countless "
documents deal with it, is one of the darkest and most
significant phases of ecclesiastical life during the Babylonian
Captivity.[3] Of course the evil began long before this period,
but it was greatly increased under the Avignon Popes. In
the services of the Church were many persons of illegitimate
birth, who got dispensations so that they could hold benefices
and be consecrated. An exceptionally large number of such
persons were priests and of course had a demoralizing effect
on the people. The Church was the best and safest means of

---

[1] Ch. 3.   [2] Sauerland, 1, lxvii–viii.
[3] Ib., i, xviii.

disposing of illegitimates. The common practice of having priests' sons succeed their fathers began in the thirteenth century.[1] Dietrich of Nieheim said that in Ireland, Norway, Sweden, Spain, Portugal, and Gascony the illegitimate sons of priests shared the benefices of the priests.[2] The great majority of those who received Papal dispensations for illegitimate birth were sons of priests. Under Benedict XII from 20th February to 29th May, 1335, 207 dispensations were granted *super defectu natalium*, and 148 of them were sons of priests. The 207 dispensations do not include the bastard sons of nobles who were bishops and who consequently received dispensations in some other form, nor those who received dispensations from bishops.[3] In Strassburg priests got dispensations for their illegitimate sons, and had them appointed as their successors.[4] The Archbishop of Trier granted two dispensations for priests' sons in 1335 ; three in 1336 ; four in 1338, and nine in 1342. The Archbishop of Cologne granted one similar dispensation in 1338, and seventeen in 1342. Archbishop Baldwin of Trier in 1343 was given power to grant dispensations to thirty sons of priests in his own diocese who wanted ordination. These dispensations were only for the sons of the clergy : those granted to the illegitimate sons of the laity were of course much larger, the ratio being one to three in 1335, and one to twenty-seven in 1342. Sauerland gives fifty-seven instances of parishes ruled over by unconsecrated priests, who either illegally remained away, or else secured dispensations (xvii). That was in the district of Cologne and Trier. In the Rhine provinces where there were 4,000 priests, 42 dispensations were granted between 1310 and 1352.[5] The Archbishop of Trier granted between 60 and 70 and in Metz 12 were granted in 35 years. At the same time, 71 dispensations were granted for illegitimacy to sons whose parents were not priests in Cologne and 1,000 in Trier.[6] This condition in the Rhine Valley was not exceptional, but typical of all Germany and probably of all Europe.[7]

Conditions grew worse as the Avignon period progressed. Under Clement VI in the year 1342–3 614 dispensations were

---

[1] Sauerland, lxx. See letter of Honor, III to Otto of Toul, 25th Feb., 1227. in ib,. lxx, n. l

[2] Nemus Unionis, Tractus vi, cap. 35, p. 378.

[3] Sauerland, I, xviii. [4] Kothe, 87.

[5] *Röm. Quartalschr*, 1906, vol. xx, p. 129. [6] Ibid. [7] Sauerland, lxix–lxx.

given out for illegitimacy, and of that number 484 were for sons of priests from 17 to 25 years of age. Only ten of them came from Cologne, and one from Trier. All of the 614 dispensations were dated on the same day, 22nd July, The dispensed appeared in person before the Pope, Clement VI, and at Avignon they saw the pomp and luxury, the dissipation and depravity, the simony and immoral living, and the shameful part money and influence played in the Papal court.[1] They saw the ease with which dispensations for all kinds of moral deliquencies could be bought. It is but natural to surmise that they carried away from the curia the worst impressions, and indeed, even the worst intentions, particularly since at the same time they knew of the immoral and illegal relations of their own parents and had come to know at the curia hundreds of their own colleagues whose parents had lived in the same relations. Indeed one can scarcely imagine a more shameful condition than the records reveal in connection with illegitimacy and dispensations.[2] Archbishop Baldwin of Trier was shrewd in obtaining from the Pope permission to deal with the 30 cases in his own diocese, because he saved them an expensive trip to Avignon, and prevented their seeing the wicked conditions in the Papal court. Besides in all probability he himself got a large fee out of the transaction.

The most extraordinary kind of a dispensation was the one granted to illegitimates excusing them from announcing their illegitimacy.[3] Most of those so favoured were the sons of the higher and lower nobility, and the higher clergy. This may have been done in part to save the reputation of those prelates who were to receive the better places in the Church and in part to avoid all disagreeable investigations about their fathers.

Another very common dispensation was for non-canonical age. The Church had repeatedly decreed that 25 years was the legal age for ordination. But for money or through influence that requirement was repeatedly overlooked. Consequently benefices large and small were often given to mere boys. Baldwin of Luxemberg was appointed Archbishop of Trier at 20. Henry Dauphin was made Bishop of Passau by

---

[1] Sauerland, xviii; Muratori, III, ii, 584, 756–7 ; Petrarch, *Epistolae* (Fracassetti), i, 302 ff.
[2] Sauerland, 1, lxxi.   [3] Ib., iii, 502.

John XXII at 20 and at 22 was transferred to Metz. Walram of Jülich was created Archbishop of Cologne by the same Pontiff at 20. Gerlach of Nassau was named Archbishop of Mainz at 24 by Clement VI. These four high prelates also by virtue of their ecclesiastical offices, held the position of electors of the Empire. In fact, the appointments were all made out of political considerations. Of course, there were numerous other cases of bishops, abbots, canons and lower clergy.[1]

In making all these dispensations the Papacy laid down two precautionary conditions : (1) That of a good character and a good education ; and (2) that of local episcopal recommendation.[2] This was a pure sham, however, because the dispensation itself in many cases absolutely ignored the conditions imposed. Theoretically every candidate for a position in the Church, for a provision or an expectancy, had to undergo an examination. A genuine civil service based on fitness would have solved many of the most pressing problems of the Church of that day, and would have prevented its decline and subsequent dissolution. Just what the examination required is not now known.[3] The character of the examination for a curate was : *bene legere, et bene construere et bene cantore ac congrue loqui latinis verbis.* Usually if the candidate promised on oath *bene cantore* within a year after appointment it sufficed. The examination was not always taken at the Curia because if the bishop or prince promised for their candidate *ut examen commitatur ad partes* the guarantee was accepted.[4] That made the attempt to determine the intellectual fitness of candidates virtually a farce. Nor did the Church make much effort to determine the moral character of the applicant. All depended upon the good-will and knowledge of the so-called executors to whom was assigned the task of bestowing offices provided they found that all conditions had been met.

Formerly the right of election had been something of a check on the fitness and character of the priesthood. But the mass of provisions and the sale of expectancies by the curia invalidated the right of election and of collation and of cooption of the various spiritual bodies and of single individuals of high ecclesiastical and secular rank. At the

---

[1] Sauerland, iii, 502. [2] Ib., i, lxxii.
[3] Ib., i, lxxi. [4] Ib., lviii.

same time the curia found in this traffic docile imitators in the bishops who permitted an exhibition of licence similar to that exercised by the curia for the whole Church. Thus Archbishop Baldwin of Trier claimed the right to grant the benefices of the canons of his collegiate churches and of all the collegiate churches in his diocese. Another time he secured from the Pope the right to grant dispensations in all nuns' and monks' cloisters in his diocese, and he exercised the right too. Archbishop William of Cologne demanded the same privilege. Thus the right of cooption was rescinded. Most of the holders of provisions and expectancies from the Pope were the favourites of cardinals, bishops, and princes. The cardinals' favourites after appointment mostly remained at the Papal court; and the candidates of the bishops and princes usually remained at the court of their patrons.[1] There they received their incomes from subordinates and lived on them. Those who held benefices requiring residence like *beneficia curata* got dispensations. It is uncertain just how far substitutes were sent out, and it is likely that the practice was more common than is generally supposed, since the laws making necessary the appointment of a vicar were very strong, and the local complaints could not be wholly ignored by those who had the interests of the Church at heart.[2]

From 1294 to 1352 in the Rhine provinces 100 parishes were priestless or at least had no resident priest from one to ten years.[3] That meant for the period of approximately 60 years that about five per cent of the parishes were not provided with resident clergy. Less than twenty of these places, or only one per cent were filled by the curia. Young noblemen, whose fathers or relatives had the right to patronage possessed the benefices. Often canons had the parishes connected with their offices. One synod after another complained of the unfortunate condition of these neglected, priestless, parishes. The causes of absenteeism were: pluralism, patronage, non-consecration, and dispensations.[4]

43. *Universal Outcry against Ecclesiastical Evils*

The Papal financial system of the Avignon period, notwithstanding its strictly business-like methods, called forth

---

[1] Sauerland.   [2] Ib., I, lix.   [3] Ib., lx.   [4] Ib., iii, 92, 572, 672.

a storm of complaints and urgent demands for reforms.[1] The unscrupulous traffic in spiritual benefits and Church offices, and the rise of the theory that every ecclesiastical service had a money value, provoked expressions of disgust all over Christendom. The Avignon fiscal policy contributed more than is generally supposed to the undermining of Papal authority.[2] The financial difficulties which confronted the Popes in the thirteenth century were seriously increased after the Popes took up their residence on or near French soil. The income from Italy was largely cut off; and other contributory powers fulfilled their obligations more irregularly because they feared that their payments would fall into the hands of France. Hence to cover deficits and to meet the unusual extravagances the Papal financiers resorted to very questionable means of raising money. The demoralizing system of *annates*, reservations, and expectancies gave rise to a multitude of abuses, which aroused a storm of protest from both clergy and laity. The pronounced success attending these financial measures incited jealousy on the part of governments and peoples. The worst effect, however, was that the Papacy became more worldly than ever before in its history and largely neglected its spiritual obligations.

The period of the Babylonian Captivity produced a group of keen, defiant letter writers and pamphleteers who were bolder and cut much deeper than the tractarians who defended the ambitions of France for national independence. They not only refuted the pretensions of the Papacy to temporal sovereignty, as the publicists in support of Philip IV of France did, but they called into question the very foundations on which the pontifical hierarchy rested and attacked the Papal assumption of spiritual supremacy. This sweeping assault paved the way, no doubt, for the ground taken by Wiclif, Huss, and Luther. The causes for this radical attack were: (1) the Babylonian exile itself under the leadership of the French party; (2) the attendant financial system and its excesses; (3) the rampant worldliness, greed for office, and corruptions among the clergy; and (4) the continuance of the extreme claims to political supremacy taken by Boniface VIII, particularly in dealing with Germany, England, and Italy.

Haller, 112 ff.　　　　[2] Pastor, *History of the Popes*, i, 73.

The Pope was denounced for not remedying the oppressive conditions which seriously demoralized the Church and weighed so heavily on the poor. The clergy were assailed for neglecting their religious duties and profiting in a financial way by the evil system. Alvar Pelayo, a Spanish official of many years standing in the Papal court and a strong defender of the Papal power, wrote :

"Whenever I entered the chambers of the ecclesiastics of the Papal court, I found brokers and clergy, engaged and reckoning the money which lay in heaps before them." [1] "No poor man can approach the Pope. He will call and no one will answer, because he has no money in his purse to pay. Scarcely is a single petition heeded by the Pope until it has passed through the hands of middlemen, a corrupt set, bought with bribes, and the officials conspire together to extort more than the rules call for." [2] There was scarcely one Spanish bishop in a hundred who did not demand money for ordination and for granting benefices. Of Clement V, John of Hacksen asserted : "This absolute simonist permits all livings and benefices to be sold through the market crier and thinks that he has a right to do it." [3] The Church was not the "Mother of the Faithful" but the mother of the money of the faithful. [4]

Catherine of Siena, who fairly worshipped the office of the Pope, with pious importunities urged Gregory XI to institute a reformation of the clergy ; to allow no simony or flattery to count in choosing cardinals and pastors and "to drive out of the sheep-fold those wolves, those demons incarnate, who think only of good cheer, splendid feasts, and superb liveries." She declared that the various rebellions against the Papacy were due to the wicked priests and begged the Pope to get rid of those false, evil clergy "who poison the garden" of the Lord.

She wrote to the Pope : "Do not come to Rome with armed troops. The sword and war will not restore the beauty of the Church, but peace alone." "Hold the rod of righteousness fast in the hand of love." [5]

As an attractive personage [6] whose "figure flits like that of an

---

[1] On the Lamentations of the Church, ii, art. 7.
[2] Ib., ii, 17 ; Döllinger-Friedrich, 86, 420.   [3] Woker, 30.
[4] Ib., 2.   [5] Monnier, Lit. Geschicht., iii, 130.
[6] Scudder, Saint Catherine of Siena as seen in her Letters, New York, 1906 ; Gardner, Life ; Gregorovius.

angel through the darkness of her time," a brief span of years from 1347 to 1380, she represents first a somewhat hysterical, ascetic, evangelistic spirit ; secondly, the profound yearning in Italy for the return of the Papacy to Rome ; and, thirdly, a devoted attitude towards the office of the Pope and consequently a burning hope for the spiritualization and purification of the Papacy and the whole Church.

At the age of twenty she renounced her retired life as a nun and in 1367 appeared in public to devote her life to charity. Her fame soon spread over all Italy. She laboured by impassioned letter and at Avignon in person to persuade Gregory XI to return to Rome. She sought to keep the peace between the Italian cities and the exiled Pontiff. She lived to see the Captivity ended. She fully understood how the Avignon period had brought the Papacy and the priesthood into general disrepute and she laboured with all her might to induce the Pope to institute reforms. She boldly told the Pope that the appointment of bad shepherds and evil rectors, who were consumed with self-love and cupidity, was responsible for the rebellion in the Church. Instead of dragging Christ's sheep away from the wolves, such bad prelates devoured the sheep themselves. The Church had become like a garden full of the foul-smelling plants of avarice, impurity, and pride, and the Pope was urged to pluck out the injurious weeds. " Your sons nourish themselves on the wealth they receive by ministering the blood of Christ, and are not ashamed of being money-changers. In their great avarice they commit simonies, buying offices with gifts or flatteries or gold." She was anxious that the Pope " consider the loss of souls more than the loss of cities, for God demands souls." Again her hope of reform was expressed in these words : " The bride, now all deformed and clothed in rags, will then gleam with beauty and jewels, and be crowned with the diadem of all virtues. All believing nations will rejoice to have excellent shepherds." Her constant theme was the corruption of every rank in the hierarchy and the imperative need of reform. She told Gregory that God would rebuke him if he did not cleanse the Church of its impurities. To Urban she said that while it was not possible to end all the evils in Christendom, still he should do all within his power. The prelates cared for nothing but pleasure and ambition, and were wolves

and traffickers in divine grace. The priests were exactly
the opposite of what they should be, corrupt in life, beasts
rather than men, wallowing in filth and indulging in the wicked
gratification of their bestial appetites, and carrying souls
to hell.[1]

The sainted widow, Birgitta (b. 1303) had journeyed from
her Scandinavian home to Rome in 1350 as a pilgrim.   Like
Catherine she devoted herself to labours among the sick and
the poor, and gained a reputation as a prophetess.   The
absence of the Papacy tried her loyalty but did not shake
her faith.   The worldliness of the Popes led her to exclaim
that Peter " was appointed pastor and minister of Christ's
sheep, but the Pope scatters them and lacerates them.   He
is worse than Lucifer, more unjust than Pilate, more cruel
than Judas.   Peter ascended the throne in humility, Boniface
in pride."   She predicted the speedy death of Urban V when,
after returning to Rome, he announced his decision to go
back to Avignon.   To Gregory XI she wrote : " In thy
curia arrogant pride rules, insatiable cupidity, and execrable
luxury.   It is the very deepest gulf of horrible simony.
Thou seizest and tearest from the Lord innumerable sheep."
She died in 1373 and her body was taken back to Sweden.[2]

Birgitta was of royal lineage, had a family of eight children,
and her husband died in 1344.   She belonged to the third order
of St Francis, but founded an order of her own which without
stressing poverty and humility emphasized the inner honouring
of the sorrows of Christ on the cross.   There were both male
and female cloisters.   The recruits came mostly from Sweden.
Much attention was given to a study of the Bible and to popular
preaching.   Her daughter, St Catherine, succeeded her as
head of the Order of the Holy Saviour.[3]

Birgitta sent the following message to Gregory XI as
a revelation from the Lord : " Hear, O Gregory XI, the
words I say to thee, and give unto them diligent attention !
Why dost thou hate me so ?   Why are thy audacity and
presumption so great against me that thy worldly court
destroys my heavenly one.   Proudly thou despoilest me of
my sheep.   The wealth of the Church which is mine, and the

---

[1] *Epistole della Santa Caterina da Siena*, Lett. 9, 13, 14, 15, 17, 18, 21 35,
38, 39, 41, 44, 50, 91, etc. (Milano, 1843).
[2] Haller, 88 ; Gardner, 78.
[3] Zökler, *Askese und Monchtum*, ii, 540.

goods of the faithful of the Church, thou extortest and seizest, and givest to thy worldly friends. Thou takest unjustly the stores of the poor and lavishest them without shame on thy worldly friends. . . . Why in thy court dost thou suffer unchecked the foulest pride, insatiable avarice, wantonness execrable to me, and all-devouring simony ? . . . Well-nigh all who go to thy court thou plungest into the fire of hell. . . . Arise and bravely seek to reform the church . . . to its former state, though now a brothel is more respected than it is. If thou dost not obey my command, know verily that thou wilt be condemned, and every devil of hell will have a morsel of thy soul."

In another revelation she was ordered to represent to the Pope the deplorable condition of the Church and all orders of the clergy. The priests were rather pimps of the devil than servants of God. The monasteries were well-nigh abandoned, mass was only celebrated in them occasionally, while the monks acknowledged their offspring, or wandered around frequently clad in armour under their frocks. The doors of the nunneries were open day and night, and they were brothels rather than holy retreats.[1]

In 1351 a Carmelite, preaching before the Pope and cardinals, inveighed against their turpitude in terms which terrified everyone and caused his immediate dismissal. Shortly afterwards a letter was found affixed to the doors of the churches addressed to the Pope and his cardinals. It was signed " Leviathan, Prince of Darkness," and was dated from the centre of hell. He greeted his vicar, the Pope and his servants the cardinals, with whose assistance he had overcome Christ ; commended them for all their vices ; and sent them the good wishes of their mother Pride, and their sisters, Avarice, Lust, and the rest. Clement was frightened and fell dangerously sick, but the writer was never discovered.[2]

Nicholas d'Oresme declared that the Church had become worse than the Jewish synagogue. The Pharisees sold doves ; the priests sold the very sacraments and ecclesiastical offices.[3]

---

[1] *Revelat, S. Birgitta*, Lib. i, c. 41 ; Lib. iv, c. 33,37, 142.
[2] Lea, *Hist. of the Inq.*, iii, 633.
[3] Haller, 8.

44. *The Council of Vienne*

The Council of Vienne, the fifteenth of the universal councils and the last to be held for nearly a century, met on 16th October, 1311, and adjourned on 6th May, 1312. Clement V opened it and stated that the three purposes of the council were : (1) to take action on the order of the Templars ; (2) relief for the Holy Land ; and (3) for the correction and reformation of the Church.[1] The Pope had no idea of a reformation in the sense in which the term was used in later councils, but thought only of remedying certain evil practices and breaches of law on the part of the clergy. He sought to enforce the ecclesiastical constitution as he understood it. He wanted the clergy and the Church freed from secular control, a moral and honest clergy, a stricter regulation of preachers of indulgences, the annual visitation of nuns' cloisters, the suppression of heretical organizations like the Beghards and Beguins, episcopal supervision of the Hospitallers, episcopal visitation of the Cistercian order, reformation of the Benedictines, the reduction of the garments of priests to a uniform type, and the prohibition of the clergy from carrying weapons, conducting butcher-shops and public-houses, and engaging in business. Farther than these mild reforms the Pope gave no hint of wishing to go.[2]

The bishops, on the other hand, had a much more radical reform programme to present to the council.[3] The most conspicuous spokesmen of the episcopal reform party were Le Maire, Bishop of Angers, and Durand, Bishop of Mende, who, in accordance with the Pope's invitation to prelates to make recommendations, wrote pamphlets which throw much light on the general conditions of the Church at the opening of the fourteenth century.

William Le Maire was a Frenchman, at home in the royal court, in his theology thoroughly orthodox, a faithful son of the Pope, and a believer in the sovereignty of councils.[4]

---

[1] Ehrle, *Archiv.*, iv, 361–470 ; Hefele-Knopfler, vi, 514–54 ; Raynaldus, 1308, No. 8 ; *Regestum Clementis*, No. 3626 ; Wilkins ii, 308 ; *Bull. Taurin.*, iv, 191.

[2] Haller, *Papsttum*, 54.

[3] Heber, *Gutachten und Reformvorschläge für das Vienner Generalkonzil*, Leipzig.

[4] Ibid. ; *Melanges Historiques*, ii, 471 ; Hefele, vi, 517 ; Ehrle, *Archiv.* iv, 427.

In his *Reform of Church Customs* he complained of the misuse of Sundays and holidays because they were used for markets, fairs, courts, and all sorts of pleasures instead of being devoted to religious services ; given to the devil instead of God. Consequently the churches were empty and the ale houses were full, while curses instead of prayers were heard on all sides. He regretted the misuse of excommunication which should be reserved for only the gravest sins and crimes, and proclaimed by the higher clergy. As it was, that power was too commonly exercised since as many as from 300 to 700 excommunicated persons were found in a single parish. So common had the penalty become that it meant nothing and had no effect. He objected to the loose method of appointing both the lower and the higher clergy. It was so easy to become a priest that many of the uneducated laity were receiving ordination. Even minor officers and parish priests were appointed by the Pope. A bishopric was cited in which there were twenty benefices, where thirty five vacancies took place in twenty years, but out of the entire number the bishop filled only two places because the Pope appointed all the rest. In consequence the bishops had little to do. To make matters worse, these appointees were frequently strangers, who did not know local conditions and problems, and were ignorant of the local language. Such clergy were all striving to misuse their power and to exceed their jurisdiction, hence the people hated them and called them Jews. They wore unsuitable ecclesiastical clothing and lived immoral lives. Mass was celebrated in a scandalously loose fashion and some priests did not even attend services. Spiritual judges solicited bribes. Good holy prelates in cathedral churches were as scarce as lilies among thorns and vacancies were continually filled by the same kind of men. Elections to office were determined by intrigue, money, and nepotism. Absenteeism was a common curse, because all who could afford it lived either at the royal or Papal court. One person frequently held from two to five offices in different churches and from ten to twelve benefices. As a result many good clergy were thrown out of office and had to enter business or become the advisers of princes and enemies of the Church. The only way to correct these flagrant abuses, which were destroying the Church, was to observe the old laws of the Church rigidly ; to abolish reservations and expectancies ; to let all the clergy from priest to Pope reform their own lives ; to trust the people to elect upright bishops ; and to let the bishops surround themselves with pious, learned, clerics who would be zealous for the souls of people and eager to save them.   The appointment of ignorant barbarians to Church offices must stop.   Pluralism was called a crime, when one benefice would support and educate fifty desirable prospective priests.   The greed for gold, so rampant among the clergy, ought to be crushed. Monastic life should likewise be improved.   The monk should remain in his cloister and not mix up in worldly business. Single, independent little cloisters should be brought under some regular rule and the monks forced to live a uniform life. The exemption of monks from their customary obligations should cease, and they should not be permitted to invade the rights of the priests.   In short, Le Maire urged the necessity of a complete reformation of the Church in " head and members " and insisted that the movement begin in the Papal court.   His whole plea was to return to the Church of the first four oecumenical councils and of the holy fathers.   Unless that was done, he warned the Pope and cardinals that the terrible condition of the Church would end in the downfall of the Church.[1]

William Durand, the Younger, Bishop of Mende,[2] wrote a tract for the Council of Vienne on the necessity of Papal and ecclesiastical reformation.[3]   He also set forth the necessity of reformation in " head and members " which was to serve as a watchword of the reform party for the next century and a half.   His cry was back to the Church of the first four universal councils.   He assailed secular princes for violating Church laws and for appropriating the money and property of the Church, and enumerated fifty different grievances and encroachments against them.[4]   For the general good he suggested the limiting of the power of both the Pope and princes.   The constitution of the Church should be changed so that the Pope could do nothing of importance without the advice of the cardinals.   Princes should consult the notable people

---

[1] Heber, 37–40 ; Ehrle, *Archiv.*, iv, 427.
[2] Coulon, No. 775, 848, 850 ; Haller, *Papsttum*, 58 ; Hefele, vi, 517 ; Scholz, 208–23.
[3] *De modo concilii celebrandi et corruptelis in ecclesia reformandis* ; Heber, 40.
[4] Cf. *Hist. lit. de la Fr.*, xx, 439.

of their kingdoms in assemblies on all important matters pertaining to the Church and state. Thus he favoured a sort of constitutional sovereign for both the Church and State.

He asserted that unless there was a thoroughgoing regeneration of the Church, the true faith would disappear from the face of the earth. The Papal court was demoralizing the whole world and the Pope was most guilty because he had no thought of saving souls but cared only for money and benefices, and was given to nepotism. No effort was made to crush simony and heresy. The Roman Church, as head of all Churches, must reform itself before it could rule other Churches rightly. He appealed to the cardinals to reform Clement V and his court as the first step in a general reformation.

He urged the restoration of the independence of the episcopal power and a revival of local synods on the ground that the bishops derived their prerogatives from God and were the successors of the apostles and the equals of Peter. The Pope was not " prince of the clergy," nor " the highest priest," nor " Lord of all the clergy," but only the " Bishop of the first episcopal see." Gregory I and other Popes forbade such presumptions. The Pope should remember the saying : " He who wished to have all, lost all." The Roman Church claimed everything, hence he feared it might lose all. It had already lost Greece. The Pope was bound to obey the laws which governed humanity in general. He possessed no right to give privileges, indulgences, and exemptions and then revoke them. Nor could he revoke the orders and acts of his predecessors. Laws pertaining to the welfare of the whole Church could be enacted only by a general council, and such a council should be called every ten or twenty years.

The Pope should surrender every semblance of simony in deed as well as in word, and give up every desire for wealth, and yet simony and greed for gold were so openly practised in the Papal court that they were not even looked upon as sins. All schemes for the promotion of cardinals in financial matter must be stopped. It was well-known how they strove for benefices even in foreign lands to the great injury of the local Churches. The cardinals did not take their offices seriously, and too many of them were unfit, while educated doctors were without places. Cardinals should be at least thirty years of age, above reproach in character and competent intellectually.

Some method should be devised for the welfare of the Church to protect the property that belonged to all Christians. Durand suggested the democratic plan of control by local communities. Persons who broke the law, or insulted an ecclesiastic, should have some easy way of being excused without excommunication and robbery of their property. Yet at the Papal court absolution could be obtained readily for almost any sin by the payment of a little coin. The result was that ecclesiastical punishments were despised. Church services and preaching were neglected, and indulgences were shamelessly misused. The ban was imposed by the Curia, or by legates, for the slightest misconduct; and the victims were ordered to appear at the Papal court. Such trivial affairs should be looked after by the bishops. Some law suits were delayed three years before a judgment was rendered.

Durand made a strong plea for the independence of episcopal power. All the apostles were given the power to bind and to loose, hence they had the same power and honour as Peter. Of their own accord they chose Peter to be the head of the Church. The bishops, not the cardinals, were the successors of the apostles, hence the Pope cannot raise himself above the bishops either in jurisdiction or in granting benefices. Yet incompetents, relatives and friends of the Pope and cardinals were promoted over the heads of the bishops to positions in the Church—a practice that violated the episcopal right of election in each diocese. The affairs of each diocese should be regulated by a local synod and one should be held at least twice a year. Only the most important cases should be appealed to Rome. There were entirely too many poor episcopal dioceses. In Sicily one bishop was too poor to have a horse and a servant. The poor dioceses should be joined to some neighbouring one. All bishops should be required to stay at home to look after Church interests, and should be expected to visit all parishes annually. All bishops ought to be doctors of theology or law. Bishops could be excommunicated only for mortal sins. It was advisable for the bishops to levy a tax for the support of teachers in connection with all important Churches to instruct the poor pupils.

The priests were unmercifully denounced because of their

greed for money, ambition for power and promotion, dissipation, immorality, envy, passion, ignorance, and neglect of spiritual responsibilities. Unless a remedy was found for such an unworthy priesthood, religion would become a mockery. He advocated an age limit of 25 years for a deacon and 30 years for a priest, and educational qualifications, and a spiritual character. Some method ought to be devised so that priests would not be obliged to handle money, for from the lowest to the highest all were corrupted by greed. He suggested the payment of a fixed salary to the clergy, and if that was not enough to support them, then let them work like the apostles. The sin of ambition was the result of the fact that all offices in the Church had a price and hence priests were eager to obtain promotion. Many priests also dressed in an unseemly garb, wore a sword and owned a horse, and were given to lewd talk, drunken carousals, gluttony, and concubinage. They neglected the prescribed fasts, attended games, theatres, and public-houses. Some were notorious criminals. A way must be found to put an end to such disgraceful characters among the priests. He urged the severe punishment of the clergy who were fathers of illegitimate children, and suggested that such offspring be given in slavery to the father's church.[1] The minds of priests should in some way be turned away from the attractions of the world, and devoted to the needs of the Church and to the care of the souls of sinners. Otherwise the laity simply followed the ways of evil bishops and priests. Hence he would secure a worthy priesthood by exercising the greatest care in ordination ; by enforced residence ; and by filling all vacancies immediately with spiritual-minded, competent men.[2] The high ideals of the early Church were to serve as a model.

This was a most remarkable picture of western Christendom coming from a man who had himself bought an expectancy and was made bishop before the canonical age. He was very active in the ecclesiastical politics of France and knew Clement V very well. In 1319 he was a prisoner at Avignon, but was soon freed and travelled in Italy as a Papal legate. He died in 1328.[3]

The historical significance of the Council of Vienne lies not in what the council did in the way of reformation, because

[1] Heber, 50.   [2] Ib., 53.   [3] Ib., 65–6.

little of value was accomplished, but in the sweeping and persistent demands for reform presented to the council by typical men like Le Maire and Durand. Their programme for reform laid before that ecclesiastical body was elaborated and never forgotten for a moment throughout the entire fourteenth century, and it became the basis for the attempts at reformation made in the three great reform councils of the fifteenth century. The effort for reform failed at Vienne simply because the heart of Clement V was not in it and Philip IV had no interest in it. The discussion of the relation of the Pope to the general council was new, and was to bear fruit a century later. Suggestions for a fixed salary for the clergy and the proposal to replace all taxes and fees by a definite income tax of 20 per cent. were not heard of before.[1]

45. *Controversy with the Spiritual Franciscans*

The controversy of John XXII with the Spiritual Franciscans called forth a group of keen, fearless, pamphleteers, who assailed the evils of the age, denounced the abuses and corruptions of the Church, and attacked the very foundations on which the Papacy rested. In the Franciscan order arose a dispute over the possession of property. One party called the Spirituals, or Observants, wished to enforce the will of St Francis which recommended absolute poverty ; the other party believed in a reasonable use of property, and were called Conventuals. Nicholas III in 1279 issued a bull in which he granted to the Franciscans the right to use property as tenants, but not to own it. The Spirituals protested and kept up the struggle. Celestine V sought in vain to settle the differences by merging the Spirituals with the order of the Hermits which he founded. Boniface VIII took a stand against the Spirituals, deposed the general who sympathized with them, and appointed a general who belonged to the laxer party. After the case was presented to the Council of Vienne without a definite decision, Clement V sought to compromise the dispute by issuing in 1313 the bull *Exivi de paradiso* [2] which forbade the order, or any of its members, to accept bequests, own vineyards, sell products from their gardens,

---

[1] See Heber, 61–2 for an excellent summary of the acts passed in the council.

[2] Hefele, vi, 550 ; Ehrle, *Archiv.*, 1885, 540 sqq.

build fine churches, or go to law ; and permitted the use of only such property as was absolutely necessary.   Members were to wear no shoes, ride only in cases of necessity, fast from 1st November to Christmas and on every Friday, and own but two mantles, one with a hood and one without it.   Even that decree so favourable to the Spirituals, did not settle the quarrel.[1]

John XXII in two bulls, 10th December, 1317, took a positive stand against the Spirituals.[2]   In a few weeks he condemned a formal list of their errors and abolished all convents under their control.   They protested that even a Pope could not modify the rule of St Francis.   Notwithstanding the fact that the general of the order, Michael of Cesena, defended them, John summoned 64 of them to Avignon and when 25 of them refused to yield they were turned over to the Inquisition. In 1318 six were burnt at Marseilles, and thirty-six men and eight women at Narbonne.   In 1330 fifty-eight men and eight women were burnt in various lands.   Under Clement VI six were put to death, under Innocent VI two, and under Urban V fifteen.   About 1317 they took the name of Fratricelli.[3]   By additional bulls John tried to force his decisions on them, or destroy them, but without success. Their three great leaders, Cesena, Occam, and Bonagratia, were imprisoned, but escaped in 1328 and fled to the Pope's enemy, Lewis of Bavaria, then at Pisa. and later joined his court at Munich.   Of course they were excommunicated.

The Spirituals under persecution became mutinous, obstinate, and defiant.   They declared that Christ and the apostles had the use, but not the ownership, of the necessities of life ;   that no priest and no Pope, in consequence, had a right to own property ;   and that hence the Pope should have only what was necessary for the life of the Church, but had no authority to dispose of it or to hoard it.   They held John XXII up as the head of a carnal Church, full of luxury and worldliness, instead of ruling over a spiritual Church,

---

[1] In 1314, 120 monks from Provence and Narbonne resolved to secede and form their own organization.   John Olivia was the leader of the movement.   They chose a guardian and decided upon a garb of cheap stuff in imitation of St Francis.   Soon they were joined by brothers from other provinces, particularly Tuscany.   Cf. Wadding, *Ad. ann.*, 1314, n. 8.

[2] *Quorumdam exegit* and *Sancta romana.*

[3] Hefele, vi, 581 ; Ehrle, *Die Spiritualen* in *Archiv.*, 1885, 509–14.

simple, poor, and God-fearing. They, therefore, busily devoted themselves to preaching and writing against the Pope and his court as anti-Christ and the Babylonian harlot.[1]

Their ideas were, of course, contrary to the common ideals and social usages of the day and particularly abhorrent to a Pope of the temperament and ideals of John. It is small wonder, therefore, that he issued bull after bull against them, and employed the fire and sword as well as the bell, book, and candle to suppress the pestilential error.

Conspicuous among the aggressive opponents of the Avignon Papacy, who were Spirituals, were the following :—

(1) Michael of Cesena [2] (1270–1342), who took his doctorate at Paris in theology, then taught in Bologna, and wrote commentaries on the Bible and on the *Sentences* of Peter Lombard. In 1316 he was elected general of the Franciscan order and at once called a chapter at Assisi for the purpose of revising the constitution in the direction of a stricter observance of poverty, simplicity in life, and appropriate clothing for the monks. He attempted to bring the two hostile parties together on the basis of a compromise.[3] In the ensuing discussion John XXII combated Michael's views and in 1327 summoned him to Avignon and threw him into prison. But he escaped and fled to Lewis of Bavaria at Pisa in 1328, where he posted on the church door an appeal from the Pope to a general council as Huss and Luther both did at later dates. He also read to the multitude Emperor Lewis' decree deposing John XXII. The Pope issued a letter warning the faithful against Michael, who answered in several pamphlets [4] in which he accused the Pope of heresy, assailed the worldliness of the Church, contrasted the life of the Pope and his court with that of Christ and his apostles, and attacked some of the very foundations of the Papal theory. Michael impeached the Popes' infallibility in matters of doctrine,

---

[1] The struggle lasted until 1517 when Leo X wisely recognized two distinct branches of the Franciscans.

[2] Riezler, *Die Literarischen Wiedersacher der Päpste zur Zeit Ludwug des Baiers*, Leipzig, 1874, is the best monograph dealing with this whole controversy. See Gudenotz, *Michael von Caesena*, Breslau, 1876, a small dissertation.

[3] Wadding, *Annales Minorum*, ann. 1317, 12.

[4] *Ad perpetuam rei memoriam innotiscat quid ego, Fr. Michael*, 25th Nov., 1330 ; *Christianae fidei fundamentum ; Litteras plurium magistrorum ; Teste Solomone*. These are given in Occam's *Dialogue*.

and denounced the religious despotism to which they had
gradually exalted themselves. He claimed that the council
stood above the Pope and that what it did the Pope could not
change. He himself appealed to a general council against
John XXII. His order in a general chapter at Paris in
1329 condemned his conduct and his writings and elected
a new general, while the Pope put him under the ban. He
followed Lewis to Munich, continued to act as general and
died in 1342.

Michael, in discussing the Papal and imperial powers, said
that since the Papal power had sunken so low and had neglected
its obvious duties, it was the duty of the Emperor to take charge
of the spiritual needs of the Church, care for the poor, and
save men's souls. Just as Paul called Peter to time for judaizing
so the Pope could be opposed and punished for neglecting his
duties, and for heresy. A sinful Pope was in a worse condition
than an ordinary sinner, since a condemned Pope had no power
above the council to appeal to. So Anastasius and Eusebius
appealed against Pope Liberius, and Hilarius against Leo.

(2) Bonagratia of Bergamo (?–1343),[1] a Franciscan
theologian and canonist, joined the strict party and in 1322 was
sent to Avignon to represent their views before the curia.
The next year he appeared before the Pope John XXII and
the cardinals and zealously opposed the Papal attitude against
the Spirituals. Instead of succeeding he was cast into prison
where he remained a year. After his release he too joined Lewis
of Bavaria in Italy and accompanied him back to Munich.
There Bonagratia died under the sentence of excommunication. Chief among his writings was his *Articuli probationum*.
He like his colleagues made a bitter attack on the spiritual
powers of the Papacy and helped to raise questions which were
opening the eyes of Europe to a new view of Papal authority.

(3) John of Jardun, a Frenchman, educated at the
University of Paris, had by 1316 attained considerable fame
as a master at the college of Navarre. The same year
John XXII conferred upon him a canonry at Senlis and he
remained there until 1323, when one of his friends, "a man
of high character and great wisdom," invited him to Paris.
There he became a person of prominence, and is best known
for his joint authorship with Marsiglio of Padua in *Defensor*

---

[1] Wadding, *Annales Minorum*, vi, 401 ; vii, 1.

Pacis. He also wrote a number of other tracts touching on the problems of his age. He died in 1328.[1] He went to Bavaria with Marsiglio about 1326, and there became one of the private secretaries of Lewis the Bavarian.

(4) William of Occam was born in England about 1280, studied at Oxford, was a master at Paris from 1315 to 1320, and joined the Franciscan Order. He was one of the leaders in advocating absolute poverty as the fundamental doctrine of the order and consequently came into conflict with John XXII. He was tried, found guilty of heresy, and was thrown into prison for four years at Avignon.[2] With Michael of Cesena and Bonagratia he escaped and fled to Lewis of Bavaria at Pisa in 1328. It is reported that he proposed the following bargain with that ruler : " You defend me with the sword and I will defend you with the pen." He went with the Emperor Lewis to Munich and apparently each faithfully fulfilled his part of the agreement. When Cesena died in 1342, he committed the seal of the order to Occam. Shortly before his death in 1347, he is said to have submitted to the Pope, Clement VI, who had offered him absolution upon condition that he abjure his errors.

Occam was easily one of the foremost scholastic thinkers of the fourteenth century. Every reformer from Wiclif to Luther was more or less influenced by his ideas. Luther gladly acknowledged him as his " dear teacher ".[3] On his contemporaries he also exerted a powerful influence. Many of his views were adopted by modern philosophers and political scientists. Among the defenders of the imperial prerogative he took first rank beyond doubt.[4] He asserted that should the Pope fall into heresy the Emperor had a right to depose him.

His two best known works were *The Dialogue*, a vast mass of almost unreadable disputation, and the *Eight Questions*. Scholz found three more of his tracts which were unprinted and practically unknown.[5] In these writings Occam cut at the very roots of the Medieval Church. He acknowledged

---

[1] Renan, *Hist. Litt. de la France*, xxxiii, 528 ff. ; Haller, 78 ; Riezler, 56.
[2] Müller, *Ludwig der Baier*, 208.
[3] *Works*, Weimar, ed. vi, 183, 195, 600.
[4] Scholz, 141.
[5] Ib., 142 ff. The first was a part of *The Dialogue* ; the second, *De dogmatibus Johanis pape* ; the third was a tract against Benedict XII. *The Dialogue* is printed in Goldast. Haller, *Papsttum*, 74, makes a plea for the publication of Occam's writings in the *Mon. Ger.*

that Peter receivedsupreme power from Christ but asserted that that supremacy was purely spiritual. Hence the Pope received from Peter only spiritual jurisdiction and was subject to the worldly power in secular affairs.[1] Jesus said absolutely nothing about a Church constitution, hence it was a human creation growing out of the needs of organization and the Church could change it as circumstances required. The Papacy was an advantageous method of ecclesiastical government, but not an indispensable necessity, because its continuance depended upon its usefulness and efficacy. Nevertheless the Papacy was upheld as the most ideal administrative system for the management of the Church. If the Pope had plenary power, then all would be slaves.[2] The Papacy was not a necessary institution, and the time might come when it would be advantageous to have several Popes. Christ and not the Pope was the true head of the Church, and a general council or even the cardinals could depose a Pope. John he called a heretic. No bishop could excommunicate without the consent of the secular power.

In his last tract, *De imperatorum et pontificum potestate*, he assailed the curial policy and the whole Papal procedure at Avignon. He showed how the Avignon Popes had departed from the ideals and practices of the early Church.[3] Christ had set definite limits to the power he transferred to Peter and those limits also pertained to the Papal power. The Pope was simply the first administrator in the Church, and was chosen to be useful and helpful to his subjects. Many evils and abuses had resulted because the Pope had not observed the limitations: Papal interference in secular affairs, unjust excommunications, and interdicts, favouritism, injustice, corruptions, frivolities, wars, and a decrease of the number of true believers. The government of the Avignon Curia was denounced for its despotism and greed and partiality. Occam insisted that the Pope should stick to the things necessary for the salvation of men and for the instruction of the faithful.[4] He asserted that neither the Pope nor the councils, nor the traditions of the universal Church, but the Gospel of Christ alone, was for each Christian the final source of faith.[5] Still

[1] Scholz, 79.   [2] Werner, iii, 120.   [3] Scholz, 182.
[4] Ib., 183.   [5] Ib., 188.

he advocated the duty of the laity to obey the Pope and to pay tithes.

In his mental attitude towards the great problems of the day, Occam was thoroughly academic.[1] He was a revolutionist rather than a reformer.[2] At the close of his career he made a fine summary of his views on philosophy, theology, political science, and Church history.[3] In some respects Occam had a keener mind than Marsiglio. When the latter went to Paris to continue his studies Occam was the dominating personality in the university, and no doubt Marsiglio received from Occam his radical theories regarding the Church and State.[4]

(5) Marsiglio of Padua (1270–1334), a descendant of an ancient Italian family, took his university degree at Padua, and then entered the services of the Church as a canon in his native city.[5] He was not a monk and apparently was never in priest's orders. His interest, it seems, was not primarily in theology, so he devoted himself to medicine. He began his medical course at Padua and completed it at Paris, whither he went in 1311. At Paris he gained such prominence that by 1312 he was the Rector of the University for three months.[6] There is some evidence that he had served in the army of the German Emperor for some time before he went to Paris. There he met John of Jandun, perhaps as early as 1311, and about 1325 or 1326 they betook themselves to the court of Lewis of Bavaria, where he acted as the Emperor's physician. In 1328 he accompanied Lewis to Rome, participated in the coronation ceremony of that ruler, and gave his support to the deposition of John XXII and to the election of an anti-Pope. As a reward for these services he was made vicar of Rome. He returned with Lewis to Munich where he died before 1343, under the Papal ban. His whole life and his attitude towards the Church were coloured by his connection with the imperial court.

Sometime between 1324 and 1326 Marsiglio in conjunction with John of Jardun wrote *Defensor Pacis* in Paris. It was

---

[1] Haller, 78.   [2] Scholz, 81.
[3] Ib., 181–9, gives an excellent analysis of his views. Haller says that Occam said nothing about popular sovereignty.
[4] Poole, 264.
[5] Renan, *Hist. Litt.*, xxxiii, 560.
[6] *Chart. Univ. Paris*, ii, 158.

completed in two months [1] and was dedicated to Lewis for his virtue, heroism, and zeal in defending science and the faith. It seems that the book was presented to that sovereign, when Marsiglio and John joined his court at Nuremberg, and was warmly applauded. In the composition John was the councillor and possibly the copyist, but the work was really the product of the brain of Marsiglio, hence he always speaks in the first person. The book clearly shows the Italian, the Ghibelline, and the physician. Both friendly and hostile contemporaries always speak of the joint authorship. John's contribution probably was the philosophical spirit seen throughout the book particularly in the use of Aristotle's *Politics*.

Defensor Pacis was divided into three parts; first, the origin and aim of the state; secondly the relations between the secular and sacerdotal power; and thirdly, forty-one conclusions drawn from the first two parts. [2]

The Scriptures were held to be the final source from which the Church derived all its authority. In case of disputes about the interpretation of the Bible, the general council was to settle the meaning. [3] With Occam, Marsiglio agreed that the Holy Book alone was infallible and that Christians could not be forced to believe anything not found therein. Canon laws were only the ordinances of the ruling class in the Church, and, if contrary to the Bible, Christians were not bound to obey them. [4]

The Petrine theory was discussed with the breadth of view of a modern Protestant. Christ did not commit the faith to the Pope, but to the Church. With Occam he asserted that Christ did not appoint a vicar. To Peter was committed no greater authority than to all the apostles. [5] Peter was called the " Prince of the Apostles " simply because he was the oldest and most steadfast. He was Bishop of Antioch, not the founder of the Roman bishopric, and there is no proof that he

---

[1] Riezler, 36; *Eng. Hist. Rev.*, 1905, 302. *Defensor Pacis* was translated into English in 1535 by Marshall. Sullivan, *Am. Hist. Rev.*, ii, 411, asserts that the work was not completed in two months, but was the result of a long period of investigation as proved by the many references to the current history of the day. He believes that it was begun between April and July, 1324. Scholz says the date was 24th June.

[2] There is a fine summary in Gieseler, iii, 29, note 15.

[3] *Defensor Pacis*, iii, 1.

[4] Ib., ii, 5.   [5] Ib., ii, 15.

was even in Rome. In sacerdotal authority his power was no greater than that of the other apostles.[1] He declared that such texts as Matt. xvi, 19, Luke xxii, 38, John xxi, 15–17, were falsely interpreted and that even if Peter had derived some primacy from Christ he never used it.[2]

In reply to the question : " What is the Church ? " he defined it as all the Christian people. Christ founded the Church and committed the faith to it ; and somewhere in it the truth had always been held and preserved. With Occam again he believed that the Church derived its authority from the Bible and not from the Pope. Occam maintained that the true church was the congregation of believers in the teachings of Jesus and differed therefore from the Roman Catholic Church, which was a priestly organization for the purpose of administering the sacraments and for showing men the way to salvation, but even that organization had not civil jurisdiction.[3] The true Church, and not the Pope and the Roman Church, was infallible. Marsiglio made the Church wholly subject to the will of a democratic community and compared the Church to a " perpetual minor " because without the permission of the community it could not legislate, exercise judicial power, or own property. He clearly differentiated between the Apostolic Church and the medieval Church. In the former Christ committed the government of the Church to all the apostles alike.[4] Hence he asserted the equality of the priesthood because the bishops and priests were originally equal. Their functions were purely spiritual and educational. The ultimate source of all authority was not in the priesthood, but in the Church, that is, the entire body of Christian men. The Roman hierarchy which had succeeded the Apostolic Church had a natural, historical development. Its origin was human and not divine. The Papacy was not absolutely indispensable to the Church. Conditions might arise to make it necessary to establish a number of national churches. Consequently Marsiglio made a bitter attack on the whole hierarchical assumptions of the Papacy.

A general council represented the entire Christian body, both priests and laity, and was elected by the people as

---

[1] *Defensor Pacis*, 14.   [2] Ib., ii, 15, 17.
[3] Kropatscheck, 55.   [4] *Defensor Pacis*, ii, 15.

the one supreme sovereign power in the Church. The council
had final authority in all matters of belief and on all questions
of organization. Only councils had the right and the power
to canonize. The Pope called the council but the council was
superior to the Pope,[1] hence the Pope was not infallible.
Even a legitimate Pope might be guilty of heresy as Peter was
rebuked by Paul for judaizing. Liberius was an Arian. Leo
was arraigned by Hilary of Poitiers for false doctrine.
Nicholas III and John XXII contradicted each other, hence
one of them must be a heretic. Even councils were not infallible
and might err. A council might try a Pope for heresy and if
it failed in its duty the cardinals might pronounce the decision.
If the cardinals failed, then a temporal prince could assume the
right to try the Pope, just as Pilate judged Christ, so the
Emperor could judge a Pope. In case the Pope refused to
summon a general council, the State should do it.

Christ did not appoint a vicar, hence the primacy of the
Pope is not of divine origin but was derived from either the
general council or from the legislature of the State. The Pope
cannot excommunicate, impose the interdict, or inflict any
kind of ecclesiastical punishment without the consent of the
civil power. Papal authority to bind and to loose was
declarative and not judicial, for God alone can forgive sins
and punish the sinner. The Pope's claim to fulness of power
contradicts the true nature of the Church. The pre-eminence
of the Bishop of Rome is due to his location in Rome. He has
no more sacerdotal jurisdiction than any other priest. His
claim to jurisdiction over princes and nations was the source
of wars and strife, particularly in Italy. Marsiglio denied
the validity of the Donation of Constantine. Obedience to
the Papal decretals was not a condition of salvation, otherwise
how could Clement V make the bull *Unam sanctam* inoperative
for the French king and people ? That bull expressly declared
that submission to the Pope was necessary to salvation.
No Pope can set aside the conditions for salvation established
by God. The temporal power of the Pope was categorically
denied. St Bernard had said that the Pope needed no wealth
nor court to be the successor of Peter. Texts of Scripture
like John xvii, 36, and Matt. xxii, 21, were cited to prove that
the Pope had no temporal power, for Christ expressly excluded

[1] *Defensor Pacis*, 17.

the apostles from all earthly dominion.[1] The Pope cannot depose the Emperor or any other prince. The imperial oath to the Pope is not one of fealty, but to protect the Church. Constantine did not confer the rule of the West upon the Pope, because he divided his empire among his sons. Theodoric and other emperors exacted dominion in Rome. Peace would never be established in the Christian world as long as the false claims of the Papacy were accepted. Even the Pope's extreme claim to spiritual functions was attacked. It was very much to be regretted that Popes and Cardinals were chosen from among the lawyers instead of the theologians. Many cardinals were youngsters who loved pleasure and were ignorant of important fields of knowledge. It is the Pope's simple duty to carry out the orders of a general council. He possessed no lordship over the bishops.

In the Apostolic Church, the bishops and priests were equal, but in the development of the hierarchy that original parity was lost. The clergy were very severely denounced for their greed and ignorance.[2] They possessed no power to excommunicate, to interdict, or to punish, since only the "congregation of the faithful" exercised those prerogatives The clergy could detect heresy, but could not punish it. They had as much sacerdotal power as the Pope. Their functions were spiritual and educational—to teach and to warn. They should practice self-denial like Christ. The various Christian communities should elect the clergy, supervise them, and control them in performing their duties. The democratic Christian communities possessed sovereign power in all local ecclesiastical concerns.

In discussing the State, Marsiglio recalls the wildest theories of the legists of Philip IV and the Caesarian lawyers like William Durand, John of Paris, Pierre Dubois, and others. But he was far more radical and revolutionary than any of them. He completely abandoned the old theocratic conception of society and made the people under God the immediate source of all authority in both the Church and the State. Sovereign law was the expression of the will of the majority of the people, and not of the will of princes. The divine right of democracy was proclaimed. The elected head of a nation

---

[1] *Defensor Pacis*, ii, 4 ; cf. Haller, 74.
[2] *Defensor Pacis*, 11, 10, 23.

had only delegated executive power. Legislative power was exercised through representatives elected by the people. The ruler was merely the instrument of the legislature. He, like all individuals, was subject to law. If he neglected or exceeded his power, the people could depose him. Marsiglio even suggested the extension of civil power to the determination of the number of men to be employed in every trade and profession. Individual liberty had no more place in his state than it had in Sparta. In the Church the faithful were the sovereign power, elected priests and bishops, and legislated. The State summoned the general council, composed of clergy and laity, elected by the people, which was the supreme legislature of the Church, created the Pope as the executive branch and appointed the college of cardinals to work with him. But in Marsiglio's Church the Emperor occupied a very influential position. He called and directed the council; he could punish priests, bishops, and even the Pope; he could tax the property of the Church[1]; he could limit the number of clergy and he controlled the patronage of the Church. In all matters of local ecclesiastical government the democratic parish held supreme control. It could choose and dismiss priests and mete out punishment to offenders. Thus, as in Calvin's system of a later day,[2] all judicial and legislative power of the Church was inherent in the people, and delegated by them to the clergy. The community and the State were everything; the Church a convenient figure of speech without power. The goods of the Church belonged to individual members for ecclesiastical uses, but ultimately to the State which decided regarding sales and purchases, and contributions to the clergy and the poor. At any time the State could secularize Church property against the will of the clergy. The State could not release priests from their civic obligations.[3] No one was bound to pay tithes to the Church. That doctrine was certainly revolutionary and subversive of all ecclesiastical and social order.

The significance of the *Defensor Pacis* lay in the fact that it comprehended the whole essence of the political and religious theories which separate modern times from the Middle Ages.

[1] *Defensor Pacis*, ii, 20.
[2] See Döllinger, *Lehr buch*, ii, 259, for a discussion of the relation of the system of Calvin to that of Marsiglio.
[3] *Defensor Pacis*, ii, 7.

The sixteenth century reformation substituted a ministry serving the Church for a hierarchical class, and brought man directly in touch with the Bible and God. It emancipated man from the ecclesiastical machine of the Papacy. The political revolutions of the eighteenth and nineteenth centuries consisted largely of the recognition of the people as the sovereign source of law and government. Marsiglio clearly saw both of these epoch-making principles. He thought them out, explained them in unmistakable terms, and stated them in such clear outline that the modern protestant and the modern publicist needed only to work them out in a practical way.[1] Hence among all the opponents of the medieval Church, Marsiglio stands head and shoulders and three-fourths of his body above them in his modernity. The Middle Ages had not seen an attack so scholarly, so keen and critical, and at the same time showing so little respect for ecclesiastical authority and tradition and making such a revolutionary assault upon the fundamentals of the Papacy.[2]

A second tract called *Defensor minor* was written by Marsiglio in 1328, without any assistance from John of Jardun. He takes as his basic fact the existence of two powers in the universe : the divine and the human. No man can in any manner change the first power ; and no bishop, or ecclesiastic can modify the human law for that right belongs to the " human legislature ", or its representative, the King of the Romans. The Pope can alter neither the divine nor the human law. In so far as the clergy claim that right, or exercise it, they have merely usurped power. No priest has authority to exercise any jurisdiction over man, and consequently cannot impose penances. He argued that the process of excommunication as exercised by the clergy was not authorized by the Bible. He declared that confession to God was much better than confession to a priest. He doubted the validity of vows. He denounced the crusades inaugurated by the Church to force infidels to accept the Christian faith, and asserted that only the Prince of Rome had that right. Indulgences and pilgrimages were pronounced useless and harmful. He accepted the rise of the primacy of the Pope as a historical fact, but denied its dogmatic authority. He

[1] Poole, *Illustrations of the History of Medieval Thought*, 275.
[2] Scholz, 1.

restated his belief in a supreme human legislature, representing a majority of the people, and in a general council of all Christian people, Greek and Latin, as the sovereign law-making power of the Church. He assailed one of the fundamental laws of the Church in advocating the appointment of competent judges to pass on petitions for divorce.[1] This treatise has just been recovered in the Bodleian Library at Oxford, but has not yet been published. It throws much light upon his larger work. A third treatise *De jurisdictione Imperatoris in causa matrimoniali* has been edited by Preher and Goldast.[2] A fourth, *De translatione Imperii Romani*, has been printed four times in German and once in English.[3]

On 3rd April, 1327, the Pope called Lewis of Bavaria to account for the reception given to " two lost sons and damned alumni ".[4] On 9th April he excommunicated them as " Those sons of Belial ", who " are so audacious as to affirm that the Blessed Apostle St. Peter received no more authority than the other apostles ; that he was not appointed their chief ; and further that Christ gave no head to His Church and appointed no vicar here below. These children of Belial do not fear to assert that the Emperor has the right to appoint, to dethrone, and even to punish the Pope. These frivolous and lying men say that all priests, be they Popes, archbishops, or simple priests, are possessed of equal authority and equal jurisdiction by the institution of Christ ". All those assertions, it was maintained, are disproved by the Scriptures, tradition, and history, as heretical and dangerous. Ten years before Marsiglio had been recommended to John XXII by two cardinal friends as a suitable person for an appointment and thanks to their influence he received in 1316 a letter creating him canon of the episcopal church of Padua. In 1318 it appears that John XXII thought of making him Bishop of Padua.[5] No doubt, therefore, to the Pontiff from whom he had received favours the unprecedented attack upon the fundamental Papal prerogatives merited the harshest punishment. In 1326 John's attention was first directed to the appearance of the

---

[1] Renan, *Hist. Litt. de la France*, xxxiii, 606 ff.
[2] Ib., 617 ; *Monarchia*, ii, c. 1283.
[3] Based on a treatise by Landolfo Colonna.
[4] Danifle, *Chart.*, ii, 301 . The bull of 23rd Oct., 1327 is given in Mirbt, *Quellen*, 152.
[5] He called John " the great dragon, the old serpent."

Defensor Pacis. Following the promulgation of the ban, a committee was appointed at Avignon to examine the dangerous tract and on 23rd October, 1327, it condemned five heretical propositions contained in it. But Marsiglio had set free certain ideas so dangerous to the fundamental pretensions of the medieval Papacy that it is impossible to estimate their effect on the thought and feeling of Europe for the next two centuries. Many prophets of a new era during the coming generations were to repeat his intellectual assaults in one form or another, until the final result was the protestant revolt.

In this conflict, carried on with the weapons of literary skill, legal lore, and historical science, first appeared in their full significance those reformatory and revolutionary ideas which in the following centuries produced such momentous results in Church and State. As the Papacy sought to extend its power without limit, it met opposition which called into question the very foundations on which it rested and threatened to destroy them. These radical writers menaced not only the Curia, but the whole hierarchy. The strongest attack was centred on the Papal claim to rule in worldly affairs, but the most dangerous assault was made on the spiritual prerogatives of the medieval priesthood. The call was not so much for a reformation as for a revolution, but two centuries were to pass by before the disruption actually occurred. The elements in the Church in the fourteenth century, favourable to a revolution were, however, more numerous and stronger than is commonly believed. Had the governments and the peoples been ready and willing to follow the leadership of these daring thinkers, it is quite conceivable that it could have taken place at that time.

46. *The Papal defenders*

The Papal court not only sought to suppress the bold rebels who had made such an unprecedented criticism of the validity of the fundamental principles upon which the entire Papal super-structure rested, but also alarmed lest the assertions spread over Christendom, supplemented the ban and excommunication with tracts which combated the heresies and condemned the false teachings. Among those who wrote answers to Marsiglio and Occam were the following :—

(1) Lybert von Beek, a Dutchman, a member of the Carmelite order, who had studied in the Universities of Cologne and Paris and was the first of his order to be made *magister theologiae*. In 1316 he became the fourth head of his order. He died in 1332.[1] Between 1326 and 1327 he wrote a tract at the order of the Pope in which he pointed out the six fundamental heresies of which Marsiglio was guilty and then explained in full why each one was heretical. The remainder of the pamphlet was taken up with a complete vindication of the traditional view of the Papacy.[2]

(2) William Amidanis, an Italian Augustinian, who studied at Paris, and became the head of his order in 1326. Later he was made Bishop of Cremona. He was a zealous but not a blind defender and adviser of the Pope, at whose request he wrote a refutation of *Defensor pacis*.[3] It was a scholarly scholastic treatise and had not a word about the need of reformation. In several other pamphlets, however, he pointed out certain abuses that needed to be corrected.

(3) Petrus de Lutra, whose life is so far unknown,[4] wrote two political tracts in which the Papal claim to temporal power was defended on theological and historical grounds.[5]

(4) Augustinus Triumphus, who had zealously defended Boniface VIII, dedicated his most important work on *The Power of the Church* to John XXII and in it defended him in his attack on the Spiritual Franciscans and in his quarrel with Lewis the Bavarian. His exposition of the unlimited powers of the Pope was so extravagant that modern Catholic historians have felt called upon to apologize for him.[7] So extensive was the Papal authority that even the Pope did not know its bounds. His jurisdiction and his judgment were coterminous with God's. He could even empty purgatory by granting indulgences, if he wished to do so. No council or any other human power could depose him. He was above all and could he judged by none. In short he exalted the Pope into a demi-God with absolute power over the whole world. As God's Vicar he could depose emperors and rulers and take away from

---

[1] Scholz, 3–6, gives his life.   [2] Ib., 6–13.
[3] Ib., 15–22.   [4] Ib., 22–4.
[5] Ib., 24–7. Five additional tracts against Lewis' *Gloriosus Deus* and his imperial coronation are analysed, ib, 28–70.
[6] Riezler, 286 ; Poole, 252 ; Haller, 83 ; Finke, 41.
[7] Pastor, i, 80 ; Alzog, 11, 14 (10th ed.) ; Döllinger, *Fables*, 130 ; Hergenröther-Kirch, ii, 75, 757.

the electors their right of election. Still it was admitted that the Pope might fall into heresy and in that event would *ipso facto* cease to be Pope. To God was due adoration; to the Pope, worship—as to the saints. Even if a bad man, his authority was none the less " of God ". To him belonged unquestioned and universal obedience. From his decision there could be no appeal, not even to God, for his voice was identical with God's. All laws emanated from him and all property and wealth belonged to him. In short his work was an encyclopedia defending Papal infallibility.

(5) Alvar Pelayo, a Spanish Franciscan, and professor of law at Perugia, fled from Rome upon the approach of Lewis the Bavarian, in 1328, and was appointed Papal penitentiary at Avignon, and later Bishop of Silves in Portugal. His *Lament over the Church* [1] exalted the Papal office and said the Church was a dwarf with a giant's head, the Pope. He who did not accept the Pope, denied Christ; and he who accepted the Pope, accepted Christ. Legally all—even pagans, Jews and Saracens—were under his jurisdiction. He will was wisdom and law. Wherever he was, there was the Roman Church, and he was not compelled to remain in Rome. To doubt his powers meant exclusion from salvation. He ruled all persons and judged all things. All princes received their power from him and were responsible to him.

Alvar was not so extravagant as his Augustinian brother, and spoke very plainly about Papal shortcomings and the evils in the Church. He denounced the exemptions and other invasions of the rights of prelates; opposed the greed for gold at the curia; scolded about nepotism; attacked the extraordinary taxes levied on the Church; and declared that the Church was rich, mighty, ruled on land and sea, made war, and strove for wealth—in short was all that she should not be. These criticisms were fundamental in his book. He charged this unfortunate condition in the Church up to Papal neglect. He said that the Church could be saved only by the " Angel Pope " who followed in the footsteps of St Francis. He was not only a Papal defender and reformer, but was the best educated representative of fourteenth century pietism. [2]

His treatise is also full of personal recollections, noteworthy things he saw, anecdotes of wonderful occurrences,

---

[1] Scholz, 151; Haller, 84–7. [2] Ib., 87.

casuistries of the confessional, experiences at the Curia, life as a student at Bologna, and experiences as a teacher of law at Perugia.

He deplored the fact that the Church had become so completely secularized that priests and monks were busy in every branch of worldly life. The prelates he compared with the fabled beast Lamia, with the body of an animal and the head of a man, which tore its own offspring to pieces and destroyed all within its reach. The bread due to the poor was given to jesters and to dogs. Faith and Justice had abandoned the earth; human kindness was unknown; the flame of wrath and greed destroyed the Church; fraud and simony killed the poor; the Scriptures and canons were declared to be fables; and iniquitous priests and prelates shed the blood of the just and opened the broad way to destruction.

(6) Konrod von Megenberg, a patriotic German, but still a defender of the Papacy, in 1438 wrote a poem in two parts in the form of a petition.[1] The policy of John XXII was bitterly satirized, yet at the same time he spoke of the Pope as " the Vice-Christ ".[2] Benedict XII bestowed upon him an expectation, which made the twelfth he possessed, and still he complained of ill-treatment! The first part of his work consists of a dialogue between the Pope and the Church, in which there is much plain talk about both the theory and practices of the Church. He suggested the possibility of the Germans breaking away from Rome and forming an independent national Church like that of the Greeks.[3] A long list of complaints is given concerning the Church in Germany.[4] He declared that the Pope was regarded as the " work-horse of the King of France and Robert of Naples "; that the Germans would rather give up their allegiance to Rome than abandon their emperor; that the laity made no distinction between the Jews and the avaricious priests. He denounced the sloth and avariciousness of the clergy and he made an assault upon the evil results of curial policy in the empire.

The second portion of the poem dealt with the injuries and transgressions inside the Church. He charged the monks

---

[1] *Planctus ecclesia in Germaniam.* See Grauert, in *Hist. Jahrb.*, xxii (1901), 631–87; Höfler, *Aus Avignon*, Prag., 1868, 24 ff.
[2] Scholz, 79.   [3] Ib., 88.   [4] Ib., 89.

with all sorts of crimes. He declared that Caiaphas, Pilate, Herod, Judas, and Simon Magus were now the real bishops of the Church. Monks no longer imitated their master, Christ, but preached false doctrines. He assailed their greed and shameless acts. He showed how monks and priests quarrelled over the right to bury rich Christians and lamented that the luxurious and wealthy monasteries had lost all their spirituality.[1] The Church Fathers were no longer obeyed, but Aristotle and Averroes ruled in their stead. He ridiculed the sale of grace and of offices. In a joking manner the people said: " A miracle for a penny "; and " A De profundis for a fresh egg ". He satirized indulgences, particularly those promises tacked up on the church doors offering 100 and 1,000 days' indulgence. He cited the instance of a peasant who tried to buy 100,000 days' indulgence for 4,000 eggs, good and bad. When the pious priest explained the error to the poor man he grew angry and denounced the whole system as a piece of priestcraft.[2]

This comical, poetical burlesque appealed to the popular mind and reflected it with surprising accuracy. It must have gone far to shake the people's faith in such institutions as indulgences. The attack he made on the monks, who left their fine monasteries to beg, many of them dishonest, unchaste, and carrying arms, and all wanting ten benefices, must have reflected the common criticism. Avignon was described as a place where the rich alone prospered and the poor got nothing. To the powerful and the wealthy alone were the doors open. He who had little in Avignon lost even that. The Pope hid in his Papal castle and was seldom seen, and the priests at the Papal court were dumb like the statues in the churches. In contrast to the life of the cleric, the career of the scholar was praised as worthy of imitation and assistance.

A second tract, almost unknown to-day, was written and dedicated in 1354 to Charles IV.[3] It was an exceptionally keen exposition of the relation of the Church and the Empire, but it was consistently pro-Papal throughout. It appeared in opposition to a tract by Lupold von Bebenburg. A third tract was written against Occam.[4]

These writings of Konrad reveal him as a sharp critic,

---

[1] Scholz, 92.   [2] Ib., 92–3.
[3] De translatione imperii Romani.   [4] Scholz, 95–127.

a satirist of exceptional cleverness, an iconoclast, a patriot, and a good Christian. He was an internal reformer and not a revolutionist like Marsiglio and Occam.[1]

No doubt the laboured exaggerations of Papal power, such as were found in the Papal defenders and apologists like Triumphus, were coached by the Avignon court. However satisfactory their extreme claims may have sounded in the ears of the Pope and his confidants, they fell far short of counteracting the attacks of political scepticism in regard to the authority of the Holy See. On the contrary they incited answers from some of the keenest brains of Europe and aroused grave suspicions all over Europe that increased in seriousness and significance as the years passed by.

[1] Scholz, 127–140.

CHAPTER VII

POLITICAL AND ECCLESIASTICAL OPPOSITION TO THE PAPACY IN EUROPE

47. *In Italy*

THE period of the Babylonian Captivity marked the decay of the feudal and hierarchical institutions of the Middle Ages. Both the Papacy and the Empire—creations of the Latin idea of the organization of human society—appeared in entirely altered relations, languishing and threatened with dissolution. The Empire fell into vassalage to the Pope and was banished from Italy. The Papacy exiled from Italy for seventy years under French influence lost, not only its claim to universal rule, for that was asserted more boldly than ever, but its grip and its recognition among the European powers. The Popes turned the absolute dominion which they had acquired in the thirteenth century upon the Church itself and mercilessly despoiled it by a thousand tyrannical abuses and corruptions. That shortsighted policy aroused the reforming and even revolutionary spirit of the west. The bravest thinkers disputed not only the secular, but also the spiritual jurisdiction of the Papacy. Germany pronounced its Empire independent of the Roman Pontiff and the genius of Germany gave indications of its declaration of separation from Rome in matters of faith.[1]

In Italy the Ghibelline idea, feudal and imperialistic, triumphed over the Guelf, or Papal idea. The Ghibellines disputed the union of the spiritual and temporal powers in the Papacy. The desertion of Rome by Clement V and the absence of the Papacy from Italy for the greater part of the fourteenth century filled the Italians with bitterness and woe. " O good beginning ! To what a vile conclusion must thou stoop " wailed Dante.[2] The disastrous effects of the Gallicized Papacy were at first chiefly felt in Italy. The fundamental principle of unity in the Italian peninsula was the Roman Papacy. Bereft of that unifying and steadying force, Italy was left a prey to anarchy, torn to pieces by irreconcilable parties, and a scene of desolation. Hence from first to last

---

[1] Gregorovius, vi, pt. 1, 1.   [2] *Parad.*, xxvii, 59, 60.

there were bitter longings for the return of the Papacy and continual protests against the desertion.

Dante sharply reproved the " Supreme Pastor of the West " for his alliance with the French monarchy.[1] When the cardinals met to elect a successor to Clement V, he addressed a severe letter to the Italian cardinals : " You, the chiefs of the Church Militant, have neglected to guide the chariot of the Bride of the Crucified One along the path so clearly marked out for her. Like the false charioteer Phaeton, you have left the right track, and though it was your office to lead the hosts safely through the wilderness, you have dragged them after you into the abyss. But one remedy now remains : you, who have been the authors of all this confusion, must go forth manfully with one heart and one soul into the fray in defence of the Bride of Christ whose seat is in Rome, of Italy, in short of the whole band of pilgrims on earth. This you must do, and then returning in triumph from the battle-field, on which the eyes of the world are fixed, you shall hear the song ' Glory to God in the Highest ' ; and the disgrace of the covetous Gascons, striving to rob the Latins of their renown, shall serve as a warning to all future ages ".[2] Dante died in 1321 but his severe arraignment of the cardinals and the Papacy was typical of Italian feeling throughout the entire exile. Dante, " consumed with zeal for the House of God," in a most emphatic tone expressed his indignation at the cupidity and nepotism of the Avignon Popes, although he always distinguished between the Papal office and its occupants.[3] He complained that the winestock which Peter had planted had become only common wood.[4]

Petrarch, the great intellectual leader of the fourteenth century, the " first modern scholar ", the " implacable enemy of ignorance and superstition ", the reformer, counsellor of princes, leader of men and idol of his age, lived his life during the Babylonian Captivity.[5] His " fate or his sins " made him a most unwilling citizen of " the Babylon of the West ". He execrated Avignon, which was " filled with every kind of confusion, the horror of darkness overspreading it, and

[1] *Inferno.*, xix, 82.
[2] *Opp. min. di Dante*, ed. P. Fraticelli (Florence, 1862), iii, 486–94 ; Wegele, 262–5.
[3] Hettinger, *Dante*, 122, 460.
[4] *Parad.*, xxiv 110 ; *Purgator.*, xxxii, 142.   [5] Robinson, *Petrarch*, 11, 15.

contained everything fearful which had ever existed or been imagined by a disordered mind ".[1] He described it as " a hell on earth " and much worse than in his youth, although even then the most foul and filthy of places.[2] Yet he called " that disgusting city of Avignon which I heartily abhorred " his " home ",[3] and was not averse to sharing in the material advantages of the Papal court and was offered a Papal secretary-ship, an honour which he refused.[4] In 1353 he left Avignon for ever, and went to Italy.[5] When the Romans sent a delega-tion to persuade Clement VI to return to Rome, it seems that Petrarch was a member, and for the remainder of his life he gave his support to the movement to restore the Papacy in the Eternal City. When that hope was finally temporarily realized, Petrarch compared it to Israel's return from Egypt. He died in 1374, a true Italian patriot. It must be remembered, however, that Petrarch did not deny the divine origin of the Papacy,[6] was outwardly on good terms with nearly all of the Avignon Pontiffs and received favours from many of them. His numerous satirical attacks on the Papacy, therefore, were probably viewed as poetical rhapsodies which have been taken too seriously by modern historians.[7]

Boccaccio in a mocking spirit was equally outspoken in his denunciations of the Papacy during the period of the exile. From the highest to the lowest, he said, everyone in the Papal court was abandoned to the most abominable vices. The very sight of it, he wittily affirmed, would convert a Jew, for he would come to the conclusion that Christianity must be of God, since it spread and flourished in spite of the wicked-ness of its head.[8]

Of all the European countries Italy was thrown into the most deplorable condition by the Papal expatriation. The struggle between the Ghibelline and Guelf parties filled a large part of its history. The Ghibellines disputed the union of the two powers in the Papacy and that idea had become so strong by the end of the period of the Captivity, that 80 cities formed a league to destroy the Pope's temporal power. In 1319 at Assisi the Ghibellines broke into the sacristy of St Francis and robbed the Papal treasury.[9]

[1] Robinson, 86–7. [2] Ib., 87.   [3] Ib., 67.   [4] Ib., 118.
[5] Ib., 119.   [6] Körting, i, 407 ; ii, 201.   [7] Pastor, i, 66.
[8] *Decamerone*, Giorn., i, nov. 2.   [9] *Archiv. f. Kirchengesch.*, i, 239.

Of all Italian cities Rome suffered most. The powerful families were in a constant feud for possession of the government of the city, and in turn had to contend with the democratic elements. The Papal legate was practically powerless at Rome. With the source of her support and chief attraction removed to Avignon, the city became poverty-stricken and fell into decay and ruin. No such thriving commerce as enriched northern Italy brought wealth and prosperity to the Eternal City and mighty Rome dwindled down to a dull, provincial town of less than 20,000 people by 1370. The monuments of classical antiquity fell into ruin, or were torn down. The costly marbles were burnt into lime; the Colosseum became a vast quarry for building feudal castles; and much of value was carted away to other cities. Churches were neglected, roofless, some destroyed by fire, others used as cattle barns. No new structures of value were erected and little was done to repair the old. The streets were full of filth and débris, and foul pools made the city offensive and unhealthy. It is small wonder that Cola di Rienzi declared that Rome was more fit in 1347 to be a den of robbers than a habitation for civilized man.

"Italy," moaned Dante, "is full of tyrants, and every peasant who joins in any enterprise is taken for a hero." Venice, Genoa, Pisa, and Florence had obtained the greatest power, but their wealth and authority did not work for either peace or unity in Italy. On the contrary the Italian peninsula was given up to almost continual strife and warfare, first within the cities themselves, and secondly among the different cities. The country districts were infested with bands of brigands. Bishops and abbots paid the price of immunity from pillage with large sums of money. Petrarch, like Dante, died disappointed and disheartened, saying: "Liberty, that precious and greatly desired boon, is never appreciated until lost."

Notwithstanding the anarchy and confusion and division in Italy during the fourteenth century, there were daring souls who dreamed of a united national state. Some wished for the realization of that hope under a restored and reformed Papacy; others believed in the quickening of the national feeling under the leadership of the Emperor; and still others thought of the possibility of reviving the Roman Republic.

The continued absence of the Popes at Avignon defeated the realization of unification from that source. Dante and others looked to the Emperor for peace and unity. Henry VII crossed the Alps in 1310, but was excommunicated by Clement V and checked by the King of Naples and the Guelfs. He was about to return to Germany, leaving Italy in as much anarchy as he found it on his arrival, when in 1313 he died. Another emperor, Lewis the Bavarian, crossed the Alps in 1327 and in Rome assumed the useless crown of the Roman Empire, but he too was excommunicated, and left Italy almost deserted by supporters. The chivalrous John of Luxemburg and King of Bohemia arrived as imperial vicar in 1330 and gave the Italians a moment's hope, but he fared no better than the others and in a few months was detested. It is a sorry spectacle to see Italy rushing with infatuated enthusiasm to welcome each newcomer, and then becoming as quickly disgusted with him and seeking to drive him out.

Passing from one illusion to another in their yearning for the realization of nationality, they finally turned to Rienzi, the Roman tavern-keeper's son, a pupil of Petrarch, imbued with his love for ancient Roman history, who thought to arouse in the people the realization of their dream of a united Italy by preaching the revival of the ancient Roman Republic. With Livy in his hand he evoked the ancient Republic, and on the steps of the Capitol, amidst the ancient monuments, he pictured to the Roman people the glory of the days of their fathers. In 1347 he was proclaimed on the Capitol tribune of the " good state ". At once he began to organize the republic by creating a citizen army and an Italian navy. He won over the refractory nobles and hanged the brigands ; he established public granaries and cared for the poor and needy. The republics of Tuscany and Romagna applauded his course, and several Lombard princes consented to receive his deputies. Amidst great enthusiasm the " Holy Roman Republic " was proclaimed and granted freedom to all the Italian cities. But Rienzi's own mystical excesses and ambitions, together with the obstacles and difficulties in the way of working out in a practical manner the new political problems, brought the fine dream of the poet-tribune to an inglorious end. The people grew tired of him and deserted him.

Petrarch hailed the tribune as the Saviour of Italy. " So

just a cause," he wrote from Avignon, " is sure of the approval of God and the world." The Pope at first acquiesced in the revolution and sent deputies to the national parliament which Rienzi had called, but pronounced hostility developed in the Papal court, largely through the fear of losing the Papal States, and a belief that the creation of an Italian national state would endanger the independence of the Papacy. Hence the Pope authorized the deposition of Rienzi as a pagan, a criminal and a heretic. On 15th December, 1347, the tribune abdicated, and Papal power was restored in Rome. The hope of the republicans had come to an end like the other dreams for unity under the Pope or the Emperor. But all these movements clearly show one thing, namely, that there existed in Italy the modern idea of nationality, although it was to be centuries before that idea was to be finally realized.

Connected with this popular revolution was an expectation of a religious reformation. No attack was openly made on the Papacy ; on the contrary efforts were made to co-operate with the Pope. Wicked priests were punished. A Cistercian monk was beheaded for crime. A puritanical spirit began to pervade the people such as existed under Cromwell in England.[1] It was hoped that the revolution would be the means of bringing back the Pope to his rightful capitol, stripped, however, of his temporal power. Rienzi would have restored the Papal election to the Roman people and thus put the Papal hierarchy on a democratic basis.

Notwithstanding the political anarchy of Italy in the fourteenth century, that country of all European nations was the farthest advanced on the path of civilization. Industry and commerce flourished. Milan was a city of 200,000 people, and supplied Europe with armour, trappings, saddles, fine cloths, and millinery. Verona manufactured 20,000 pieces of cloth a year. Florence, a city of 30,000 inhabitants, and ruling over as many more outside of the city, had 30,000 workers in wool and wove 80,000 pieces of cloth annually. Agriculture in central and northern Italy was well advanced and very lucrative. The men of Lombardy, Florence, Genoa, and Lucca were the bankers of Europe. Italian commercial enterprises, connected with the Orient, monopolized a large amount of the business of the Western World. Dante,

[1] Gregorovius, vi, pt. i, 257.

Petrarch, and Boccaccio formed a renowned triumvirate in literature, and ushered in the Renaissance. The Italian universities vied with Paris and Oxford. In art it was the age of Niccola Pisano, Cimabue, Giotto, Masaccio, and other famous architects, sculptors, and painters—the celebrated pioneers and teachers of the modern world. Unfortunately, this very wealth in literary, artistic, and material fields went far to explain the indifference of the Italians to a thorough-going religious reformation and the perpetuation of political decentralization and provincialism.

The long period of exile from Rome and Italy not only shattered the influence of the Pope throughout the Italian peninsula, but its whole claim as a universal power was greatly weakened in the eyes of Christendom. Other nations became distrustful of the independence of the Pope and his court. Under such conditions there was a strengthening of the yearnings for both a national State and for a national Church.

48. *Hostility in Germany*

Another result of the Babylonian Captivity was the inevitable alienation of the powerful European rulers, with the exception of the King of France, who felt that he was reaping many benefits from his influence at the Avignon court. In proportion as the Pope was shorn of power by the French monarch he was all the keener to assert his political supremacy over the other states of Europe, and particularly over the comparatively weak German Emperor.[1] Pope John XXII not only reasserted all the old stock arguments advanced to prove the subjection of temporal to spiritual authority, but assumed more than Innocent III had ever done. Indeed his political ideas resembled those of an Oriental despot. He spoke not alone for the Papacy but likewise for the French king in dealing with imperial claims.

When King Albrecht of Germany took the humiliating oath of vassalage to Boniface VIII in 1303, it looked as though Papal lordship had been re-established in Germany. Henry VII (1308–13), who was greeted by Dante in 1310 as the Messiah of the storm-swept Italian fatherland, was asked by Clement V to take the oath of feudal fealty. Hoping

---

[1] Kirsch, *Die Päpstlichen Kollektorien in Deutschland*, xi.

to win the Pope away from French influence, he appeared not unwilling to comply with the request, but was carried off a victim of fever before the question was definitely settled. Then followed the long but very significant conflict between Lewis the Bavarian (1314–47) and the Popes John XXII, Benedict XII, and Clement VI.

After the death of Henry VII the imperial electors met in 1314 to choose a successor. Lewis the Bavarian received five votes and Frederick Hapsburg four votes.[1] Consequently Frederick disputed the election. Lewis was crowned at Aachen by the Archbishop of Mainz; Frederick at Bonn by the Archbishop of Treves. Both claimants appealed to the new Pope, John XXII, for recognition and imperial coronation. Lewis was beyond doubt the legal king and was regularly crowned. Pope John, however, saw a golden opportunity to win a victory for the Papacy over the Empire and withheld his decision. Meanwhile civil war broke out in Germany and in 1322 Frederick was defeated and captured. Lewis then thought that surely the Holy Father would recognize him as the rightful claimant, but John did not appear to be impressed by the decisive battle as a means of settling an apostolic question.[2]

Lewis, feeling, no doubt, that his crown was now secure, ignored the Pope's demand that the question should be arbitrated, and proceeded to exercise all the prerogatives of his office, as claimants successful on the battlefield usually do. Early in 1323 he sent a vicar-general and other officials over the Alps to safeguard his Italian imperial interests. Thereupon John XXII broke loose. He had already chosen an Italian vicar-general and saw his ambition for Papal supremacy in Italy threatened. He bluntly told Lewis that he had no right to assume either the title or power of king or emperor until Papal confirmation had first been given, and threatened him with the ban unless he laid down the reigns of government and presented himself within three months before the Papal throne. John took particular pains to let the whole Church know of his actions.[3] Lewis gave no heed to these commands and threats, however,

---

[1] Müller, *Der Kampf Ludwigs des Baiern mit der römischen Curie.* Tübingen, 1879, 2 vols.

[2] Hauck, *Kirchengeschichte Deutschlands,* v, 483.

[3] Müller, 8, 61 ; Hauck, v, 485.

and consequently was excommunicated on 23rd March, 1324, and his whole kingdom put under the interdict.

The fundamental principle involved in the controversy was the old one so clearly set forth by Dante, namely, the relation of the Church and the State, of the Papacy and the Empire. John strove not to destroy the Empire, but to subject it to his will as Pope. He lived in the disappearing world of disappearing medieval imperialism, not in the newer emerging world of national states.[1] Besides he had no personal affection for Germany, and took keen delight in lording it over the German ruler whom he hated. Like Philip IV in his controversy with Boniface VIII, Lewis was backed up in his defiance of John by the German nation, by the Italian Ghibellines, and by a group of educated churchmen and skilled publicists such as Michael of Cesena, Occam, Marsiglio, John of Jardun, and Lupold of Bebenburg, who made a powerful defence of the German ruler and of course, were cursed by the Pope as heretics. The jurists were the natural allies of the German Emperor, and not all canonists agreed with the extreme claims of the Papacy.[2] At the outset of the trouble the majority of the German people, princes, nobles, and clergy were in sympathy with Lewis notwithstanding his outlawry. In addition Lewis had the memorable historical triumph of the Hohenstaufens, not so far away, to cite in support of his course. Emboldened by all this support, Lewis publicly declared that the Empire was independent of the Pope; that the Pope was a heretic who sought to destroy the Empire to the injury of the Church as well; and that, therefore, like Philip of France, he appealed to a general council to try the Pope and to depose him.

Meanwhile, the Ghibellines in Italy, the anti-Papal party, were urging Lewis to cross the Alps for imperial coronation. The temptation was one he could not resist. He had greatly strengthened his position in Germany by defeating Leopold of Austria in 1325-6, who was working in the interest of Charles IV of France and the Pope. He felt it safe, therefore, to leave for Italy and suddenly decided in March, 1327, to do so.[3] He received the iron crown of Lombardy from two

[1] Hauch, v, 486. [2] Gieseler, 111, 27.
[3] Müller, i, 164.

deposed bishops and then marched without any opposition to Rome, where on 17th January, 1328, in front of St Peter's, Sciarra Colonna " in the name of the Roman people " put the imperial crown on the head of Lewis, and the two outlawed bishops administered unction. Lewis was the first medieval emperor crowned by the people of Rome. Things seemed to be moving away from the past very rapidly and very significantly. This popular coronation was in accord with Marsiglio's idea of a democratic empire. Villani, a contemporary, expressed horror at the unprecedented ceremony performed without the presence of the head of the Church.[1] A similar coronation had never before been seen in Rome.[2]

The new Emperor was not slow in exercising his prerogatives. In accordance with his conception of imperial responsibility for Papal misrule and unfitness, he instituted a formal trial of Pope John XXII, and " James of Cohors who calls himself John XXII " was deposed as a heretic, usurper, oppressor of the Church and anti-Christ in a public meeting in front of St Peter's.[3] Lewis no longer thought of a general council, but felt quite competent with the approval " of the people " to do the business himself. A straw image of John was dragged through the streets of Rome and then publicly burned. This work was completed finally when Lewis permitted the Roman people to choose Nicholas V [4] as an anti-Pope—the first since Barbarossa—and he himself put the Papal crown on his creature's head. The Bishop of Venice performed the ceremony of unction. Nicholas V appointed seven cardinals and it looked as if the Church was confronted by a formidable schism. At Pisa in the Emperor's presence the new Pope excommunicated John XXII for heresy and called a general council to meet in Milan. This Pope also began to sell offices and preferences in a genuine Avignon style. Contented with this apparent victory and revenge, Lewis in 1330 thought of returning to Germany.

By this time, however, the floodtide of Lewis' triumph began to ebb. Italy was fatal to his plans as it had been to many a predecessor. The fickle Romans resisted their people-crowned emperor when he called on them to pay $25,000 in

---

[1] Villani, x, 55.   [2] Hauck, v, 510.
[3] Muratori, xiv, 1167–1173 ; Gregorovius, vi, 153.
[4] He was a humble, inoffensive monk, divorced from his wife. Villani, x, c. 68.

taxes, so he left Rome and went north. The Ghibelline party which had given him such an enthusiastic support began to dwindle away. On 25th August, 1330, after Lewis had withdrawn from Italy, Nicholas V, with a rope around his neck, submitted to John XXII at Avignon. The Germans themselves had grown weary of the conflict and the long absence of Lewis had given his enemies an opportunity to organize and gather strength. Meanwhile John XXII, enraged at the course of Lewis in Italy, was absolutely relentless and unconciliatory. He hurled a whole series of bulls at the Emperor and his followers. In 1328 a crusade was preached against Lewis in Italy and liberal indulgences were promised to all who would participate in it. The Pope left no stone unturned to stir up rebellion in Germany against Lewis. The sentence of excommunication was not only repeated in stronger terms, but he was also deposed and all his subjects were released from obedience to him. The German princes were called upon to elect a new ruler. The climax was reached in the bull of 1334, the most violent ever hurled by a Pope against an emperor,[1] which repeated all the old censures and added new curses, and which arbitrarily severed Italy from Germany. Thus was accomplished that Papal programme which had been begun under Innocent III and furthered in the conflict between Gregory IX and Frederick II.

Under these circumstances, with Italy lost and Germany in a state of defiant rebellion, Lewis was ready for a reconciliation, although not at the cost of his imperial crown. John XXII died in 1334 and the quarrel was inherited by Benedict XII who was not permitted by Philip of France to make peace with Lewis. The Emperor succeeded in forming an alliance with England against France in 1337 and thus strengthened his position. Furthermore the German princes, in defence of their own constitutional rights, drew up the famous constitution of Rense,[2] which was approved in 1338 by the Diet of Frankfurt. The Diet declared that all the proceedings of John XXII against the Emperor were void, and the Emperor was requested to annul the interdict placed upon Germany ; to reestablish public worship throughout the Empire ; and to punish all rebels, lay or cleric. The

---

[1] Müller, 336, 376, 406.

[2] Vogt, *Reichspolitik des Erzbischofs Baldwin*, 1328, 1334, Gatha, 1901 ; Rymer, *Foedera*, I pt.

electors resolved to maintain all German and imperial laws against all powers and persons without exception and to force all their vassals to do likewise. They asserted that imperial power was derived directly from God and did not depend upon Papal grant. These articles were declared to be the fundamental and immemorial laws of the Empire and all persons were bound to obey them on pain of treason, forfeiture of property, and loss of citizenship. Encouraged by these measures of national protest, Lewis at once promulgated decrees for their execution. It will be perceived that these enactments amount to an absolute rejection of the Papal claims against the Empire. This was the first time an independent assembly in Germany dared to assert the independence of the Empire. The gain, however, was to the Empire and not to the Emperor as the sequel proved.

Lewis' sun was rapidly setting. The English alliance languished. Philip VI pursued his game of guile and intrigue in Germany with success. The Emperor gradually lost his staunch supporters. An interdict was still hanging over the German Diet. Lewis made overtures to Avignon, but word was received that absolution could be granted only in case he submitted to all canonical penalties that might be deemed necessary and gave convincing proofs of genuine penitence and future obedience. The pacific Pontiff Benedict XII died at this juncture in 1342, and was succeeded by Clement VI, who turned a deaf ear to the vacillating and deserted monarch, and in 1343 ordered him to renounce his imperial dignity. Lewis at length yielded and signed 28 articles. The conditions imposed seemed so hard that the Diet in 1344 rejected them, but there was little fight left in either the Emperor or the nation. Consequently, when in 1346 a final bull calling upon God to strike Lewis with blindness and insanity ; invoking the curses of Peter and Paul upon him in both this world and the next ; summoning the elements of the universe to combat him ; and damning his house and his children to destruction,[1] summoned the electors to choose a successor to Lewis they gave way and elected Charles IV. Lewis was mercifully killed in a bear-hunt the next year, still under the Papal ban. He died in defeat it is true, but it must not be forgotten that the resolutions of the Diet of

---

[1] Müller, ii, 214 ; Mirbt, *Quellen*, 153.

Frankfurt stood upon the statute book of the Empire as a legal and constitutional refutation of Papal pretensions. Lewis the Bavarian was the last emperor whom the Holy See ventured to excommunicate and the interdict of John XXII and Benedict XII and Clement VI was the last Papal experiment of that sort on the German nation. The sceptre of empire finally dropped from the hands of the Pontiffs of Avignon.

The Emperor Charles IV (1346–78) had the council of electors draw up and the Diet of Metz approve in 1356, the celebrated Golden Bull without the remotest references to the pretensions of the Papacy. The Golden Bull confirmed the statutes of the Diet of Frankfurt and laid down precautions that ensured their execution for the future. This epoch-making constitution excluded the Pope from all participation in the election of emperors in the ages to come.[1] This was the last struggle between the Pope and the Emperor. Creighton well says that with this struggle the history of the Medieval Papacy came to an end. Never again did any Pontiff make an open attack upon an emperor. Verily a new age had dawned.

The conflict of John XXII with Lewis the Bavarian was a weak imitation of the Papal struggle with the Hohenstaufens and of the bitter quarrel between Boniface VIII and Philip IV.

The significance of the quarrel between the Papacy and Lewis lies in the fact that its continuance produced new ideas which worked a great change in the spirit of the age. The allegiance of thousands to the Papacy was shaken to the point of revolt. The spiritual bonds which had attached them to the Church were wellnigh disrupted. The general feeling of the people towards the Papacy had undergone a pronounced transformation. All these results were dangerously prophetic for the future.[2] On the surface of things, however, it seemed as if the Pope had won and the Empire had lost, but the contrary was true.

In no country in Europe in the fourteenth century was the opposition to the Avignon financial system and all its accompanying evils and abuses so pronounced as in Germany. It was complained that all kinds of ecclesiastical oppressions, which were denounced by reforming Popes like Gregory VII

---

[1] Henderson, 220.
[2] Pastor, i, 86 ; Müller, ii, 266 ; Lorenz, *Päpstwahl*, 195.

and Innocent III as deadly evils, were now practised in a greater degree by the Avignon Popes. Demands for reforms were heard on all sides. The Papal collectors' reports were full of instances of resistance and refusals to pay the Papal exactions levied on benefices.[1] During the first half of the century it was planned, therefore, as an additional pressure, to have all who owed the *annates* pay them directly to the camera at Avignon, and regular books were kept for that purpose, but it did not work well. The Germans were in no mood to give their loyal support to the French Popes who had done their utmost to humiliate the German Emperor.[1]

One is not surprised to find written in 1351: " The Ledger of Satan to his dear Sons, The Bishops and Prelates." [2] From one quarter came the complaint: If you don't know the practices of the Roman Curia, listen. It loves law-suits, strife and litigation, because nothing can be carried through without gold. Gold alone obtains appeals to the Pope. Dispensations are secured only for pay. This greed and laziness of the court has aroused the whole Church. Long has it been since another than a French Pope has filled Peter's chair. Clement V was known everywhere for his mercenary dealings. He raised large sums for a crusade and then never proclaimed it. He plundered the churches and the poor and gave it to the French king. It was better to have no Pope at all than to endure such taxes. Why should the Pope take more from the clergy than the ruler from the laity ? The Emperor asks for money only for legitimate purposes ; the Pope demands it whenever he pleases. " O, Jesus ! Relieve us of the Pope. Or at least decrease his power which he uses to the undoing of the people ".[3]

Matthias von Neuenburg declared that the Papal curia at Avignon was a veritable " stable of greed ". [4]

The German opposition to the manner in which the Avignon Popes amassed money and levied taxes is reflected in many of the city records, which clearly shows that the resistance was open and universal.[5] In 1372 the monasteries and abbeys in Cologne entered into a compact to resist Gregory XI in his proposed plan to levy a tithe on their revenues : " In

---

[1] Kirsch, *Annaten*, p. v.   [2] Haller, 8.
[3] Haller, 67.   [4] *Fontes rer. Aust.*, iv, 205.
[5] *Chroniken der deutschen Städte*, iv, 306 ; vii, 189 ; ix, 583.

consequence of the exactions with which the Papal court
burdens the clergy, the Apostolic See has fallen into such
contempt, that the catholic faith in these parts seems to be
seriously imperilled. The laity speak slightingly of the
Church, because, departing from the custom of former days,
she hardly ever sends forth preachers or reformers, but rather
ostentatious men, cunning, selfish and greedy. Things have
come to such a pass, that few are Christians more than in
name." [1] Similar protests were issued by the clergy from
Bonn, Xanten, Soest, and Mainz.[2] Duke Stephen of Bavaria
and his sons addressed a letter to the clergy of their land in
1367 informing them " that the Pope lays a heavy tax on the
income of the clergy, and has thus brought ruin on the
monasteries ; they are, therefore, strictly enjoined, under
severe penalties, to pay no tax or tribute, for their country
is a free country, and the princes will not permit the introduction of such customs, for the Pope has no orders to give
in their country ".

49. *Opposition to the Avignon Captivity in England*

The attitude of the English king, nobles, clergy, and people
towards the Avignon Papacy is both interesting and instructive,
and significant. During the Babylonian Captivity the hostility
of England towards France was quite as pronounced as in
Germany and when the Papal government came under French
influence, there grew up in England a decisive resistance
to Papal oppressions—an opposition that was not confined
to the English government but struck its roots deep in the
nation. The scandals of Avignon were favourable to the
Crown's assertion of supremacy in reference to benefices
and taxes.

For a fundamental explanation of the conflicting relations,
one must go back to the reign of Edward I (d. 1307) which
Stubbs called the " golden age of English church history ",[3]
the period of the great ecclesiastical princes. With Edward I
it had passed.[4] For the first 24 years of his rule he was friendly

---

[1] Lacomblet, *Urkundenbuch für Gesch. des Nieder-rheins*, Dusseldorf,
1853, iii, 627-9..
    [2] Freyberg, *Gesch. der bayerischen Landstände*, Sulzbach, 1828, i, 265.
    [3] *Const. Hist.*, ii, 310.   In 1301 in the Lincoln letter Edward declared his
independence of the Pope in all worldly affairs.   Makower, *Const. of Ch. of
Eng.*, 32.   [4] Haller, 375.

with the Pope and a battle with Rome was not a part of his programme. Conscious of his position in a strong national state, he was as determined to uphold his royal prerogatives as was Philip IV of France. He treated Church property as a part of the national domain. He regarded the higher clergy as sustaining the same relation to him as the nobles and princes.[1] He claimed jurisdiction over all endowed benefices. The clergy might obey the Pope, but he held the Church property in his hands and thus could control them. He was the first English ruler to tax the Church.[2] The Monk of St Albans complained that the English Church was crushed between the upper and lower millstones, between Scylla and Charybdis, between the Pope and the King.[3] The King began to grind more heavily than the Pope. In 1300 the clergy were very loyal to Boniface VIII and in 1302 they refused to pay the 15 per cent demanded by the King without Papal authorization.[4] On the other hand they gave the Pope a free-will gift of 2,000 marks sterling and promised more.[5]

Clement V had been a subject of the English king as Archbishop of Bordeaux. He allowed the primate Winchelsea to be suspended in 1306,[6] and permitted the king to collect tithes, but at the same time demanded the payment of *annates* for three years.[7] Clement V's unheard of use of provisions and expectancies aroused great opposition in England, which culminated in the epoch-making laws of the Carlisle Parliament held in 1307. Those acts (1) forbade the taxation of monastic orders by foreign heads of the orders ; (2) forbade Papal collectors from collecting money and carrying it out of England ; (3) appointed an ambassador of the king and

---

[1] Stubbs, *Chronicles*, ii, 10.   [2] Haller, 378.
[3] Mat. Par., iv, 559.   [4] Wilkins, ii, 274.
[5] Ib., Stubbs, ii, 148, 158.   [6] Rymer, i, 983.
[7] Haller, 382.

The noble English bishop Grosseteste (1175-1253) had raised a bold voice against the transference of Church lands to monastic and knightly orders because the practice impoverished the parishes and left them without care. He tried to stop the Papal practice of giving " Italian rascals " English benefices, since they drew the incomes and yet never set foot in the country. He scathingly denounced the " bad pastors " in a famous memorial to Innocent IV in 1250, and said that the cause of the miserable condition of the Church was the Holy See itself—" its dispensations, provisions and collations." He begged the Pope to stop those disorders, and to root out the corruptions of the Papal court. He denounced the appointment of the Papal nephew to the prebendary of Lincoln merely to give him the revenue and went so far as to say that the commands of the Apostolic See were to be obeyed only when given for the edification of the Church.

Q

nation to carry the protests and complaints to the Pope ;
and (4) ordered sheriffs to look into complaints and report
to the king.[1] These acts of Carlisle became classic and were
cited again and again in the fourteenth century as legal
justification of resistance to Avignon financial tyranny. They
were occasioned by a conviction that Papal rules and
pretensions exhausted the English Church, weakened divine
services, injured and dishonoured the judicial authority,
the property, and the royal prerogatives of the English king ;
violated the original will of the founders of benefices ; and
jeopardized the independence and constitutional law of
England. They represented a sharp conflict between two
systems of law, namely, the canon law of the Medieval Church
and the law of the English national state.[2]

" Peter, the son of Isidore," in a remarkable chronicle
that appeared in England at this period, spoke the mind of
the pious clergy against the use of the income of the Church
for illegal purposes. He showed the widespread opposition
to the worldly lordship of the Pope, and the patriotic loyalty
and hatred of the English clergy against those foreigners
who cared only for English gold. He summed up the sentiment
of opposition in England to the claims and demands of the
Avignon Papacy and curia. " Your Roman princes," he
said, " have become your deadly enemies." They " impose
upon you heavy, unendurable burdens and allow you, who were
once free, to be subject to many taxes." " Look at the
unheard of deeds of your so-called father, who separates
the good shepherd from the stables of the sheep and puts
his own nephews, cousins, and relatives in the offices—some
of whom cannot even read ; others so deaf they cannot hear
the bleating of the sheep. So is the priesthood of our day
degenerated ; obedience to God forgotten ; the general welfare
of the Church neglected ; and the pious purposes and wishes
of the king, princes, and people nullified ". He professed
astonishment that the Pope as the representative of every
Christian should be ambitious to rule the world and subject
every monarchy to his will. Not content with a tenth of
the income of the Church, he demanded the *annates* from the
servants of the Church without any regard to the wishes of
the founders. He was a Nebuchadnezzar who robbed the

---

[1] Haller, 386–7 ; Gee and Hardy, 92–4.　　　[2] Ib., 390.

temples. He would help France subdue England. Hence
it was the duty of England to resist the Pope who ruled not
in God's will, but in the will of his relatives, to rob England
of her gold.[1] This document appears to have been part of
the plan to free England from Papal oppression in order to
enable the English Government to tax Church property and
to free benefices from Papal control.[2]

Edward II meant to uphold this lofty position. His
Parliament of 1309 went even farther than the Carlisle Parliament. The lords in the name of the whole kingdom wrote
the Pope a protest against provisions and *annates*. They
declared that the Papal exactions vitiated the will of the
founders of benefices by giving the incomes to foreigners;
by robbing the needy poor of alms; by weakening the faith
and injuring the souls of men; by decreasing piety and disrupting divine worship; by impoverishing the kingdom and
bringing the crown to open shame. They promised that the
nation would make free-will grants to the Pope and thus
enable him to accomplish his objects of taxation. Clement V
answered with a long list of complaints about the violation
of Papal rights and the secularization of the Church. Robert
Winchelsea was restored to power and he laboured to recover
England for the Pope. Meanwhile a costly war compelled
Edward II to ask aid from the Pope, who lent him 160,000
florins against the royal income in Aquitaine. In return the
Pope was given a free hand for the *annates* and other exactions
in England. John XXII, who was also wise enough to give
aid to Edward II against the Scotch rebels, had full sway in
England, indeed Edward II even bargained with the Pope for
an equal division of the *annates*.[3] In 1317, the king was given
the right to levy a tithe for three years on the Church.[4]

The career of John XXII produced a most unfavourable
impression in England. It was said that he " was spotted
with greed ", and that bloody gold was poured out before
him daily. Everything was for sale and the Pope cared more
for money than he did for souls.[5] Adam Murimuth denounced
the misrule, provisions, dispensations, reservations, and many

---

[1] Hemingburgh, *Chronicon*, ed. Hamilton, *Eng. Hist. Soc.*, vol. 2, Lond.,
1848; cf. Prynne, *Records*, iii, 914; Haller, 383–4.
[2] Haller, 385.   [3] Wilkins, ii, 464; Haller, 401–2.
[4] Wilkins, ii, 464.   [5] *Flores Histor.*, iii, 192.

other abuses connected with the curia at Avignon where anything could be accomplished with money.[1]

With the deposition of Edward II in 1327 the long rule of Edward III for half a century began. At the outset his relations with John XXII seemed to be amicable. In 1330 the King was permitted to collect tithes and was given 50 per cent of the *annates* for four years.[2] In 1330 he had the statutes of Carlisle repealed.[3] In that same year the back tributes due to the Pope from England amounted to 33,000 marks, and the obligation was apparently recognized by the payment of 1,000 marks.[4] In 1333 John received 1,500 marks in tribute. A complete list of all benefices in the hands of foreigners was drawn up by order of the king in 1334 with the intent, no doubt, of ousting them when the time was opportune.[5] Benedict XII followed John XXII in 1334 but there was no open breach until Edward III formed an alliance against France with Lewis of Bavaria in 1339, when under French pressure the Pope commanded Edward to renounce all intercourse with the excommunicated heretic and usurper. In retaliation Edward refused to pay the crusade tithes and confiscated them. As a further resistance to the Papal invasion of royal prerogatives, the first lay chancellor was appointed in 1340, and thirty years later the Parliament restricted that high office to laymen. When the war broke out with France in 1337 the incomes of all French monks and clergy had been confiscated. It was also ordered that all trials over benefices in dispute were to be held in England.[6] The vicar-general of Canterbury declared that the Papal income from England was as large as that of the king. At the Avignon curia it was said : " The English are brave asses ; they bear all burdens which one puts on them." The feeling against the Pope was becoming acute and he was spoken of as a foreigner, a term that meant in English, an enemy. The spirit of a modern nation was ready to assert itself once more.[7] Edward III said in 1339 that it broke his heart to see French troops paid with Papal funds.[8] Consequently the Avignon Popes were regarded as foreign enemies and allies of France.[9]

[1] Haller, 114, 115, 174 ; Wharton, i, 761.
[2] Bliss, *Calendar*, ii, 494 ; Murimuth, 63.
[3] Wormuth, 44.   [4] Haller, 403.
[5] Wilkins, ii, 574.   [6] Rymer, ii, 982 ; Knighton, ii, 2.
[7] Haller, 410.   [8] Walsingham, *Hist. Angl.*, i, 200.
[9] Makower, 13.

Benedict XII died in 1342 and was succeeded by InnocentIV who took up the controversy. The storm broke in the Westminster Parliament in 1343, when it was complained that as a result of the provisions and reservations rich benefices were in the hands of foreigners ; alms were neglected ; no native could secure a position ; the national treasury was used for the French enemy, and state secrets were betrayed to the French monarch. The king was urged to write the Pope about these matters. With the general denunciation of *annates*, provisions, and reservations as oppressive to the English people and Church, it was decreed that all persons who brought bulls into the country, or received them, should be punished with imprisonment.[1] Two cardinals were sent out of England at once.[2] Two letters were sent to Avignon : one from the Lords and Commons in May and another from the King in September. Both letters appealed to the Papal sense of right and justice. They pointed out that it was the duty of the Pope to tend the sheep, not shear them ; to stop provisions and reservations ; to cease giving benefices to unworthy foreigners who knew no English and had no interest in the spiritual welfare of the English Church ; and to do something to improve public church services and to arouse a deeper piety among the people.[3] The Pope complained bitterly of this hostile attitude which he called " rebellion ", sought to justify provisions, and threatened to use the ban.[4] A long controversy followed, in which the people stubbornly persisted in their demands although the king became more moderate.

On the face of things the climax was reached when the following decrees were issued defining the attitude of England :

(1) Statute of Provisors of Benefices in 1351 which reserved to the king the right to appoint the benefices, and thus forbade provisions and reservations, and all the abuses that accompanied them as contrary to the customs of England.[5]

(2) Statute of Praemunire in 1353 which forbade all cases within the king's jurisdiction from being tried before a foreign court.[6]

---

[1] *Rotul. Parl.*, ii, 144 ff. ; Knighton, ii, 28.
[2] Haller, 413.   [3] Haller, 414.
[4] Bliss, iii, 9 ; Murimuth, 149 ; Walsingham, i, 259.
[5] Gee and Hardy, 103.   [6] Ib., 112.

(3) Statute prohibiting Papal collectors from entering
England.[1]

It was one thing to pass these laws and thus lay down a definite
principle of procedure; and it was quite another thing to
enforce the laws. In practice they remained little more than
a theory, for the old methods continued,[2] and the King and
his parliament were the first to break them. Of course, the
Pope was diplomatic enough to appoint court candidates
and sometimes the King could force his own candidates
on the Pope.[3] Provisions and reservations in no wise ceased,
but were given out at the request of the King and Queen.
In 1353 four expectancies were bestowed at the Queen's
solicitation and one at the King's; and in 1357 fourteen
expectancies were given at the request of the Prince of Wales,
and fourteen more to satisfy the Count of Arundel, the royal
ambassador.[4] The Pope thus still named bishops and made
reservations. Provisions were wellnigh countless : 1352 York
and Worcester ; 1356 Ely and Emly ; 1362 Ely and London ;
1363 Ferne, Lincoln, and Cloufert ; 1364 Bath and Rochester ;
1367 Winchester ; 1369 Canterbury and Worcester ; 1370
Chichester, Hereford and Norwich ; 1371 Bangor and Ossary ;
1373 Cashel ; 1374 York, Ely, and Achonry ; 1375 Canterbury, London, and Hereford.[5] Yet in 1365 the statutes of
1351 and 1353 were solemnly renewed.

One House of Commons after another complained about
the non-enforcement of the rights of the Crown against the
Pope, but to no avail. The King seemed to be content with
Papal concessions such as the 100,000 florins allowed to be
taken in tithes from the Church in 1362.[6] In 1366 Parliament
refused to pay tribute to the Pope. There was a continual
outcry against the King for his indifference towards the
statutes.[7] When in need of funds to carry on war with France
Edward did not hesitate to seize the imposts of ecclesiastical
benefices, even those belonging to non-resident cardinals.
The cardinals' revenues were restored to them, however,
much to their joy. In 1372 a law was enacted forbidding
gold to be taken out of a benefice by either a native or a foreign

---

[1] Haller, 425.   [2] Cf. Bliss, ii, 345 ; iii, 54.
[3] Wharton, i, 44 ; Higden, viii, 356.
[4] Bliss, *Petitions*, i, 139, 291, 278.
[5] Haller, 426, n. 4.   [6] Wilkins, iii, 48.   [7] Haller, 430.

incumbent.[1] The next year Parliament again complained of the great injury to the kingdom of the reservations and provisions. The King said that he had sent messengers to the Pope about the matter. When the Pope demanded a large gift of the English clergy, they raised objections and asked the King to protect them and answered with a demand for the redress of ecclesiastical grievance.[2] They pointed out to the King that the money would go to the King of France, the enemy of England. In 1374 another inquiry was made into the number of foreigners holding English benefices in order to arrive at some understanding with the Pope.[3]

Pope Clement VI, elevated to St Peter's chair in 1370, sought in 1375 to placate England. Hence bulls were issued revoking reservations, allowing royal appointments to benefices to remain,[4] and remitting the *annates*. It was thought that these concessions would settle the complaints which had become more insistent each year, but they did not. On the contrary the nation seemed incensed at not having secured a complete reformation of all abuse. The Good Parliament of 1376 reviewed all the old complaints and made new ones. They said that the Papal income from England was five times as large as that of the King. These taxes put the clergy in debt and injured both the Church and the state. Many persons used the revenues of their benefices only to purchase richer benefices from "the wicked city of Avignon". Thus by simony and the use of money many an evil person held benefices worth 1,000 marks, while worthy doctors of theology and masters of godly learning had to content themselves with benefices of only 20 marks income. So the educated lost all hope of advancement; people no longer sent their children to school; and scholarship, the pride of the Holy Church, was in danger of being lost. Foreigners and enemies held the best places in England. The Christian rulers of the Church were worse than the Jews and Saracens. God gave the Pope his sheep to tend, not to shear. If the continuance of these conditions was tolerated, the freedom of England would be destroyed. Finally it was urged that the Pope and the King get together and settle all the issues for the best interest of each.[5]

[1] *Rotuli Parl.*, ii, 311.   [2] Wilkins, iii, 97.   [3] Haller, 431.
[4] Rymer, iii, 1037-9.   [5] Haller, 432; *Rotuli Parl.*, ii, 337 ff.

About the same time appeared the " Lettre de Lombard ". It repeated the same old song, heard ever since the Carlisle Parliament in 1397, in attributing the ruin of the English Church and State to the machinations of the Avignon Papacy. The ecclesiastical establishments, endowed by kings, princes, and rich people, constituted about one-third of the wealth of the kingdom, and were intended for local needs. But sin-cursed Avignon sought to upset those sacred old arrangements by making a traffic of the English benefices. Greed and simony predominated throughout the Church ; hence war, hunger, famine, oppression, plague of man and cattle, smote the world. Nothing but a pure, learned priesthood, spiritual preaching, honest visitations, and a clean confessional would save the English kingdom, make the country rich in good people, promote scholarship and chivalry, and bring quiet, peace, and protection. " Since the Holy Church, from whom we receive baptism, which is the gate of Heaven, and through which we hope to be saved—since she rules in so wicked a manner, therefore, God sends us, since he sees such great injustices and so much unrighteousness ruling among us, so many misfortunes that we can hardly endure them." He prayed the King and lords to restore the Church to its original purity and simplicity as in the days of Gregory and the other saints. He was advocating something more fundamental than the abolition of provisions and reservations, namely, the condemnation of the whole ecclesiastical system ; the repudiation of the Papacy ; the secularization of Church property. He stood forth as the representative of a new age and prepared the way for Wiclif, by preaching a genuine religious revival and a revolution in the fundamentals of the Medieval Church.[1] The movement he led was little seen at the time, but it was momentous, and would soon thrust into the background those petty politico-religious quarrels of the period.

The statutes of Richard II in 1390 and 1393 renewing and enlarging the laws of 1351 and 1353 completed the immediate political results of the Babylonian Captivity in England.[2] By the close of the fourteenth century the English Church had become virtually a state Church. It was like a house all completed but the roof, with the scaffolding not yet taken

[1] *Rotuli Parl.*, ii, 337, 339, 434.   [2] Makower, 46.

away. Wiclif and Henry VIII tore down the scaffolding and put on the roof. The real national Church, however, was completed in the fourteenth century as a result of the transfer of the Papacy to Avignon. In 1400 Froissart wrote : " England is the best ruled land in the world." [1] From Edward I to Richard II (1272–1399) the English Government asserted its rights and through strong laws and ordinances sought to restrict the Church to the limits laid down by the political science of the age. [2] The inevitable outcome of that policy under the existing conditions was an ecclesiastical organization dependent upon the English state.

50. *Attitude of Spain*

In Spain, Alfonso, King of Castile, made a show of resisting the Papal provisions, but he was more easily silenced than the King of England. [3] That monster of cruelty, Peter of Castile, was in constant conflict with the Papacy and in 1356 actually confiscated the property of certain cardinals in his kingdom and cared but little for the censures laid on him. [4] The Spanish rulers were too busy with their crusades against the Mohammedans and their own petty quarrels to give much attention to the shortcomings of the Avignon Papacy. [4]

51. *Hostility in Switzerland*

The free Swiss in 1370 by the Pfaffenbrief, or Priests' Law, put an end to the encroachments of ecclesiastical tribunals by declaring that no ban in cases of debts and other purely secular matters was to be endured. No priest was permitted to seek a foreign court, either ecclesiastical or temporal; otherwise he would be socially and economically outlawed. [5]

52. *The Neo-mysticism*

Another portentous result of this period, when scholastic theology was giving way to modern methods of thinking, when the Papacy at Avignon had attained its summit of secularization and materialization, when good men everywhere

---

[1] Haller, 464, 469.
[2] Makower, *Die Verfassung der Kirche von England*, Berlin, 1894, 13.
[3] Raynaldus, *Ann.*, 1344, No. 54 ; 1348, No. 14.
[4] Ib., 1356, No. 40 ; 1359, No. 2.
[5] Tschudi, *Schweitzer Chronic.*, i, 472 ; Müller, *Schweizergesch.*, ii, 287.

in Europe were denouncing the scandals in the Church and
crying for reformation, when the very foundations of the
Medieval Church were giving way under one bold onslaught
after another, and when the new age of inquiry and readjustment of social, religious, and political relations was gradually
coming in, was the appearance of the new type of mysticism.
It was both the outcome of and a reaction against the Middle
Ages, and it in turn helped to pave the way for the evangelical
ideals of the Reformation.   Its home was in Germany, where
the opposition to the worldliness of the Avignon Papacy was
most pronounced, and its connection with the medieval
period was shown by the fact that most of the mystics belonged
to the Dominican Order.   Strassburg and Cologne were the
centres of mystic activity, and the most conspicuous leaders
were : Meister Eckhart, John Tauler, Henry Suso, John
Ruysbroeck, and Geritt Groot, all of whom died between
1327 and 1384.   Their activity corresponds, therefore, with
the Babylonian Captivity.[1]

They stressed a conscious, personal, religious experience,
an intimate contact of the soul with God, a pure heart, and
a clean helpful life.   That was in sharp contrast to the emphasis
placed by the Church upon dependence on the ecclesiastical
machinery, rites, ceremonies, and sacraments of the priesthood for salvation.   There was no revolutionary effort to
discard the sacraments of the Church, or to dispute the
authority of the Church.   They simply preached a purer,
more helpful, religious experience within the Church—a life
of love and conversion from worldliness to spiritual values.
The new mysticism was a soul-saving oasis of piety and
devotion in an age of corruption and strife, and it had a burning
human sympathy for humanity in a life of toil and struggle.
Its appeal was made to the laity and clergy alike through
preaching, writing, godly living, charitable works, schools,
and emphasis laid on the New Testament.   To reach the masses
Latin was discarded and the propagandism was carried on
in the vernacular.

Eckhart, who died at Cologne in 1327, was a university-
trained man, who occupied responsible positions in the
Dominican order in Germany.   He was charged with heresy

---

[1] Cruel, *Geschichte der deutschen Predigt im Mittelalter*, Detmold, 1879,
pp. 370–438.

in 1325 on the ground that he was leading the people astray, and in 1329 John XXII announced that of the 26 articles against him 15 were heretical and the others were tinged with heresy. He was one of the most popular and original preachers of the age.[1] In his theological thinking, he was still somewhat under the influence for the scholastic methods.[2] While he did not preach justification by faith, at the same time he did not stress the medieval penitential system, and that fact may have given grounds for suspecting his orthodoxy. He himself had come into the joyous consciousness of a new religious life, hence we find him preaching to his age almost in the words of Luther. He was not professedly a reformer, and yet in spirit and influence he was potentially both a heretic and a revolutionist.

John Tauler,[3] whose life came to an end in Strassburg in 1361, was educated in Cologne and at Paris, and entered the Dominican Order in 1315. He admired Eckhart and was in close touch with the Friends of God. He laboured in Bavaria and Basel, but Strassburg was the chief scene of his activity. He was a plain, blunt, practical preacher, very popular with the masses. At the age of fifty he experienced a very remarkable spiritual exaltation, and from that time on spoke continually of the necessity of conversion by faith, and gave good works and the sacraments a subordinate place. He praised the dignity of honest labour. No charges of heresy were made against him. Luther read his sermons and as early as 1516 declared that he had found neither in Latin nor German a saner theology, or one more in harmony with the Gospel.[4] "Among the moderns," said Melanchton, "Tauler is easily the first." In the Protestant Church his sermons were more widely read than those of any other medieval preacher.

Henry Suso, who died at Ulm in 1366, was an emotional, poetical, Dominican, who had studied at Cologne and Strassburg. From his eighteenth year on he gave himself up to almost incredible ascetic practices, described in his famous Autobiography.[5] He spoke of Eckhart as his "high teacher"

---

[1] Pfeiffer, *Deutsche Mystiker*, 192 ; Büttner, *Echchortis Schriften*, 14.

[2] Deutsch, in Herzog, v, 15. Cf. Delacroix, *Mysticisme*, 277, for an opposite view.

[3] Winkworth, *The Hist. and Life of the Rev. John Tauler with 25 Sermons*, N.Y., 1858.

[4] Köstlin, *Life of Luther*, i, 117, 126. Cf. Preger, iii, 194 ; Schmidt, 160.

[5] Diepenbrock, *Suso*, 137–306.

and was closely associated with the Friends of God. He advocated in his writings an experimental theology based on God's love for man. He made no attack on the teachings of the Church.[1]

The Friends of God were a group of pietists scattered along the Rhine from Basel to the Netherlands, composed of laymen and priests, unorganized, who sought in the Bible a satisfaction for spiritual longings not found in the customary church services. They did not break with the Church, but observed its ordinances, and fought the heretical Beghards.[2] In 1377 one of them visited Gregory XI in Rome and begged him to purify Christendom.

John Ruysbroeck, who died in 1381, was a Belgian mystic who served as a priest until he was sixty and then entered the Augustinian monastery near Waterloo. He was not a popular preacher like Tauler, but gave himself up to religious contemplation and writing. He advocated ascetic practices and asserted that the soul found God "without an intermediary". Although he denounced heretics for their hostility to the rules and doctrines of the Church, yet he himself was accused of the heresy of pantheism.[3] He was closely allied in spirit with the Friends of God although not regarded as one of them.

Gerrit Groot (1340–84) was a Dutchman, educated at Paris. He taught at Cologne, was appointed a canon, and lived a worldly life, rich in benefices, until converted by a Carthusian prior, Kalkar, when he renounced his ecclesiastical livings, put himself into touch with Ruysbroek, and at the age of forty began to preach without ordination to throngs in Holland, clergy and laity alike. He denounced the simony and the loose morals of the clergy, incited people to a life of prayer, purity, and charity. In 1374 he gave the house he had inherited from his father as a home for widows and unmarried women, who, without being under a vow, devoted themselves to a secluded pious life, and to labour and charity. The Bishop of Utrecht forbade him to preach because he was a layman, so he gathered about him some young monks and began to copy manuscripts. Their earnings were put into a common fund and thus began about 1380 the

[1] Schaff has an excellent sketch of Suso, v, Pt. ii, p. 262.
[2] Preger, *Deutschen Mystik*, iii, 290–337.   [3] Engelhardt, *Ruysbroeck*, 265–97.

" Brothers of the Common Life ". Similar societies were soon organized in Holland and Germany. The brotherhood included laymen of all kinds and degrees, and priests. The members took no irrevocable vows but remained unmarried and renounced worldly possessions. They copied books, taught the young, and laboured with their hands. They represented a pronounced protest against both the scholasticism and the sacerdotalism of the age. They proved that a life of pure religious devotion was not monopolized by the old monastic orders, and that education and deeds of charity were no longer wholly in the hands of the clergy. They helped to prepare the way for the coming of the Reformation and some of them joined that new movement.[1] The rector was chosen by the community and was not necessarily a cleric. Members were obliged to earn their livelihood, for no begging was allowed. Patterned after the first house established by Groot at Deventer in the house of Florentius Radewyn in 1380, in rapid succession 40 more for men and 80 for women were founded. These houses occupied a sane middle position between the old monastic institutions and a free society. They were attacked by both monks and priests as Beghards, and the controversy was carried to the legal faculty of the university of Cologne, which gave a decision strongly in their favour. Thomas à Kempis lived from 1392 to 1399 in the original house at Deventer and left a beautiful description of the manner of life pursued.[2]

The Windesheim congregation was founded at Windesheim, 20 miles north of Deventer, in Holland in 1386 to give men a greater opportunity to cultivate religious ideals. The members became canons regular of the Augustinian Order, and spread rapidly over Netherlands, and North and Central Germany. In 1394 two more houses founded by the Brothers of the Common Life united with the Augustinian Order under the prior of Windesheim, and the next year Papal approbation of the arrangement was obtained. One of the most famous of these monasteries was that of St Agnes at Zevolle, where

---

[1] Kettlewell, *Thomas à Kempis and the Brothers of the Common Life*, N.Y., 1882 ; Lea, *Inquisition*, ii, 360 ; Uhlman, *Reformers before the Reformation* ; see Schulz in the *Realencyklopädie*, who shows that only one community joined the Lutheran movement.

[2] Kempis, *Lives of Groot and his Disciples*. Tr. by J. R. Arthur, *Founders of the New Devotion*, 1905 ; Kettlewell, *Thomas à Kempis and the Brothers of the Common Life*, 1882 ; Cruise, *Thomas à Kempis*, 1887 ; Herzog-Hauck.

Thomas à Kempis and Gansfort found peaceful retreat and congenial labour. Cloisters for women were also established with canonesses. Altogether these Augustinian establishments numbered more than 100, and they remained very closely connected with the houses of the Brothers of the Common Life until the middle of the fifteenth century. They led the way for the series of reforms undertaken by the monastic orders of Germany preceding the Reformation and had much to do with preparing the people for that great movement.

The Carthusians, "never reformed because they never deformed," preserved their earlier simplicity, purity, poverty, and spirituality from the days of St Bruno, their founder. During this period they assailed the prosperity and excessive wealth of the Church and their leaders were popular preachers all over Europe. They had a powerful influence in the reformation of the other monastic orders. The most widely known representative of the time was Henry Aeger Kalkar (1328–1408), who wrote works on rhetoric, music, and asceticism, and in his sermons attacked the worldliness and sins of the day. Hendrik von Coesfeld (d. 1410) wrote on monastic ideals, and Jacob Juterbogk and Dionysius Richel were other prominent members of this order.

Among new organizations of this period were the Alexians, a union of lay brothers, on the basis of voluntary poverty, begun in Netherlands in the fourteenth century, who cared for the poor, visited those in prison, succoured and nursed the sick, buried the dead and cared for the graves. Female societies were also formed. Members wore a black monkish dress, so the women were called the "black sisters". They spread over Netherlands, and Western and Central Germany and in their ministrations replaced the regular monks who had come into considerable disrepute. Consequently the monks and priests attempted to discredit them and denounced them as vagabonds parading under the false guise of spiritual helpers. An effort was also made to stigmatize them as heretical Beghards. Hence the bulls of Gregory XI and Boniface IX against the Beghards were frequently enforced against the Alexians, although the city magistrates sought to protect them. They were also called Cellites, from dwelling in cells, Matemans, Lollards, and in Germany Nöllbruder.

The Jeromites started as four independent cloisters in

Spain and Italy and spread to other lands. They were dedicated to learning and the dissemination of knowledge. The order was recognized by Gregory XI in 1374 and at the thousandth anniversary of St Jerome they came into considerable prominence.

The Jesuits were a lay brotherhood founded by a pious merchant of Siena named Colombini, who died in 1367, the year in which Urban V approved the order. The members served the poor, cared for the sick, and preached repentance. The name was given to them as a term of derision because they promised to begin every call to repentance with the name of Jesus. They adopted the Augustinian rule, and had a female branch.[1]   The Birgittians, named after St Birgitta, of Sweden, were founded at Vodstena with 70 monks, 60 nuns, 13 priests and 4 deacons for the purpose of conducting popular preaching and encouraging the people in industry, agriculture, and other lines.   In 1379 Urban VI approved of the order.

The significance of these Orders lies in the fact that, first most of them were lay societies; secondly, that they were pledged to assist the common people in ways neglected by the Church; and, thirdly, that they promulgated a higher conception of spiritual life than inculcated by the ordinary priest or monk. Their life was also a protest against the evil influences of wealth and lucrative benefice in the Church. The very evident approbation given by the people and the Pope shows that the clergy were neglecting both their duty and their opportunity.

"Where the feet of generations passed the oftenest traces of their forerunners were easiest lost."[2] It is not always a simple task to reconstruct the life and ideas of a man of the fourteenth century, but the career of Richard Rolle of Hampole, England, is fairly clear. He attended Oxford University where he gave himself up to religious rather than scholastic studies. At the age of 19 he returned to his father's house where he improvised a hermit's garb, and set out in the world to lead a contemplative life. He explained with great definiteness how he passed through the preliminary stages of purification and illumination, which took three years, when his eyes were opened to the divine vision. He belonged to no order and conformed to no rule. He wandered about,

---

[1] Mansi, iv, 566.   [2] *Camb. Mod. Lit.*, ii, 42.

staying wherever he found friends or sympathisers. He desired to found an order for hermits, but met with opposition, and had to be content to see many recluses follow his example in north England. At length he settled down as a hermit, advised with those who came to see him and began to write songs and tracts, through which he exercised the greatest influence. He died in 1349 at Hampole, and it was reported that many miracles were wrought at his shrine.

At Oxford a rule of Grosseteste devoted the first morning lecture to the Bible, which had come to furnish the material for most of the theological teaching. Rolle, in this way, became profoundly interested in the Bible, and based his religious experiences upon its inspiration. By exalting the spiritual side of religion over the forms, by his enthusiastic celebration of the love of Christ, and by his assertion of the individualistic principle, he had a great influence on his own, and the next, generation. He represented the best side of those influences which produced the Lollard movement, but he was a faithful son of the Church and would have repudiated the political activity of Lollardism. He spoke his mind freely about the evils of his day and in *The Pricke of Conscience*, a popular summary in 9,624 lines, he covered the whole range of medieval theology, condemned the evils of individual licence, opposed the misuse of riches, denounced the vices and worldliness of the day in a very practical way, and flayed the social life about him. He made free use of the Bible and the Church Fathers. He did much and said much to strengthen the crude democracy of his time. His reform ideas were sane and moderate, and were written in both English and Latin. No doubt he deserves some of the fame later attributed to Wiclif for it was said that the " evil men of Lollardy " tampered with his writings to quote him in their own support.[1]

The historical significance of this new mysticism lies in the fact that it held up before Europe a higher type of a practical, personal Christianity than was either taught or practised at Avignon and generally throughout the Church ; that it taught salvation by faith and a pure life without openly seeking to overthrow sacerdotalism ; and that it produced within the

---

[1] Eng. Text Soc., 1896, gives his English writings : Morley, *Eng. Writers* iv, 263–9; Kribel, *Eng. Studien.* viii; Horstmann, *Yorkshire Writers* ; Morris, *Pricke of Conscience*, 1863.

Church, without making any objectionable attack on the Church, a genuine spiritual revival and reformation, which would either win over the Church to a realization of the necessity of such a change generally, or would help to produce the disruption which came two centuries later. One must have a short vision who cannot see the connection between this fourteenth century movement and the Protestant Revolt.

53. *Heretical Sects*

The fourteenth century was a period of considerable spiritual unrest. The Church was kept busy dealing with the Beghards and Beguins, who originated in the preceding century, the Brethren of the Free Spirit, the Fratricelli, the Flagellants and the Waldenses. Luciferans were burnt in Passau and Salzburg in 1312, 1315, and 1338.[1] The Beghards, notwithstanding accusations of heresy and prohibitions, seem to have increased throughout the Babylonian Captivity. By 1400 scarcely a German town existed without its beguinage. In 1368 Erfurt had 400 Beghards. They had spread to Holland, France, Italy, and England, or at least were confused with other similar organizations.[2] The synods of Treves and Mainz in 1310 forbade clerics from entering beguinages and Beghards from explaining the Bible to the ignorant.[3] In 1312 the Council of Vienne accused them of heresy, and prohibited their communal life.[4] In the latter part of the fourteenth century, the Inquisition destroyed many houses in Germany and appropriated their property. Gregory XI in 1377 admitted, however, that many of the Beghards were leading worthy lives and Boniface IX in 1394 recognized those who were devoted to godly lives of voluntary poverty.[5] These sectaries without doubt greatly influenced the mystics and Brethren of the Common Lot.

The Brethren of the Free Spirit, at times confused with the Beghards and Beguins, were infected with pantheistic ideas, free thought, and libertinism. Margaret of Porete was burnt for heresy in 1310 at Paris. The Men of Reason at Brussels were charged with errors.[6] The Fratricelli were active in Germany, France, Holland, Italy, and Spain. They

---

[1] Döllinger, *Sectengeschichte*, i, 174; Alphandéry, *Hétérodoxes Latins*.
[2] Haupt, in Herzog, ii, 519.
[3] Hefele, vi, 490, 500.　　　　[4] Ib., 543, 544.
[5] Döllinger, ii, 381–3.　　　　[6] Fredericq, *Inquisitie*, i, 267–79.

defied Papal edicts, so bull after bull condemned them to harsh
punishments.   The Inquisition ran them to earth, and burnt
them.   The Flagellants covered Europe in one wave of
religious fervour after another in 1333, 1349, and 1399.   In
1333 an eloquent Dominican led 10,000 of them to Rome.
In 1349 they appeared in nearly all parts of western Christendom, and even bishops, princes, and women joined them.
In 1317 there were 30 houses in Strassburg, and from 1300
to 1400 over 70, some of them aristocratic private houses.
They were filled with the unmarried daughters from 6 to 24.
Eckhart often preached to them.[1] Clement VI pronounced
their movement as a work of the devil,[2] after a mob of 2,000
of them had visited him in 1349, and called upon the bishops
and the civil rulers to assist in suppressing them.   Kings,
cities and the higher prelates sought to stamp out the religious
outbreaks which grew out of a craving which the Church of
the day could not satisfy and which included mostly the laity
imbued by a strong religious and ethical purpose.

54. *Public Opinion*

One of the most significant results of the Babylonian exile
and the assumption of a harsh imperialism and an unprecedentedly corrupt fiscal system, was to arouse against
the Papal hierarchy public opinion throughout Europe—a
force that had once been the staunchest ally.   In the conflict
with Lewis the Bavarian, the people for the most part sided
with the Emperor ; in England the people upheld the independence of the Church and State ; in Italy the people
joined their rulers in resisting Papal demands ; and in short
wherever the state came into open controversy with Papal
exactions and prerogatives the people showed themselves to
be hostile rather than friendly.   Everywhere the people
denounced the prevalent evils, corruptions, and abuses of
the clergy in general, and sympathized with every demand
for reform.   This popular attitude continued until the
sixteenth century, when, largely through its support, the
Protestant Revolt became successful in compelling a reformation and reorganization of the Church.   It must be borne
in mind, however, that although public opinion did not hesitate
to criticize severely the Pope and the clergy, there was little

<hr />

[1] Kothe, 52.   [2] Schaff, v, ii, 506.

thought among the masses of either disloyalty or revolution, because they believed in the Church and needed its services. " No good Catholic Christian doubted that in spiritual things the clergy were the divinely appointed superiors of the laity, that this power proceeded from the rights of the priests to celebrate the sacraments, that the Pope was the real possessor of this power and was far superior to all secular authority." [1] The dogma was universally accepted that salvation could come only through the mediation of the priesthood.

55. *General Effects of the Babylonian Captivity*

At the beginning of the thirteenth century the cardinals had possessed the right, as a closed corporation, to elect the Pope. The Babylonian Captivity permitted a secular ruler to interfere and partially dictate the election. As a result of the exile, the setback of Papal absolutism, both externally and internally, decreased the power of the cardinals and led them to seek to develop an oligarchical government of the Church. They were extremely jealous of their prerogatives and always insisted upon their share of the income of the Papal court. Popes Celestine V, Clement V, and John XXII gave them half of the income, but as a rule they seldom received their full portion.[2]

The effects of the Babylonian Captivity may be summed up as follows :—

1. It supplied both the opportunity and the occasion to the keenest thinkers of Europe—English, German, and Italians particularly—to make an attack upon first the abuses and corruptions in the Church ; secondly, upon the Pope's claim to temporal authority and to his financial system ; and, thirdly, upon the spiritual authority of the whole Roman hierarchy.

2. It alienated the obedience and support of the various states of Europe, like England, Germany, and Italy ; drove them to take measures to ensure their independence of Papal interference by organizing national states hostile to the Papal monarchy. Even France, so closely allied with the Avignon Popes, refused to surrender a whit of its claim to national sovereignty. The resulting aspirations towards political

---

[1] Harnack, *Hist. of Dogma*, vi, 132 n. [2] Souchon, i, 2–4.

nationality in Germany and Italy, and the actual development of national states in England, France, and Spain,
threatened the creation of national Churches and two centuries
later succeeded in accomplishing this in northern Europe.

3.   It called forth a discussion everywhere of the fundamentals
on which the Medieval Church rested, of the divine character
of the sacraments and the priesthood, and of the validity
of the rites and practices of the Church.   This in turn led to
heresy and disbelief resulting in the rise in various parts of
Europe, of dangerous and troublesome sects which multiplied
as the years passed by and paved the way for the Protestant
sects two centuries later.

4.   It produced a cry for reformation from one end of Europe
to another from scholars, priests, and laity that became more
insistent and bolder as the time ran on until the Church
attempted to do something officially in the great reform
councils and failing had to see the schism of the Reformation.

5.   It aroused public opinion to the point where it could never
again be content to accept medieval theology in its entirety,
or to conform unanimously without protest to the exactions
of the medieval hierarchy.   A new and conscious democracy
had been born, feeble and timid it is true, which attempted
to democratize the Church by putting sovereign power in
the hands of a general, representative council and by restoring
episcopal independence.

6.   Finally no one can fail to see that forces, old and new,
positive and negative, were at work to bring about the decline
of the Medieval Church.

In the atmosphere—in the hearts and heads of Western
Europe—was brewing a conflict that could not be suppressed.
It was the clash between medievalism and modernism—between
a system which stood for universal absolutism and ignored
or suppressed the individual, on the one hand, and a system
which sought by every possible means to develop to the utmost
the latent possibilities within every individual on the other.
Medievalism was represented by the Papal system, the empire,
scholasticism, and asceticism.   Modernism sought to democratize
the Church ; to replace the world-empire by the national
state ; to dispel scholasticism with a rational system of thought
and knowledge based on experience, experimentation, and
natural science ; to drive out the ascetic view of life and culture

by a normal conception of man's rights and duties. The fourteenth century was something more than a period of unfortunate transactions and happenings in Church and State ; it was a period of positive progress in many directions, intellectual, political, religious, social and economic, and contained within itself the germs of our own age.

PART II

THE GREAT WESTERN SCHISM

CHAPTER VII

The Great Western Schism

56. *Causes of the Schism*

THE Great Western Schism is the name given to the period of ecclesiastical history from 1378 to 1417—an epoch of nearly forty years—during which there was a serious disagreement in Western Europe about the true headship of the Church. For thirty-two years there were two rival claimants to the Papal throne—one at Rome, the other at Avignon—each one claiming to be the divinely appointed and constitutionally chosen successor of St Peter ; each with his own college of cardinals and extensive Papal court ; each with loyal supporters among the states and peoples of Europe ; each sending his appointees to every vacant office in the Church ; each attempting to raise large sums of money from all Christendom to meet his heavy expenses ; and each fulminating bulls against the other as usurper and anti-Christ with all the harsh epithets found in the rich ecclesiastical dictionary of that day. Then, to make matters still worse, the Council of Pisa in 1409, with praiseworthy motives but questionable foresight, succeeded in adding a third aspirant to the headship of the Church, so that during the last eight years of the schism, the misunderstanding was further complicated by three claimants to the triple crown.

During this period of conflicting claims, demoralizing disputations, and uncertainties, the Church was vainly seeking its true head. The situation was further complicated by medieval politics, aroused passions, and the greatest forms of selfishness. The conflict of rival ambitions and the novelty of the situation rendered a frank understanding and unanimity of action impossible. Salembier says, with truth, that this was not in reality a schism, since there was no culpable revolt against Papal authority in general and no scorn of the sovereign power of St Peter. No one wished to separate from the head of the Church as in the Protestant revolt ; in fact, all were

seeking unity. Hence the so-called schism was in reality
" a deplorable misunderstanding concerning a question of
fact "—in other words a most unfortunate historical complica-
tion founded on ignorance and selfishness that was not settled

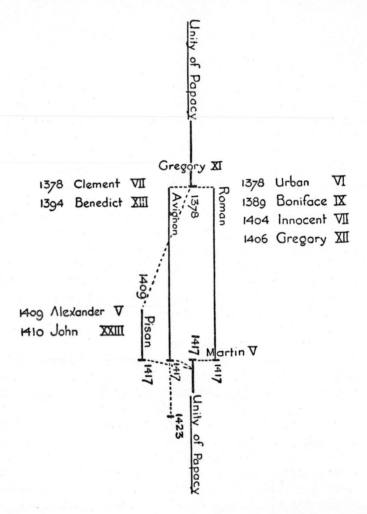

for forty years, because of the state of perplexity existing among
cardinals, bishops, theologians, canonists, and princes.[1]

The above diagram and the following lists will show the

---

[1] *Cath. Encyc.*, xiii, 539.

rival lines of Popes until Martin V, elected in 1417, was
recognized as the universal head of the Roman Church.

Roman.	Avignon.	Pisan.
1378 Urban VI	1378 Clement VII	
1389 Boniface IX		
	1394 Benedict XIII	
	Deposed at Pisa, 1409	
	Deserted by his cardinals, 1415	
1404 Innocent VII	Deposed at Constance, 1417	
1406 Gregory XII	Died 1423	
Deposed at Pisa, 1409		
Resigned at Constance, 1415		1409 Alexander V
Died 1417		1410 John XXIII
		Deposed at Constance, 1415

Martin V
Elected at Constance, 1417
Generally recognized as Pope.

The causes which produced this deplorable breach in the
unity of Western Christendom are neither obscure nor difficult
to understand, and may be summarized as follows :—

1. The fundamental cause was the Babylonian Captivity
and its unfortunate results. During that period of seventy
years the French party was dominant in the Roman Church.
All the Popes had been French, the cardinals and the higher
clergy in the Papal court had been predominantly Gallican,
and the entire ecclesiastical polity had consciously and
unconsciously coincided with the interests and ambitions of
the French monarchy. Consequently the French party in
the Church, supported by the French Government, was
determined to retain their supremacy even at the risk of
a schism, which they believed could in some way be adjusted
to their advantage.

2. Italian sentiment and the power of the Roman mob
constituted no small factor in creating and in continuing
the schism. The Eternal City was the acknowledged historical
capital of the Roman Church. The Romans in 1378 were so
determined to have a Roman, or at least an Italian Pope,
that their zeal ran away with their discretion and thus supplied
an excuse for the assertion that the election of Urban VI was
the result of threats and force.

3. The occasion and immediate cause of the schism was
the irritating personality of Urban VI himself and his well-

meaning but short-sighted policy. Had he either yielded to or compromised with the French party the schism would not have occurred. Had he even been more politic, more tactful, more polite and more considerate of the prerogatives of the aristocratic cardinals, or had he possessed the wisdom and diplomacy with which to deal with men in public affairs, the schism might have been averted. Upon Urban VI, therefore, must rest the blame as the provocative cause of a condition of ecclesiastical disturbance in Latin Christendom much more disastrous in its results than the Babylonian Captivity.

4. Another cause, which has been commonly overlooked, was the inevitable conflict bound to come between the strong absolutism of the Papal rule, on the one hand, and the growing oligarchical tendencies in the college of cardinals, on the other. Even before the Babylonian Captivity signs of this significant revolution were not lacking ; and during that exile adequate proof of the intentions of the cardinals appeared in both the literature and in the transactions of the Papal curia. It grew primarily out of a conflict of incompatible interests, which were concerned with finance, patronage, and administration.[1]

Since Urban VI played such a leading rôle in inaugurating the Great Schism, careful consideration must be given to his character, the circumstances attending his election as Pope, and his acts afterwards. Gregory XI had re-established the Papacy in Rome in 1377[2] to the great joy of all the Italians, and especially of the Romans, but contrary to the wish of the French. Seeing that confusion was likely to follow his death, he sought in consequence to avert such a catastrophe, particularly a disputed election, by decreeing only eight days before his death that any election, whenever and where-ever held, would be valid.[3] Consequently, the rule that the conclave should be held in the place where the Pope died was thus set aside, apparently to the intended advantage of the French party. That Gregory XI died in Rome on 27th March, 1378, was an accident, for had he lived he intended to return to Avignon.

The choice of a successor to Gregory XI was a serious question. Whether Rome or Avignon would continue to be

---

[1] Souchon, i, 5.   [2] Raynaldus, *Annales Eccles.*, 1378, No. 2.
[3] Mirbt, *La politique pontificale et le retour du Saint-Siège à Rome en* 1376, Paris, 1899.

the Papal residence depended upon the result of the election. The French party had every reason to expect the selection of a French Pontiff, who would return to Avignon, or at least would rule in their interest at Rome. The Romans and Italians, on the contrary, whose interests and rights had been so long neglected, were determined to have a Roman Pope, or at least an Italian, who would not remove the seat of the Papacy to the banks of the Rhone. The days immediately following the death of Gregory XI, therefore, were full of nervous excitement. No sooner had the spirit departed from the body of the dead Pontiff than the Roman municipal officials appeared before the cardinals with a petition that a Pope should be chosen who would remain in Rome, the seat of St Peter and his successors for so many centuries. The Babylonian Captivity, they said, had left Rome in a pitiable condition—in ruins and deprived of her glory. God had at last brought the Pope back to Rome and when he thought of returning to Avignon had taken his life. The cardinals were begged to give some promise favourable to the Eternal City before going into conclave, for, if they did not, the officials said they could not answer for the peace of the city. The cardinals gave no direct reply, as of course they could not, but assured the officials that they would endeavour to select the best man for the welfare of the Catholic Church. At the same time they requested that the crowds of peasants be sent home and that the great square of St Peter's be kept free, otherwise they threatened to leave Rome.[1]

On April 7, 1378, ten days after Gregory's demise, the conclave met in the Vatican.[2] It was composed of 16 cardinals —11 French, 4 Italian, of whom 2 were Romans, and 1 Spaniard.[3] The French party had a large majority and could easily have chosen their candidate had they not been divided into two hostile groups. The 6 Limousin cardinals united to elect one of their number Pope [4]; but the other 5 French cardinals and the 4 Italians were determined not to choose a Limousin cardinal as Pope. The Spanish cardinal apparently

---

[1] Gayet, ii, 4 ; Jahr, *Die Wahl Urbans VI*, 1378 ; Halle, 1892, 24.

[2] Six French Cardinals were still in Avignon caring for ecclesiastical affairs, and one cardinal was absent on a mission to Florence.

[3] Jahr, 5–18, has an excellent brief survey of the sources covering this election.

[4] This was the faction to which Gregory XI and his predecessor belonged.

was not committed. Rome was full of wily politicians and wire-pullers, both ecclesiastical and lay. The customary practice of walling up the doors giving admission to the conclave chamber was dispensed with, but the cardinals were locked in after a long delay and considerable trouble. Soldiers filled the room below the chamber in which the cardinals met and even thrust their spears through the floor above them. The city gates were closed and guarded in order to prevent the cardinals from fleeing. A Roman mob surrounded the Vatican, broke into the Papal wine cellar and increased their boisterous patriotism with its liquid contents, rang the bell of St Peter's, and yelled, " A Roman, a Roman, or at least an Italian for Pope." Late in the night, when the cardinals were attempting to get a little rest, the city officials called on the cardinals and begged some assurance that a Roman, if possible, or at least an Italian, would be chosen Pope, but received nothing except a merited rebuke. The two Roman cardinals were Tebaldeschi, an old man, and Giacomo Orsini, the youngest member of the college, who was eager for election to the high honour. One of these the mob wanted for Pope and loudly declared their preference. There is no doubt that the Romans endeavoured to influence the decision of the cardinals. Whether this attempt actually did rob the cardinals of the necessary freedom of mind requisite to make the election valid is the question on which the legitimacy of the Roman, or the Avignon line of Popes, rests.[1]

On 8th April, at eight o'clock in the morning, the voting began in the chapel with the mob still shouting " Give us a Roman ". It was soon apparent that neither a Frenchman nor a Roman could be elected. Consequently, no doubt with some consideration for the demands of the mob outside, the cardinals accepted the lesser evil and compromised on a Neapolitan, the Archbishop of Bari, who was supposed to have French tendencies.[2] He was a subject of the Countess of Provence, the ruler of Naples, and therefore, was a sort of a Frenchman, who, it was believed, might be induced to go to Avignon while at the same time his election would placate the Romans. His name had been mentioned from the

[1] For an account in English favourable to the French cardinals see Froissart, *Chronicles*, ch. 326–7 ; partly quoted in Robinson, *Readings*, i, 506.
[2] He had spent considerable time at Avignon, and was well known to the cardinals ; Scheuffgen, 3.

first as a possibility, although he was not a member of the sacred college. At this time he was the temporary vice-chancellor of the Roman Church, and was regarded as the enemy of vice, simony, and extravagant display.[1] He had bought a home in Rome in order to qualify as a Roman citizen.[2] In the conclave little was said against him, which is pretty good evidence that the French cardinals were favourable to his appointment under the exceptional circumstances. Müller contends that his election was a foregone conclusion and generally recognized as such, before the cardinals entered into conclave.[3]

While the cardinals were waiting for the arrival and consent of the Pope-elect, the mob outside grew impatient and threatening. To quiet them the youthful Roman cardinal, Orsini, intending to send them into St Peter's to await the announcement of the election, shouted to them out of a window "Go to St Peter's!" The mob misunderstood and thought that the aged Roman cardinal of St Peter's, Tebaldeschi, had been chosen Pope. Hence, wild with joy, they rushed off to loot his palace, as was customary when a cardinal was elevated to the Papacy, and then broke into the room of the conclave, seized the gouty old cardinal of St Peter's, seated him on a stool, placed a white mitre on his head, threw a red cloak about his shoulders, and for several hours bowed before him, and kissed his hand before he could convince them that he was not the new Pope.[4]

Meanwhile, in the tumult and confusion the cardinals fled—some within the walls of Castle St Angelo, and four beyond the walls of Rome. Only five dared to remain in their own palaces. As the cardinals were fleeing, the real Pope-elect arrived to find himself deserted by all but the old cardinal of St Peter's. The next day, however, all the cardinals except those who had escaped from Rome, recovered their self-possession sufficiently to reconvene when one of them in the customary manner proclaimed from the window: "I announce to you a great joy. You have a Pope and he calls himself Urban VI." During the next few days all the cardinals offered the new Pontiff their respectful homage

---

[1] Niem, i, 1.   [2] Scheuffgen, 47.   [3] Müller, ii, 49.
[4] For the so-called second election after dinner on the 8th, see Gayet, 1, 357 ; Valais, i, 49 ; Bliemetzrieder, 57.

and asked and received of him many favours.[1] Then they adored him, and enthroned him first at the Vatican and later at the Lateran.[2] On 10th April he was escorted to St Peter's, where he conducted mass accompanied by the cardinals.

He held consistories three times a week and with the consent of the cardinals granted provisions and conducted the affairs of the Church.[3] Finally they solemnly crowned him on 18th April in front of St Peter's, Cardinal Orsini performing the ceremony and placing the Papal crown on his head. On the following day they officially notified their six colleagues at Avignon of Urban's accession in these words: " Since important matters are often misrepresented through false reports, we notify you that freely and uncontrolled we chose the Archbishop of Bari to succeed Gregory." [4] The Avignon cardinals recognized the new Pontiff and sent him their congratulations.[5] The Roman cardinals then sent the information to the head of the Empire and to other Catholic sovereigns. Cardinal Robert of Geneva, later Clement VII of Avignon, wrote the news to his relative, the King of France, and also to the Count of Flanders. Cardinal Pedro de Luna of Aragon, the future Benedict XIII, sent similar intelligence to several Spanish bishops. Urban VI for his part notified all the rulers of Europe of his election ; and entered immediately upon his duties as Pope, aided in all ways by the cardinals. On them and others he bestowed bishoprics and benefices without a sign of dissatisfaction. Up to this point, therefore, there was not a single objection, hesitation or dissatisfaction with the election of Urban VI, and it seems clear that his selection had been due solely to the division in the sacred college and not to either his own electioneering or to terror of the mob.[6] The adoration and enthroning of Urban VI were performed in an irregular manner and gave the cardinals some excuse for contesting the validity of the election.[7]

[1] Scheuffgen, 4 ; Souchon, ii, 6. He granted them the customary patronage of the " rotuli ".
[2] Valois, i, 43 ff.   [3] Souchon, i, 8.   [4] Bulaeus, iv, 465.
[5] The guardian of the Castle of St Angelo had received the strictest orders not to give up the key to the new Pope until the consent of the six cardinals at Avignon had been received. They ordered the keys to be placed in Urban's hands. Raynaldus, ann. 1378, No. 24 ; Baluzius, *Vitae*, ii, 813. Cf. Pastor, i, 1, pp. 681–3.
[6] Jahr, 5.
[7] Burger, ii, 201. Cardinal Flanders' account of the election of Urban VI is given in German in Souchon, i, 10 ff.

Within a few months, however, there was a pronounced change in the attitude of the cardinals toward their new creation. Either Urban's true character was in reality unknown when he was elevated to the supreme office in the Church, or else his character underwent a profound change after his election. As Pope at that critical time he had an opportunity such as fell to the lot of but few of the successors of St Peter, namely, to establish permanently the Papacy in its ancient seat, to recover the loyalty of united Latin Christendom, to end the great eastern schism, and to purify and spiritualize the Church. The role was too much for Urban VI ; a Hildebrand or an Innocent III alone could fill it ; and in consequence Urban made a miserable failure of it.

Urban VI was 60 years of age when made Pope, having been born in Naples in 1318. He was a university man and bore the title of doctor of canon law. He had early gone to Avignon to seek his fortune, as was the custom, and was there about ten years.[1] At the age of 46 he was made bishop, and in 1377, just a year before his election, he was translated to the Archbishopric of Bari by Gregory XI and placed in charge of the Papal chancery, a position of honour and importance. He bore the reputation of a strict disciplinarian, of severity in morals, and of pronounced hostility to simony. He was reputed to be a scholar in law and theology.[2] It was reported that he wore a hair shirt and retired at night with the Bible in his hands. Such a pedantic puritan and reformer with the necessary supplementary qualifications, might have left a great name behind him. His elevation to the See of St Peter evidently turned his head and brought out all that was sinister in the man. The picture one gets of him as Pope is that of a short, stout, swarthy, obstinate, arrogant, stiff-necked, hot-blooded, bigoted old man without tact or prudence, lacking in even the common courtesies of life, and entirely too prone to give his ear to obsequious flatteries. He showed himself whimsical, haughty, suspicious, supercritical, and at times choleric in his dealings with those about him. He was wholly wanting in good common-sense and could act, when he pleased, and that was often, with the ferocity of a barbarian. By nature he was dull and had no clear perception of his own interests, to say nothing of the interests of the great

---

[1] Souchon, i, 32.   [2] Niem, *De Schism.*, lib. 1, c. 1.

S

organization over which he presided. He possessed the talent of displeasing everybody.[1] Dietrich von Niem, his secretary of briefs, said : " There was in this man a hard and restless nature, no humanity, no conciliation of disposition. He was contumacious, threatening, rough, more willing to be shunned and to be feared than to be loved." Catherine of Siena advised him as a friend : " Mitigate a little, for the love of Christ, these sudden impulses. You have a great heart, but these hasty passions are the plague of your soul." Had he acted firmly but graciously, as became his high office, and had he quietly appointed the best men in the Church as cardinals to offset the predominant influence of the French party, he could easily have avoided the schism.[2] Urban VI was not wholly free from nepotism. At least five, and possibly eleven of his 52 cardinals appointed, were known to be his relatives. Some of them were only 21, 22, and 25 years old. His new cardinals were given 50 per cent of the *census*.[3]

From the outset of his pontificate he absolutely refused even to entertain the idea of returning to Avignon and thereby offended and reunited the French party. A wise, sane, tactful policy would soon have converted this decision into genuine strength by the creation of a powerful Roman party to offset the French faction. He did threaten to increase the Italian cardinals so as to deprive the French cardinals of their majority, but his manner of doing it was offensive to both Italians and French.[4] In his undiplomatic zeal for reformation he estranged and insulted the cardinals. He publicly reprimanded them for their worldliness and for living away from their episcopal sees. He forbade pluralism and simony among them. He charged the nuncios in the consistory with taking bribes. The cardinal of St Marcello hotly replied : " Since you are Pope, I cannot answer you, but if you were still the little Archbishop of Bari, I would tell you that you lied." He called the noble-born Cardinal Orsini a fool, and commonly addressed the cardinals with such phrases as " Shut up " and " Stop your gabbling." [5] He scolded them for their vices and even sought to limit their food and drink. He ordered that their

[1] Krüger, ii, 201.
[2] Scheuffgen, *Beiträge zur der Gesch. des grossen Schismas*, 3.
[3] Souchon, i, 26, 29.
[4] Muratori, iii, ii, 724 ff. The French cardinals sought to have relatives promoted to the college. Baluze, i, 834.
[5] Bulaeus, iv, 503 ff.

customary share of the *servitia* should be used for the restoration of their titular churches.[1] He forbade their acceptance of pensions, provisions, gifts of money, and other favours on the ground that the ecclesiastical interests were thereby injured.[2]

As a result of Urban's decision to stay at Rome, of his over-zealous reformatory endeavours, and of the personal indignities heaped upon the cardinals, there was aroused a strong opposition in the college of cardinals among both Italians and French. Those haughty, aristocratic princes of the Church were not slow to express their anger at the low-born indiscreet Pontiff, who seemed to be determined to be master and not servant. Incensed at the attack made upon their personal habits, upon their official prerogatives and perquisites, and disappointed in their expectation of a return of the Papacy to Avignon, the French cardinals, by 24th June, had all gone,[3] one by one, on leave to the Papal summer resort of Anagni on the specious plea that Rome was too hot and unhealthy. They invited the Pope to join them there but he refused, and went instead on 26th June to Tivoli with the Italian cardinals, but they soon deserted him with the exception of the venerable Cardinal of St Peter's, who soon died.[4] No Pontiff was ever left more completely alone.

In July the cardinals removed to Fondi, in Neapolitan territory, under the protection of Queen Joanna of Naples, and a guard of 200 Gascons.[5] Meanwhile they secretly plotted the Pope's deposition and wrote letters to eminent jurists to secure opinions on the illegal and forced election of Urban, but they received cold responses because the general opinion was that the choice had been perfectly canonical. Two trusty prelates were secretly sent on 15th July to France to explain to the king the plan of the French cardinals.[6] The determined purpose of the French party was no longer in doubt [7] : they demanded the resignation of Urban VI. On 2nd August the

---

[1] Baluze, *Vitae*, i, 998. [2] Bulaeus, iv, 508.

[3] Souchon, i, 9, says that 12 French and 1 Spanish cardinals went to Anagni. All of them but three were university men. Six were doctors of law, and one was a doctor of theology.

[4] In his will he strongly asserted the legality of Urban's election.

[5] Scheuffgen, 5.

[6] Denifle, *Chartul*, iii, No. 1610 ; Bliemetzrieder, 33.

[7] Bliemetzrieder, 32. As early as 24th April, 1378, a cardinal had written to the French king declaring the election of Urban VI invalid. Scheuffgen, 9.

13 ultramontane cardinals issued a manifesto [1] which denounced him as an apostate ; asserted that his election was void because forced by the Roman mob ; and anathematized him as " anti-Christ, devil, apostate, tyrant, deceiver, elected-by-force " and other ugly epithets in the rich and expressive vocabulary of that day. [2]   On 15th July messengers were sent to France announcing the election of Urban VI ; on 27th July an account of the tumult in Rome was sent ; by 21st August the dissenting cardinals wrote of the " invasion " of Urban VI ; and on 7th September the Archbishop Peter wrote to the University of Paris that the Papal throne was vacant. [3]   The Italian cardinals at first suggested a general council to settle the dispute, but soon acquiesced in the French programme. [4]

The reasons set forth by the cardinals for their action were :—

1.   That when they voted for Urban VI they were in fear of their lives from the Roman mob ; and hence the election being under restraint, was invalid according to the canon law. Constraint had invalidated the election of Paschal because of concessions made to Henry V.

2.   That they had fully intended to elect one of their own number but the tumult in Rome became so violent that in self-protection they precipitately chose the Archbishop of Bari and then were forced to flee from Rome to save their lives.

3.   That the individual testimony of the cardinals corroborated these facts and had been freely made.

4.   That as princes of the Church they had power to depose as well as to elect a Pope ; consequently they merely exercised a constitutional prerogative in acting as they did.   Had not the sacred college received the abdication of Celestine and elected his successor while still living ?

The historical fact seems to be, however, that the cardinals were guilty of a cowardly act, prompted by the fear of the loss of their power and the curtailment of their luxurious living, and not by their love for the higher interests of the Church. Thomas d'Acerno, a contemporary, gives these reasons for their procedure :—

[1] The document is given in Hefele, vi, 730–34 ; Baluze, i, 468 ;   Thatcher and McNeal, No. 167.

[2] The six Avignon cardinals approved of the act in Nov., 1378. Baluze, i, 852.

[3] Denifle, *Chartul*, iii, 555, 556.

[4] Souchon, i, 14.

1. The Pope's determination to invade their personal liberties by a reduction of high living in the college, and particularly in forbidding their expensive food and drink.

2. The rigid prohibition of their pet sin, simony.

3. The threat to offset their influence by creating Italian cardinals.

4. The insulting and abusive language hurled at the cardinals.

5. Urban's refusal to go to Avignon and his determination to remain in Rome.

No one can doubt that these reforms were sadly needed, and Urban deserves only praise for daring to attempt to enforce them. His coarse words and tactless acts were regrettable, to be sure, but constituted no excuse for the vindictive course of the cardinals. Self-interest, and the knowledge that the King of France and the Queen of Naples would back them up, alone guided them in their unwarrantable action. To them, therefore, must be charged the Great Schism in the Western Church with all its dire consequences.

Urban VI, deserted by his rebellious cardinals, who demanded his resignation of the Papal office, felt himself put on the defensive and answered the cardinals with a document called the *Factum* in which he vindicated the validity and constitutionality of his election. He went back to Rome alone to uphold his rights. He possessed no genius for intrigue, and revealed the poorest judgment in advancing his own interests. For instance the Queen of Naples at first recognized Urban, and apparently was anxious to aid him, but she was alienated from him by his haughty demeanour and hostility to her wishes.[1] It is difficult to understand why he did not use the thunderbolts of his office to defeat his adversaries, and why he did not at once surround himself with a new college of sympathetic cardinals to uphold his claims. One can only think that it was due to his short-sightedness, to his deplorable lack of wisdom, and to his ignorance of good ecclesiastical politics. It was not until 18th September that he appointed 29 new cardinals.[2] He had not yet deposed the old cardinals, hence there were 51 cardinals. According to tradition he could depose cardinals only with the consent

---

[1] Niem, i, 8; Raynaldus, *Ann.* 1378, No. 46.
[2] Baluze, i, 1239; Scheuffgen, 8; Souchon, *Anhang,* ii, 257.

of the college and it may be that he wanted a college first before taking that action.

At Fondi the cardinals formally deposed Urban with bell, book, and candle.   The Archbishop of Arles stole all the Papal insignia from the Castle of St Angelo and put them in the cardinals' hands.   On 20th September, two days after Urban created his new college of cardinals, they went through the mad and guilty function of choosing one of their own members Pope.   That was undoubtedly rebellion, and a rebellion produced by selfishness and revenge.   The three Italian cardinals did not vote for, nor did they oppose the new Pontiff.[1]   Indeed at different times they declared their belief in the validity of the election of Urban.[2]

The new Pontiff was Cardinal Robert of Geneva, an intellectual and influential prince of royal blood, a relative of the King of France, only 26 years old, a soldier born to fight and rule, rather than a priest whose mission was to preach the gospel of the Prince of Peace.   With him as with Urban the moral values were the least conspicuous—at least, in his public career.   The blood of the massacre of Cesena was still on his hands, and he was known as a shrewd politician and a fast liver.   On 31st October he was consecrated as Clement VII and many were the bitter gibes at the name that warrior Pontiff assumed.   It was said that Urban wept at the news and regretted his mad course, and that his gusts of uncontrollable passion were pitiable.   With his own sacred college he tried to parry the blow at his office, but it was too late to avoid the disgraceful and ominous schism which a wise Pontiff might easily have averted.   In this matter the hostile cardinals acted as if their own powers were on trial and asserted their independence and supremacy by deposing the Pope they created and by electing another in his stead as head of the Church.   Clement VII, as a militant Pope, sought first to overthrow his rival by force, but failed in his attempt and then on 29th June, 1379, returned to France with the lily of France in his Papal seal.

The question of the legitimacy of the pontificate of Urban VI, and consequently that of his successors during

---

[1] Bliemetzrieder, 61 ; *Hist. Jahrb.*, 1892, xiii, 193 ; Baluze, i, 1039, 1050· Niem, i, 9. They still advocated a general council to settle the disputed election.
[2] Baluze, i, 1100, 1144, 1140 ; Bulaeus, iv, 600, 586 ; Scheuffgen, 24.

the period of the schism, has never been officially decided by either a Pope or a council. It may be cited in Urban's behalf :

1. The contemporaries of the fourteenth century, who could speak with recognized and disinterested authority, were divided into two pronounced camps, but a majority of them defended the cause of Urban and his successors. Niem, who was in Rome at the time asserted : " No one can honestly deny " that Urban was canonically elected Pope.

2. Modern scholarship has become practically unanimous in defence of the Roman line of Popes during the schism. Hergenrother, Hefele, Bliemetzrieder, Hinschius, Kraus, Bruch, Funk, Scheuffner, and Pastor in Germany; Marion, Chenon, de Beaucourt, Denifle, Valois, and Salembier in France; Kirsch in Switzerland; Albers in Holland; Rinaldi and Palma in Italy—all have openly championed the legality of the election of Urban VI.

3. In 1904 the " Gerarchia Cattolica " compiled a new and corrected list of the legitimate sovereign Pontiffs. This official list omitted both the Avignon and the Pisan Popes, thus emphasizing and recognizing the legality of the Roman Popes as the true line.

4. The names of Clement VII and Benedict XIII were taken by two later Popes, whose legitimacy was not questioned, in 1523 and 1724, thus virtually classifying the two Avignon claimants as illegal anti-Popes.

57. *Western Christendom divided into two Hostile Parties*

A complete victory for either Urban VI or Clement VII depended wholly upon the political powers of Europe, hence both Popes sought in every way to win the support of the clergy, princes and peoples of the various European nations.[1] Western Christendom was quickly divided into two almost equal parties.

Nations ranged themselves on one side or the other largely for political reasons and national interests. The Italian and the German states, for the most part, for reasons of patriotism, self-interest, and imperial connections, supported the Pope in Rome. The German Emperor was glad to support a Pontiff free from French influence. Bohemia, Denmark, Sweden, and Poland, under more or less German influence, also championed

---

[1] Scheuffgen, 8.

the Roman line of Pontiffs. England and Flanders,[1] because of their hostility to France, decided for Urban VI and his successors. Portugal likewise cast her lot in with Rome. On the other hand, France and all the nations in the orbit of France defended Clement VII and the Avignon Popes. Through dynastic connections, Sicily and Sardinia gave their allegiance to Avignon. Scotland hated England and hence became a defender of the French Pope. Spain, as an ally of France, followed her lead, and parts of Italy and Germany did the same. Thus all of Western Europe was divided into two hostile political camps, each expecting to gain some positive political advantage out of the unhappy Papal rift.

Scholars, literary men, canon and civil lawyers, and the universities took sides, usually following their countries, and thus added fuel to the flame of controversy. Theologians in Germany like Henry of Hesse, Langenstein, and Conrad of Gelnhausen, were inclined to Urban. On the contrary Pierre d'Ailly, his friend Philippe de Maizieres, his pupil John Gerson, and Nicholas of Clemanges, together with the whole school of Paris, defended Clement VII. The most famous doctors of law, however, were mostly in favour of Urban VI. The saints themselves were not of one mind on the perplexing situation. Catherine of Sweden,[2] Catherine of Siena, Peter of Aragon, Ursilina of Parma, Philippe d'Alençon and Gerard of Groot were in Urban's camp ; while Vincent Ferrer, Peter of Luxemburg, and St Colette arranged themselves on the side of Clement.

Archbishops, bishops, abbots, priests, monks, and nuns were divided likewise in their allegiance which tended largely, though far from universally, to follow the national attitude. Thus there were factions and counter-factions among the clergy high and low in all parts of Christendom.

The common people in city and country, so far as they could intelligently take sides, followed their rulers, or ecclesiastical leaders.

Europe was confronted by the sorry spectacle of two

---

[1] Valois, in vol. ii, gives a detailed account of the allegiance given to the Popes. Flanders was closely connected with England in trade and industry.

[2] " I have heard," she wrote to Urban, " that those devils in human form have resorted to an election. They have chosen not a vicar of Christ, but an anti-Christ. Never will I cease, dear father, to regard you as Christ's true vicar on earth."

Popes, elected by the same college of cardinals without a dissenting vote, each claiming all the prerogatives of the supreme head of Christendom, each cursing the other as a schismatic usurper, and each calling upon the whole Church for recognition and obedience. For forty years—for two entire generations—the Church was rent by that schism, which called forth everywhere hateful words, bitter accusations, lies, perjuries, and blows. At the same time there were two colleges of cardinals, two expensive Papal courts to support, two sets of legates swarming over Europe, two appointees for every vacant benefice, and two levies of ecclesiastical taxes with the invention of many new devices for raising money to meet two sets of expenses. It is not at all surprising, therefore, to find Western Europe during this period embroiled in both political and ecclesiastical quarrels. Emperors had often set up anti-Popes; but such resistance generally left the Pope on whom the attack was made stronger than before. Now a new thing had occurred : the cardinals themselves broke up the unity of the Church and half of Europe supported them in the deed. No similar movement was to be seen until the sixteenth century revolt of Northern Europe from Rome.

At the outset of the Schism the Papal States and Naples constituted the chief theatre of the conflict between the rival Popes. Joanna, Queen of Naples, and Louis of Anjou, at that time regent of France, whom she had chosen as an adopted son and heir to her throne in 1380, gave their allegiance to Clement VII. Urban with characteristic courage declared that Joanna had forfeited her crown, made war on Naples, and freely used the treasure of the Roman Churches to finance the military operations. Louis of Anjou was deposed and Charles of Durazzo, of the Hungarian royal house, Joanna's natural heir, was appointed in his place and in 1381 crowned as King of Naples by Urban. In a short time Charles made himself master of the whole kingdom, took the wicked Joanna prisoner and in 1381 had her put to death. Clement VII created parts of the Papal States into the duchy of Adria, and appointed Louis of Anjou as its ruler. In 1382 he appeared in Italy with an army, but made little headway and died in 1384. Charles conferred upon Urban the overlordship of Capri, Amalfi, Fondi, and other places, which the Pope in turn conferred upon his worthless nephew. Meanwhile differences arose between Urban and Charles. The head-strong, tactless Pontiff went to Naples, put the city under an interdict, excommunicated and deposed the King, who in turn besieged the Pope in his castle near Salerno in 1385. Urban succeeded in escaping in 1386 by ship and proceeded to Genoa, although the crew threatened to carry him to Avignon and had to be bought off. Five of his cardinals were executed for treasonable conspiracy and two Italian cardinals fled to Clement VII. The cruel, hard-hearted Pope then went to Perugia, raised an army, and again started for Naples. Charles in the meantime had been called to the throne of Hungary, but in 1386 was assassinated. His son, Ladislaus, succeeded him, but found his claim to the throne of Naples contested by Louis of Anjou, Joanna's heir. Urban went no further south than Feretino, and then returned to Rome in 1389 only to die in a few months as a result of a fall from his donkey. He had won a victory in the Papal States, but had failed in Naples.

Whatever his virtues were before his election, as Pope he proved himself to be an absolute and utter failure and wholly unfit to rule the Church. He lived and ruled as if there had been no schism. He cared so little for the unity of Christendom that he would not make a single concession. He possessed no sense of statecraft and could not conceive of compromise for the welfare of the Church. His bigoted conduct alienated his cardinals and brought on the unholy Schism.[1]   It may be true, as Niem affirms, that he never made ecclesiastical offices the object of sale, but he was certainly guilty of the sin of nepotism. Crusades were set on foot against the Clementine Party with a profuse expenditure of indulgences. In 1383 the Bishop of Norwich in England led a religious expedition to Flanders with the hope of striking France. "There he destroyed in warfare some nine thousand men of that land who sided with the French heretics" but in the end was forced to flee to England.[2] John of Gaunt joined Portugal in a holy crusade against

Souchon, i, 43.   [2] Thompson, *Usk's Chronicle*, 146.

Castile with such a lavish use of bulls of indulgences as to amaze and disgust the minds of sober men.[1]

58. *Perpetuation of the Schism*

The successor of Urban VI was Boniface IX (1389–1404), a member of an impoverished Neapolitan family.[2] He was an ignorant man, a poor theologian, and lacked skill in the conduct of curial business, but fortunately differed from his predecessor in being by nature mild, tactful, and prudent though firm enough when occasion demanded it. He was a man of fine personal appearance and only 35 when elected Pope through the influence of Ladislaus, whose claim to the throne of Naples he wisely championed. At Gaeta in 1390 he crowned that young monarch, and for the next decade aided him in effectively expelling the Avignon claimant, the tool of the Avignon Pontiff, from Italy.

He firmly believed that he was the true Pope. Shortly after his election he excommunicated Clement VII, who of course immediately returned the compliment. Boniface defended with vigour his own legitimacy and spurned all suggestions from his own supporters of abdication for the peace of the Church.[3] In a letter written on 1st May, 1391, he declared that every other suggestion for healing the schism, except the overthrow of his opponent, was useless. A general council, he held, would be an interference with the ordinances of God.[4]

In the Papal States Boniface gradually regained control of the chief cities, which had recognized Clement VII, and through his administrative reforms became the true founder of the government of Peter's Patrimony as it endured down to the Reformation. In Rome he replaced municipal independence by Papal supremacy and compelled obedience by fortifying anew the Castle of St Angelo, the various bridges and other points of strategic advantage. He also took under his personal rule the port of Ostia from its cardinal-bishop.

---

[1] Poole, 129.

[2] He was elected 2nd Nov., 1389, by the fourteen cardinals of his obedience. Niem says that he could neither write nor conduct services well, 130.

[3] Communication to Richard II, 1396; the Diet of Frankfurt, 1397; king Wenceslaus, 1398.

[4] Kneer, *Konzil. Theorie*, 97.

It is true that the faithlessness and violence of the irrepressible Romans frequently caused him to reside at Perugia, Assisi, and elsewhere, but as a rule he was the master, and at his death had the satisfaction of seeing all Italy except Genoa acknowledge his leadership.

In foreign affairs he played an active but conciliatory rôle. The English Parliament more than once confirmed and extended the statutes of Provisors and Praemunire of Edward III.[1] Boniface protested and stood out for his prerogatives, but yielded in 1393 and victory was with the English crown. The anti-Papal virulence of Wiclif increased the opposition of the people, clergy, and government to the methods of Boniface in granting English benefices. Nevertheless in 1396 the synod of London condemned the teachings of Wiclif and the University of Oxford in 1398 issued a document in favour of Boniface.[2] At least one Englishman and probably others found favour at the Papal court. Adam of Usk in 1402 was raised by the Pope and the Rota to the dignity of Papal chaplain and auditor of the Papal palace, and judge of the city of Rome. Within a week thirty " great causes " were submitted to him for decision.[3] Benefices in England were conferred upon him the same year, and in 1404 he was appointed Bishop of Hereford.[4]

In Germany the electors in 1400 deposed the unworthy Wenceslaus, and in his place chose Rupert, Duke of Bavaria, who sent a solemn embassy to the Pope for confirmation.[5] At first Boniface was cautious, but in 1403 he approved of the action of the electors.[6]

In 1398 and 1399 Boniface appealed to Western Christendom to support the Emperor Emanuel of Constantinople, threatened by the Turks, but Europe was in no mood to heed the appeal.

Boniface's Pontificate was strengthened by the enthusiasm and the substantial contributions of two jubilees in Rome. The first one took place in 1390, as arranged by Urban VI, and was largely frequented from Germany, Hungary, Poland, England, and Italy. Several German cities obtained the

---

[1] Lingard, ii, ch. 4.
[2] For the statutes cf. Thompson, *Usk's Chronicle*, 256.
[3] Ib., 243.   [4] Ib., 246, 256.   [5] Ib., 245.
[6] Ib., 248–52 gives the document.

privileges of the jubilee, but the preaching of indulgences gave rise to abuses and impositions on the part of unaccredited agents to such an extent that the Pope was obliged to proceed against them with severity. In 1400 Boniface decided to take advantage of the opening of a new century and hence proclaimed another jubilee. Great crowds of pilgrims from all over Western Europe made their way to Rome, particularly from France, to obtain the special centennial indulgences. Notwithstanding the outbreak of the plague in Rome, and throughout Italy the large crowds continued to visit the Sacred City and of course large sums of money were contributed to the Papal treasury.

Next to John XXII Boniface IX was one of the shrewdest financiers of the Pontiffs of this period. Because of his limited constituency, he was compelled to resort to new financial devices, and he was exceptionally successful, and showed special cleverness in extending the *annates*.[1] Niem, who was quite disappointed in not securing office under Boniface, accused him of avarice and greed ; and Adam of Usk, who was exceptionally favoured, said that he was like a thin greedy fox, " though gorged with simony, yet to his dying day was never filled." [2] He was notoriously guilty of nepotism. His brothers held large tracts in the kingdom of Naples, Spoleto, Ancona, and the Papal States,[3] and his nephews were given good places in the Church.[4]

Boniface IX died in 1404 with the Roman line in the ascendancy. His contemporaries praised him for his labours in behalf of education in founding the universities of Ferrara in 1391, and Fermo in 1398, and for confirming the University of Erfurt in 1392 ; for his political virtues ; for his personal purity and his nobility of spirit. But they also charged him with an inordinate love of money ; dishonest traffic in benefices ; the extravagant sale of indulgences and dispensations ; the invention of questionable devices for raising money ; and nepotism.[5]

Innocent VII, who followed Boniface IX in 1404, was

---

[1] Phillips, v, 573 ff.   [2] Thompson, *Usk*, 259.
[3] Gregorovius, vi, 522 ; Theiner, iii, 9. 39.   [4] Souchon, i, 56.
[5] Niem, 119 ; Thompson, *Usk's Chronicle*, 259 ; Creighton, i, 98–161 ; Pastor, i, 164 ; Jansen, *Papst Bonifatius IX, und seine Beziehungen zur deutschen Kirche*, Freiburg, 1904 ; Gregorovius, vi, part ii, p. 566 ; *Cath. Encycl.*, ii, 670.

68 years old when elected Pope and ruled but two years. He came of humble parentage in the Abruzzi. He was a university man, a doctor in theology and law, having studied at Perugia, Padua, and Bologna. He taught law at the first two universities and then was called to the Papal Curia by Urban VI, who sent him as a Papal collector to England, where he remained ten years. In 1386 he was appointed Bishop of Bologna and the next year became Archbishop of Ravenna. In 1389 he was created cardinal and sent as a trusted legate to Tuscany and Lombardy. He was universally esteemed for his learning and piety and was an able manager of finances.

Before his election all the Roman cardinals took an oath, if elected Pope, to leave nothing undone even to the point of abdication, in order to end the schism.[1]   To carry out that purpose Innocent called a council, but disturbances in Rome brought his good intentions to nought. The Romans rebelled against the Pope's absolute rule in the city; and he called King Ladislaus of Naples to suppress the insurrection. That ambitious monarch took advantage of the occasion to extend his own rule over Rome and the Papal territory. This and the indiscretions of a nephew, whom Innocent had made cardinal, forced the Pope to flee to Viterbo, until the fickle Romans called him back in 1406. King Ladislaus was excommunicated and withdrew his troops from Rome. These local disturbances and the short reign of the Pope prevented him from taking positive measures for the healing of the schism.[2]

Gregory XII, the last of the Roman Popes during the schism, came of a noble Venetian family and was elected Pope in 1406 at the advanced age of 79. He had been made bishop in 1380 and Patriarch of Jerusalem in 1390. Under Innocent VII he served as apostolic secretary, then legate of Ancona, and finally in 1405 was promoted to a cardinalship. His reputation for great piety and his zeal to end the disintegrating schism, now in progress for 28 years, resulted in his unanimous election. Before the choice of a Pope was made, each cardinal swore that, if chosen, he would abdicate provided his rival at Avignon did the same, in order to heal the disastrous

---

[1] Thompson, *Usk's Chronicle* 262, gives a vivid picture of the coronation ceremonies which he himself witnessed.

[2] Kneer, *Zur Vorgeschichte Papst Innocenz VII* in *Hist. Jahrb.*, xii, 347–51; *Cath. Encyc.*, viii, 19.

breach. Gregory XII was so much in earnest that he repeated the oath after his elevation and so notified Benedict XIII. But all his relatives and King Ladislaus, for selfish political reasons, exerted all their efforts to prevent a meeting of the two Pontiffs for the purpose of a joint abdication. When his disappointed cardinals threatened to desert Gregory XII in 1408, he summoned them to Lucca, ordered them not to leave the city under any pretext, and created four of his nephews cardinals, contrary to his promise, to name no new cardinals. Seven of his cardinals secretly left Lucca and negotiated with the cardinals of the Avignon Pontiff concerning a general council to depose both Popes and to elect a new one. This conference resulted in the famous Council of Pisa held in 1409, in which the two absent claimants to the headship of the Church were deposed and Alexander V was elected. Gregory meanwhile created ten new cardinals, and called a council of his own at which both Benedict XIII and Alexander V were pronounced schismatics, perjurers, and devastators of the Church. Rupert of Germany, Ladislaus of Naples and other Italian princes still recognized him as a true Pope. The Council of Constance in 1415 received his resignation by proxy and appointed him Bishop of Porto and perpetual legate of Ancona. Two years later he died " in the odour of sanctity ". He had failed to realize the high hopes which Christendom, immeasurably wearied of these endless divisions, had placed in him. As an old man of fourscore it was believed that ambition would not supplant the desire for peace and unity, as might be true of a younger Pontiff. These hopes were blasted simply because Gregory became little more than the mouthpiece of the selfish Italian political party.[1]

The Avignon Pontiffs during the schism numbered but two. The circumstances attending the election of Clement VII have been described.[2] He was a brother of Peter, the Count of Geneva, and was connected by blood or by marriage with most of the sovereigns of Europe. This fact alone made him a formidable rival of Urban VI. He had been educated under French influences and had accepted favours from the hands

[1] Finke, *Papst Gregor XII und König Sigismund im Jahre* 1414 ; *Rom. Quartalsch.*, i, 354–69 Rome, 1887 ; Salembier, 218–58.
[2] Valois, *La France et le grand schisme d'occident*, Paris, 1896 ; Baluze, i, 486.

of the Avignon Popes ; canon at Paris, apostolic prothonatory
at the age of 17, bishop at 19, archbishop at 26, and cardinal
at 29. in 1377 as Papal legate he had directed the savage
suppression of the revolt of the people of Cesena against the
Papal authority.   When elected Pope in 1378 he had the
support of Charles V of France and Joanna of Naples, as well
as several Italian barons, and he succeeded later in retaining
the allegiance of a considerable portion of Europe and a part
of the Latin East.

His first plan was to overthrow Urban VI by force, seize
Rome, and establish his authority in Italy.   Unable to
maintain himself in Italy, however, he took up his residence
in Avignon in 1379, although he never surrendered his supreme
purpose of making himself master of Western Christendom.
To that end he lavished the gold of his supporters with lavish
hands.   He carved the principality out of a portion of the
Papal States and held it, together with the kingdom of Naples,
as a bait before the eyes of the Duke of Anjou, the eldest brother
of Charles V to lure him to attack Rome.   This tempting
bait led to a series of military expeditions to Italy at the
expense of Clement, but accomplished nothing more than
momentary successes.   Before his death Clement was forced
to open his blind eyes to the bitter fact that the supreme
purpose of his strenuous life was doomed to failure.   Brute
force, in the form of French arms, could not break down the
opposition to his plans simply because that opposition was
founded on the conviction of the greater part of Catholic
Europe that his cause was wrong and his deeds unwarranted.

He incurred a general reproach because of his vast expenditures for the useless Italian wars, for the defence of the
Comtat Venaissin, for the attack on Raymond of Turrenne,
and for his incessant embassies ; because of his luxurious
tastes and princely habits which outdid any of the Avignon
Popes.   The five day visit of Charles VI in 1389 cost 70,000
gulden.[1] Hostility to his cause was aroused because he
persistently refused to refer the hateful schism to a general
council with the view of securing a restoration of unity in
the Church.   He resorted to simony and extortion to meet
the financial needs of his court, his extravagant life, and his
illusive dreams of Papal conquest.   Clemanges said that his

[1] Souchon, i, 179.

greed and his ambition were unbelievable.[1] He disposed of monastic and secular benefices of all orders, grades and conditions, and gave single individuals not merely one benefice, or two or three, ten or twelve ; but 100, 200, 400, and even 500.[2] Langenstein said that one cardinal received from 200 to 300 benefices.[3] These offices were sold at the whim of the Pope.[4] Bankers of the old days once more set up their establishments in Avignon.[5] Clement was also much more dependent upon the will of the French court than any of the Avignon Popes.[6] He died in 1394 at the age of 52, five years after the death of Urban VI.

Benedict XIII, a Spaniard by birth, at the age of 69 succeeded Clement VII. Like so many of the ecclesiastical leaders of the day he was a university man, studied law at Montpellier, received his doctorate, and taught canon law in his alma mater. Gregory XI had made him cardinal in 1375, because of his noble lineage, his austere life, his reputation for prudence, his untiring energy, and his learned mind. He saw the Papacy restored to Rome and voted for Urban VI as Pope. He refused to flee before the mob saying : " Even if I die, I will fall here." He distinctly championed the validity of Urban's election at first, but later changed his mind and in 1378 helped to elect Clement VII. He proved to be a zealous adherent of that Pontiff and energetically defended his legitimacy. Clement sent him to Spain to win over those states, and he succeeded. In 1393 he was named legate to France, Flanders, Brabant, and England.[7] He was easily the most important man among the Avignon cardinals, and perhaps one of the ablest men of his age.[8] He was strongly in favour of unity in the Church and consequently a coolness sprang up between him and Clement.

Before election, which was unanimous, he had declared that if necessary he would renounce the Papal dignity to heal the schism, and after his coronation he solemnly renewed the promise.[9] His election was popular in France because much was expected from him in peace efforts.[10] But he refused

[1] Von der Hardt, i, 3, 15.   [2] Souchon, i, 180.
[3] Ib., 181.   [4] Martène-Durand, *Thes.*,i, 1612.
[5] Souchon, i, 181.   [6] Pastor, i, 132-3 ; Döllinger, ii, i, 281.
[7] Haller, 524.   [8] Ib., 214.
[9] Bourgeois du Chastenet, 21 ; *Religieux*, iii, 602.
[10] Valois, iii, 439.

T

to receive orders from either the French clergy or the French king and proposed to follow his own course in bringing about a reunion of the distracted Church.[1]   He believed himself to be the rightful Pope and hoped to persuade his Roman rival to resign and thus realize unity, but negotiations with Boniface IX failed.   Benedict's obstinacy finally led France in 1399 to withdraw obedience to him.   The French clergy at Avignon were ordered to leave the curia under penalty of the forfeiture of their benefices in France, and 17 cardinals deserted Benedict and took up their residence at Villeneuve in France, and urged him to listen to reasonable advice.   He declared that he would rather suffer death than accept the humiliating terms proposed.   Thereupon all the cardinals but five withdrew their obedience.

Avignon was besieged with French troops to bring the stubborn Pope to his senses, and he was at last forced to treat with his enemies.   He agreed to renounce the Papal office, if the Roman Pope would do the same, though he secretly protested that this pledge had been extracted by force. Meanwhile, public opinion in France spoke in favour of the Pope, and theologians like Gerson and Clemanges became his champions.   In 1403 he fled to Louis II of Anjou.   Avignon immediately submitted to his terms, his cardinals likewise recognized him anew, and in a short time all France was again loyal.

At the outset Benedict was anxious to observe the wishes of France.[2]   France called a synod on 2nd February, 1395, at Paris, to determine the best way to heal the schism.   The University of Paris at the same time advised the abdication of Benedict as the best method of bringing peace.   Thus France and the University of Paris threw down the gauntlet to the Pope and he took it up.[3]   In 1404 Benedict renewed negotiations with Boniface IX for a joint meeting, but the latter obstinately refused to listen to the proposition.   The next year he went to Genoa to treat with Innocent VII but failed of results.   Then he planned to drive that foe out of Rome, but strong opposition in Italy and disaffection in France, because of the taxes levied on benefices and his departure from Avignon, caused him to give up the project and go to

[1] Haller, 219.
[2] Ehrle, *Archiv.*, vi, 153 ; Valois, iii, 18.
[3] Haller, 219.

Marseilles, where he declared himself ready to assemble a council of his constituents to settle the problem of unification. After a fruitless effort to come to some agreement with Gregory XII, Benedict, once more deserted by France, fled to Roussillon in 1408, summoned a council of his own at Perpignan, which of course was utterly useless. There he resided until 1415, when he retired to his family castle of Pensacola in Spain, where he died in 1422 still clinging to his Papal crown.

Of all the Popes of the period of the Great Western Schism Benedict was undoubtedly the ablest. He had the spirit of Gregory VII and the ability of Innocent III. Had he been in the Roman line with a free field he would have had a noteworthy career. He was keen, alert, independent, willing to compromise for the general good, and never yielded an iota of his Papal prerogatives. He maintained his office against three Roman Pontiffs and that in the face of the desertion of the King of France. He outlived two reformatory councils, still asserting his Papal claims in grand isolation until death removed him from the schismatic controversy. A mere handful of his Spanish adherents elected Munoz as his successor and for a short time he continued a feeble schism.[1]

---

[1] In addition to many ecclesiastical documents he also wrote the following pointed tracts ; *Tractatus de concilio generali* ; *Tractatus de novo subschismate* ; and *Tractatus de principali schismate*. Denifle-Ehrler, *Archiv.*, vii, 515 ff.

CHAPTER IX

EFFORTS TO HEAL THE SCHISM

59. *By the Popes and their Advisers*

WHEN the Schism began in 1378 the people of Europe quite generally believed that the methods and means of healing it rested in the hands of the rival Pontiffs and their immediate advisers, the cardinals. Many times had the Church witnessed the appearance of an anti-Pope, but no serious breach had ever resulted commensurate with this one. Many contemporaries deplored the condition of a divided Papacy, but at the outset no one suspected its seriousness, or thought that it would continue beyond the lifetime of Urban VI or of Clement VII. Had it been fully realized that the ugly and disastrous division would drag its weary course along for four decades, no doubt some action would have been taken to bring about an early and a speedy ending.

At the outset Urban VI, feeling himself outraged at the secession and rebellion of his college of cardinals, smote them and their newly elected anti-pope with the heaviest curses of his office. Urban VI at the beginning favoured a council, but soon surrendered the idea.[1] These fulminations made a loud noise, but produced little in the way of desired results. Clement VII returned the courtesies in language just as forceful and choice, but in addition resorted to armed force to crush his adversary. More considerate of public opinion than Urban, he even proposed a general council as a means of settling the contest and very chivalrously promised, in case of his re-election, to accept Urban as his chief cardinal.

One of the first acts of Boniface IX was to excommunicate Clement VII in strong terms and of course, the latter replied with similar compliments. Boniface also very magnanimously agreed to appoint his opponent apostolic legate and vicar-general of the Roman Church for life.[2] In vain Clement looked for recognition by the Roman college of cardinals when Urban died. After Clement's death it was reported that he had already

---

[1] Scheuffgen, 58.　　　　　[2] Giesseler, iii, 91.

decided to abdicate voluntarily and was only prevented from doing so by his sudden death. Haller declares that that report was spread for the sole purpose of embarrassing his successor.[1]

By this time the schism had taken on a dreaded appearance, and had become notoriously serious. Hence Innocent VII, Gregory XII, and Benedict XIII, before election, took an oath to employ every means, even abdication if necessary, to bring peace and unity to the Church.[2] Once crowned, however, each one of these Pontiffs stood stoutly on the defensive and called upon his antagonist to surrender. Innocent VII followed his two predecessors at Rome in outlawing Clement and his cardinals as schismatics, heretics, pirates, and brigands. Clement in turn fired shot just as hot into the Roman camp. To each Pope's mind the solution of the difficulty was simplicity itself, namely, the resignation of his illegitimate opponent. Boniface IX wrote to all the sovereigns of Europe declaring that he very much regretted the schism, that he earnestly desired to see it ended, and that it could be easily done if only Clement, that " son of Belial ", would resign his ill-gotten power. He opened negotiations with Charles VI of France, but his motive was simply to win France away from his rival.[3]

It was also suggested that when one Pope died the other should be universally recognized. Upon the demise of Urban VI and Boniface IX, Clement VII endeavoured to bring about such an adjustment but, of course, the Roman ecclesiastical politicians spoiled his unselfish plans.[4] Another way out of the difficulty was to have both claimants resign and thus open the field for a new election; but again the Popes themselves thwarted the project. When Innocent VII died in 1406, it was hoped, in case a new Pope was not chosen at Rome, that Benedict XIII would at last carry out his promise of abdication. To such a suggestion, however, Benedict returned only evasive answers, so Gregory XII was elected.[5] Benedict sent an embassy to Rome to confer with Boniface IX and to arrange for a joint meeting to discuss the whole subject. Boniface would receive them only as Pope,

---

[1] Haller, *Papst.*, 214 ; Valois, ii, 428, n. 1.
[2] Souchon, i, 296 ; Haller, *Papst.*, 214 ; Ehrle, *Archiv.*, v, 403 ; Baluze, *Vitae*, i, 567.
[3] Poole, 131.   [4] Souchon, i, 65.   [5] Ib., 89.

and said : " Very well, but remember that I am the true Pope ! Your master is an anti-Pope." " That may be true," replied the angry deputies, " but at all events he is not a simoniac." All these Popes were strong in words suggesting great sacrifices, but short in deeds ; and so the schism went on, leaving in its train an increasing rancour, hatred and evil results.

Gregory XII immediately after his election in 1406 wrote to " Peter de Luna, whom some people in this wretched schism call Benedict XIII ", declaring that, like the woman who was ready to renounce her child rather than see it cut asunder, each of them should be willing to surrender his claim rather than see the Church rent in twain. He announced that he was ready to abdicate, on condition that Benedict did likewise, and suggested that afterwards the two colleges of cardinals should unite for a unanimous Papal election. Benedict addressed his reply to " Angelus Carrer, whom some, adhering to him in this pernicious schism, call Gregory XII ". With suspicious eagerness he accepted the proposals. " We are both old men," he wrote, " Time is short, hasten, and do not delay in this worthy cause. Let us both embrace the ways of salvation and peace." [1]   An agreement was soon drawn up : (1) Savona was to be the place of joint abdication ; (2) the cardinals were to unite at the same place to elect a new Pope ; and (3) each Pope agreed to lay aside his insignia of office. Of course each Pope expected to win a victory over the other. Gregory, in his first consistory, had asserted that for the sake of peace and unity in Christendom, he would travel by land or sea, with a pilgrim's staff if necessary, or in a fishing smack, in order to come to an agreement with Benedict.

The two Popes with their cardinals at length started for the designated city. Benedict reached Savona, but Gregory stopped at Lucca just 50 miles away, and made 22 formal excuses for not proceeding further. Among them he said that Savona was French territory, and hence proposed Pisa. Besides he had no funds and the country was unsafe for travel. Another objection was that Benedict had the best ships. The other points were equally trivial. This was a sorrowful and disgusting spectacle. Here were two old men dodging, parrying, and making excuses for the fear of losing power.

---

[1] Niem, 209–13, gives both letters.

" There are two masters in the vessel, who are fencing with and contradicting each other," said Jean Petit in the council of Paris. Leonard of Arezzo compared one Pope to a land animal refusing to approach the shore ; the other to a water animal refusing to leave the sea. Niem declared that they were like two knights in a sham battle ; they appeared in earnest but all was vain display. That was the last scene in which the two Popes appeared as the leading actors. As the two supreme leaders of the two factions in the Latin Church, opportunity passed from their hands. The Papal attempt at reconciliation and pacification had proved to be an absolute failure. Other actors in this schismatic drama then stepped forward to play the heroic rôle. But even when the council of Pisa was called the two rival claimants sought to defend their prerogatives by calling councils of their own ; Benedict at Perpignam, Gregory at Aquileia. It was too late, however, and no attention was paid to the two Pope-called councils.

60. *By the Cardinals*

The original college of cardinals under Urban VI was personally responsible for the beginning of the schism. The two colleges at Rome and Avignon were likewise guilty of perpetuating the breach by electing successive schismatic Popes. Many of the cardinals themselves and influential individuals outside of the colleges believed and declared that the duty of unifying the Church rested with the two colleges acting jointly. But the cardinals were, if anything, more obstinate and persistent than the Popes. The Avignon college claimed to be the original one and therefore, the only canonical body with power to create a head for the Church, as well as to depose him for good cause, as it had done in the case of Urban VI. The Roman college, on the other hand, contended that their Pope was the original, genuine Pontiff with absolute power to cut off and to create cardinals. He had repudiated the rebellious Avignon cardinals and created a new college of cardinals, which was duty bound to continue the original and legal line of Roman Popes.

Cardinals in both lines early and keenly realized the disastrous results of the schism and clearly saw that the following courses were open to them : (1) one college could, on the death of its Pope, refuse to elect another, and either recognize the survivor, or await his abdication or death ; (2) both colleges could induce the two Pontiffs to abdicate and then unite in the choice of a new Pope ; (3) both colleges could depose the two Popes and then unite under a common head ; and (4) the cardinals could call a general council to depose the Popes, or to determine which was the legitimate Pope, and thus clear the field for unity.

The danger of conspiring to overthrow a Pontiff, however, was shown in the case of the six cardinals who conspired to dethrone Urban VI. They were seized, tortured, five were executed, and the sixth imprisoned.[1] Two more, Italians, deserted to Clement VII and were graciously received. Upon the death of Clement VII, the King of France sent a letter to the cardinals calling upon them to postpone the election of another Pope. Suspecting the contents of the communication, they left it unread until they had chosen Benedict XIII.

The most hopeful method of healing the breach, which the cardinals attempted, was to have each cardinal in the conclave held to elect a new Pontiff, swear that if chosen head of the Church, he would do everything within his power to bring about unity—even to the surrender of his office. Such an oath was taken by two Roman and one Avignon Popes.[2] The cardinals feebly insisted upon the fulfillment of the obligation and then left the matter to the Pope's own discretion. The Avignon cardinals met without the Pope's permission and strongly advised him to adopt one of the three means of healing the schism suggested by the University of Paris. Clement VII at once condemned his cardinals for presuming to possess the right to give such advice. When delegates from the King of France called upon both Popes to abdicate, all but two of the Avignon cardinals supported the proposition ; but Benedict XIII issued a bull against such a course. When the Council of Paris in 1398 withdrew the obedience of the French clergy from Benedict, the cardinals deserted him, but in 1403 they once more recognized him. In September of 1404, Benedict sent a messenger to Boniface IX suggesting that the two Popes and their colleges meet to adjust matters, but the proposal came to naught.[3]

When the peace blusterings of Benedict and Gregory in

---

[1] Niem, 91, 103, 110.   [2] Souchon, i, 67, 94, 212, 280 ff.
[3] Scheuffgen, 104 ; Souchon, i, 270.

1407 proved to be such a miserable and ridiculous fiasco, the cardinals with the mutterings of a European storm in their ears, stepped to the front and, contrary to all canonical precedent, took the revolutionary course which resulted in the reunion of the whole Church under one recognized head. Benedict XIII had suggested to Gregory XII that the cardinals of both obediences should meet to talk the matter over in order to see whether it might not be arranged for one Pope or the other to resign.[1] Gregory's cardinals continually reminded him of his pompous promises. They even tried to bribe him— offered him the patriarchate of Constantinople, two Venetian bishoprics, the bishopric of Exeter, and the archbishopric of York, if he would give up the contest. He answered that it was his intention to create four new cardinals contrary to his plighted word.

Finally, 7 of the Roman cardinals, who were unionists, in May, 1408, broke away from Gregory XII at Lucca, went to Pisa,[2] and issued a manifesto to Gregory and all Christian princes, appealing from a poorly informed Pope to a better informed one, from Christ's vicar to Christ himself, and to the decisions of a general council.[3] Two more cardinals followed this secession from Gregory.[4] At the same time 4 Avignon cardinals deserted Benedict and went to Leghorn. Negotiations were opened with the Roman cardinals, and these 13 cardinals from the two colleges, acting as if the two Popes had been deposed, retired to Leghorn and on 29th June took upon themselves as rulers of the Church the duty to summon a general council to meet at Pisa on 25th March, 1409, to heal the unholy schism.[5] This act seemed to be as much of a rebellion as the course of the college in deserting Urban VI in 1378. The cardinals who would not hear of a council in 1378 were forced to call one thirty years later.[6] They then wrote to the sovereigns and universities of Europe letters in which they freely applied such terms as " perjurers and liars " to their former masters, and compared them to the Roman soldiers who divided the seamless robe of Christ. From this time onward the cardinals strove to make the council a successful ending of the schism and to win over all the secular princes.[7]

---

[1] Niem, 209.   [2] Scheuffgen, 118 ; Souchon, i, 155, ii, 3.
[3] Souchon, i, 277 ; ii, 8.   [4] Ib., ii, 6 ; Mansi, xxvii, 165.
[5] Souchon, ii, 15 ff. ; Scheuffgen, 119.   [6] Souchon, i, 162.   [7] Ib., ii, 34.

This unprecedented act by the cardinals was approved by
universities like Paris, Oxford, Cologne, and Heidelberg,
by most of the leading prelates, by the most distinguished
doctors like Gerson and D'Ailly, and by most of the princes
who no longer relied on the good will of the rival Popes and
were determined to act without them and if necessary against
them.   The cardinals gave their masters a last opportunity
by inviting Gregory to go to Pisa to carry out his oath to give
the Church peace,[1] and by urging Benedict to go to Leghorn
for the same purpose.[2]

61. *By the European Rulers*

The inability and unwillingness of the Popes and cardinals
to take positive measures to heal the schism gave the secular
rulers an excellent opportunity to intervene.   But at the outbreak of the schism scarcely a country was in a position to
stop it.   England was governed by a boy ; France was shortly
to pass under the rule of another youth, and a madman at
that ; Germany was in the hands of the drunken Wenzel ; Naples
was ruled by a wicked woman ; and the smaller states were
powerless.   Through division into two powerful groups of
supporters of rival Popes the European nations were in large
measure responsible for the continuation of the schism,   if
not for its inception.   France in particular could be charged
with actually having instigated the election of Clement VII
and his removal to Avignon.[3]   Had there been really one
powerful ruler in Europe the schism might have been prevented.
Political selfishness as much as anything perpetuated the unholy
division for nearly two generations.   Each government was
expecting to reap some national advantage from the confusion
and dispute.   There can be no doubt that the self-consciousness
of some states like France and England was promoted by the
schism.

During the early stages of the schism, so far as the secular
powers interfered, the purpose was not so much to bring unity
and peace to the Church as it was to obtain political advantage
in crushing the Pope of a group of hostile opponents, and in
winning the gratitude of their own candidate.   At the outset
of the schism some of the European statesmen opposed a

---

[1] Souchon, ii, 6.   [2] Mansi, xxvi, 1132, 1180 ff.   [3] Valois, i, 144.

general council because the Roman Pope would in that case have an accidental majority in such a body, and also because national honour demanded the *via cessionis*.[1] It was with such expectations in mind that France sent her armies at the servile Clement's request to Italy to conquer Naples and to overthrow the Roman Popes. Had success attended these efforts, the schism might have been ended, it is true, but the Babylonian Captivity undoubtedly would have been repeated. The whole plan failed, however, and the kingdom of Naples remained loyal to the Roman obedience. Indeed, it was due to the preponderant influence of King Ladislaus that the two successors of Urban VI were Neapolitans. When the University of Paris in 1381 appealed to the regent of France to call a general council to end the schism, that institution was told to mind its own business and the spokesman, John Ronce, was thrown into prison and released only on promise to recognize the claims of Clement VII. The rector was threatened with similar punishment for having read to his students a letter from Urban VI.[2]

As the schism progressed, however, the French monarch discovered that the Avignon Papacy was a burden rather than a help. England, Germany, and Italy paid their ecclesiastical taxes to Rome, while France almost single-handed had to support the expensive Avignon Papal court. Costly Italian wars in behalf of Clement had ended in failure. Frenchmen no longer had the pick of European benefices. The French clergy, nobility, and people were dissatisfied. The King was convinced that a mistaken policy had been followed. At Clement's death in 1394, therefore, the King of France, urged on by the University of Paris, attempted to prevent the election of a new schismatic Pontiff.[3] His letter ordering the postponement of the election found the cardinals in conclave at Avignon. Suspecting the contents of the communication, they refused to open it until after the election. The French court in 1395 told Benedict XIII that he was elected to resign and not to rule.[4]

[1] Krüger, ii, 200, 201.
[2] Bulaeus, iv, 583 ; *Religieux*, i, 86 ; *Chartul*, iii, 1637, 1640 ; Rashdall, i, 543. Both the rector and Ronce eventually took refuge in the court of Urban VI. The university was again rebuffed in 1390 and 1391. It seems very clear that the university wished to remain neutral at the outset. *Chartul*, iii, 559, 560.
[3] *Amp. Coll.*, vii, 479 ; *Religieux*, ii, 188.
[4] Ehrle, *Martin de Alpartils*, 217.

In 1395 six theses were posted upon the doors of the Papal palace, saying that Benedict XIII, having broken his oath, was declared by a council to be a heretic.[1] A little later the University of Paris passed nine theses of the same purport.[2] It was generally believed that the salvation of the Church depended upon the deposition of Benedict in a general council.[3]

Consequently, in 1395 Charles VI, still urged on by the University of Paris, called a council of the higher clergy in Paris to consider the grave situation. That body by a vote of 87 to 22 requested Benedict XIII to resign, as the only way to bring about reunion, but he adroitly proposed that the two colleges and both Popes meet in a council under the French monarch, so the controversy continued.[4] King Wenzel of Germany in September, 1390, wrote to the University of Paris to labour to end the schism, and thus bring peace to the Church.[5] In 1398 Charles VI and Emperor Wenzel, both feeble rulers, held a conference at Rheims, and resolved to have both Popes resign. On the contrary, Ladislaus of Naples found it to be to his advantage to perpetuate the breach.[6] By the treaty of Calais in 1396 England and France agreed to demand the abdication of both Popes.[7] Wenzel and other rulers were asked to join in the good work. Castile did so. In 1397 the resolutions were sent to Avignon and Rome, but with no results. Richard II of England also favoured this course of having both Pontiffs abdicate.[8] Pierre d'Ailly was despatched to Avignon and Rome to inform the Popes of this resolution. Each Pontiff insisted that his rival should set the holy example of abdication, and the proposal came to nought. Not long after this the English and German rulers were both deposed, and France was left to carry out the laudable project alone. Charles VI then called a general assembly of all prelates, canons, and professors in France, who by a vote of 247 to 38 refused to recognize Benedict XIII.[9] An ecclesiastical council, consisting of eleven archbishops and sixty bishops, held in

---

[1] Döllinger, *Sectengeschichte*, ii, 351.
[2] Bulaeus, iv, 753 ; Valois, iii, 71, n. 4.
[3] Martène-Durand, *Thesaur*, ii, 1135.
[4] Haller, 222, 220, 356 ; *Religieux*, ii, 226 ; Valois, iii, 36 ; Ehrle, *Archiv.* vi, 194.
[5] *Chartul.*, iii, 595.   [6] Kugler, ii, 202.
[7] Ehrle, *Archiv.*, vi, 242 ; *Religieux*, ii, 470 ; Valois, iii, 198 ; Haller, 224.
[8] Valois, iii, 69 ff.
[9] Ehrle, vi, 274, 283 ; Valois, iii, 172 ff. ; Haller, 228, 234.

Paris the same year, resolved to withdraw their obedience and that of the French Church from the Avignon Pope. The King thereupon issued a decree forbidding any one in his kingdom to obey the Pope, to pray for him or to pay him money.

Charles VI after 1392 was so generally recognized as incompetent and at times insane that his uncle, Philip of Burgundy, and his brother, Louis of Orleans, assumed the regency. Both had a good reason for wishing unity in the Church : Philip because his duchy of Flanders recognized the Roman Pope ; and Louis because of his possessions in Northern Italy.[1] These political considerations explain why the French monarch gave ear to the University of Paris and permitted the national synod of 1398 to withdraw all obedience and financial support from Benedict XIII.[2] At the same time, the cardinals at Avignon and also the states of Castile and Navarre withdrew their recognition ; but financial needs soon drove the cardinals back to the Pope. Louis of Orleans, suspicious of the purposes of his uncle, likewise renewed his support of Benedict. The University of Toulouse offset the influence of the University of Paris. This action of France was virtually a schism within a schism. By this act of separation the chancellor of France, already viceroy, became to all intents and purposes vice-Pope. Consequently, in 1403, all France had again recognized the Avignon Pontiff and was forced to pay heavier Papal taxes than ever before.

In 1407, however, after the murder of Louis of Orleans by the son of Philip of Burgundy, a national synod resolved " to return to the old freedom " of the French Church, to restore the rights of the French clergy, and to curtail Papal prerogatives. That action was followed the next year by a declaration of neutrality for France, which meant, of course, a desertion of Benedict. The Gallican Church then proceeded to organize itself through synods and bishops.[3] The sentiment for union and peace throughout France was well nigh unanimous.[4] The King summoned his assembly at Paris. At the open session the preacher denounced Benedict as a

[1] Behind Orleans stood the feudal nobility ; and behind Burgundy were the citizens of the large cities and especially Paris ; Müller, ii, 52.

[2] Raynaldus, *Ann.*, 1398, No. 25.

[3] Kehrmann, *Frankriech's inner Kirchenpolit.*, 1890 ; Müller, *Frankreich's Unionsversuch*, 1393–98, 1881 ; Ferry, *La vie polit. de Louis de France duc d'Orleans* (1372–1407), 1889 ; Haller, *Papst.*, 197–308.

[4] Haller, 367.

heretic, schismatic, and an enemy of Christ. The two bulls of Benedict were pronounced illegal and treasonable, and then torn to pieces by the princes and university professors. The Pope's messengers were seized, dressed in fantastic costumes, and mounted on a high scaffold amidst popular derision. An armed force was sent to capture Benedict, but he escaped to Perpignan. The die was cast : at last France had proclaimed her neutrality to the world. The master mind in bringing about this decision was John Gerson. Of course, Benedict excommunicated all who participated in these proceedings, but that bull was publicly destroyed. France was at last free to act in the great councils soon to engage the attention of Europe. Her ultimatum was issued on 12th January, 1408 : in case the unity of the Church had not been restored by 24th May, 1408, France would publicly declare her neutrality and no longer recognize either Pope.[1] By 13th May almost the whole college of cardinals had deserted Gregory XII.[2] On 18th April Benedict returned a dignified and conciliatory reply and the King received it on 14th May. The threatened declaration of France went into effect at the end of the specified date.

In England the laws of 1380 made it practically impossible for ambitious outsiders to secure benefices in that country.[3] The laws were not strictly observed, however, for in 1381 and later there were countless complaints about provisions in abbacies and priories.[4] The king was given power to fill benefices and the government promised to enforce the laws.[5] Richard II at first praised Urban VI for his conduct,[6] but the regency quarrelled with him about taxes [7] and forbade the payment of money to the Roman curia.[8] Urban ordered England to receive his appointees under the ban and ignored English laws.[9] Boniface IX prolonged the conflict. The Commons continued to assert opposition to Papal taxes and appointments to benefices, and enacted the strictest laws to uphold their rights.[10] In a plain-spoken letter to the Pope the monarch said : " Thus is the Christian religion lowered ; the piety of the people disappears ; hospitality and alms cease ; houses of worship have become desolate ; the incomes of

---

[1] Haller, 294 ; Bulaeus, v, 151 ; Bourgeois du Chastenet, 259 ; Valois, iii, 597.
[2] Valois, iii, 588 ff. ; Bulaeus, v, 152.
[3] *Statutes of Realm*, ii, 14 ; *Eulog. Histor.*, iii, 349.   [4] *Rotuli Parl.*, iii, 117.
[5] Ib., 138, 162, 163.   [6] Rymer, iii, 4. 18.
[7] *Rotuli Parl.*, iii, 246.   [8] *Statutes*, ii, 60.
[9] Malverne, 205.   [10] *Statutes*, ii, 69 ; Gee and Hardy, 112.

churches disappear through absentee holders ; scholars leave the universities, who were once useful to the king and kingdom because all hope of advancement is cut off, and thus the clergy daily diminish ; and science and knowledge are almost lost." [1] When Richard II married Isabella, the daughter of Charles VI of France, in 1396, he agreed to unite with France in renouncing both Popes. When that plan failed, he favoured a general council to heal the schism.

Henry IV took a deep interest in Arundel's efforts to heal the schism. He attended at least one council called for that purpose by the archbishop. He was indignant at Gregory XII's breach of faith and wrote him a strong letter.[2] In 1408 he made a three year's peace with France, and co-operated with that nation in bringing peace to the Church. When the Council of Pisa elected Alexander V, he at once transferred his allegiance to him. When the English Parliament proposed to confiscate the temporalities of the Church, he opposed such a revolutionary scheme.[3]

The attitude of the English towards the schism is shown in the chronicle of Adam of Usk, who wrote in 1400 : " One thing in these days I grieve to tell, to wit, that two Popes, like a monster in nature, now for two and twenty years, most wickedly rending the seamless coat of Christ, contrary to the words of the Song of Solomon : ' My dove is but one,' have too sorely vexed the world by leading men's souls astray and racking their bodies with divers terrors." [4]

About the same time in 1408 Bohemia and Hungary withdrew their obedience from the Roman Pope.

The fact seems to be that the kings throughout Europe were for the most part tired of the schism and of the wobbling efforts of the Popes and cardinals to get rid of the double-headed monster which possessed the Papacy. They were eager, therefore, to see the general council convened and were prepared to take a prominent part through their representatives in its proceedings. Hence in the end the same states which had done so much to perpetuate the schism had to step in to bring it to an end.[5]

[1] Rymer, iii, 5. 58.
[2] Walsingham, *Hist. Angl.*, ii, 279.
[3] *Dict. of Nat. Biog.*, xxvi, 40, 41.
[4] Thompson, *Usk's Chronicle*, 218.
[5] Krüger, ii, 201.

62. *By the Universities*

The universities of Europe regarded the problems of the schism as suitable subjects for academic discussion and settlement. In the main the various universities took the side of the Pope supported by their sovereigns. Some of them at first and towards the end of the period, assumed a neutral attitude. As early as 21st November, 1378, Urban VI, in a letter to the University of Paris praised them for their loyalty to him.[1] In May of that year the University recognized Urban VI as Pope and sang the *Te deum laudamus*[2] after the arrival of the nuncios in Paris telling of Urban's election. On 12th June the University sent three professors as deputies to Rome, apparently to arrange about benefices.[3] In July the cardinals sent messengers to the University to explain the dissatisfaction with Urban.[4] After the election of Clement VII the University was divided in its loyalty to the two claimants, and hence decided to remain neutral.[5] The news of the election of Clement produced a pronounced difference of opinion among the doctors and a paper warfare took place between the defenders of the two Popes, which ended by a decision not to recognize either Pope without the unanimous vote of all faculties and nations. To the University streamed students from all European nations, hence neutrality was regarded as the best policy.[6] The University had three faculties—law, medicine, and theology—and was divided into four nations—French, Picards, Normans, and English. At the outset the French and Normans were against and the Picards were for Urban VI. Practically all of the professors and students were either holders or expectants of benefices.

The University of Paris was a great international institution, and had within its own constituency a schism like that in the Church and the states.[7] When the King of France forced the University to recognize the legitimacy of Clement VII, a large number of German students and professors left for their native land. One of the results of this exodus was the organization of a number of German universities.[8]

[1] Bulaeus, iv, 565.
[2] *Chartul*, iii, 552.
[3] Ib., 553.
[4] Ib., 553.
[5] Kneer, 9.
[6] Burger, ii, 202.
[7] Krüger, ii, 201.
[8] Kneer, 40, 85 ; Thornbeeke, 1, 9 ; Müller, ii, 52 ; Henderson, 262, gives the foundation charter of Heidelberg (1386).

On 16th November, 1378, Charles V declared for Clement VII.[1] About Easter, 1379, quite a few of the cardinals went to Paris to champion Clement's cause. They were present in the third French council held on 7th May, 1379, to urge the recognition of their candidate, but although the French king agreed with them, the clergy of the University and the people opposed such recognition.[2] Hence the monarch, on 21st May 1379, ordered the University to take a stand for Clement.[3] On 22nd May the Picards and English recognized Clement,[4] and on 24th May the Gallic nation and the faculty of medicine sent him the "rotulus".[5] By 1380 practically the whole University had declared for Clement VII. Some of the professors, however, like Henry of Langenstein, resigned rather than give him their support.[6] On 20th May, 1381, the University urged the King to summon a council, but he told the professors to mind their own business and imprisoned their spokesman.[7] Undaunted, they again and again urged that the representatives of the Church be called to heal the schism.[8] Indeed, it was the pronounced division in the University of Paris itself that led to the suggestion of a general council to settle the schism.[9] Nevertheless, on 3rd February, 1383, and again on 9th February, 1387, the University of Paris issued a declaration for Clement VII.[10] The English nation remained neutral till 1382.[11]

As the schism began to assume alarming proportions in Europe it spurred the University of Paris on to greater intellectual activity. Most of the pamphleteers of the period were connected in one way or another with that institution. On its faculties were many enlightened and conscientious men. Indeed, it was called the third great power in Europe—after the Pope and the Empire.[12] It certainly took the lead in agitating remedial measures. It urged the French King again and again to take active means, force if necessary, to heal the schism. It collected ten thousand individual opinions on the best methods of settling the ruinous controversy. It called upon

---

[1] *Chartul.*, iii, 562.
[2] Ib., 563.
[3] Ib., 564.
[4] Ib., 565.
[5] Ib., 563, 580.
[6] Ib., 561–75 ; Valois, ii, 394.
[7] Bulaeus, iv, 568 ; *Chartul.*, iii, 582.
[8] *Chartul.*, iii, 583.
[9] *Chartul.*, iii, 562.
[10] *Chartul.*, iii, 589, 592.
[11] Bulaeus, iv, 591, 592, v, 65.
[12] Rashdall, i, 546.

Clement to summon a general council ; he gave them an ear, but to no purpose.[1] The idea of forcing an end of the divided Papacy certainly belonged to that University. When Clement died, the King was memorialized to prevent the election of a successor, and when Benedict XIII was chosen he was urged to fulfil his vow to abdicate if necessary, or to take other steps to bring peace and unity, but he gave only polite words in reply.[2]

The University said : " What would Christ advise two disputing brothers to do ? Why first to try to settle the differences between themselves ; secondly, if that was impossible, to summon witnesses to compromise the dispute ; and thirdly to let the Church take it up." Hence nothing was left but to call a general council to settle the schism.[3] The University kept that idea alive.[4]

On 6th June, 1394, the University wrote a long and celebrated letter to the King of France suggesting three possible methods of effectually getting rid of the schism : (1) the abdication of both Popes ; (2) the appointment of a commission to pass on the respective claims and thus settle the contest by arbitration ; and (3) the summoning of a general council to settle the whole controversy.[5] The University preferred the first method as the simplest, and suggested that after the abdication of both Popes either the original college of cardinals of 1378 should then elect a new Pope, or the two schismatic colleges should unite for that purpose. The third method was recognized as being irregular, and the most difficult.[6] though under the unusual circumstances thoroughly justifiable. In the end the third plan proved to be the wisest, although the first was far more popular, and was definitely adopted in 1395.[7] The King sent the proposals to the cardinals at Avignon and they at once declared that one of the plans must be adopted.[8] Benedict XIII was angered at the officiousness of the University and denounced it as " a daughter of Satan, mother of error, sower of sedition, and the Pope's defamer." When Benedict

---

[1] Bulaeus, iv, 699.
[2] Bulaeus, iv, 714 ; Bourgeois du Chastenet, 123.
[3] Scheuffgen, 59.   [4] Kneer, 97.
[5] Chartul., iii, 608 ff. ; Thatcher and McNeal, No. 168 ; Bulaeus, i, 688.
[6] It was feared that a general council would be composed of ignorant bishops and that the Italians would have a majority, while the place and the composition would be questions hard to settle. Bulaeus, iv, 817, 818.
[7] Bulaeus, iv, 729, 732, 747, 773.   [8] Poole, 131.

sought to interfere with the University and to deprive its members of their benefices the faculties in 1396 appealed to the " future, sole, true, orthodox, and universal Pope." The doctors seem to have had a special hatred for Benedict, whom they repeatedly called a schismatic and heretic and " treated worse than a Jew."[1] The fight against Benedict seemed to be largely a personal one, and he was generally spoken of as " stubborn Benedict ". On penalty of expulsion all members of the University were forbidden to ask favours from him.[2] Special representatives were sent to England in 1395 and to Spain and Germany in 1396 urging action against him.[3] Yet in 1398 the University declared that the pope recognized no superior on earth, and that there was no court that could judge him.[4]

From 1394 until the Council of Pisa was called, the University of Paris never ceased its agitation to bring peace and unity to the Church.[5] It persuaded the national synod of 1395 to vote 87 to 22 in favour of Benedict's resignation, and to send a committee to him with the recommendation, but he absolutely scorned the well-meant advice. Then it decided to send trusty men to the various Kings of Europe to induce them to join in suppressing the dual Papal government, but little came of that effort. In 1395 a letter was sent to all the universities of Europe to join in advocating the *via cessionis*.[6] In 1396 the University wrote : " He who searches hearts knows that the French Church recognizes no difference between a Greek, Roman, Spaniard, German, or Frenchman, provided only that the Church is ruled in a holy manner."[7] As time passed and the futility of abdication voluntarily or of arbitration became more apparent, the University stressed the necessity of a general council, and deserved much credit for the successful issue of that plan. When the two colleges of cardinals at last seceded from the Popes and called the Council of Pisa for 1409 full confirmation for the legality of the course was given by the University of Paris,[8] along with Bologna and Florence. The University had greatly suffered by a depletion

[1] Bourgeois du Chastenet, 201 ; Valois, iv, 80.
[2] Denifle, iv, 13 ; Valois, iii, 11.
[3] Ehrle, *Archiv.*, vi, 200 ; Valois, iii, 87, 141.
[4] Bourgeois du Chastenet, 26, 29, 39.
[5] *Chartul.*, iii, 627 ff.   [6] Kneer, 98 ; Hartwig, i, 70 ff.
[7] Bulaeus, iv, 818.   [8] Ib., v, 163.

of students as a result of the schism and felt the loss very keenly. It is interesting to note that the very elements in France upon which the Babylonian Popes had depended for support were now hostile to the Avignon Papacy.

The conspicuous example of the University of Paris in attempting to solve the demoralizing problem before Europe was followed by other universities. The University of Toulouse gave its hearty support to Benedict. In the national assembly of 1398 a professor from that institution upheld the cause of Benedict.[1] The scheme of French secession was opposed and in 1402 a strong memorial was sent to the King of France urging him to return to the obedience of Benedict.[2] Still the University was in favour of calling a general council. Oxford University gave its cordial approval to the call of a general council.[3] On 5th February, 1398, in an opinion given to Richard II, it recommended that Boniface IX call a council of the Church and invite Benedict and his obedience to attend it.[4] At the University of Paris the English nation voted to expel Peter d'Ailly for his views on the schism.[5] The University of Bologna was rather inclined to side with the Roman Pontiff, but laboured zealously for peace. It advised the union of both colleges for the purpose of calling a general council.[6] In 1407 the faculties of theology, canon law, and civil law voted that it was the holy duty of the cardinals to withdraw from the two Popes, who had violated their oaths to work for unity and thereby heretically encouraged the schism, for the purpose of summoning a general council.[7] The University of Vienna responded to the appeal of the University of Paris to join in the *via cessionis*.[8]

63. *By Prominent Individuals*

The sorry spectacle of two Pontiffs dividing between them the outward allegiance of Latin Christendom was most humiliating to all true churchmen. That neither Popes, cardinals, nor secular princes would take measures adequate to cure the evil, as decade after decade passed by with the

---

[1] Haller, 249.   [2] Bulaeus, v, 4–24 ; Valois, iii, 265.
[3] Poole, 132.   [4] Raynaldus, 1398, 32.
[5] Denifle, *Auctarium*, i, 708.   [6] Souchon, ii, 7.
[7] Martène-Durand, *Amp. Coll.* viii, 894–7 ; Mansi, xxvii, 219–23 ; Souchon, i, 146, ii, 7.
[8] Kneer, 99 ; Müller, ii, 52.

continuance of the double-headed Papacy, and all its attendant abuses and oppressions, called forth individual critics and reformers among both the clergy and laity such as the Church had never experienced. Christendom looked upon the scandal helpless and depressed, and yet impotent to remove it. With two sections of Christendom each declaring the other lost, each cursing and denouncing the other, men soberly asked who was saved. The longer the schism lasted, the more difficult did it seem to heal it, and yet people generally felt that for that very reason positive action was all the more necessary. The very sublimity of Papal pretensions made earthly jurisdiction and compulsory abdication seem very difficult. Still the fact stared Europe in the face that the schism itself, with the cupidity, selfishness, and meanness accompanying it, had shattered the sanctity of Papal claims in breaking up the unity of Christendom. Hence it was easier to deal with these very pretensions and, if necessary, restore unity and peace at their expense. The attacks made on Papal prerogatives and the endeavour to change the Papal constitution did not come from the revolutionary element in the ordinary sense, but from the very leaders and authorities among the ruling class—the most conspicuous prelates, university professors, and princes. The question of the relation of the Papacy to the Church so boldly raised in this period was to continue to our own day. The leading personalities of the period were with but few exceptions canonists.[1]

Among the prominent men of the day who laboured with their pens to restore the Church to its earlier unity and power were :—

Conrad of Gelnhausen, a German, born about 1320, who went to the University of Paris in 1344. There he joined the English " nation " and began his studies in the theological faculty. After qualifying as a master, he took up theology, and earned his doctor's degree. From Paris he went to the University of Bologna, probably as an instructor.[2] When the schism broke out, he had returned to Paris and was a professor of law. Together with other German professors in the University he helped to create a sentiment in favour of Urban VI, and thus for a while induced the University to take

---

[1] Ehrle, *Martin de Alpartils*, 462.   Kneer, 36-7.

a neutral attitude. When the King of France forced the University to recognize Clement VII, Conrad and other German colleagues, and students left the University and returned to their native land. He was soon called to the University of Heidelberg, founded in 1386, served as the second rector, and died in 1390,[1] bequeathing his library and property to the University.

He took a deep interest in the scandalous schism, lived through twelve years of it, and was one of the most original, creative minds in suggesting remedies. As early as 31st August, 1379, less than a year after Clement VII was elected and shortly before his arrival in Avignon, Conrad wrote his *Epistola brevis* in which he declared that nothing short of a general council could adjust the claims of the rival claimants to the chair of St Peter. He called attention to the fact that Church history furnished numerous instances where general councils had settled questions of canon law and cited the cases of Leo III, Leo IV, Marcellus, Sixtus III, Gregory IV, and Innocent IV as precedents. The leading canonists of the Church, he asserted, made necessity an excuse for calling a general council. Since such a necessity confronted the Church at that time, he urged the King of France and the Emperor of Germany, together with princes, bishops, and doctors, to summon such a body for the purpose of uniting the " separated brothers ".[2]

In May, 1380, appeared a second and more important pamphlet called *Epistola concordia*.[3] He addressed the letter to the King of France, Charles V,[4] and stated that his love for his " spiritual mother ", the Church, prompted him to write it. All were clamouring for the crushing of the schism, yet nothing had been done. He again urged necessity as a valid reason for calling a general council. Necessity had called the first four universal councils. Just as a local synod was called to meet local needs, so a general council should be held to solve the grave dangers confronting the whole Church, since only

---

[1] Bliemetzrieder, *Die wahre hist. Bedeutung Konrads von Gelnhausen*, in *den Stud. u. Mitt. a. d. Benedict u. Cist. Orden*, 1907, 549 ff. This work shows the errors held hitherto about Conrad.

[2] Bliemetzrieder, *Lit. Polem.*, 66.

[3] Martène-Durand, *Thesaur.*, ii, 1200–1226 ; Wench, *Hist. Zeitschrift*, lxxvi, 1 ff. ; *Chartul.*, iii, 581.

[4] A copy was sent to the Elector of Palatinate and to the Roman King in 1381.

such a body was superior to both the Pope and the cardinals.[1] Neither Pope was in a position to summon a council, hence there must be an extra-legal call,[2] or what under ordinary circumstances was not permitted became obligatory under necessity. He defined a general council as the meeting of the whole Church, that is of all true believers, through their representatives.[3] The cardinals could not settle the schism, since their testimony would be so contradictory and they might even be guilty of falsehood. One of the Popes was the true Pope, otherwise there would be a vacancy, but only a council could settle the doubt.[4] In plain, clear, sensible, conservative words this eminent canonist, basing his arguments like a modern man on a wide range of authorities, made it evident that if the established law did not provide means to heal the schism, then other methods would have to be devised. His solution was a general council.[5] Gelnhausen practically originated the theory of conciliar church government, which was further elaborated by Langenstein, Gerson, d'Ailly, Niem, Zabarella, and others, and which blossomed in the councils of Pisa and Constance.[6]

Henry of Langenstein, a German theologian and mathematician, born in 1340, was a contemporary of Conrad of Gelnhausen. He also went to the University of Paris at least as early as 1363, where he first qualified as master in philosophy, and then by 1376 as doctor in theology. He became a member of the English " nation " and was one of that powerful coterie of German professors at Paris.[7] At one time he served as vice-chancellor of that institution.[8] He was a progressive in many fields of thought and stubbornly fought superstitions and astrology. In 1368 he wrote *Questio de cometa* in which he exploded the theory of the prophetic character of comets, and before 1376 he had written three more pamphlets on the same subject.[9] He was also entrusted with numerous official embassies of an important character.

When the schism broke out in 1378 he joined the group of German professors and students who defended the Roman Pope against Clement VII, and who persuaded the University to take a neutral position.[10] In 1379 he wrote his *Epistola*

---

[1] *Epistola concordia*, chap. i. See summary in Scheuffgen, 77–82 ; Kneer, 60.
[2] Ib., chap. ii.   [3] Ib., chap. iii.   [4] Ib., chap. iv.
[5] Bliemetzrieder, *Lit. Polem.*, 90 ; Kneer, 60 ff. ; Scheuffgen, 91 ; Haller, 337 ff.
[6] Kneer, 126 ; Scheuffgen, 91.   [7] Denifle, *Gesch. der Univ.*, i, 617.
[8] Aschbach, *Gesch. der Univ. Wien*, i, 372 ff.   [9] *Cath. Encycl.*, vii, 236.
[10] Kneer, 60.

pacis, a clever dialogue between an Urbanist and a Clementine in 88 parts.[1] In it were given a number of clear definitions of terms connected with Papal elections and Church government. A strong case was made out for the legitimacy of the election of Urban VI. The cardinals were upbraided for their cowardly action and were told that their existence was an accident and not founded upon Biblical warrant, since they were not even mentioned in the Bible. Clement's election was declared invalid for many reasons, but chiefly because it was not unanimous since the Italian cardinals had refused to vote. Still he recognized the schism as an accomplished fact and proposed the following methods of getting rid of it :—

1. The University of Paris, which was famous throughout the world for solving perplexing problems, might bring about a solution and adjustment. That plan was not strongly urged however.

2. A commission of 15 or 20 members made up of representatives of the three parties in Christendom, namely, (*a*) Urbanists, (*b*) Clementines, and (*c*) neutrals, should be appointed either by the two Popes, or better still by the unprejudiced neutrals. God, he believed, would help such a board to conclude peace.[2]

3. A general council was suggested as the *via communis et regia ecclesia* and the most feasible way to settle the trouble, because that body was the sovereign power in the Church, represented all the faithful, and worked for the welfare of Christendom. The council should be summoned by (*a*) the two Popes acting jointly, or if they refused, by (*b*) the original cardinals and the leading prelates, or if they declined, by (*c*) the other clergy in the Church, because in the early days the bishops sat in judgment over Marcellus and John XII, or in case they would not act, by (*d*) the princes since both the Scriptures and Church history justified such a course. The cost of such a council should not be counted against the perpetuation of the schism. He believed that all moderate and honourable thinking men were heartily in favour of a council.

In the latter half of 1381 appeared at Paris the *Epistola concilii pacis* in which the arguments of the conciliar theory

---

[1] Bulaeus, iv, 574 ff. ; Scheuffgen, 43 ff. ; Kneer, 66.   [2] Part 58.

and even whole phrases were borrowed from Gelnhausen's
Epistola pacis of two years previous. The work was divided
into five parts and contained twenty chapters.[1] In arguing
about the powers and authority of a general council, he stood
squarely upon the shoulders of Gelnhausen.[2] He emphasized
the fact that all prominent men in Europe were in favour of
a general council to heal the schism. The right to choose
a Pope belonged primarily to the Church, but the Church had
delegated that right to the cardinals. In doubtful cases,
however, the exercise of that right reverted to the Church
represented in a general council. The Popes were powerless
to put an end to the divided Papacy, hence the duty devolved
upon all Christians to restore unity, purity, and power.[3]
Effectively to heal the breach, three steps were necessary :
(1) every Christian should return repentant to God and do
penance for his sins ; (2) the whole Church should pray for
forgiveness and relief ; and (3) the general council should
convene under the grace of the Holy Spirit to remove the evils
afflicting the Church.[4]

The duty of calling the council rested with the princes,
who should adjust their differences, set the example of duty
and piety, and work for the peace of the Church as in the past,
because they were the leaders of the Church [5] ; and upon
the prelates whose first duty it was, as the successors of the
Holy Fathers, to restore and preserve the unity and purity
of the Church.[6] Then he enumerated eight reasons against
calling a council and fourteen reasons for one based upon
the history of the Church.[7] After dealing with the right of
the council to choose a true Pope, and to sit as a supreme
court,[8] he gave a summary of his arguments in favour of a
general council to deal with the schism.[9]

When the French monarch compelled the University of
Paris to recognize Clement VII, Henry with a number of
Germans at Paris then severed his connection with the Uni-
versity, and in 1383 entered a Cistercian monastery near

---

[1] Von der Hardt, ii, 3–60, gives the tract except Chaps. 1–2, which were
published later in *Discrepantia mss. et editionum*, Helmstadt, 1715, 9–11.
Cf. Du Pin. *Opp. Gerson*, ii, 810. Kneer, 76, gives excellent reasons for using
the title given above instead of *Concilium pacis*. Scheuffgen, 61–75.

[2] Kneer, 84, 110.   [3] Part i, chap. 3.   [4] Part i, chap. 4.
[5] Ib., chap. 4, 6, 7.   [6] Ib., chap. 8, 9.   [7] Part ii.
[8] Part iii.   [9] Part iv.

Wiesbaden.   While there he wrote a letter *De schismate* [1]
to the Bishop of Worms, in which he continued his efforts
for peace.   He was invited to the University of Vienna in
1384, where he helped to organize the theological faculty,
spent the rest of his days teaching theology and canon law,
and wrote numerous treatises.   Roth attributes to his pen 7
works on astronomy, 18 historical works on the Schism, 17
polemics, 12 epistles and sermons, and 50 ascetic tracts.[2]
He was one of the most advanced men of his day, a pronounced
liberal in theology and philosophy, and used both the synthetic
and analytic method.   Compared with him Gelnhausen was
a conspicuous conservative, who never departed from a safe
legal footing.   He died in 1397,[3] as rector of the University
of Vienna, after having seen the schism continued for a
generation.

Two treatises written towards the close of his interesting
career are worth noting in this connection.   In 1393 he wrote
his *Investiva contra monstrum Babylonis*, a work of 900 lines,
in which he still believed in the possibility of a voluntary
abdication of the two schismatic Popes and the election of
a true Pope, but urged a more practical and more certain course,
namely, the general council.   The double-headed monster
of a schism could be killed only by blood-letting, not with
the sword of iron, but with the sword of spirit.   The Church
could wait no longer for miracles   The German Emperor and
the French King ought to call the council and cure the horrible
disease.[4]

Two years before his death he wrote *Epistola de cathedra
Petri* in 163 verses to Bishop Berthold of Freising.   He
deplored the sad schism and said that a whole army of evils
were resulting from it every day.   A stop must be put to that
devilish condition.   Many methods had been proposed, but
leaders were wanting to carry out any of them.   A general
council had at first seemed to him to be the best course to
follow, but both Popes so stubbornly resisted it that he now
proposed : (1) That the two Popes take away the power to
choose a Pope from the two colleges of cardinals and transfer
it either to a small commission of four or six prominent men

[1] Edited by Sommerfeldt, *Hist. Jahrb.*, Munich, 1909, xxx, 46–61.
[2] *Cath. Encycl.*   [3] Aschbach, i, 372 ff.
[4] Kneer, 94 ff. ; *Chartul.*, iii, 598.

who should accept the resignation of the two claimants and elect a true Pope, or to the Roman Church ; (2) that in case the Popes refused this plan, or the commissioners proved a failure, all princes, bishops, priests, abbots and Christians should withdraw their allegiance and withhold their contributions from both Popes until they took some positive remedial action ; or in the event of the fruitlessness of that arrangement, then let the princes and prelates take matters into their own hands and consult as to the next step to be taken. That, of course, would lead directly to a general council. This last tract was short, sharp, clear, and to the point ; and summed up without any verbiage practically all his previous arguments.[1]

Peter of Ancarno, born in 1330 of a branch of the Italian Farnese house, was one of the most celebrated canonists of the period of the schism. He studied law at Bologna, Siena, Padua, and Venice. In 1392 he was called to Bologna as one of the most renowned teachers of canon law in Europe.[2] Students from Spain, England, France, Netherlands, and Germany as well as Italy, flocked to his classroom. He knew Innocent VII intimately,[3] and was on friendly terms with cardinals and princes. The Roman Pope frequently called upon him to give advice and to fill important missions. He suggested six means of healing the schism : (1) the disputed question of law should be submitted to the scholars of Europe for decision ; (2) a general council should be called ; but he was not certain as to how such a body should be convened, and rather doubted the right of the cardinals to call it. The terrible scandal, however, led him to change his mind and to favour a council called by the cardinals on the ground that the emergency justified such a course ; (3) a commission of five or six princes and prelates from each nation should bring about some compromise out of the entanglement ; (4) all Christendom should pray that God would direct the schismatic Popes and cardinals to make a direct settlement of the controversy ; (5) both Popes should agree to a mutual resignation and then the united cardinals should elect a new Pope ; and (6) secular princes should use force to secure unification. This plan should be used only as a last resort after all the other

---

[1] Kneer, 102 ff.
[2] He seems to have been in Ferrara from 1403 to 1405.   Souchon, ii, 241.
[3] Kneer, *Hist. Jahrb.*, (Görres), xii, 345 ff.

plans had failed. He had little faith in the first and fourth plans because the raven of discord had eaten up the dove of the Holy Ghost. He laboured hard for the fifth proposition. The schism, he declared, was contrary to the fundamental doctrines of the Christian Church and led the common people to think that the plan of salvation as preached by the Church was a frivolous thing. The Pope who did not use all means to heal the schism was guilty of deadly sin and fell into heresy. Such a disgraceful squabble was contrary to both the Bible and the Church history, hence all Christians were urged to labour for peace and unity.

In 1405 Cardinal Cossa, who lived at Bologna, asked Ancarno for advice about the best way to secure union. He replied that nothing was to be gained from a discussion of the legitimacy of Urban's election. The Popes, one or both, must be persuaded to resign for the good of the Church without regard to the question of right. If they refused then the only course open was to force them to be removed. Should the Popes withdraw, then the cardinals could unite as the repre-sentatives of the law of continuity and choose a new Pope. No man on the Roman side had spoken with more boldness or with more wisdom.[1]

He went to the Council of Pisa in 1409 as the representative of the University of Bologna and took a prominent part. He also attended the early sessions of the Council of Constance until driven home by disease,[2] and was about the only friend John XXIII had in that body.[3] He made no attack on the office of the Papacy, but on the contrary championed Papal absolutism. He said the Pope as God's representative stood above canon law and the councils. The Emperor was subject to the Pope. The Pope had to yield to a council only in the case of heresy. The Pope and cardinals were inseparably united like man and wife, hence the cardinals enjoyed the Pope's privileges and prerogatives. The Pope should always advise with them. In the case of a schism, therefore, the jurisdiction devolved upon the cardinals. In case the Pope died and there was no college of cardinals then the duty of electing a new Pontiff would devolve upon the general council, or perhaps upon the Roman clergy which would be still

---

[1] Souchon, i, 82–84, 85 ; ii, 242, 244.   [2] Ib., ii, 242.
[3] Finke, *Forschungen*, 257 ff.

better. But by 1407 he was hot for a council as the only way out of the perplexing difficulty.[1]

Peter d'Ailly, a French theologian and philosopher, was one of the most conspicuous personalities in the negotiations to unify the Papacy. He was born in Compiègne in 1350 and died at Avignon in 1420. He entered the College of Navarre in 1372 as a theological student and finished his education at the University of Paris, where at the age of 30 he received his doctorate in theology. In 1375 he prepared a commentary on Lombard's *Sentences*, but was recognized as a pronounced liberal. In 1381 in an eloquent address before the regent, the Duke of Anjou, he sought to win the French court to favour a general council to end the schism. His appeal failed, however, and he retired to Noyen, where he wrote *Epistola diaboli Leviathan* [2]—a satirical letter purporting to come from the devil in which his satanic majesty ordered his vassals, the priests, to continue their activity in promoting the schism. He warned them in their own interest to oppose all efforts to bring about peace through a general council, otherwise eternal shame would be their lot. He urged them to follow his example more industriously in making the Church a house of barter, in tithing anise and cummin, in wearing gaudy clothing, and in enlarging their kingdom and in increasing the number of their subjects.

He championed the cause of Benedict XIII at first, but gradually withdrew his support, urged the two Popes to resign, and agitated for a general council. In 1384 he was made director of the College of Navarre, where he had Nicholas of Clemanges and John Gerson as pupils, and gained great fame for his eloquent sermons and lucid discussions. Five years later he was chosen chancellor of the University of Paris, became the confessor of the King and treasurer of the Saint Chapelle, and was recognized as a man of power and influence in the French court.[3] He visited the court of Clement VII to persuade him to uphold the University in a controversy over the immaculate conception and succeeded. When Benedict XIII was elected he was sent by the French

---

[1] Souchon, ii, 165.

[2] Tschackert, Appendix, 15–21, gives the text. The list of his writings is on pages 348–65, and an estimate of their value on pages 303–35. Ehrle, *Martin de Alpartel*, gives two unused tracts of D'Ailly on the Schism (1395-1404).

[3] Ehrle, *Martin de Alpartel*, 462.

King on a secret mission to Avignon.[1] He was on very intimate
terms with that Pontiff and did not hesitate to accept from his
hands the appointment as Bishop of Le Puy in 1395 and as
Bishop of Cambray in 1397. Clement VII and Benedict XIII
stopped his mouth with benefices, and almost bribed him to
become a defender.[2] He was one of the richest ecclesiastical
princes of the day.[3] There was something of the opportunist
in d'Ailly, for in 1398 he heartily approved the action of France
in subtracting its obedience from Benedict and then in 1403
he counselled submission again in a strong sermon at Paris,
although he made certain reservations in the interest of France.
In 1405 he was once more with Benedict at Genoa, and in
1407 he accompanied him to Savona in the hope of a joint
abdication.   Meanwhile France had once more withdrawn
its obedience.   D'Ailly was seized and taken to Paris, but was
protected by the King.   In January, 1409, in the synod
of Aïx he made a powerful appeal for a general council in
which he asserted that since the Church had both a natural
and a divine right to its unity, it could and ought to call a
council without Papal sanction.   He declared that disunion,
if continued, would destroy the Papacy itself.[2] A few months
later the Council of Pisa was summoned.

At Pisa he sanctioned the acts which deposed the two Popes
and elected Alexander V.   John XXIII made him a cardinal
in 1411 and he assisted in the Council of Rome in 1412. He
played an important rôle in the Council of Constance, presided
over it on March 26, 1415, and saw the schism finally healed
by the Election of Martin V in 1417.[4] He was sent to Avignon
as Papal legate and passed his last days there. He was easily
one of the half dozen greatest men of that day, and was deeply
interested in all the great questions of the age as is shown by
the 154 treatises on the Schism, Church government, theology,
philosophy, history, astronomy, geography, and meteorology.[5]
He was a nominalist and drew many of his ideas from Occam.[6]
He believed in astrology and wrote a *Concordance of Astronomy
with History* to prove its truth.   His geographical work
Picture of the World, following Roger Bacon, asserted the
rotundity of the earth and expressed the belief that Cathay

[1] Valois, iii, 25 ; Ehrle, *Martin de Alpartel*, 469.   [2] Souchon, ii, 158.
[3] Ib., 218.   [4] Hübler, 74 ; Finke, *Forsch.*, 103.
[5] Ehrle, *Martin de Alpartel*, 462.
[6] Haller, 342 ; Müller, *Occam in Allg. deutsche Biog.*, xxiv, 125.

could be reached by sailing westward. Columbus owned a printed copy of that work and it is still preserved with his marginal notes in the Columbian Library at Seville.[1]

John Gerson, the "Most Christian Doctor", was born near Rheims in 1363, and became the most influential theologian of this period of division and reform councils. He entered the College of Navarre at the age of 14 and there came under the influence of Peter D'Ailly and Peter de Aliaco. He took his doctor's degree in theology in 1392, and soon became conspicuous for his brains and his capacity for leadership. At the age of 20 he was chosen procurator of the French "nation" in the University of Paris, and in 1387 was sent as one of the delegation to Clement VII to secure the condemnation of the Dominican, John of Montson, for denying the immaculate conception of Mary. In 1390 he was lecturing on the *Sentences* in the University. The next year he wrote a tract on the best means of securing ecclesiastical unity in which he proposed three ways of healing the schism: (1) By compromise; (2) through a general council; and (3) by the resignation of both Popes.[2] He always exercised a sober and moderate opinion in dealing with the two Papal claimants and opposed violent proceedings.[3]

When d'Ailly was promoted to the episcopate in 1395 Gerson fell heir to his position in the University of Paris as professor of theology and chancellor, and received his appointment at the hands of Benedict XIII. In that important office he was soon recognized as the most influential intellectual leader in Europe. From 1397 to 1401 he was in Bruges as dean of Saint Donatien and there wrote *Sententia de modo se habendi tempora schismatis*.[4] He was one of the first to show that Benedict XIII should not be regarded as either a heretic or a schismatic.[5] In 1398 he fought the "total subtraction" of France, but was not opposed to the curtailment of the Pope's temporal power and wealth.

In the discussions over the Schism, in which the University of Paris took such a dominant part, Gerson was the leading spirit. His voice and pen carried great weight in moulding public opinion in the Church in reference to the settlement

---

[1] Cf. "La découverte de l'Amerique et Pierre d'Ailly" by Salembier in *Revue de Lille*, 1892, v, 622; Fisk, *Discovery of America* i, 372.

[2] *Chartul*, iii, 595.   [3] Valois, iii, 71, 180.

[4] Schwab, 97, 152.   [5] *Opera*, ii.

of the schism and other pregnant questions growing out of it. No one deplored the disgraceful bickerings more than he, and no one saw more clearly the long train of disasters that were bound to follow unless something was done to settle the quarrel. He took the ground that peace and unity were necessary to enable the Church to fulfil its mission, since all Church authority was established for the purpose of preserving peace and unity. All members of the Church should be ready, therefore, to make any sacrifice of position or office to restore and to preserve that peace and unity. It was better to have peace without a Pope than disunion with two uncertain claimants, because salvation was possible without a Pope. At first he hoped much from the diplomacy of princes, but was keenly disappointed, and then developed his conciliar theory as the most certain method of obtaining peace.[1] In 1407 he and d'Ailly as members of a delegation went to Benedict XIII to persuade him to resign by a formal bull but failed, hence after 1408 he was thoroughly committed to a general council as the wisest course to pursue. With d'Ailly he took a sort of middle position between Benedict XIII and the University of Paris and tried to bring them together.[2]

In the opening address to the Council of Rheims in 1408 he stood forth as a strong champion of the council. In two famous tracts, *De unitate ecclesiastica* and *De auferbilitate papae ab ecclesia*, he unified public opinion into the conviction that the Church must be unified and that a general council was the most practical means of accomplishing it. Just as Aristotle asserted that for the good of all a people could depose its prince, so the Church could set aside obstinate, schismatic Popes for the sake of peace and unity.

At the Council of Pisa, at which official business prevented his attendance, he saw his theories put into operation. He was also unable to attend the Council of Rome. At the Council of Constance he took a leading part and again and again, by voice and by pamphlet, he advocated his ideas and was gratified to see that body accept them. He gave his unqualified support to the condemnation of the heresies of Wiclif and Huss.[3] To his mind heresy was a terrible, contagious cancer

---

[1] These ideas were set forth in a sermon preached in 1404 before Benedit XIII, and the Duke of Orleans. Du Pin, ii, 54–72. Cf. Schwab., 171–8.

[2] Souchon, ii, 159.   [3] Schwab, 540–609.

which must be cut out to save the life of the Church.[1] In the controversy over giving the cup to the laity, he strongly defended the position of the Medieval Church.[2] As a result of the displeasure of the Duke of Burgundy over Gerson's opposition to Jean Petit's theses that the murder of a tyrant or of a traitorous vassal, was justifiable,[3] he was not permitted to return to France until the Duke's death in 1419. Then he went to Lyons and spent his last days in monastic seclusion, dying in 1429.[4] After d'Ailly was created cardinal in 1411, Gerson was recognized in France as the leader of the liberal party in the Church. Although he was in sympathy with the progressive spirit of his age, he was in no sense an extremist.

Nicholas of Clemanges, a French humanist and liberal theologian, was born at Champagne about 1367 and entered the College of Navarre at the age of 12,[5] where his ideas were moulded by d'Ailly and Gerson. In 1380 he became a licentiate, later he received the degree of master of arts, and in 1393 that of bachelor of theology from the University of Paris. His advanced work was done in the faculty of arts rather than in theology.[6] Upon the election of Benedict XIII, he wrote a letter to him appealing to him, as the one who no longer occupied the position of one boatman among others, but stood at the rudder of the ship, to act in the interest of all Christendom. He began to lecture at the University in 1391 and served as rector from 1393 to 1395.

In the discussions over the "pestiferous" Schism, he was a timid but nevertheless, a prominent leader. He asserted that God alone knew whom the Holy Ghost had elected as Pope. Hence under the circumstances a general council was the only infallible power in the Church capable of settling the problem. By 1394 he began to insist upon the voluntary resignation, or the compulsory abdication, of both Popes. The next year he was forced to give up the rectorship of the University, and then became canon of St Codoald and later canon and treasurer of Langres. In 1397 Benedict took him as his secretary and he remained at Avignon with that Pontiff till 1408, when, " weary of the vices and tumults " of Avignon, he abandoned the Pope and retired to a Carthusian monastery,

---

[1] Du Pin, ii, 207.   [2] Ib., i, 457–68 ; Schwab, 604 sqq.
[3] *Opera*, ii and v ; *Chartul.*, iv, 261–85, 325 ff. ; Schwab, 609 ff.
[4] Schwab, 767 ff.   [5] Rashdall, i, 491 ff.   [6] *Chartul.*, iii, 606.

where he gave himself up to the study of the Scriptures, regretted that he had spent so much valuable time on the classics, and wrote his best treatises.[1]

Such a man could not remain hidden in a monastery, however, in the fifteenth century, hence in 1412 he was persuaded to return to Langres and was named archdeacon of Bayeux. He attended neither the Council of Pisa nor the Council of Constance, although he wrote to the latter body urging unity of thought and action. In 1425 he was teaching rhetoric and theology in the College of Navarre, and probably died there in 1437. He was a forerunner of the reforming humanists. At the University he was one of the leaders in classical studies and wrote that in Paris Virgil, Terence, and Cicero were often read in both public and private.[2]

Francis of Zabarella, born in Padua in 1339, took his university course at the University of Bologna, and then after 1391 taught canon law with marked success at Padua and Florence. He was chosen Archbishop of Florence, but Boniface IX called him to Rome instead as an adviser on the Schism.[3] He soon returned to Padua and became with Peter of Ancarno the leader of the progressive ecclesiastical party in Italy.

He wrote three tracts on the problems confronting the Church, of which *De schismate sui temporis*, penned in 1403, was the most famous. At first he believed that the Schism could be healed by one of five methods : (1) through compromise by a commission ; (2) by an agreement between the two Popes ; (3) by the resignation of both claimants and the election of a true Pope ; (4) by an arrangement whereby each college of cardinals would recognize the surviving Pope, or wait until both died and then unite to elect a Pope ; and (5) by compulsory deposition either by a council, or by the Emperor, on the ground of heresy and obstinacy.[4] As the Schism continued to the injury of the Church, Zabarella, failing to see any of his suggestions materialized, became more radical. He then advocated the exercise of the right of " subtraction ", such as had been used by France against Benedict XIII,

---

[1] *De fructu eremi* ; *De fructu rerum adversum* ; *De novis festivitatibus non instituendis* ; and *De studio theologico* ; Schuberth, *Nicolaus von Clemanges als Verfasser der Schrift de corrupto ecclesiae statu*, Leipzig, 1888.
[2] *Chartul.*, III, 606.   [3] Scheuffgen, 100.
[4] *Ib.*, iii ; cf. Kneer, 58 ff. ; Souchon, i, 84 ff.

by all true Christians on both sides. He argued that since the Popes were both dangerous heretics and stubborn schismatics, every single member of the Church possessed the right of rebellion against the Popes and was not bound to obey them—nay, it was his duty not to render obedience and not to give any material support. The general good was paramount to that of the individual. Thus deprived of all obedience and all means of subsistence, the Popes would be forced to surrender and to give the Church unity and peace. This was by far the most radical course suggested, and showed to what extent the unrest, suspicion, and disgust produced by the Schism encouraged the best men to go.[1]

He was the first to emphasize the necessity and legality of calling a council through the union of the two colleges of cardinals.[2] As early as 1403 he advised that course and derived their constitutional competence to call a council representing the whole Church out of their right of election, Biblical authority, canon law, the Church Fathers, Gratian, and the decretals.[3] He said that if the Popes could not or would not agree, then the cardinals were under obligation to find a way out of the dilemma, since they were the only organization representing the whole Church that possessed the power to call a council. The universal Church had delegated to the cardinals the authority to elect a Pope, hence in the event of a disputed election it was their duty to give the Church a single head even if they were forced to exercise their right to depose the two schismatic Popes.[4] The old idea that the Pope himself was the supreme judge and hence could be judged by none was denied. The supremacy of the Pope was not in the person of the Pope but in the office of the Pope and the cardinals, because both represented the universal Church. The Pope was not immune, nor did he possess absolute power except as he acted in the name of the universal Church with the co-operation of the cardinals.[5] By 1408 he was still using these arguments, but as time passed he stressed more and more the simple plan of calling a general council to settle the difficulties.[6]

He defended the supremacy of the council over the Pope who, in case of error, should be corrected by the superior power.

[1] Scheuffgen, 98.   [2] Souchon, ii, 36.   [3] Ib., 37.
[4] Ib., i, 86–7; ii, 36 ff.   [5] Ib., 37–8.
[6] Niem, 554–70 gives the tract.

He denounced the Popes as " oath-violators, schismatics, and heretics ", whose dignities and powers should be taken from them by a council called by the cardinals. God, not the Pope, was the true head of the Church, and in the case of an unholy schism the Church through a council should decide which Pope was a good representative and which one was a bad representative—a power which beyond doubt was given it by canon law.[1]

In 1411 Zabarella entered the services of John XXIII as cardinal, but his appointment to that honour did not prevent him from helping to arrange for the Council of Constance, nor from actively participating in it. He deserted John and remained loyal to the Council as the supreme power in the Church. He died on 26th September, 1417, before the new Pope, Martin V, was elected.[2]

Pierre Leroy, a Norman by birth and a Benedictine monk, appeared at the University of Paris in 1379.[3] He was so radical in his efforts to heal the Papal Schism that he was put under the ban and the curse was not removed until 1383. He was generally recognized as the leading canonist in France towards the end of the fourteenth century. He also held the office of Abbot of Mont St Michel. No man in France was more active in Church politics than he, for he sat in all synods, had a place on all committees, and was connected with all important embassies. Clement VII denounced him as a skilled author of trouble. He was bold, shrewd, and full of ideas, a very eloquent speaker, and the type of a man who would grace any parliament. So far as is known, he left no writings behind him, but made two noteworthy addresses in the national councils of 1398 and 1406 in which he contended that the best way to kill the monstrous Schism was to withhold the revenues which kept it alive. He was a strong supporter of a general council and believed that the rulers of Europe had authority to call it. He set forth his ideas with a clearness and energy of thought that chains one's attention.[4] Alexander V appointed him his *referendor*. He died in Bologna in 1410.

Simon Cramaud, another product of the University of Paris, the Patriarch of Alexandria and a royal adviser, was a prominent

---

[1] Souchon, ii, 38 ff.   [2] Scheuffgen, 100.   [3] Denifle, 248, 573.
[4] Bourg. du Chastenet, 164–176 ; Haller, 350.

leader of the liberal party in the Church against the two rival Popes. He was a master politician, easily captured the ear of prelates, princes and kings with his cleverness, and consequently exercised a powerful influence in that day. He presided over the French synod in 1395 and did more than any single individual to cause the French " subtraction " in 1398. He also advised the independence of the French national Church. He laboured with might and main to stop the breach : (1) by preventing the election of a successor when Clement VII died ; (2) by attempting to persuade both pretenders to resign ; (3) by uniting the two colleges for a new election ; and (4) by calling a council to settle the whole problem.

He saw his endeavours triumph in the secession of the two colleges of cardinals, in their united action in calling a council, and in the election of a new Pontiff at Pisa.[1] He was a member of that council and could flatter himself that he had had a large share in bringing about the unity of the Church. Unfortunately he could not at the time see that the Schism was worse than ever. He was made a cardinal in 1413, and after 1417 he took a part in the Council of Constance and there saw peace and unity permanently realized. He was a Church revolutionist who deserves to rank with Gelnhausen and Langenstein.[2]

Matthew of Cracovia, not a Pole as has been held, but a German from Cracow in Pomerania, a student at Prague where he received his master's degree in 1367, completed his education in the University of Paris, and served as dean in the university faculty.[3] He belonged to the German party, and when the University, under royal pressure, voted to recognize Clement VII, he left Paris and accepted a call to the University of Heidelberg.[4] In 1403 he was sent by Ruprecht as an ambassador to Boniface IX, and in 1406 he went on a similar peace mission to Gregory XII. The German Emperor sent him to Pisa in 1409 where he died in 1416.

Early in the fifteenth century he wrote *De squaloribus curiae Romanae* in twenty long chapters portraying the sad conditions of the Church as a result of the Schism.[5] He accepted

[1] Souchon, i, 247, 272 ; ii, 11, 161 ; Finke, *Forsch.*. 14 ff.
[2] Souchon, ii, 161 ; Haller, 357 ; Bourg. du Chastenet, 218.
[3] Bulaeus, iv, 975 ; Franke, *Matth. von Krakau: Sein Leben, Charakter und sein Schr*. Greifswald, 1910.
[4] Thorbecke, *Gesch. der Univ. Heidelberg*, i, 20.   [5] Niem, i, 68.

the Petrine theory, but declared that the Pope and curia were in the state of damnation on account of their vices and simony.[1] The Church had one head and one capital, not two. Christ was the true head of the Church, not the Pope, who was only its custodian. The Church was the society of true believers and had both the right and the power to restore the true Pope and to preserve the unity of the Church. It could settle controverted elections and if necessary even depose a Pope. The special organ through which the Church acted was the general council. Such, he insisted, was the historical constitution of the Church.[2]

Jean Petit, the born demagogue of the period, a Franciscan professor at the University of Paris, who upheld the murder of tyrants as natural, moral, and approved of God, cried out in a speech delivered in 1406: "He who obeys a doubtful Pope is himself a schismatic, and sins against the dominion of God."[3] He declared that Christians should shun Benedict XIII as a priest who lived in guilty consciousness of concubinage. "Let me die", he cried out, "rather than obey that man any longer!" "I belong to Christendom, hence I dare to punish Benedict."[4] Petit's views on murder were not approved by the University of Paris. The Bishop of Paris and a commission of the Inquisition condemned him and his views. He died in 1411, but his ideas created some discussion at the Council of Constance and were partially upheld.[5]

John Juvenel, a royal official in the French synod of 1406, said: "The Church has become poorly ruled; we are here to remedy it."[6]

Peter of Aliaco, the Bishop of Cambray and the teacher of Gerson, was strongly in favour of a general council after 1408 because it alone could cure the evils in the Church and heal the Schism.

Peter Ternario, the Archbishop of Toledo, wrote a long tract[7] in which he suggested that the two Popes and the two colleges of cardinals unite in calling the council because then there could be no doubt of its legality and authority.[8]

---

[1] Chap. xvi.   [2] Scheuffgen, 91-7.
[3] Bourg. du Chastenet, 222.   [4] Ib., 224, 228; Haller, 350.
[5] Schwab, 609 ff.; Gerson's works, vol. v; *Chartul.*, iv, 261-85, 325 ff.
[6] Bourg. du Chastenet, 229.   [7] Martène et Durand, *Thes.*, ii, 1100.
[8] Kneer, 71. John Lemoine, a cardinal under Boniface VIII and founder of a college in Paris, a French commentator on canon law, whose "Glosse" was often referred to in the discussions during the Schism, asserted that a

64. *Final Settlement by a General Council*

These demands for peace and unity in the Church, accompanied by intelligent and feasible solutions of the serious problem, came from the leading men in Italy, Germany, England, and France. They show that the Church was in desperate earnest and was ready as a last resort to take the matter into its own hands. All these men supplied the building materials for the revolutionary structure to be erected by the great reform councils.

After thirty years of wearisome discussion and fruitless endeavours, a general council accomplished what neither Popes, nor cardinals, princes, and reformers succeeded in doing, namely, took decisive measures to get rid of the double-headed Papacy. This plan had been proposed from the very beginning of the Schism, and the idea was held up before Christendom throughout the entire period as a possible solution. Urban VI had at first expressed himself in favour of a council but he was not in earnest, or thought only of a council to oust his opponent and soon gave up even that idea.[1] The three Italian cardinals held steadily to the hope of a council before an anti-Pope was elected. Orsini on his deathbed urged a general council.[2] European princes favoured a council. Charles V at the outset suggested a council to judge the election of Urban VI and on his deathbed in 1380 expressed the wish that the breach be closed in that manner.[3] The clergy, high and low in synods and in letters and pamphlets, advocated a council. Prominent theologians, doctors of both civil and canon law, and leading laymen raised their voices for a council. The universities like Paris, Oxford, Bologna, Vienna, and Heidelberg outlined the most feasible plans for a general council, and repeatedly resolved that it be summoned. Even cities like Florence and Ghent took action in favour of a council. In these various ways the idea gradually spread over all Europe,

Christian believer was not subject to the Pope as a servant to his master. The Pope was fallible, as was also a general council, for the Church alone was absolute and must see that the true faith was never lost. Haller, 337.

[1] Baluze, i, 1110 ; Scheuffgen, 58.

[2] Baluze, i, 1100 ; Kneer, 70 ; Souchon, i, 14 ; A. a. O., 797.

[3] Charles V called an assembly on 8th September, 1378, of prelates and scholars to send an answer to the cardinals who had informed him of the breach with Urban VI. He suggested a general council of prelates and princes, to be called by the secular rulers, for the purpose of adjusting matters. That idea was adopted thirty years later. *Chartul.*, iii, 558 ; Bliemetzrieder, 36, 93.

and became the settled conviction that a council was the only way out of the serious difficulty. And yet it was not called for thirty years simply because : (1) the Popes were at heart opposed to it through fear of defeat ; (2) the cardinals refused to take the initiative in calling it ; (3) the rulers could not be brought to act ; and (4) there was so much diversity of opinion as to the legal course to pursue under the unparalleled circumstances.[1] At last with all these demands ringing in their ears, in sheer desperation the cardinals of both Popes deserted them in 1408 and called the Council of Pisa for 1409.

With Gregory XII at Rimini and Benedict XIII at Perpignan, both opposing the council with all their might, which, after all, with the wholesale desertion of Europe, counted for little, the Council of Pisa met in 1409. Following the leadership of Gerson and Langenstein, and backed up by the universities of Europe, as well as the people generally, the Council decided that under the unusual circumstances, it was the sovereign power of the Church. A formal trial of the two Popes, lasting two months, was instituted. Though absent both were deposed as "notorious schismatics, prompters of schism and notorious heretics, errant from the faith, and guilty of the notorious and enormous crimes of perjury and violated oaths."[2] Then the cardinals reunited in the college under the influence of the Burgundian party, and on 26th June, 1409, elected the Archbishop of Milan as Pope, who took the name of Alexander V. A Greek by birth, educated by the Franciscans in Italy and at Oxford, created a cardinal by Innocent VII, he was 70 years old when elevated to the headship of the Church.[3] His rule lasted but a year, when the cardinals chose John XXIII to succeed him in 1410.

On the face of things it looked as if the unity of the Church had been realized at last. The two obstinate rival claimants had been disposed of, and the cardinals had elected a true Pope to rule over Latin Christendom, but Gregory and Benedict refused to recognize the right of the Council to depose them, and denied the power of the joint college of cardinals to elect a new sovereign for the Church. Spain and Scotland

[1] There were prominent prelates like Peter Flandrin who denounced the calling of a council on the ground that it would be null and void without the Papal authority. Kneer, 70–1.

[2] Mansi, xxvi, 1147, 1225 ff.

[3] Niem, 320 ff. gives a sketch of Alexander's early career.

were still loyal to Benedict, while parts of Italy and Germany
still recognized Gregory.   Alexander V, therefore, had only
a part of Christendom, although the major part, to acknowledge
obedience to him.[1] He had the support of the united cardinals
to be sure, but Gregory and Benedict both had created cardinals
of their own, and each had held a universal council of his
adherents to offset the Council of Pisa.   Hence the result of
the Council of Pisa was in reality to increase the Schism by
adding a third Pope instead of curing it.   The situation was
more deplorable than ever, and all Christendom fairly groaned
for relief.   The " infamous dualty " had become the " cursed
trinity ".   For five years the triple-headed monster kept
Europe stirred up until finally, after many conferences,
discussions bitter and violent, interventions of the civil powers,
and catastrophes of all kinds, the Council of Constance
deposed John XXIII, the Pisan Pope ; received the abdication
of Gregory XII ; and deposed the obstinate Benedict XIII.
On 11th November, 1417, Oddo Colonna was elected and took
the name of Martin V.   He was recognized as the undisputed
head of the whole Church, and thus at last after forty years
the Great Schism of the West was ended.

[1] K. Müller ii, 54.

CHAPTER X

SIGNIFICANT RESULTS OF THE SCHISM

65. *Continuation of Financial and other Abuses*

ONE of the most noticeable results of the period of the Schism was the continuation of the financial system, which came into existence during the Babylonian Captivity, with all its aggravating excesses and abuses. Furthermore the financial policy was made all the more burdensome by the fact that Christendom was called upon to support two expensive courts. In consequence the weight of Church taxes was felt more keenly than ever before in the history of the Church. Every opportunity was taken to exploit Christendom and many new schemes were devised to raise money. Every office, preferment, privilege, and service within reach of Papal or curial jurisdiction was put on a financial basis. Reservations, expectations, and provisions; Peter's pence, *annates*, and tithes; appointments, offices, and spiritual services; procurations, feudal tributes, and dispensations; fees, gifts, and subsidies—all these methods and practices of the earlier period were perpetuated and exploited so far as possible to raise money.

From the standpoint of an available income the Roman Popes had a big advantage over those at Avignon, because: (1) the Roman Pontiffs controlled the Papal States which were a source of considerable revenue; (2) the Roman " obedience " geographically was more extensive—it included more people and more wealth—and consequently there were more lucrative offices to dispose of; (3) the loyalty of the supporters of the Roman line was more consistent and more pronounced, hence the tithes, *annates*, and other contributions were paid more regularly and more cheerfully; and (4) the jubilee of 1390 and 1400 and the many sacred spots in the Eternal City with annual pilgrimages to them brought thousands of Christians to Rome from all parts of Europe, and resulted in numerous free-will offerings to the treasury of the Roman Church.

Urban VI, although he possessed the unfortunate talent of displeasing everybody, had a lofty conception of the spiritual obligations of his office, and did not convert it into a money market.[1] In fact, his financial reforms were a potent factor in alienating the cardinals to the point where they elected an anti-Pope. In the interest of better service for the Church he forbade them receiving pensions, provisions and money gifts.[2] A few days after his election he ordered Cardinal Aigrefeuille, the treasurer of the curia, not to pay to the cardinals their customary portion of the *servitia*, but to use it for the restoration of the titular churches in Rome.[3] These privileges had been enjoyed so long by the cardinals that they were viewed as canonical prerogatives, hence the summary measures of Urban VI were denounced as revolutionary.

The ordinary sources of income were not disturbed by this Pope, nor was any effort made to correct the evil methods employed in collecting money for the Church. Provisions were granted in consistories as hitherto,[4] and his newly appointed cardinals were given fifty per cent of the *census*.[5] He did not restore the right of free elections, and he received the *annates*.[6] Nor was Urban VI free from nepotism, for out of 52 cardinals appointed by him, 5 are known to have been his relatives and 6 more are believed to have been his kinsmen.[7] Nevertheless, the Pontificate of Urban as a whole was remarkably free from innovation of financial corruption. The most serious charge that can be made against him is that the *status quo* was preserved.

The successor of Urban VI had no such record. Next to John XXII Boniface IX was one of the shrewdest financiers of all the Popes. Adam of Usk said that he was like a lean fox " though gorged with simony, Boniface to his dying day was never filled." [8] Niem declared that he was insatiable and in avarice for money had no equal.[9] He showed special skill in increasing *annates* to the limit. His agents throughout Europe did a wholesale business in indulgences, dispensations, and special favours of all sorts for which money would be paid

---

[1] Krüger, ii, 201. [2] Bulaeus, iv, 504.
[3] Baluze, *Vitae*, i, 998. [4] Souchon, i, 8. [5] Ib., 29.
[6] Walsingham, *Hist. Angl. ad. ann.* 1382; Kurz, *Oestr. unter Herzog Albrecht III*, Th. 2, p. 119; *Albrecht IV*, Th. 2, p. 245.
[7] Souchon, i, 26. [8] Thompson. *Usk's Chronicle*, 259.
[9] Niem, 119.

and as a result turned large sums into the Papal treasury. A tax was put on every religious grace and service. Places in the Papal court and benefices throughout the Church were openly sold to the highest bidder. The curia at Rome became a veritable stock exchange. Boniface IX hard pressed for money to pay his army suddenly deposed nearly all the prelates who chanced to be at the Papal court, together with many absent ones, or translated them to titular sees, and then disposed of the places thus vacated to the highest bidders. In this way he filled many important places with unfit and useless persons.[1] All the practices which the worldly lords of France, Germany, and Italy had employed in the tenth century in dealing with churches and cloisters, and against which the clergy and Popes had so stubbornly fought, were used by Boniface and his Curia. The jubilees of 1390 and 1400 were exploited to their utmost as money raising schemes, and pilgrimages to Rome were encouraged at all times because of their monetary value. Boniface was notorious likewise for his nepotism. His brothers were enriched by large tracts of land in Naples, Spoleto, Ancona, and the Papal States,[2] while his nephews were given lucrative positions in the Church.[3] In simoniacal dealings he far surpassed the Papal court of Avignon,[4] and even defended his nefarious transactions without any sense of shame.[5]

The pontificate of Innocent VII was rather colourless, and about all that can be said is that the evil practices of his predecessor were continued. He was also accused of gross nepotism.

When Gregory XII came to the Papal throne the treasury was empty, and, indeed, during the conclave money had to be borrowed to meet current expenses. To send messengers abroad to announce the election of Gregory, another loan had to be negotiated.[6] The income of the cardinals caused much complaint and some open disloyalty. The revenues were in various ways so curtailed and reduced that both the Pope and the cardinals were driven to the desperate device of selling and pawning Papal property to raise enough gold to meet the customary expenses. In 1407 a Papal mitre was pawned

---

[1] Lea, *Hist. of Inq.*, iii, 627–8.
[2] Gregorovius, vi, 532 ; Theiner, iii, 9. 39.　　[3] Souchon, i, 56.
[4] Niem, *De schismate*, ii, c. 7.　　[5] Ib., c. 9, 32.
[6] *Archivio stor. ital.* (1884), 37 ff. ; Souchon, i, 120–1.

to the merchants of Florence for the sum of 7,400 gold gulden.[1]
The vicarate of Rome was sold to Paul Orsini for 10,000
gulden.[2] Henry Bowet, a favourite of Henry IV of England,
was appointed Archbishop of York for a stipulated sum of
money.[3] The churches and cloister of Rome sold or pawned
their gold and silver vessels, their houses and vineyards, to
raise the taxes levied on them by the Pope.[4] A number of
valuable manuscripts belonging to the Church were sold to
Cardinal Gaëtani for 500 gold gulden.[5] Indeed, it was even
reported that Gregory sold the city of Rome to King Ladislaus [6]
—at all events the Pope had to hire troops to defend himself
against Ladislaus and his retainers. Paul Orsini was authorized
to raise money by taxing the Church lands.[7] Gregory was
also notoriously guilty of nepotism.[8]

The Avignon Popes found it to be much more difficult
to finance their government than did the Roman Popes
because : (1) their obedience was neither so large geographically
nor so wealthy, nor so loyal; (2) the Papal court,
particularly under Clement VII, was as luxurious and as
extravagant as during the Babylonian Captivity [9]; (3)
numerous costly military campaigns, especially under
Clement VII, were carried on—in 1380 to create a German
league hostile to Urban VI ; in 1382 to subdue Provence ;
in 1382, 1390, and 1392 to conquer Naples ; and against
Raymond de Turenne [10]; (4) the cardinals insisted upon
receiving their customary 50 per cent of the income of the
Church which they had enjoyed under Gregory XI.[11] The
servitia were paid directly into their treasury.[12] Thus it will
be seen that the Papal budget was in nowise curtailed, but
the revenues were aggravatingly meagre.[13] Castile had
practically asserted its independence in ecclesiastical taxation
as well as in appointments to benefices.[14] Scotland was weak
and poor and consequently made small contributions. The
sections of Italy and Germany true to Clement were of no great

---

[1] Theiner, iii, 95.

[2] Niem, iii, 22.

[3] Ib., 21.

[4] Ib., 22 ; Raynaldus, *Ann.* 1409, 59.

[5] Theiner, 98.

[6] Niem, iii, 18, 23 ; Souchon, i, 121.

[7] Theiner, 99, 100.

[8] Souchon, i, 122.

[9] Souchon, i, 179.

[10] Ib., i, 178.

[11] Ib., 79 ff.

[12] Ib., 177 ; Baluze, i, 1311, 1331.

[13] Haller, *Papst.*, 206.

[14] Raynaldus, 1381, § 33, speaks of a " compact " with Clement VII.
Cf. Valois, ii, 203 ; Ehrle, *Archiv.*, vi, 299.

consequence. Hence practically the entire burden of supporting
the Avignon Papacy—Pope, curia, and cardinals—fell upon
France. Although receiving only about 30 per cent of the
benefit, France paid nearly 100 per cent of the expenses of
the Avignon ecclesiastical government. Tithes were repeatedly
levied on France and collected.[1] In 1400 the Pope received
a larger income from France alone than he received in 1350
from the whole Church.[2] In the Council of Basel it was said
that the French clergy did more for the Church than all the
other clergy together, and practically bore the whole burden
of support.[3] Still the Avignon Pope was always hard pressed
for cash.

The price paid for these large money contributions was
a far greater subserviency to France on the part of Clement VII
than had been the case during the Babylonian Exile. Frenchmen were appointed to all places high and low, within the
Avignon " obedience " and out of it. A Norman abbot
complained in 1406 that he could not appoint his candidates
to even the smallest benefices.[4] With Papal permission the
King of France at one time disposed of 750 benefices and at
another time he named an archbishop.[5] What was desired
in Paris happened in Avignon and he who wanted a position
in the Church operated through the French court.[6] Even
those next to the Pope himself could get nothing unless
recommended by the French monarch. A contemporary
called the Pope a " servant of the servants of the French king "
and said that every court favourite was more of a Pope than
Clement VII who bore the title.[7] The monk of St Denis
and the University of Paris made the same complaints.[8]
The king was permitted to levy taxes for political purposes
on clergy and laity alike without distinction.[9] For these
concessions to the secular ruler, the Pope in turn was allowed
to squeeze funds out of the French Church. Indeed in 1386
a formal " pragmatic sanction " was drawn up and signed
to protect the churches and cloisters from the greedy oppression
of the Pope and the cardinals,[10] but it did not alter the real
conditions very much.[11] The Pope was so completely in the

[1] Souchon, i, 178.
[2] Haller, 208.
[3] Bourg, du Chastenet, 466, 468.
[4] Ib., 171.
[5] Kehrmann, 29, 34.
[6] Haller, 209.
[7] *De ruina eccles.*, ch. 13.
[8] Bulaeus, iv, 693.
[9] Valois, ii, 375 ; Haller, 210.
[10] Valois, ii, 391.
[11] Haller, 211.

hands of the French ruler that he did not even protest.[1] It remained for the University of Paris in a memorial to the monarch to expose the extortionate and corrupt business and the open, bloody simony of the Papacy at Avignon.[2] In 1389 Charles VI visited the Papal court for five days and the visit cost the Pope 70,000 gulden. But the King forced the French clergy to bear the expense.[3]

Clement VII did not depend upon tithes, numerous as they were, for his income, but resorted to all the methods of the Captivity. There were numerous instances where Papal castles were either sold outright or were pawned to raise funds. The castle of Diano d'Alba in Piedmont was sold to the Duke of Savoy. The castle of Borbantane was pawned in 1382 for 20,000 gold gulden; and three castles were pawned to Turenne.[4] He borrowed from his cardinals.[5] At Fondi in 1379 he borrowed 35,000 francs of Louis I of Anjou [6] and had to make good the 100,000 francs borrowed by Gregory XI. He borrowed a large sum from the Duke of Burgundy in 1391 and paid him with the right to nominate 120 canons. As an incentive to capture Naples he offered the followers of the Duke of Anjou all the gold and silver articles in the churches of that region. He did a wholesale business in selling offices.[7] He extended the *annates*, after the example of Boniface IX at Rome, reserved many of the best places under his jurisdiction, and collected the *spolia* from the bishops and abbots.[8] Expectations were openly and extensively sold without regard to qualifications.[9] The clergy had monastic and secular benefices of all kinds—not two or three—ten or twelve—but up to 500 which had been purchased at public auctions.[10]

From contemporaries like Clemanges, Langenstein, the Monk of St Denis, Gerson, and von der Hardt, one gets a picture painted in lurid colours of the unscrupulous greed of

[1] Haller, 212.
[2] *Chartul.*, iii, 617; Bulaeus, iv, 687; Relig., ii, 136; *Chronographia*, iii, 110.
[3] Souchon, i, 179.
[4] Niem, ii, 4: Hardt, *De nec. reform.*, i, 297.
[5] Souchon, i, 181.
[6] Martène-Durand, *Thesaur*, i, 1610; Ehrle, *Archiv.*, vii, 246.
[7] Ehrle, *Archiv.*, vii, 75 ff.
[8] K. Müller, ii, 51. Collected from deceased prelates.
[9] *De ruina ecclesia*, ch. 18; ch. 42; Baluze, *Vitae*, i, 537; Niem, ii, ch. 4.
[10] Hardt, ii, 1, 52.

Clement VII, and of the army of collectors and sub-collectors that overran France and other lands gleaning the field so faithfully that the original intentions of founders of religious institutions were violated; oppressing abbots to the point where they scarcely had enough left to feed their monks so were forced to sell or pawn the precious possessions of the monasteries; and threatening all who were slow in paying with the penalties of the Church.[1] So successful were the methods employed that it was reported that the cash balance found in the Papal treasury upon the death of Clement VII was 300,000 gulden.[2]

Benedict XIII asserted and for the most part maintained his independence of the French monarch. Nor did he so openly and so notoriously traffic in the honours and services of the Church; still his career was far from being spotless. He purposely left the best benefices vacant for years in order to receive the income.[3] In collecting the *spolia* of the deceased prelates he even surpassed Clement VII.[4] His collectors not only gathered in the tithes but also took money for the right of suspension from divine services, interdicts, and anathemas.[5] Justice was openly sold at his curia.[6] Cardinals were often permitted to appropriate as many as 500 benefices,[7] and were guilty of the most flagrant simoniacal practices.[8] The *annates* were managed so skilfully that they yielded 20,000 francs annually in France alone.[9] Leroy declared in 1406 that the Pope cared much more for money and benefices, for provisions and expectancies, than he did for converting the unbelievers, or for teaching the faithful, or for managing the difficult affairs of the Church.[10] The author of *De ruina ecclesia* in bitter terms assailed the simony at Avignon where all things sacred were prostituted for gold and luxury. The evils arising from *annates* and expectancies, he declared, surpassed the power of description. To make matters worse the financial tyranny was perpetuated by "an abominable fornication" of leagues with princes. Many bishops caring only for their incomes, purchased the privilege of turning

---

[1] Kehrmann, 19. [2] *Religieux*, ii, 186. [3] K. Müller, ii, 51.
[4] Martène-Durand, *Thesaur.*, ii, 1295; *Preuves des Lib. de L'Egl. Gall.*, ch. xxii, No. 9.
[5] *De ruina ecclesia*, ch. 9. [6] Ib., ch. 10. [7] Ib., ch. 14.
[8] Ib., ch. 15. [9] Hardt, *Concil.*, I, xiii, 780.
[10] Haller, 359 ff.

their sees over to incompetent subordinates; canons and vicars did the same. Priests bought the privilege of living with their concubines to the disgust of the laity.

The Schism threw many bishops out of their positions, particularly among the adherents of the Avignon Popes, and hence they went to Avignon to seek aid and money. The Papal accounts show that some of them were pensioned, others were given positions as ambassadors, and still more of them were supported by contributions directly from the Papal treasury. A list still preserved gives a brief biography of 89 of such bishops at the Papal court.[1]

Alexander V was elevated to the Papacy in the Council of Pisa as the head of reunited Christendom and with the hope that he would correct the flagrant evils and commonly recognized abuses. It was his intention to carry out a thoroughgoing reformation of the whole financial system of the Church, because so many of the running sores of the Church were connected in one way or another with that system.[2] He likewise declared that he did not intend to reserve to himself the spoils of deceased bishops, nor the revenues of vacant benefices. The council made him promise not to sell or mortgage any of the goods, lands, or estates of the Roman or any other Church before the next general council at which it was hoped that a complete reformation of the Church in head and members could be instituted. He also promised to shun nepotism. The council stipulated that translations should be abolished and that no important changes should be made without the consent of a majority of the cardinals.[3]

But Alexander was a feeble old man, not in robust health, and soon came so completely under the influence of the cardinals that they practically took over the rule of the Church. It is not surprising, therefore, that the income of the cardinals was soon in better condition than it had been for a long time.[4] They received their share of the income of the Papacy, as in the days of Clement V, together with the *servitia communia*. Payments were made directly to the college and the books were kept so as to show just what the Pope and the cardinals as a whole received. This arrangement guaranteed to an absent cardinal his full share. Since the cardinals shared so liberally

[1] Schäfer, *Röm. Quartalschr.*, 1904, vol. 18, pp. 176–89.
[2] Souchon, ii, 81.   [3] Ib., 83–4.   [4] *Arch. stor. ital.* (1884), 325 ff.

in the income of the Papacy, they were willing to have that income increased as much as possible. From this Pontiff dates the oath taken by appointees to the higher offices in the Church to pay the customary fees to the Pope and the cardinals—except the *servitia minutia*, which went to their servants.[1]

No sooner was Alexander promoted to the headship of the Church than the customary disgraceful scramble for offices began. Indeed, on the very day of his election there was a grand rush for curial offices.[2] The cardinals, of course, had a big advantage over all other candidates. They not only had all their old benefices renewed, but they got more than their share of the honours, livings, and benefices at the command of the Pope. The Pope lived in a splendour which resembled that of Boniface IX, so that men like Niem spoke of the conditions as scandalous. He bestowed favours with such a prodigality that Niem said: " Alexander denies none—he pays great and small, let it be who it may, and makes no discrimination of persons. The result was that the curia was filled with a crowd of useless persons, and that the Pope, who was so deficient in business matters, soon lost completely the oversight and power over the curia." [3] He " was so completely befuddled over the rules and duties which imposed upon him authority in respect to his high honour ", that the " cardinals could demand what they pleased and he granted it without a word because he did not have the courage to deny them anything. So shameful were the requests with which they daily besieged him that he sometimes completely lost his head. But they were utterly insatiable ".[4]

John XXIII was an expert financier, did everything in a businesslike manner and found Christendom a fruitful field for exploitation. He held formal auctions of offices and sold benefices to the highest bidders.[5] He sold the same offices to several different persons and for an additional sum would pre-date the sale. He granted concessions of every kind for money. The benefices in Sicily were handled in a shameful manner.[6] The cardinals were given benefices with a lavish

[1] Souchon, ii, 81.   [2] Martène-Durand, vii, 1115 ff.
[3] Niem, iii, 51, 52.
[4] Hardt, *De diffic. reform.*, i, 6, 262 ff. ; Souchon, ii, 82.
[5] Hardt, iv, 231, § 13 ; Souchon, ii, 119.
[6] Niem, ii, 373.

hand. Curial offices were openly disposed of for cash.[1] The sale of expectancies was very common, and those granted in Florence in 1413 were notorious.[2] Plenary indulgences were worked with profit, particularly in Germany.[3] Against all canonical rules he gave a dispensation to the illegitimate son of Henry IV of England to enter clerical orders in 1412 under the name of E. Leboarde.[4] He forced gold from the Romans, sold the churches and the treasures in them, and took with greedy hands whatever he could and used the money for both ecclesiastical and worldly uses.[5] He mortgaged the income of the Church to meet present needs. He gave his sister's son, a young man of vile habits, a cardinal's hat, but was thwarted in an effort to bring a second relative into the college of cardinals. He bestowed upon his numerous relatives costly gifts, honours, and benefices. Michael Cona was made admiral of the Papal navy. He sent clothing, boots, and a green upholstered chair to his nephews and 100 gulden to his mother.[6] His expensive gifts, luxurious living, and the many wars made on Church property kept the Papal treasury low and put John to his wits end to collect funds. Hence he pawned his Papal crown in Florence for cash, and borrowed money from Florentine bankers and from his cardinals. Cardinal Broguy lent him 27,000 florins, and John promised him as security all his benefices or his estate in case of the cardinal's death.[7] The fees on bulls alone from January, 1411, to March, 1414, amounted to 45,000 gulden.[8]

John was the first Pope to make a regular division with the cardinals of the income of the Church.[9] No doubt pressure was brought to bear on him to assure them a fixed income. Many favours were bestowed upon them. Thus Cardinal Isolani, a married man not in priest's orders, received a yearly pension of 4,000 scudi.[10] Henry IV of England gave John permission in 1410 to bestow on a cardinal four benefices in England.[11] With the cardinals' consent he gave out provisions, called the councils of 1412 and 1414, created bishops, regulated the *census*, and took steps for the unity of the Church. The cardinals never had

[1] Niem, ii, 366 ff. [2] Ib., 383.
[3] Hardt, ii, 340, 371 ; iv, 241 § 22.
[4] *Eng. Hist. Rev.*, 1904, 96 gives the document.
[5] Souchon, ii, 119. [6] Ib., 113.
[7] Duchesne, ii, 514–524. [8] Souchon, ii, 111.
[9] Ib. [10] Ib., 113.
[11] Rymer, *Foedera*, iv, 19 ff.

more power than under John XXIII, a fact probably due to the Schism. Of his thirty-five cardinals, seventeen were sent out over Christendom on various missions as legates. Yet Filastre said : " It is true that the cardinals fear this simoniac." [1]   When John realized the possibility of his deposition by the Council of Constance he set aside large sums of money to his private account in Florence.[2]   He favoured the old cardinals in every way and permitted them to change their titles. All his accounts were kept in a very businesslike manner. He was anxious to build up an Italian party in the Church as is shown by the fact that from 1410 to 1415 he made 231 promotions of lower clergy to a higher rank and out of that number 117 were Italians.[3]

The practice of the Pope in making handsome gifts to the cardinals on election to the Papacy was continued during the Schism. The gifts of Innocent VII, Gregory XII, Alexander V, and John XXIII must have amounted to approximately $1,000,000.[4]

Simony was the " corroding cancer " of the fourteenth and fifteenth centuries, and afflicted all classes from King to common layman and from the Pope to the humblest parish priest. Those who had only the sacrament and the simpler religious services to sell made a traffic of them. Those who had rich benefices and chances of high preferment, as well as dispensations and justice, in their hands were not ashamed openly to seek the highest bidders. Is it any wonder that the Church came to be in the hands of mercenary and rapacious men who thought only of filling their pockets by extortions ? Yet the canon law characterized simony as heresy and punishable as such, but the Inquisition was never instructed to prosecute simoniacs.[5] Indeed the Holy See practically issued dispensations for heresy habitually. John XXII systematized the sale of absolutions in the hands of the Papal penitentiary, when pardon for simony cost a layman six *grossi*, a cleric seven, and a monk eight. Simony was not commonly regarded as heresy.[6] Simony corrupted every fibre of the Church, and filled its offices high and low with ignorant and worldly men who thought only of profit and not

---

[1] Finke, *Forsch.*, 209 ; Souchon, ii, 119.   [2] Souchon, ii, 113.
[3] Hübler, *Konstanzer Reformation*, 318.
[4] Schäfer, *Röm. Quartalschr.*, 1907, vol. 21, p. 47.
[5] Lea, *Hist. of the Inq.*, iii, 625.   [6] Ib., 626.

of service. In a sermon preached before the Council of Constance, Stephen Palecz made the sweeping statement that nearly every church in Christendom was stained with simony and that this system resulted in the promotion to office in the Church of wicked, weak, and ignorant men who could not find jobs as shepherds or swineherds. Canon lawyers and jurists went so far as seriously to contend that the Pope could not commit simony. Niem declared that the Italian clergy gave thought to nothing but enriching their families and themselves, yet at their death the camera regularly collected the *spolia* to the destruction of the cathedrals and monasteries. The officers of the camera had hard heads, stony bosoms, and hearts steeled against mercy or charity. They were as pitiless as Turks or Tartars against Christians and robbed newly promoted prelates of everything.[1] Those who could not pay immediately, purchased delay at usurious rates, and if the money was not forthcoming at the end of the stipulated time the bishop became a simple priest, and the abbot a simple monk again. Niem said that these insatiable simoniacs should find a place with the infernal furies, with the foul harpies, and with the tortured Tantulus.[2] Poggio, Papal secretary for forty years, asserted that the curia was swamped with clamouring applicants who were idle, unlettered, greedy, useless for all good purposes, and avariciously seized any favour they could get.[3] Many paid ten times more for their benefices than former holders. Some archbishoprics brought 40,000 florins, others 60,000 and still others 80,000.

The lucrative method of raising money by means of tithes was continued during the period of the Schism. Of the first two schismatic Popes, Clement VII worked the system more diligently than Urban VI. The Monk of St. Denis said : " Under Urban the Church was free from tithes ; Clement, on the other hand, was the worst foe of the churches, and ruined their possessions through frequent tithes." He gave the French kings permission to collect the tithes and levied tithes in the name of the curia about every two years.[4] Urban VI in 1382 proclaimed a twentieth tithe for one year on the clergy of the Polish bishoprics and on the sees of Breslau and Lebus, and the next year extended it to Germany and Bohemia.

---

[1] Hardt, i, xvi, 841.
[2] Ib.
[3] Poggio, *Dialogus contra Hypocrisim.*
[4] Hennig, i, 82, 83.

Collectors were named and some money was secured, although no record of the amount has come to light.[1] In 1385 Urban levied a sort of secret charity tithe on Germany, Bohemia, Poland, Hungary, Italy, and other lands, and even the Knights of St John and the Teutonic Knights were included, but the results are unknown.[2] The conflict with Naples in 1386 emptied the Papal treasury of the Roman Pope, so he levied a genuine three-year tithe on Poland and appointed the customary collectors. The clergy of Cracow and Gnesen refused to pay, but finally those of the latter place compromised on a two-years' tithe. The Breslauers were put under the ban and finally released upon promising to pay a two-years' tithe. This tithe seems also to have been imposed upon Germany and Bohemia, but nothing further is heard of it.[3] In 1390 Boniface IX put a tithe on six German bishoprics, Prague, Gnesen, and Cambrai for two years. Bishop Pavo of Tropea was named collector at a daily salary of ten florins, and bishops were ordered to gather in the tithe and turn it over to him, but the results are unknown. In the year 1400 the same Pontiff levied a second tithe for three years on the province of Prague. John XXIII in 1414 decreed a three-years' tithe on Gnesen and Kulm and named two collectors, but that was the last tithe during the schismatic period. At the end of the Schism, however, the old practice was revived and Hussite, Tartar, and Turkish tithes were levied. In 1453 the impending dangers from a Turkish invasion led to a powerful revival of the system. A comparison with the period of the Babylonian Exile reveals the fact that tithes were much more numerous than during the Schism, due, no doubt, to the fact that the times were so unsettled.[4]

66. *Demands for Reformation*

The occurrences under Boniface VIII and what followed immediately thereafter, namely, the Babylonian Captivity and the Great Western Schism, greatly injured the power and respect of the Church, and produced social and religious results everywhere injurious in the general conditions.[5] The Exile and Schism, coupled with an evil financial system, were disadvantageously commented on everywhere. At the same

[1] Hennig, 41–2.   [2] Ib., 42.   [3] Ib., 43.
[4] Ib., 44.   [5] Knöpfler, 473.

time there was an unaccountable indifference regarding the education as well as the social status of the lower clergy, and that resulted in a notorious neglect of pastoral duties. In consequence of these conditions there appeared an ever increasing demand for improvement and reformation. The fiscal system of the Babylonian period had aroused a storm of protest and denunciation. The continuation of the same policy, but in an aggravated form by the double-headed Papacy, made it seem more offensive and more unendurable as time passed, and created a powerful sentiment which resulted in a definite concrete effort to purge the Church of those evils through the great reform councils of Pisa, Constance, and Basel. The fact must not be overlooked that the then popular cry for a general council was as much for the purpose of getting rid of these intolerable evils and abuses connected with the financial administration of the rival Papal curias as to unify the Church.

Unfortunately, however, the prospective reformation was chiefly one-sided and external. The supreme purpose was to decrease expenses and to enforce economy rather than to improve morals and to cultivate holiness in the Church by curtailing the power of the Pope. If the conspicuous individual leaders like Gerson, D'Ailly, Nicholas of Cusa, and others expressed the typical ideas of the age, then most of the criers of reform actually wanted least of all a genuine spiritual reformation. The chief reform of which they always spoke was " pay less," while at the same time they wanted more for themselves. Hence injurious luxury, worldliness and many other evils remained in ugly bloom. Of course, it was very difficult to reform the bishops, simply because they were mostly worldly princes who cared only for their secular duties. Also the Popes, fearing the loss of power and income, often actually worked against reforms. In fact, no one wanted to see reformation begin with himself, although he was quite willing to see his neighbour reformed. Even the great reform councils did not comprehend just what was most needed and approached the problem wrongly, hence it was no wonder that the councils on which so much hope was put failed miserably.

Meanwhile heresy grew everywhere, especially in England and Bohemia, caused in part by the evils in the Church, and in part by the new spirit of the times. The rise of mysticism, more conspicuously in Germany and the Netherlands, was a standing protest to the worldliness of the Church and significant of future developments. The appearance of humanism, chiefly in Italy, portended an intellectual revolt against the medieval system of thought. The complaints against the Church and its representatives steadily grew, and resulted together with other forces in preparation for the great catastrophe of the sixteenth century which shattered the unity of the Church for ever. If the mistakes and evils of the political and religious life of the fifteenth century, after thousands of complaints and warnings had been made, could not be cured by Popes, reformers, and general councils representing the whole Church, then the destructive and reconstructive storm was bound to come.[1]

In looking over the tracts and speeches of the leading men of that day it is interesting to see what a large place is given to a description of the financial shortcomings of the Papacy and clergy and to demands for their correction. Langenstein denounced the clergy for demanding gold for all sorts of religious services.[2] The priests in many cases had become regular shopkeepers to make money. Some prelates held from 200 to 300 benefices. The clergy were so hard pressed from above that they had to mortgage Church property to pay the taxes demanded by the bishops. Most of the money of the Church, instead of being used for the salvation and care of human souls, poured into the Papal curia. The ease with which exemption from duty and from punishment for violation of ecclesiastical law could be bought brought the ban into contempt and ridicule. Bishops, canons, abbots, and monks had become financial officials instead of Christian shepherds. The best places in the Church were too often sold to the sons of rulers and nobles without regard either to local conditions and needs, or to the fitness of the appointees. All discipline and spirituality were lost because too many dispensations and privileges were sold for cash. The old churches were falling into ruin and decay, because the Pope and the cardinals were grabbing up their revenues. Langenstein's tract was the first to demand a general council for the purpose of correcting these evils as well as for healing

---

[1] Knöpfler, 474.   [2] Langenstein, *Epistola pacis*, Hardt, ii, 3, 61.

the division in the Papal office.[1] He argued that the council should get rid of the old evils which the schism perpetuated as well as the new abuses to which it gave birth. The double purpose in calling the council, as urged by Langenstein, was taken up and advocated by all the leading men in the Church.[2]

In his first tract, *Epistola pacis*, Langenstein drew a sad picture of the Church under the Schism, which not only gave Latin Christendom two rival Popes, but also two episcopal claimants in every diocese, two abbots in every cloister, and two priests in every parish, each outlawing and cursing the other; each attempting to seize the revenues; and each appealing to the people for support. Such an unchristian and scandalous condition, he exclaimed, would let the enemies of the Church triumph. Hence either the princes must step in, or else a general council must be called, to purify the Church. The scheme for a conciliar reformation, however, was more convincingly elaborated in his second tract, *Epistola concilii pacis*.[3] In it he deplored the fact that as a result of the confusion in the Church over the true Pope, the faith of both the clergy and the laity was lost. Gross immorality was rampant and affected all classes. The whole social and political order was weakened, and if this continued long it would result in open rebellions and revolutions of the people against the clergy, and of subjects against their princes. In fact, the pride and insolence of the masses had already become almost unendurable.[4] The Church must be restored, not alone to its original power, but also to its earlier purity.[5] Every Christian must return repentant to God, do penance for his sins, and pray for forgiveness and relief.[6] The leaders of the Church, prelates and princes alike, should set the example of duty and piety.[7] The Church Fathers were quoted to prove that in the early days there was far greater zeal for the integrity and welfare of the Church.[8] It was suggested that perhaps God had permitted the Schism to curse the Church in order to force the reformation of the Church. Even without the Schism, Langenstein contended that a general council was needed to correct the abuses and to purge Christendom.[9]

The closing portion of Langenstein's tract surpassed even

---

[1] Kneer, 82–3.
[2] Kneer, 72; Scheuffgen, 43–58.
[3] Scheuffgen, 61.
[4] *Epistola concilii pacis*, Part i, chaps. i–ii.
[5] Ib., chap. iii.
[6] Ib., iv.
[7] Ib., vii.
[8] Ib., chap. ix.
[9] Ib., part ii.

John Wiclif in its bitter and sarcastic portrayal of the ills that afflicted Christendom. Neither the secular nor the spiritual clergy studied the Holy Scriptures, or the Church Fathers any more. The cardinals were nothing but secular lords with fine horses, packs of hounds, and retinues of servants to eat up the wealth of the Church and rob the poor. Hence the churches, even the Roman basilicas, were in ruins. The cardinals were nearly all of one nation, France, and did not adequately represent the various parts of Christendom. The higher offices in the Church, with the larger incomes, were sold to the sons of princes and nobles ; hence the prelates of good character, fine education, and an excellent knowledge of theology and law had to obey the incompetent aristocrats as subordinate officials. Such bishops did not live in their dioceses and seldom even visited them, but thought only of levying heavy burdens on them. This curse of absenteeism entailed a whole series of evils all over Christendom. The bishops aped the secular rulers in their dress, carried weapons, waged war, surrounded themselves with luxurious courts, and sold ecclesiastical privileges to worldly tyrants to the disgrace of the Church and to the oppression of the poor. They cared much more for financial matters than for their spiritual duties. On Christmas Day they joined the princes in celebrating *Ludo taxillorum*. Instead of punishing the parish priests for voluptuous, immoral lives, and for drunkenness, the bishops set them an example in these things. Nepotism was rife among all prelates without regard to the fitness of candidates for their places. The clergy held heathenish superstitions, consulted fortune-tellers, and gave heed to astrologers. Gold was demanded for every religious favour and service openly and shamelessly. It was recommended, therefore, that bishops revive the provincial synods, which were no longer held, at least twice yearly to correct all these crying evils.

The parish priests, likewise, neglected their spiritual duties, since they were no longer held accountable by the higher clergy, and became merchants and shopkeepers entirely controlled by mercenary motives. They were seldom present at Mass on Sundays; no longer observed the rules of fasting ; and in many cases, owing their appointments solely to the influence of relatives, did not even understand the Church office. They gave themselves up to riotous living, attended the theatres, visited the winehouses, drank to excess, and were notoriously voluptuous and immoral. Of course, there were some notable exceptions, thank God ! and not all were guilty of these sins, but still the general condition of the Church was terrible.

The canons were as bad as the bishops and like them imitated the secular lords in dress, carried swords, and lived worldly lives. The abbots as a rule were equally bad. Even the monks regarded money-gathering as more important than their spiritual obligations. The number of monastic orders was entirely too large and they were not regulated with sufficient strictness.

All moneys collected in the Church poured into the curial treasury instead of being used to save souls and carry out the needs of charity. The ban was held in contempt and ridicule. Permits were given for sins and misdeeds, and too many exemptions and privileges were granted. An ordinary law-suit over a trivial matter lasted an eternity and involved endless fees, so that poor litigants were impoverished. Officials were appointed by the Pope without considering local conditions, or the fitness and worthiness of the candidates. The old, wealthy, established churches were neglected because the Pope and cardinals appropriated all the revenues.

The laity deprived of the right spiritual guidance, openly disobeyed the rules of the Church. Festal days were given up to gaudy bazaars. The festivals of new saints were celebrated with greater pomp and zeal than those of the apostles. Polygamy was rampant. The pictures in the churches had more influence than the priest in inducing the simple country people to a purer religious worship.

Langenstein besought God to let his words be heeded so that Christendom would be restored to its original purity.[1] He was a very keen observer of the social and religious conditions of his day and wrote about the necessity of reformation from a personal knowledge. His remedy for the ills affecting the Church was very simple : (1) let a general council initiate a complete reformation of the Church " in head and members "; (2) let efficient local synods be restored to abolish the minor

---

[1] *Epistola concilii pacis,* Part v. Summarized in Scheuffgen, 61–75; Kneer, 80 ff.

evils ; (3) let conciliar and synodal reformation be supplemented by individual personal purification and consecration. The cry raised by this John the Baptist was taken up by his contemporaries and successors and never ceased until the sixteenth century reformation. In his later writing he continued to portray the " whole army of evils " resulting from the Schism and to plead for their correction.[1]

D'Ailly, the eloquent, constructive ecclesiastical statesman, the " Eagle of France ", denounced the ignoble, mercenary character of the priesthood,[2] and assailed all the abuses of his day. His biting satire made Europe laugh and at the same time see with clear vision whither the evils of the clergy were tending. In the councils of Pisa and Constance he laboured with indefatigable zeal to enact a programme of thorough reformation. Just before the Council of Constance met he wrote *Tractatus agendorum* in which he summed up his previous utterances and added new facts. Simony with all its attendant abuses was named as one of the chief causes of the Schism and he declared that it afflicted the French Church from top to bottom. He denounced the widespread reservations, *annates*, and the sale of benefices, offices, and honours. He exposed the custom of proclaiming jubilees for their immoral effects and chicanery. The episcopal power was largely nullified because the Pope monopolized the bishops' power of patronage and sold the places for his own benefit. The system of visitations was abused in a most deplorable manner, because all the higher clergy who had to pay the visitation fee recuperated their depleted purses at the expense of the lower clergy. The Papal visitors always left three scandals where they found one, and consequently did no good. Money was the key that unlocked every privilege to the rich—even freedom from excommunication. It was common to buy dispensations from the Church bans at Eastertime. No religious service of any sort could be had without gold. For burials, baptisms, and marriages large sums were demanded—even of the poor. If a servant died in a place where he was not born, a burial place had to be bought—otherwise he lay unburied. Big sums were collected for executing wills. France was impoverished by these excessive fees and d'Ailly thought that

---

[1] Kneer 94, 101.
[2] *Epistola diaboli Leviathan* is printed in Tschackert, appendix, 15–21.

they should be reduced to at least a tenth of the current prices.
A simple visitation cost five scudi.   In France thousands of
priests were under the curse of the Church ;   thousands were
unburied ;   children died without baptism ;   and adults
perished without confession.[1]

In the time of Clement VII, d'Ailly struck hard blows at
the cardinals and the Pope, the enemy of the council, the false
shepherd who promoted schism, and against the luxury of
the curia and the moral degeneration of the higher clergy who
were the champions of all sinful and unworthy practices.[2]

Nicholas of Clemanges, the famous classicist and moralist,
as Papal secretary had both the opportunity and the vision
to comprehend the vast difference between the real Church
of the fourteenth and fifteenth century, on the one hand, and
the ideal Church, on the other.   His criticism of the prelates
for simoniacal practices was very severe.[3]   In scathing terms
he denounced the corrupt morals of the clergy, high and low.
He complained bitterly of the widespread absence of piety
and of the abuses of the Lord's Day.   Religious festivals were
multiplied until working men no longer had time for their
ordinary tasks and the increase resulted not in spirituality,
but in love for pleasure and show.[4]   The fundamental cause
of the disgraceful conditions he attributed to the neglect
of Bible study, and declared that the mass, processions, alms,
pilgrimages, festivals, fasting, and other similar practices.
were of little value unless the heart was purified by faith.[5]
He complained about the disappearance of all discipline
and order, and predicted the complete disintegration
of the Church unless a thorough-going reformation was
instituted.[6]   His remedy sounds like sixteenth century
preaching : (1) back to the Scriptures as the source of all
piety, holy living, and salvation ; (2) personal purification
by faith ; (3) the correction of general abuses ; and (4) the
institution of a holy, consecrated priesthood by a general
council.   He complained of Clement VII's greed for gold and
told almost unbelievable tales about him.[7]

He has been credited with the authorship of the work

---

[1] Finke, 103 ff.   [2] Souchon, ii, 158.
[3] *De praesulibus simoniacis.*   [4] *De fructu rerum adversum.*
[5] *De studio theologico.*   [6] *Epistolae,* 104.
[7] Hardt, i, 3, 15 ; Schubert, *Nic. von Clemanges,* Leipzig, 1888, a doctor's
thesis.

De corrupto ecclesiae statu, a violent attack on the morality and discipline of the Church of his day, but most of the modern scholars dispute his authorship.[1]

The author of the celebrated tract *De ruina ecclesia*,[2] next to Langenstein, made the fiercest onslaught on the dark side of the Church. It was a complete catalogue of the vices, shortcomings, and corruptions of the clergy from the Pope to the humblest priest, monk, and nun ; and was equally severe on the impious laity. A sharp contrast was drawn between the ideal conditions of the Church of the first century, with its spiritual-minded clergy and obedient laity, and the fourteenth century Church with its wealth and power, its pride and luxury, its avarice and ambition, and its neglect of all spiritual obligations. The Popes, steeped in the sin of simony and private vices, prostituted all things holy for gold and luxury. In guilty pride they exalted their authority above that of the Empire, usurped the right to appoint all prelates, and to fill all benefices in Christendom. The evils arising from *annates*, expectancies, and reservations were unspeakable. By bargaining with princes, they perpetuated their ungodly power.

The cardinals, like the Popes, were worldly-minded, so greedy that they possessed in some instances 500 benefices, proud, arrogant, tyrannical, and licentious. They countenanced the deplorable condition of the Church because they could all the more easily carry on their exploitations. The bishops, abbots, canons, and vicars imitated the cardinals and divided their time between idleness and sensual pleasures. The common priests were grossly ignorant and squandered their time in brawling, drinking, gambling, and fornication. They bought the privilege of keeping concubines ; and many parishes sanctioned this arrangement as the best means of protecting their own wives and daughters. Scarcely one priest in a thousand was true to his vows and obligations, or filled the spiritual mission of his office. The mendicant monks were as bad as the priests and were likened unto the

---

[1] Schubert, *Ist Nicolaus von Clemanges der Verfasser des Buchs De corrupto Ecclesiae statu ?* Leipzig, 1888, gives the best discussion. Müntz, 1846, was the first to deny Clemanges' authorship. Knöpfler follows him. Bess is in doubt. Schwab defends the traditional view.

[2] Schwab, 493 ff. maintains that the tract was written in 1401 or 1402, but was not made public till 1409. Cf. Souchon, ii, 156.

Pharisees in the synagogue. Nunneries were not dedicated to God, but were shameful brothels of Venus and the resorts of unchaste and wanton men. It was " about equal to sending a girl to prostitution to have her take the veil ".[1]

In short, the Christian Church was drunk with the lust for power, glory, pomp, and bestial pleasures. Regeneration and purification must come or God's wrathful judgment would smite the Church. The author's plan of reformation was to have the whole Church humble itself in prayer, repentance, penance, processions, and fasts. God would then rectify the evils and save the Church.

The bishops had to pay so much money to obtain their sees that they devoted themselves exclusively to extortionate practices to recover the cost, and hence wholly neglected their pastoral duties and the spiritual welfare of their flocks. If by chance one of them should give some attention to his duties he was despised as unworthy of his class. Preaching was regarded as disgraceful. All preferment and every sacerdotal function was sold, as well as episcopal ministration, laying on of hands, confession, absolution, dispensation, and other services, on the ground that they had to pay for their offices and had a right to collect such fees. They bestowed benefices without payment only to their bastards and to jugglers. Justice was abused since the greatest criminals could purchase pardon. Often false charges were trumped up against the innocent in order to compel them to pay money, and frequently citations, delays, and threats of excommunications added enormous charges to the original fines. So bad were conditions that men preferred to live under the most cruel tyrants rather than under the bishops, Absenteeism was a crying evil and the rule. Many bishops never saw their sees ; and, indeed, that was perhaps better after all, since their presence only contaminated the people with unworthy examples. The canons imitated the bishops and committed all sorts of crimes with impunity.

As for monks, they openly violated their vows of chastity, poverty and obedience, and were licentious and undisciplined vagabonds. The mendicants, who pretended to do the work neglected by the secular clergy, were Pharisees and wolves in sheep's clothing. Everywhere they sought after temporal

[1] Hardt, i, 38.

gain, and gave themselves up to the pleasures of the flesh, feasting, drinking, and polluting all things with their burning lusts.[1]

These words were put into the mouth of Christ : " The supreme Pontiffs, as I know, are elected through avarice and simony ; and likewise the bishops are ordained for gold. The old proverb ' Freely give, for freely ye have received ' is now most vilely perverted and runs ' Freely I have not received and freely will I not give for I have bought my bishopric with a great price and must indemnify myself impiously for my outlay '. If Simon Magus were now alive, he might buy with money not only the Holy Ghost, but God the Father and Me, God the Son." [2]

It is exceedingly interesting to note the comments and criticisms contained in the records of the various German cities concerning the Schism, which had produced a conflict in many dioceses between rival episcopal candidates representing each obedience. The contest extended to abbeys and even to the country parishes and thus affected all classes of people and produced a great outcry.[3] The great majority of the princes and people accepted the Roman line of Popes and called the French Pope " a sworn foe of the Church ".[4] The origin of the Schism was charged up to the devil.[5] The longer it lasted the louder was the clamour for ending it as " the greatest division and error that ever happened in the history of the priesthood ". It was denounced as a " horrible schism, scandalous and miserable, detestable and cursed ",[6] the " wicked injurious breach," [7] and the " damned division ".[8] The sun of the Papacy was strangely divided and " each sun burned so strongly with its own rays that on earth no fruit could be reaped for our Lord." Each Pope excommunicated the other and his followers, " hence all Christendom was excommunicated." [9] Out of the Schism came, fire, murder, Papal wars, conflicts in countries and kingdoms, misfortunes

---

[1] *De ruina ecclesia*, cap. xix-xxxvi.   [2] Hardt, i, 104 ff.
[3] Loserth, 406.
[4] Théremin, *Beiträge zur öffentlichen Meinung über Kirche und Staat in der städtischen Geschichtsschreibung Deutschlands von 1349–1415*. Halle, 1909. Quotations from the various chroniclers of German States as shown below and on pp. 335 and 336 are explained on p. 70.
Detmar, 26, 79, 67 ; Königshoren, 593 ; Limburg, c. 114 ; Magdeb., 278 ; Oesterreich, 210 ; Posilge, 188.   [5] Oester., 200.
[6] Korner, c, 688, c. 721, c. 800.   [7] Oester., 199.
[8] Rufus, 28, 42.   [9] Oester., 201.

for all the faithful, the increase of heretics and the multiplica-
tion of wretched conditions.[1] " No one can estimate how much
evil has resulted, because on account of it souls have been
lost, heretics have grown powerful, bishoprics and churches
have declined and all Christendom has been injured." [2] It
" gave rise to many evils in Christendom and numerous
battles, feuds, and injuries for spiritual people " and ranged
country against country and city against city.[3] The Church
was ruined by those who should have saved it.[4] Men died
" in need " as a result. " Both sides asserted that their
cause was right and the other wrong, hence both were wrong." [5]
Pilgrims reported that the heathen made fun of Christianity,
saying : " At first the Christians had an earthly God, who
forgave them their sins, but now they have improved their lot,
for they have two Gods. If the one will not forgive them,
they go to the other." [6] To hold the support of princes the
Popes did for them " what was shameful ", and to win
supporters gave them " many liberties and unusual favours
and all they asked for ".[7] The people were urged to pray
God to end the Schism and unify the Church.[8] A council
was suggested as a means to heal the Schism. The bishops
and clergy of Germany were begged to confer as to means
for ending the Schism, but they refused to act because the
Pope " was a wise man, and had many learned clergy with
him. He would know what he had sworn to and what he could
and ought to do ".[9] In refusing to carry out their oaths to
heal the Schism, the Popes were " obstinate and heretical ".[10]
Each at first was " very zealous " for union, but " he was
changed by bad advice of friends and by wicked people,
so that he would not do it " in spite of his vow, so that the
whole Church remained in error.[11] It was a shame that the two
old Pontiffs held on to their offices solely because they and their
friends wished to retain power. The stubbornness of
Gregory XII, " always true Errorius," was condemned.[12]
" All sins are given up by old people except avarice, which
grows and increases ; although these two Popes were nearly

[1] Oester., 163.
[2] Ibid., 201.
[3] Detmar, 19, 561.
[4] Bern, c. 345, p. 209, c. 347.
[5] Ibid., c. 346.
[6] Ibid., c. 345, p. 210.
[7] Magdeb., 281 ; Königsh., 615.
[8] R.A., vi, n. 290 291.
[9] Königsh., 601, 606.
[10] Detmar, 26, 135.
[11] Posilge, 283, 290, 299.
[12] Korner, c. 800 ; Rufus, 28, 42.

a hundred years of age, yet they cared not whether it went well or ill with Christendom, so long as they could continue to rule." [1] They named new cardinals and thus " prolonged the Schism from day to day " and were " obstinate, greedy, abettors, and creators of schism, destroyers of holy Christendom, and hence heretics in faith ". To act in this manner they must be tools of the devil.[2] The council of Pisa was lauded as a " beautiful council " [3] and Alexander V was called " a wise, godly man " whom " God had favoured in order that through his wisdom and efforts the Holy Church should become united ".[4] A poet of the day, however, deplored the fact

> " Dass aus einem werden drei
> as zeucht sich vost auf Ketzerei." [5]

The University of Paris was praised for its " unprecedented industry " in behalf of unity, and the German princes were lauded for meeting in Aachen in 1396 and at Frankfurt in 1397 to encourage a compromise.[6] The secular princes assembled again in 1410 to entreat Sigismund to end the Schism, and this action was highly commended.[7] A contemporary poet commended the advocate of unity in these words :—

> " Er allain der lobfürst ist
> der das concili uf die frist
> zu weg mit fleiss hat erdacht
> und mit gotes hilf hat zesammenpracht." [8]
>
> Man wil sin rechten papast erwelen
> und ain ainig haubt creieren
> got well sein cristenheit florieren
> dass ain ainger papst werd
> gemacht uberall welt auf erd
> dass die cristenheit werd ergeczt." [9]

A pronounced anti-curial reform movement grew up in Germany as a result of the Schism and financial abuses. In 1384 the Archbishops of Mainz, Cologne, Trier, Lüttich, Breslau were pious loyal men who refused cardinal's hats.[10] Nieheim,[11] a German at the Papal court, wrote his *Hist. de schisma* in 1409–10, which gave full information about the

---

[1] Königsh., 613.
[2] Ibid.
[3] Bern, c. 345.
[4] Detmar, 26, 138.
[5] Liliencron, i, n. 50 ; v, 975.
[6] Detmar, 26, 80 ; Posilge, 212.
[7] Liliencron, i, n, 50 ; v, 95.
[8] Ibid.
[9] Ibid., 96.
[10] Souchon, ii, 147.
[11] Dietrich von Nieheim was born at Paderborn about 1343, and died in 1418. He studied canon law and theology, then in 1372 went to the curia at Avignon, where he was an officer in the Papal chancery, and then became *Abbreviator literorum Apostolicorum.* He accompanied Gregory XI to Rome

Roman Papacy. He painted a strong picture of the cardinals from the time of Urban VI on, and said that few of them bothered to go to Germany to improve the Church.[1] He described the wretched financial system, the greed of Boniface IX, the despicable character of John XXIII, nepotism, the crooked Church politics, and other flagrant evils, and put all the blame for the sad condition of affairs on the cardinals. He declared that the schismatic Popes should have nothing to do with councils and thought that only a strong Emperor could bring peace to the Church by deposing both Popes. The Popes and the cardinals had too much at stake to surrender any part of their power, hence they would do nothing. What could be expected from avaricious Popes like Boniface IX and John XXIII ? In 1410 he wrote a pamphlet on unity in which he was still more bitter against the cardinals.[2] He insisted that the reformation of both the Popes and the cardinals was the most essential thing in the Church. " See how cloisters and bishoprics are given to them as commendations to the injury of the care of souls " he exclaimed. " See how they and their kindred, proud in their silks, care only for the incomes they can collect to indulge in sensual enjoyments, to assure to themselves always more power and display ; or how they hunt for gold and lands for themselves and their relatives as aristocratic princes." [3] If their incomes could be taken away, the weakness and disorders of the Church would disappear. If the constitution of the Church could be changed so as to deprive the Pope and the cardinals of their excessive wealth, then the cardinals would return to their original status as servants of the Church, as unselfish advisers of the Pope, as protectors of the faith and morality of Christendom, and as the enemies of heresy. In 1414 he wrote a work on the necessity of reformation in which he denounced the whole series of financial abuses, the immorality of the clergy, and the nepotism of the Pope and cardinals ; demanded the reformation of the method of electing a Pope by the cardinals ; and advocated the appointment of a committee to co-operate

in 1377, and was intimately acquainted with Urban VI before his election. In 1380 he became his Papal secretary, and was popular and efficient. In 1395 he was named Bishop of Verdun. Sauerland, 8–12.

[1] Erler, 300 ; Souchon, ii, 149–50.
[2] Hardt, i, 5, 68–141 ; Lenz, *Drei Traktate*.   [3] Hardt, i, 151.

with the college of cardinals.[1] The next year he penned an invective against John XXIII.

Matthew of Cracovia denounced the financial abuses such as simony, the sale of indulgences, the granting of special privileges for money, and the general exploitation of the faithful by the curia for the sake of gain.[2] The Popes were assailed as wolves who sought only to devour their flocks and not to protect them.[3] The general assertion was made so often during the first thirty years of the Schism that the Schism was due entirely to the greed, avarice, and covetousness of the Popes and their courts that it was a matter of common belief that the Papacy was too rich and too powerful. As early as 1395 the University of Paris recommended that all taxes be withheld from Benedict XIII as the best means of forcing him to submit, and it was soon quite generally advocated throughout Christendom that all taxes should be taken away from the Popes as the most effective method of unifying and purifying the Church.[4] Leroy asserted that the ecclesiastical property belonged not to the Pope, but to the Church, and that benefices belonged to the local communities.[5] Hence the traffic in benefices, reservations, *annates*, expectancies, and other injurious practices should be forbidden either by the general council or by the secular princes.[6] The wealth of the Church, it was maintained, prevented the Pope from overseeing the affairs of the Church.[7] Taxes depended not upon the will of the Pope, but upon the consent of the clergy, and he had no right to ask for more money than was actually needed to administer his office in an honest, economical manner.[8] He should not demand 100,000 florins when 25,000 would meet his needs, and all simoniacal practices should be discarded.[9] Tithes could not be converted into fixed annual taxes and collected by Papal collectors; but should be equitably and legally apportioned. Under existing methods some churches had gone to pieces simply because they had no resident incumbents, still they were taxed as before, while others were absolutely impoverished because forced to bear

---

[1] Hardt., i, 6, 255–309 ; Lenz, 44 ; Fink, *Forsch*, 133.
[2] *De squaloribus curiae Romanae*, Niem, i, 68.
[3] Bourg. du Chastenet, 142 ; Valois, iii, 159, n. 3.
[4] Haller, 228.   [5] Bourg. du Chastenet, 166.
[6] Ib., 169.   [7] Ib., 170.
[8] Ib., 171.   [9] Ib., 175.

a burden out of all proportion to their ability to pay.[1] The only remedy for the prevailing conditions, he argued, was to restore local self-government to the churches.[2] He was so anti-curial that he refused to receive a cardinal's hat from Gregory XII in 1408.[3] His *De squaloribus* [4] pointed out all the evils of the ecclesiastical system of the Middle Ages. He did not hesitate to assert that because of simony, nepotism, commendations, usurious practices, pomp and luxury, the sale of indulgences and privileges, and particularly the exploitation of the faithful for financial profit the schismatic Popes and curias were in a state of damnation.[5] He insisted that the society of believers possessed the power of self-purification.[6]

George of Liechtenstein, in 1411 Chancellor of the University of Vienna, was an advocate of reformation, and influenced the Hussite movement.[7]

Filastre had championed the cause of Benedict XIII against suggestions of the independence of the Gallic Church. For that loyalty, probably, John XXIII made him cardinal. But meanwhile, Filastre had gone over to the reform party and wanted to begin the movement with John himself.[8]

A favourite theme of the writers of this period was the spoliation of the clergy. This was a result of the avarice and simony of the clergy, which produced a growing hatred against them. In Mainz in 1401 the cry "Death to the priests" resounded through the streets.[9]

Under John XXIII Cardinals Castiglione, Challout, and Adimori favoured reforms and apparently had some little influence with that Pontiff.[10]

Telesforo, the hermit of Cosenza, in 1386 could only explain the Schism by the wealth and worldliness of the clergy, whom God could reform only by stripping them of their temporalities and thus forcing them to live according to the gospel.

Henry of Hesse ascribed the Schism to the simony, avarice, pride, luxury, and vanity of the Church which God permitted to test his servants. He looked for the complete destruction

---

[1] Bourg. du Chastenet, 175.   [2] Ib., 166, 172, 176 ; Haller, 368 ff.
[3] Souchon, ii, 147.
[4] In Walch, *Monumenta* (1757), i, i, p. 25, 32, 48, 74.
[5] Niem, i, 68 ; Somerlad, 92.   [6] Scheuffgen, 97.
[7] Souchon, ii, 147.   [8] Ib., 161.
[9] Lock, 213.   [10] Souchon, ii, 117.

of the Church and the appearance of anti-Christ whom the evil and wicked priests and bishops would join. He wrote a letter to the princes of the Church in the name of Lucifer, Prince of Darkness—a communication similar to the one which disturbed Clement VI so much in 1351.[1]

Theodoric Vrie said that hell and purgatory would be emptied if only money enough could be found.

Meyer in his annals of Flanders, under date of 1379, said that it was impossible to give a true sketch of the perjuries, blasphemies, adulteries, hatreds, brawls, debauchery, murder, rapine, thievery, gambling, whoredom, avarice, oppression of the poor, rape, drunkenness, and similar vices. In Ghent within ten months 1,400 murders were committed in the brothels, gambling-houses, and taverns. Evidently the Church which should have been a model and protector of the people was false to all its obligations and responsibilities.[2]

Luke Wadding described Italy in the first part of the fifteenth century in these words : " At that time Italy was sunk in vice and wickedness. In the Church there was no devotion, in the laity no faith, no piety, no modesty, no discipline of morals. Every man cursed his neighbour ; the factions of Guelf and Ghibelline flooded the streets of the towns with fraternal blood ; the roads were closed by robbers ; the seas were infested with pirates. The world was full of sorcery and incantations ; the churches deserted, the gambling-houses filled."[3]

Francis of Zabarella, an Italian, believed that a general council alone could inaugurate the reformation so necessary to enable the Christian Church to perform its great mission on earth. Since Popes fleeced bishops, bishops priests, and priests their flocks, it was wittily said that while Peter's presence in Rome might be doubted, there could be absolutely no doubt of the presence of Simon Magus there. Peter of Ancorano stigmatized monkery, pluralism, greed, fornication of the clergy, dispensations, absenteeism, misuse of the chancery, benefice-hunting, and extortions.[4]   John Treviea, an Oxford man, said of the monks : " They are too rich and fat—the worst of all—and care more for secular business than for ghostly offices."[5] Treviea was a fellow at Queen's

[1] Lea, *Hist. of the Inq.*, iii, 636.   [2] Ib., 642.   [3] Ib., 643.
[4] Souchon, ii, 164.   [5] *Cam. Hist. Mod. Eng. Lit.*, ii, 76.

College when Wiclif was there and was expelled in 1376. He had scant reverence for Popes, monks and nuns, but found little fault with the regular clergy. He advocated the confiscation of the superfluous possessions of the monasteries by the secular authority for the use of the needy, because the wealth of the monks was the cause of their idleness and evil deeds. Although scrupulously orthodox, he was very critical and sarcastic about ecclesiastical abuses. As chaplain to Lord Berkeley, reputed to be a Wiclifite, he found himself in disfavour with the clergy. Richard Ullerton, an Englishman, wrote the *Petitions for the Reform of the Church Militant*. He preached reformation in Oxford in 1408, and the University before the Council of Constance was convened drew up a list of reforms that were imperative.[1] John Gower, another Englishman, who disclaimed sympathy with the Lollards, in 1382 wrote *Vox clamitas*, in which he assailed the coarseness and excesses of city life, and criticized the avarice of merchants, the vices of the lawyers, the heavy taxes, and the sensual indulgences of the people. He believed that the social corruptions of human society were the cause of all the evils in the world. He denounced the sins of all ranks of the clergy, emphasized the necessity of a pure religious faith, and pleaded for a complete reformation of the Church from top to bottom.[2] The Pope and cardinals were said to have taken out of England annually the sum of 20,000 marks.[3]

Gerson raised his powerful voice in behalf of a complete reformation of the Church. He used Langenstein's tract on the necessity of a thorough cure of all ecclesiastical abuses.[4] Although over zealous in crushing the heretics, Wiclif and Huss,[5] yet he was one of the most ardent of the sincere, influential, internal reformers. He denied Huss' basic doctrine that nothing was to be accepted as truth not found in the Bible, and condemned the appeal to private conscience as against Church authority, canon law, and the decrees of a general council.[6] As a mystic he taught the "perception of God through experience" by humility and penance. Following Christ meant contemplation plus action in the " art of love ". He emphasized the necessity of making the

---

[1] Wilkins, iii, 360–5 ; Hübler, 208.
[2] *Cam. Hist. of Mod. Eng. Lit.*, ii, 143 ; *Dict. of Nat. Biog.*, xxii, 300.
[3] Schwab, *Gerson*, 530 ff.   [4] Kneer, 83.
[5] Du Pin, ii, 207, 277, 387.   [6] Schwab, 599, 601.

Bible the foundation of the Church's rule and lauded Bonaventura and St Victors. He stressed the value of religious
feeling but was no visionary. He demanded a reformation
of theological studies as well as of Church life. He advocated
preaching and himself set an excellent example, because
his great sermons, delivered in French as well as Latin, were
topics of practical value and on ethical themes. His teachings
had a pronounced evangelical spirit and he well deserved
the title of " Most Christian doctor ".

In his *Tractatus de symonia*, Gerson argued against the
sin of simony and proved that the Papal demand for the
first-fruits of preferments was simony.

The period of the Schism saw numerous wandering preachers
in England, whose sympathies were with the poor people, who
scoured the country and attracted the crowds with harangues
such as the unfortunates always like to hear, and who went
" from county to county, and from town to town, in certain
habits under dissimulation of great holiness ", " without the
licence of the Holy Father, the Pope, or of the ordinaries
of the place, or other sufficient authority." They preached
" not only in churches and churchyards, but also in markets,
fairs, and other open places where a great congregation of
people is ". Their message was not so much a spiritual gospel
as a social revolution, for it was said that they " do preach
divers matters of slander, to engender discord and dissention
betwixt divers estates of the said realm as well spiritual as
temporal, in exciting the people, to the great peril of all the
realm ". When cited to appear before the ecclesiastical
authority, they refused to " obey to their summons and
commandments " so that the king's officers had to take the
matter in hand.[1]

Typical of these roaming preachers was the priest John
Ball, whose theme was the social revolution. His argument
was somewhat as follows : " At the beginning we were all
created equal ; it is the tyranny of perverse men which has
caused slavery to arise, in spite of God's law ; if God had
willed that there should be slaves, He would have said
at the beginning of the world who should be slave and who
should be lord." [2] He based his assertions on the Bible and

[1] *Statute* 5, Richard II, 2 cap. 5.
[2] *Chronicon Angliae*, 1328–88.   Rolls Series, 1874, p. 321.

appealed to man's reason to confirm their truth. Froissart described his activity as consisting of preaching in the open air, especially on Sundays, when the peasants stood in the churchyard after mass, in these words : " All ye good people : the matters goeth not well to pass in England, nor shall not do till everything be common, and that there be no villains nor gentlemen . . . What have we deserved or why should we be thus kept in serfdom ? We be all from one father and one mother, Adam and Eve : whereby can they say or show that they be greater lords than we be, saying by that they cause us to win and labour, for that they dispend . . . they dwell in fine houses, and we have the pain and travail, rain and wind in the fields ; and by that that cometh of our labours they keep and maintain their estates . . . Let us go to the king, he is young, and show him what serfdom we are in." And so the people " would murmur one with another in the fields and in the ways as they went together, affirming how John Ball said truth ".[1] But this dreamer of " equal liberty, equal greatness, equal power " was taken, drawn, hanged, beheaded, and quartered.[2]

Chaucer, who died in London, in 1400 saw service in the army of Edward III in France in 1369 and between 1370 and 1380 was employed on various political missions to Flanders, France and Italy, had an excellent opportunity to observe conditions in the Church at the outbreak of the Schism. In 1386 he sat in Parliament as a knight of Kent. His long connection with the royal court of England enabled him to study the shortcomings of the English higher clergy, monasticism, and the common priesthood. With wit and ridicule he indicted the mendicants and described the typical friar as an—

> . . . " easy man to yeve penaunce,
> Ther as he wiste to have a good pitaunce
> For unto a powre order for to give
> Is signe that a man is well y-shrive.
>
> His wallet lat biforn him in his lappe
> Bretful of pardoun come from Rome all hoot,
> A voys he hadde as small as hath a goot
> Ne was ther swich another pardonour
> For in his male he hadde a pilwe-beer
> Which that, he seyde, was our Lady's veyl :
> And in a glas he hadde a pigges bones." [3]

---

[1] Berner, *Froissart*, 641. [2] *Chronicon Angliae*. 322.
[3] Skeat's ed., 4, 7, 21.

He described the prior of a monastery as

> . . . " a lord full fat and in good point ;
> His eyen stepe and rolling in his head
> That stemed as a fornice of a led ;
> His botes souple, his hors in gret estat,
> Now certainly he was a sayre prelat.
> He was not pale as a forpined gost ;
> A fat swan loved he best of any rost ;
> His palfrey was as broune as is a bery."

An ideal priest was described as

> " A good man . . .
> That was a pore Persone . . .
> But rich he was of holy thought and werk ;
> He was also a lerned man, a clerk,
> That Christes gospel trewly wolde preche.
>
> This noble ensample to his shepe he gaf.
> That first he wrought and after that he taught.
>
> He waited after no pompe ne reverence ;
> Ne maked him no spiced conscience,
> But Christes lore and his apostles twelve
> He taught, but first he folwed it himselve." [1]

Apparently he had no reverence for the heresy of the Lollards of whom he wrote :

> " This loller wol prechen us somewhat
> He wolde sowen some difficulte
> Or sprenge cokkle in our clene corn." [2]

One might charge these extreme utterances up to rhetorical enthusiasm and intentional exaggeration of soured ascetics, disappointed office seekers, and self-righteous purists were they not so unanimous and so universal.

The immunity enjoyed by the clergy from secular jurisdiction was another potent cause of demoralization. Hence clerical murderers and criminals of all sorts were often set free after the mere mockery of trial in a secular court, much to the disgust and scandal of the laity. This immunity of the clerical class was an extra inducement for many base and worthless men to seek tonsured security from justice in the clerical ranks.[3]

Most of the reformers produced by the Schism, such as Gelnhausen, Langenstein, Clemanges, D'Ailly, Gerson, Zabarella, and similar spirits accepted the Papal system and busied themselves with the problems of unity and internal

---

[1] This has often been quoted as describing Wiclif, but apparently without any positive proof.

[2] Prologue of the *Shipman's Tale*.   [3] Lea, *Hist. of the Inq.*, iii, 629.

reforms. None of them were as radical as Marsiglio and Occam of the fourteenth century. The University of Paris was the centre from which emanated this moderate internal reformation. But from Oxford University there sprang a reformatory movement which was positively revolutionary in its tendencies.

67. *John Wiclif*

John Wiclif was the inspiring genius of the radical Oxford outbreak and consequently has earned the significant title of the " Morning Star of the Reformation ", and even at his death was known in England and Bohemia as the " evangelical Doctor ".[1] He was born in 1324 at Wyclif, Yorkshire, of Saxon parentage, took his university course at Oxford and entered the services of the Church.[2] He studied canon law and took his doctorate in theology. He held several livings as was the custom of that day and so was guilty of pluralism. Until 1366, or until his forty-second year, he devoted himself to his duties as a master and doctor at Oxford, and to his parish work. In that year he was appointed one of the King's chaplains and as such entered political life. Urban V had aroused considerable anti-Papal feeling in England, already hostile to the Avignon Papacy under French influence, by demanding the payment of the 1,000 marks which King John had agreed to pay to the Pope annually, and which had remained unpaid for 33 years. Wiclif seems to have had some part in influencing Parliament to renounce the compact of John as unconstitutional, which was expressed so emphatically that Urban did not press the claim. In 1374 he went to Bruges as one of the seven prominent commissioners to negotiate peace with France and to treat with the Pope's representatives over ecclesiastical appointments in England.[3]

Returning home without having settled the question of appointments, Wiclif, in sermons at Oxford and London began to " bark against the Church "[4] and the Pope's claim to secular sovereignty. In one of his tracts he denounced the successor of St Peter as " the anti-Christ, the proud, worldly priest of Rome, and the most cursed of clippers and

---

[1] *Fasciculi*, 362.
[2] His livings were Fillingham, 1363 ; Ludgershall, 1368 ; and Lutterworth, 1374, which was valued at 26 pounds.
[3] An excellent account of Wiclif is given in *Cam. Hist. of Eng. Lit.*, ii, 49 ff.
[4] *Chron. Angl.*, 115.

cut-purses ", who " had no more power in binding and loosing than any priest ". When the Duke of Lancaster led a movement to confiscate Church property, Wiclif gave him unqualified support, and in 1375 he urged the Good Parliament to make open charges against the Papal hierarchy.

The English prelates were not slow to retaliate, and in 1377 summoned Wiclif before the episcopal court at London, but powerful political friends protected him, and then his case was reported to Gregory XI, who issued five bulls against the errors of Wiclif, condemning 19 sentences from his writings. Two prelates were appointed to examine into the charges against him and he was ordered to be imprisoned meanwhile until the Papal court could pass final sentence on him as a follower of the heretics Marsiglio and John of Jardun.[1] Wiclif was cited to appear before the Archbishop's court at Lambeth, but a sympathetic mob and royal orders broke up the sitting. Meanwhile, the masters of theology at Oxford pronounced the 19 condemned assertions as true. The death of the Pope and the schism that ensued ended the question of Wiclif's trial for the time being.

The Papal persecution and the evils of the Schism developed Wiclif into a radical doctrinal reformer. Up to this time he had done little more than to defend the rights of the English state against Papal encroachments ; but now after 1378, he began to assail with telling blows the theological and ecclesiastical system of the medieval schoolmen and Popes. In sermons, tracts, and books, in Latin and English, with sarcasm and trenchant invective, and using the Bible and common-sense as his authorities, he spoke to England and through England to all Europe. He sought to give England the pure gospel and to that end sent forth his " poor priests " as a body of itinerant evangelists without any definite organization. They were denounced by Bishop Courtenay as " itinerant, unauthorized preachers who teach erroneousness, yea, heretical assertions publicly, not only in churches, but in public squares and other profane places, and who do this under the guise of great holiness, but without having obtained any episcopal or Papal authorization."

In 1381 in 12 theses he made an attack on the fundamental teachings of the Church as unscriptural and false.[2] He

---

[1] *Fasc.*, 242–4 ; Gee and Hardy, 105 ff.   [2] *Fasc.*, 104.

repudiated the dogma of transubstantiation. The monks became violent in their opposition and the Oxford authorities, acting on orders from the higher clergy, instituted a trial. The chancellor and a dozen doctors, without using Wiclif's name, condemned the denial of the dogma of transubstantiation. But Wiclif appealed to the King's Council and went on preaching and lecturing at the University. The King's council ordered him to drop the subject in his discussions at Oxford, but apparently without any effect on his actions. The same year the peasants' revolt broke out, instigated no doubt by the writings and sermons of Wiclif and similar spirits, although it does not appear that Wiclif had any personal sympathy with the movement. He had written : " There is no moral obligation to pay tax or tithe to bad rulers in either Church or State. It is permitted to punish or depose them, and to reclaim the wealth which the clergy have diverted from the poor." At any rate he was accused of having fomented the insurrection. The contemporary chronicler, Adam of Usk, wrote : " Amongst all other misfortunes, nay, amongst the most wicked of all wicked things, even errors and heresies in the Catholic faith, England and above all, London and Bristol, stood corrupted, being infected by the seeds which one Master John Wycliffe sowed, polluting as it were the faith with the tares of his baleful teaching. And the followers of this Master John, like Mahomet, by preaching things pleasing to the powerful and the rich, namely, that the withholding of tithes and even of offerings and the reaving of temporal goods from the clergy were praiseworthy, and, to the young, that self-indulgence was a virtue, most wickedly did sow the seeds of murder, snares, strife, variance, and discords, which last unto this day, and which, I fear, will last even to the undoing of the kingdom. Whence in many parts of the land, and above all in London and Bristol, they, like the Jews at Mount Horeb on account of the molten calf, turning against each other, righteously had to grieve for 23,000 of their fellows who suffered a miserable fate. The people of England, wrangling about the old faith and the new, are every day, as it were, on the very point of bringing down upon their own heads rebellion and ruin." [1] He feared a popular

---

[1] *Chronicle*, 140–1, 300.

uprising in which the two factions would rush " at each others throats ".

A synod convoked by the Archbishop of Canterbury in 1382, at which Wiclif was not present,[1] condemned 24 articles ascribed to him because 10 were heretical and 14 were contrary to canon law.[2] The chief heretical doctrines were : (1) denial of transubstantiation ; (2) that oral confession is not necessary for a soul about to die ; (3) that the English Church, after Urban VI's death, should acknowledge no Pope but govern itself like the Greeks ; and (4) that it is contrary to Scriptures for ecclesiastics to hold temporal possessions.[3] The Chancellor of Oxford was ordered to suppress the heretic and his teachings. Parliament supported the Primate, now Courtenay. After some difficulty the new preaching was suppressed, but Wiclif, undaunted, then sent a " Complaint " of four articles to the King and Parliament pleading : (1) for the supremacy of English law in dealing with Church property ; (2) for the liberty of the friars to forsake the rules of their orders and follow the rule of Christ ; and (3) for the more sensible interpretation of the dogma of transubstantiation.[4] Richard II peremptorily ordered the Chancellor of Oxford to carry out the orders of the Primate, and Wiclif was prohibited from preaching and retired to his rectory at Lutterworth, while his writings were sought out for destruction. Some of his strongest supporters recanted and made their peace with the ecclesiastical authorities. The reform party received a blow which staggered it and almost killed the freedom of teaching at Oxford.[5]

At Lutterworth Wiclif continued his labours on the translation of the Bible, and condemned the crusade which Urban VI had proclaimed in England against his rival Clement VII, in connection with which indulgences to the dead as well as the living were granted, which Wiclif pronounced " an abomination of desolation in the holy place ". In this

---

[1] The Lollards flocked to London from all parts of the land, and " thought to utterly destroy the clergy there at that time assembled ", but " my lord of Canterbury, forewarned of their evil design, found fitting remedies." Adam of Usk, Thompson, 300.

[2] Gee and Hardy, 108–10.

[3] In urging the confiscation of Church property, it was his idea to give it to the upper classes, and not to the common people. Trevelyan, 199. Kriehn, 254, 458.

[4] *Select Eng. Writings*, iii. 507–23.   [5] *Fasc.*, 272–333 ; Shirley, p. xliv.

period was written his most important theological work, *Trialogus*, which lays down the principles: (1) that the Bible takes precedence over the Church in all cases of conflict; and (2) that conscience rather than human authority must be obeyed in case of dispute.[1] In reply to a summons to appear before the Pope, he replied that Christ, the poorest and most humble subject of worldly authority, alone commanded the obedience of all men. The Pope of all men was under most obligation to obey the law of Christ. No Christian had a right to follow Peter, Paul, or any of the saints unless he imitated Christ. Hence the Pope was urged to renounce all worldly authority and compel his clergy to do the same. If wrong in these views, he was willing to be corrected even to death, and if his presence in Rome would help advance these ideas, he would gladly go thither. God had taught him to obey Him rather than man. He closed with the prayer that God would persuade Urban VI to imitate Christ in his own life, and teach his clergy to do the same.

He was struck the second time with paralysis, while saying mass in his church, and died a few days later on 29th December, 1384. The feeling of the hierarchy was expressed by the chronicler Walsingham: " John de Wyclif, that instrument of the devil, that enemy of the Church, that author of confusion to the common people, that image of hypocrites, that idol of heretics, that author of schism, that sower of hatred, that coiner of lies, being struck with the horrible judgment of God, was smitten with palsy and continued to live till St Sylvester's Day, on which he breathed out his malicious spirit into the abodes of darkness." His writings were suppressed, the Lateran decree of 1413 ordered his books to be burned, and the Council of Constance condemned his memory and directed that his bones be dug up and " cast at a distance from the sepulchre of the church ". The order was carried out in 1429, as described in the classic words of Fuller: " They burnt his bones to ashes, and cast them into the Swift . . . Thus this brook hath conveyed his ashes into Avon, Avon into Severn, Severn into the narrow seas, they into the main ocean. And thus the ashes of Wicliffe are the emblem of his doctrine, which now is dispersed the world over."

So strongly did Wiclif feel about the deadly Schism with

[1] *Fasc.*, 341 ff. ; cf. Lechler-Lorimer, 417.

its whole train of vituperations and abuses that the omission or reference to it is an accepted test for the date of his works.[1] At first he seemed to accept Urban VI as the legitimate Pontiff because England did so, but after that Pope proclaimed the crusade against Clement VII with indulgences to all who participated—after the friars preached it and took collections for it, and the Archbishop of Canterbury ordered prayers to be offered up for its success—Wiclif turned his vindictive fire on that Pope as anti-Christ.

Wiclif's direct influence on the fourteenth century was not very great and no prominent religious or political leader of his age would have named him as one of the constructive forces of the period. The full significance of his teachings was not understood. It remained for peoples of later centuries to assess the work of this " first reformer ", as Green calls him, at its full value and to assign him a place as one of the foremost men of the fourteenth century—one of the most eminent scholars at Oxford, a patriotic political reformer, the most notable English preacher before the Reformation, a revolutionist in theology, translator of the Bible into English, and a keen-visioned reformer of the evils of his day. His beliefs are in the main those of the great majority of Protestants to-day. His study of the Bible forced him to take a position directly contradictory to the whole ecclesiastical system of the Medieval Church and to make daring attacks on the Papacy and its teachings, the significance of which he did not clearly comprehend himself.

He upheld the sovereignty of the English national state,[2] opposed the Papal claim of jurisdiction over England, advocated the exclusion of the clergy from secular offices, and questioned the right of the Church to hold any land except at the will of the State. If the Church abused its property rights, the king could confiscate it. The tithes were not warranted by the New Testament, but were merely an expedient to enable the priesthood to perform its mission. He constantly championed the rights of the laity and repeatedly urged that the goods of the lazy, idle friars be seized and given to the needy classes.

His numerous sermons, of which 294 in English and 224

---

[1] *Cam. Hist. of Eng. Lit.*, ii, 57.

[2] His political ideas are set forth in *De domino divino, De domino civili* and *Dialogus*. The first two were edited for the Wyclif Soc. by Pool, Lond., 1885, 1890. The *Dialogus* was edited by Pollard, 1886.

in Latin have been preserved,[1] based on the New Testament, were full of references to the current ecclesiastical abuses, and contained stirring attacks on the greedy Popes and the worldly prelates, who were denounced as anti-Christ, servants of Satan, and false shepherds of Christ's flock.   Pilgrimages and indulgences were condemned as unscriptural.   The rich friars who had nothing but contempt for the poor, were unmercifully flayed.   The bishops were assailed for neglecting their duty to preach, a condition which Wiclif said was notorious.   He described the ideal priest in the following words : " A priest should live holily, in prayer, in desires and thoughts, in godly conversation and honest teaching, having God's commandments and His Gospel ever on his lips.   And let his deeds be so righteous that no man may be able to find fault with them."

Wiclif's doctrinal reforms may be found in the lists of heresies and errors drawn from his works by his enemies. From the 19 errors charged against him by Gregory XI the list grew until the number was 303 as recorded by Cochlaeus. The Council of Constance found only 45, of which the most serious were the following :

1. He denied transubstantiation as interpreted by the Medieval Church.

2. He declared that baptism, ordination, and consecration were void in the hands of a bishop or priest in mortal sin.

3. He advocated the abolition of the Papacy after Urban VI's death.

4. He said that the clergy should have no temporal possessions.

5. He urged monks to live by daily toil and not by begging.

6. He asserted that the election of a Pope by the cardinals was an invention of the devil.

7. He announced that it was not necessary to salvation to believe in the supremacy of the Roman Church.

8. He maintained that all the religious orders were introduced by the devil.

Wiclif had a very clear conception of the Church and he discussed it in nearly all of his writings.   He defined the Church as the body of the elect—dead, living and unborn—with Christ

---

[1] Wiclif's English sermons are edited by Arnold, *Select Eng. Works*, i–ii ; and the Latin sermons are edited by Loserth in 4 vols.

at their head. The Pope was only the head of a local church, namely, Rome. Cardinals and Popes who believed that their election to office gave them a primacy over the Church were guilty of blasphemy. He called Gregory XI a "horrible devil" and declared that a curia that did not follow Christ was a fountain of poison and utterly useless.

Up to his time no one had been so outspoken in his denunciation of the abuses of the offices of the Pope. He denied the necessity of the Papacy to the life of the Church and impugned the Pope's infallibility. He called the Pope antichrist, the chief vicar of the fiend, and a false "most holy father". The Pope had no right to pose as the supreme interpreter of the Scripture, or to decree the supreme law of the Church. Many of the Popes were among the damned, and if both schismatic Popes and their cardinals were cast into hell, the faithful would be saved without them. Christ alone could absolve from sin. The keys of heaven were not metal keys, but spiritual keys, and were committed not to Peter alone but to all the saints. Since Christ paid tribute to Caesar, the Pope had no dominion over kings, but his sole duty was to feed the flock committed to his care. The practice of kissing the Pope's toe was both contrary to the Bible and to reason. Constantine, incited by the devil, foisted his "Donation" on the Church and thereby started all the evils that afflicted it. Apparently Wiclif did not wish to cast aside the Papacy altogether, but only insisted on having the Pope follow Christ's law. Repeatedly he called on the Pope, bishops, and priests to return to their purely spiritual functions.

The financial abuses of the Papal court and of the clergy were bitterly assailed. The Pope and his advisers were denounced as the "most cursed of all coin-clippers and cut-purses". They robbed the English king and "took poor men's livelihoods" on the pretence of granting spiritual favours. The "proud and worldly priest-collector" would soon bank-rupt England. Men should follow the Pope only as he really represented Christ who "was the most poor" of men. None were true priests who did not follow Christ, and their real function was to show forgiveness not to impart it. A sentence of excommunication was worse than murder, for Christ said bless, not curse. Confession was a new invention of little value, for true repentance was sufficient to remove sins. The dangers of confession to immoral priests were pointed out. Pilgrimages were dangerous sources of immorality. Celibacy was unscriptural and the Church would be better off with a married priesthood. Lying was intolerable in clergy and laity alike, because sinful; and no dispensation could alter its character. Not even the Pope was justified in misrepresentation for even a good cause.

The lazy, lying friars came in for the sharpest invectives and entire tracts were written on their evil lives and base practices. They were called foul minions of the Pope's will, who trafficked in indulgences and privileges, corrupted the innocent, particularly the women, and were agents of the devil rather than servants of God. The monastic life, as commonly lived by the monks and nuns, was a delusion, and he demanded the right of the monks who saw their mistake to withdraw from the vows of their orders, so that they might lead useful lives. He painted the friars as the tail of the devouring dragon, ravenous wolves, the sons of Satan, the agents of antichrist and Luciferians, worse than Herod and Judas.

Transubstantiation was denounced as a recent doctrine of the medieval theologians, and Wiclif thanked God that he had outgrown such a ridiculous dogma. The idea of the change of the bread and wine into the body and blood of Christ he pronounced an idolatrous, lying fable, and said that the belief that the very body and blood of Christ were consumed in the sacrament was too shocking to contemplate. He based his repudiation of this sacrament on reason and natural science. His own conception was more nearly like Luther's idea of consubstantiation. His hope was that " over all the truth of reason would conquer ". Indulgences, confession, extreme unction, and ordination were all rejected by Wiclif in a revolutionary fashion.[1]

Wiclif's *Truth of Scripture*,[2] made the Bible the Christian's rule of faith and morals as was done by all the Protestant reformers. He believed that every syllable of the Bible was true and that the scribes were all inspired. Hence nothing was to be believed which was not founded on its authority. He advocated the acceptance of " the literal verbal sense "

---

[1] Pastor, i, 160.
[2] *De veritate Scriptura* was edited by Ruddensieg in 3 vols., Leipsig, 1904.

as the true one. To his mind heresy was simply the contradiction of the Scripture, and he was ready to follow it even unto martyrdom. He stood forth as the champion of the right of the laity to have the Bible, and said that to withhold it from them was a sin. He particularly recommended to all the study of the New Testament. With these convictions it was quite fitting that Wiclif should be the first to give to his people the Bible in their own tongue, translated from the Latin Vulgate. Shortly after his death it was revised by Purvey, a Lollard, closely associated with Wiclif. Copies in manuscript of these two Versions were circulated in considerable numbers, and 170 copies are extant to-day, but there was no complete printed edition until 1850.[1]

In 1391 the clerical party attempted to have the English Parliament condemn these versions, but failed, although an Oxford synod in 1406 ruled that under pain of the greater excommunication no man should, on his own authority, translate the Bible into English or into any other language. In 1414 the reading of the English version of the Scriptures was forbidden upon pain of forfeiture " of land, cattle, life, and goods from their heirs forever." But Wiclif's Bible was read secretly and helped greatly to keep alive the reform movement which he had begun, and which was grounded firmly upon a deep study of the Scriptures. The Bible of Wiclif explains why his conception of the organization, the priesthood, and the sacraments of the Christian Church corresponded so completely with the sixteenth century reformers.[2]

Wiclif did not attempt any ecclesiastical organization of his followers, nor did the movement he led result in any permanent organization. Those who accepted his views and endeavoured to spread them were known as Wycliffites or Lollards,[3] a term that came from the Continent and was applied to certain groups of heretics before the time of Wiclif.[4] In 1394 the disciples of Wiclif were sufficiently numerous and powerful to present a petition to Parliament in which the twelve " Conclusions " were given,[5] setting forth the ideas of the reformer. The number increased so rapidly that a con-

---

[1] Printed at Oxford in 4 vols. after 22 years of painstaking labour.
[2] For an excellent discussion of " Wyclif and the Scriptures " see David S. Schaff in Schaff, *Hist. of Christ. Church*, v, part ii, § 42.
[3] Schaff, v, part ii, 350.
[4] Fredericq, i, 172 ; *Cam. Hist. of Eng. Lit.*, ii, 47, n. 1.
[5] Gee and Hardy, 126–32 ; *Fasc.*, 360–9 ; Gairdner, *Lollardy*, i, 44–6.

temporary chronicler declared that of every two men met on the road one was sure to be a Lollard.[1] The ecclesiastical authorities in England sought to suppress the heretics. Most of those brought to trial immediately after Wiclif's death, recanted so that the total number who suffered death up to 1401 was not large. The fifteenth century saw many Lollard trials and martyrdoms, which also extended into the sixteenth century. The movement spread likewise into Scotland and across to the Continent, particularly in Bohemia through the labours of Huss and Jerome of Prague. Recruits came from the common people and lowly priests, although up to 1400 a number of laymen of prominence [2] favoured the reform ideas. From 1450 to 1517 Lollardy was almost entirely restricted to the rural districts and little mention was made of it in the records of the time.

There can be no doubt whatever that Wiclif and his followers set in motion a whole set of ideas which paved the way for the Reformation.[3] The most striking characteristic of the movement was the fact that it was distinctly a lay revolt against the Medieval Church. Although many priests were identified with it not one higher prelate joined it. In the sixteenth century both the leading reformers and the prominent members of the old Church were conscious of the connection between the teachings of Wiclif and those of the protestant reformers. In 1524 the Bishop of London wrote to Erasmus that the Lutheran movement was not " some pernicious novelty " but only a re-statement of Wiclif's heresy.[4] Pastor declared that all " the errors of the Apocalyptics and the Waldenses of Marsiglio, Occam and others, were all concentrated in his sect, which prepared the transition to a new heretical system of a universal character, namely, Protestantism." [5]

68. *Adam of Usk*

The Chronicle of Adam of Usk gives a vivid although somewhat scrappy and disconnected picture of the political and ecclesiastical conditions of Europe from 1377 to 1421. He was a Welsh priest and lawyer, born in Monmouthshire about 1352. From Oxford University he received the degree of doctor of laws and for some years held the chair of civil law in that institution. From 1392 to 1399 he practised law in the

---

[1] Knighton, ii, 191. [2] Ib., 181 ; *Chron. Angl.*, 377 ; Walsingham, ii, 244.
[3] Gairdner, i, 14. [4] Trevelyan, *Age of Wycliffe*, 349.
[5] Pastor, *Hist. of the Popes*, i, 159.

court of Canterbury. Evidently he gained considerable fame
as a lawyer and statesman, for he sat in the Parliament of
1397 and served on various important boards and commissions.
In 1402 he went to Rome and was taken under the protection
of the notorious cardinal, Balthasar Cossa, the future Pope
John XXIII, who secured his appointment as Papal chaplain
and auditor under Boniface IX. He returned to England
in 1408 where he died probably in 1430. Like so many of the
clergy of his day he was guilty of gross pluralism and held
numerous benefices in Wales and England. Nothing in his
Chronicle indicates that he regarded the system of pluralism
as an evil; on the contrary he openly boasts of his preferments
and particularly of his influence at the Papal court which
enabled him to secure them.

In 1381 he mentioned Cardinal Rileus, who falsely feigned
himself a Papal legate with power to " exercise the Papal
offices ", and thus collected " countless money ", " idly trusting
that the Pope would approve his acts." [1] The Bishop of
Norwich revealed his taste for fighting by crossing over to
Flanders in 1383 during the Schism, where " he destroyed some
9,000 men of that land who sided with the French heretics ". [2]
He quotes two verses received from a certain priest, which
appealed to his mirth rather than to his indignation :

" These two evils shalt thou bear, if that thou be Simon's heir :
    Thou shalt burn when thou art dead ; living, thou shalt want thy bread.''

Of his experiences in Rome he wrote : " On the 22nd day
of December (1402) abuses of indulgences, unions, exceptions,
pluralities, and other things which brought scandal on the
court, were, while I was present, revoked ; or more truly,
I may say they were renewed, for alas ! a new sale of reinstate-
ments of what had been revoked grew up."   Then he recites
how, " contrary to the revocation of unions, the Pope conferred
on me " various benefices. [4] He heard that in Rome " everything was bought and sold, so that benefices were not given
for desert, but to the highest bidder. Whence, every man who
had wealth and was greedy for empty glory, kept his money
in the merchants' bank ready to further his advancement.
And therefore, as, when under the Old Testament the priesthood
were corrupted with venality, the three miracles ceased, to wit

---

[1] Thompson, Usk's *Chronicon*, 139.   [2] Ib., 146.
    Ib., 223.   [4] Ib , 245–6.

the unquenchable fire of the priesthood ; the sweet smell of sacrifice which offendeth not, and the smoke which ever riseth up, so I fear will it come to pass under the New Testament. And methinks the danger standeth daily knocking at the very doors of the Church." [1]

The chronicler, although patronized beyond ordinary by Boniface IX, did not hesitate to denounce him openly as a greedy simoniac.[2] In strong contrast to Christ who " was meek, and his vicar a lowly fisherman ", he described Innocent VII :

> " Proud he wears the triple crown
>   Whose vassals throng his foot to kiss ;
> For king or kaiser's angry frown
>   Not a woght cares aught, I wis.
> Christ his pardon freely gave,
>   Gave his grace without a price ;
> He who here will favour have,
>   To mammon's god must sacrifice." [3]

Of conditions in the Eternal City he moaned : " O God ! how much is Rome to be pitied ! For, once thronged with princes and their palaces, now a place of hovels, thieves, wolves, worms, full of desert places, how pitifully is she laid waste by her own citizens who rend each other to pieces ! " [4]

In quoting from a poem on the Last Judgment, he upbraids

> " The priests who softly feed and lie
> On beds of down and tapestry ;
> Ye richly feast, and bid the door
> Be shut against the hungry poor ;
>
> Your flesh with flesh ye stuff and fill,
> And hoarded wealth ye spend and spill ;
> Rare wines from goblets large ye drain,
> And stretch your maw for food again.
>
> ' In works of pity,' saith the Lord,
> ' All ye who wrought have gained reward ;
> Who cared not for my poor, depart !
> But ye who cared, be glad of heart ! ' " [5]

This English chronicler wrote in 1400 : " One thing in these days I grieve to tell, to wit, that two Popes, like a monster in nature, now for two and twenty years, most wickedly rending the seamless coat of Christ, contrary to the words of the Song of Solomon : ' My dove is but one,' have too sorely vexed

---

[1] Thompson, Usk's *Chronicon*, 247.   [2] Ib., 259.
[3] Ib., 261.   [4] Ib., 264.
[5] Ib., 295.

the world by leading men's souls astray, and racking their
bodies with divers terrors. And woeful it is, if it be true what
I call to mind in the text of Scripture : ' Ye are the salt of
the earth ; but if the salt have lost its savour, wherewith
shall it be salted ? It is thenceforth good for nothing, but to
be cast out, and to be trodden under foot of men. Whence,
seeing that the priesthood was become venal, did not Christ,
making him a scourge of small cords, drive out them that bought
and sold in the temple ? And hence I fear lest we, with many
stripes and spurnings, be cast out of the glory of the priesthood. For I take heed that in the Old Testament after that
venality had corrupted the priesthood, the cloud of smoke,
the unquenchable fire, and the sweet smell which hurteth
not ceased in the temple. In short, lo ! the virgin mother,
according to the word of Revelation, hath fled with the man
child into the wilderness from the face of the beast that sitteth
upon the throne." [1]

On another occasion he exclaimed: " My God ! how
grievously now are Church and Empire harassed and laid waste
with internecine slaughters, the one with two, the other with
three rulers." [2]

69. *The Waldensians*

The Waldensian heresy had found a foothold in Bohemia
at an early date although there was no foundation for the
legend that Peter Waldo spent the last days of his life there
as a missionary. In 1245 Innocent IV declared that the heresy
embraced not only the common people, but also the princes
and magnates, and that it was so well organized that its leader
was looked up to as a Pope. Hence he excommunicated all
the Bohemian heretics, confiscated their lands, and ordered
them to be punished.[3] But the heresy continued to spread
so that King Otokar II in 1257 asked Alexander IV for aid
in its suppression, which request resulted in the first introduction of the Inquisition in Bohemia, but no traces of its
activity remain. That the heresy continued unchecked is
shown by the fact that in 1301 a synod of Prague deplored
the spread of the evil and commanded all who knew of heretics
to report them to the local bishop, but again little was done
for in 1318 John XXII called the Bishop of Prague to Avignon

---

[1] Thompson, Usk's *Chronicon Adae de Usk*, 218–9.   [2] Ib., 246.
[3] Palacky, *Beziehungen der Waldenser*, 10 ; Potthast, No. 11818 ; Lippert,
Socialgeschichte Böhmens in vorhussitischer Zeit, Wien, 1896–8.

to answer certain accusations against him as an abettor of heresy. The complaint set forth that the heretics, apparently both Waldenses and Luciferans, who were not distinguished, had an archbishop and seven bishops with 300 disciples each ; that they considered oaths unlawful ; that confession and absolution could be administered by laymen as well as priests ; that rebaptism was allowed ; that the divine unity and resurrection of the dead were denied ; that Jesus had only a phantasmic body ; that the foulest sexual excesses were indulged in ; and that Lucifer was finally expected to reign. For a time episcopal, Papal, and royal power were employed to crush out heresy, but in spite of all efforts the number of heretics increased. In 1344 Prague was separated from the Archbishopric of Mainz and erected into a separate archbishopric under Arnest, and three years later the University of Prague was founded.[1]

The intellectual activity of the University of Prague, like the universities in France and England, was producing a number of men distinguished not alone for their learning and piety, but also for their bold attacks upon the corruptions of the Church and even upon its most sacred dogmas. The earliest of these reformers was Conrad of Waldhausen (d. 1369), an Austrian monk called to Prague by Charles IV to curb the religious orders, who created a profound impression by his attacks in sermons upon the vices of the clergy and the evil lives of the monks, although he never departed from the path of strict orthodoxy. Another prominent reform leader was Milicz of Kremsier, who in 1363, resigned his position as private secretary to the Emperor, gave up his office as corrector bestowed upon him by Archbishop Arnest, in order to assail the sins and crimes of the clergy and laity. He preached in Latin, German, and Czech against the general wickedness of the age and predicted the advent of antichrist between 1365 and 1367. He boldly went to Rome to place his views before Urban V, where he was at first imprisoned, then released by the Pope and treated with distinction. Returning to Prague he was preaching more violently than ever, when the clergy drew up twelve articles against him, accusing him of teaching that antichrist had come, that the Church was

---

[1] Lea, *Hist. of the Inq.*, ii, **427**, has an excellent discussion of the conditions in Bohemia.

extinct, that the Pope and clergy possessed no light of truth, and that his followers could surrender themselves to unbridled gratification of their passions. These charges were sent to Gregory XI who issued bulls in January, 1374, denouncing him as an obstinate heretic. During Lent of the same year he went to Avignon, where he easily proved his innocence of the charges, and on 21st May was permitted to preach before the cardinals. He died on 29th June before his case was definitely dismissed. A third reformer preparing the way for Huss was Mathias of Janow, a disciple of Milicz, who fiercely denounced the disorders among the clergy and taught that the images of Christ and the saints gave rise to idolatry, that relics and the intercession of saints were useless, and that all should take communion daily. In the local synod of 1389 he was forced to recant publicly, and was suspended from the right to conduct service in his church for six months. He continued to teach his heresies more audaciously than ever, and even urged that the laity be admitted to communion in both elements.

Mathias was a great student of the Bible, and called it his " Friend, his bride, his mother, his darling ". On one occasion he said to the people : ." You wish to be righteous and to believe in the power of works, in the strength of anxiety, to receive salvation through always following new ceremonies and by having a little piety. Did not Christ die for your sins ? You have nothing of His spirit and your eyes are of no use in seeing. Trembling you follow the letter of the law, but know nothing of the freedom of the spirit which the spirit of the Lord gives. And yet the whole Scriptures call us to see that Christ the Crucified One is the only Saviour— that whoever believes in him will be saved—that in faith in Him rests all wisdom of the Christian." He also declared that a priest would accomplish more if he preached and prayed than if he read his Breviary.[1]

Other men, like the priests Andreas and Jacob, Henry of Oyta, Thomas of Stitny, John of Stekno, and Matthew of Cracow, took up the work of these three pioneers and spread the heretical teachings far and wide over Bohemia, Moravia, Austria, Hungary, Thuringia, Brandenburg, and Pomerania. Huss, therefore, like Luther, merely led a movement already under headway.[2]

[1] Monnier, 173–4.   [2] Lea, *Hist. of the Inq.*, ii, 436, 439.

The Bohemians were intensely nationalistic and hated the Roman Church largely on that ground. They denounced the German priests sent to rule over them, both because they were foreigners and because of their immoral lives. They were continually resenting German control of the University of Prague. A century before Huss, a chronicler wrote: "If I heard even from a bird that you had taken up the study of German, I would have you put in a leather bag and thrown into the Moldau. I would rather mourn my friend than mourn the shame of my mother tongue." Patriotism, therefore, was a big factor in the Bohemian question of that day, for the Bohemians wanted the restoration of their own tongue and flag as well as a reformation of the Church to meet their own nationalistic needs. It was a case of a nation attempting to recover its lost independence.[1]

Another product of the period of the Schism, whom chance forced to play a conspicuous rôle in the ecclesiastical history of the fifteenth century was John Huss, the Bohemian reformer and martyr. He was born in 1369 at Husinec in Southern Bohemia of humble Czech parents.[2] Ambitious for an education he worked his way through the University of Prague by singing and manual labour. In 1393 at the age of 24 he received his A.B. and the next year took his bachelor's degree in theology. After two more years of study he was made master of arts in 1396, but was never promoted to the doctorate. He began to lecture in the University in 1398, and apparently based his lectures on Wiclif's works.[3] In 1400 he was ordained as a priest. The next year he served as dean of the philosophical faculty, and in 1402 at the age of 33 he was chosen rector of the University for one semester. These promotions and honours would indicate that Huss was held in high esteem in university circles. Meanwhile, in 1402, he was chosen preacher of the Czech Church of Bethlehem to which he drew large congregations by his sermons delivered in the Czech tongue. He also filled the place of court chaplain and was the confessor of Queen Sophia.

The radical-reform ideas of Wiclif had early been carried to Bohemia. Bohemian students had gone to Oxford

[1] Monnier, *Literatur Geschichte*, Nördlingen, 1888, 172–3.
[2] Loserth, 69.
[3] A university rule said that no bachelor could lecture on any master's work except those of Prague, Paris, and Oxford.

University, where they came under the direct influence of Wiclif, and of course carried his teachings back to the University of Prague.[1] English students also frequented the University of Prague.[2] This avenue of communication was greatly promoted by the marriage in 1382 of Anne, the sister of the Bohemian king Wenzel, to Richard II of England. Consequently the teachings and writings of Wiclif were known in Prague at least as early as 1381, when the theologian, Nicolas Biceps, made a strong attack on them, and thenceforth they were used more or less in that educational centre, the oldest and most famous in Germany, and at times caused quite a controversy among the students and professors.

Compared with other parts of Europe the religious atmosphere of Prague was very wholesome. Under the first archbishop, Arnest, and his successor, Ocko, an honest effort was made to correct ecclesiastical abuses. By 1355 the demands for popular education in religious matters were so strong that a law was passed ordering parish priests to preach in the vernacular. A group of popular preachers basing their sermons on the Bible urged the people to frequent communion, and to lead a pure life, in an evangelical spirit. In these ways the religious atmosphere of Prague was prepared for the work of Huss.[3]

Huss wrote : " I regret that in my youth I took part in a masquerade. A singing student was clothed like a bishop put on an ass, his face turned towards the tail. Thus he was led to mass. Before him was carried a plate of soup and a mug of beer, and I saw that in the church they were put under his nose. I saw that he defiled the altar and heard him, with his foot raised in the air, cry ' Bu '. Instead of candles the students carried great steins of beer before him and thus he went from altar to altar defiling every one, whereupon the students turned their caps around and began to dance in the church. The people looked on and laughed and believed that a regular holy rite. What desecration ! What profanation ! In my youth I took part in such foolishness, but when God revealed his word to me I stopped it." [4]

From 1402 to 1410 Huss led a distinct reform movement at Prague with the hope, aided by the higher clergy, of correcting ecclesiastical abuses. He was the recognised

[1] Loserth, 70.   [2] Pastor, i, 161.   [3] Ib., 434–5.   [4] Monnier, 175.

exponent and champion of Wiclif's teachings. He was made synodal preacher and as such was requested to report on the evils of the clergy. In 1403 he preached a sermon to the annual synod denouncing the worldliness and filthiness of the clergy. The same year he was a member of a committee of three appointed to investigate the alleged miracles performed by a relic of Christ's blood at Wilsnach, which had aroused a great discussion as far away as Erfurt and Vienna, and which drew large crowds to the village. The report condemned the relic as a fake, but the fraud was too lucrative to be suppressed.[1]

The condemnation of Wiclif's teachings in England by the Church soon found a response in Prague. In 1403 the University condemned 45 articles extracted from the reformer's writings and forbade teaching or preaching them, but they had taken too deep root to be so easily suppressed. Among the new defenders who sprang up were Stanislaus Znaim and Stephen Palecz. Indeed, the movement had become so vigorous that Innocent VII in 1405 ordered Archbishop Sbinsko, who had been appointed in 1403, to seize Wiclif's writings and use severe measures to stamp out his teachings. The Prague synod thereupon condemned the 45 articles again and forbade the promulgation of the views contained in them. But Huss kept on preaching in the Bethlehem Church, often to 3,000 people, demanding reforms similar to those advocated by Wiclif. Hence in 1408 Huss was deposed as synodal preacher at the request of the clergy, and the University decreed that no lectures or discussions be held on Wiclif's doctrines. Several masters were tried before the Archbishop for heresy.

In 1409, because of a wrangle over voting by four " nations " the Germans and Poles withdrew from Prague, and founded the University of Leipzig— leaving only 500 Czech students behind.[2] In the strong nationalistic movement with its cry " Bohemia for Bohemians " Huss was the recognized leader. More and more he began to unite the demand for national rights with the cry for a pure Church, and both his religious and political ideas were based on Wiclif, whose statements were frequently embodied in Huss' writings. Huss also translated the *Trialogus* into Czech. Throngs turned out to

---

[1] In 1552 the pyx containing the blood was broken and burnt by a Lutheran zealot.

[2] Rashdall, i, 211–42.

hear the eloquent reformer. " Wherever, in city or town, in village or castle," he wrote " the preacher of the holy truth makes his appearance, the people flock together in crowds to hear him in spite of the clergy".[1]

Up to 1410 Huss had attacked only the abuses of the local clergy and had no idea of leaving the Church. He wanted a reformation without a schism. He desired to abolish false miracles, to stop the excesses of pilgrimages, to expose fraudulent relics, to revive the Gospel spirit, to purify the clergy, to destroy the pride and luxury of the priests, to check the worship of Mary, to drive commercialism out of the Church, and to have the people realize that God alone forgave sins, and that no human absolution could do it. He likewise had denied the validity of the Donation of Constantine and the secular power of the Papacy founded upon it. But he was not nearly so radical as Wiclif. He never denied the dogma of transubstantiation, although he was accused of doing so.

But he had aroused the hostility and suspicion of the orthodox clergy who felt the sting of his lash. In 1408 they drew up charges against Huss and laid them before the archbishop, and the next year they repeated the charges and called upon him to answer them, namely, that he had defamed the clergy ; that he had praised the doctrines of Wiclif ; and that he had kindled trouble between the Germans and the Czechs. But Huss paid no attention to the summons.

On 20th December, 1409, Alexander V issued a bull calling upon the Archbishop of Prague to burn Wiclif's writings and to stop preaching in unauthorized places by unlicensed preachers. On 21st June the University solemnly protested against the bull and Huss and others protested to the new Pope, John XXIII, that such a wholesale order was silly because it included many harmless works on logic, philosophy, and the Church Fathers. Nevertheless 200 manuscript copies of Wiclif's writings were publicly burned on 16th July as the bells of the city were tolled. Two days after the burning Huss and all who had refused to give up their heretical writings were excommunicated. Huss defied the excommunication and continued to preach in his church. A popular tumult broke out in the city—priests were stoned for speaking against Wiclif, and satirical songs were sung in the streets against

---

[1] Workman, *Huss Letters*, 36.

the Archbishop. Huss through handbills announced that he would preach a sermon based on Wiclif's definition of the Trinity before the University on 27th July. King Wenzel and many Bohemian noblemen pledged their honour to John XXIII, who had ordered Huss to appear before him for trial, that he was no heretic. The Pope appointed Cardinal Colonna to investigate the case, and he put Huss under the ban for refusing to obey the order to appear before the Pope as ordered.

The sentence was read in all the pulpits of Prague except two. When Huss still continued his preaching Sbinsko put the city under the interdict, but it was withdrawn when the King promised to crush heresy within his realm. Huss was not disturbed, however, and the archbishop agreed to notify the Pope that all traces of heresy in Bohemia had disappeared. In September, 1411, Huss wrote a letter to the Pope professing his full accord with all the doctrines of the Church and asking that the citation to appear before him be withdrawn.[1] But he said that he was bound to speak the truth and expressed himself ready to die rather than to deny Christ and his Church. It was false that he had repudiated transubstantiation or that he had said that a priest in mortal sin could not celebrate the eucharist. Meanwhile, John Stokes, an Englishman, a Cambridge graduate, who was a pronounced foe of Wiclifism, arrived in Prague and privately ventilated his views to the enemies of Huss. The reformer challenged him to a public disputation, but Stokes declined to enter into it on the ground that he was the representative of a friendly nation.[2]

About this same time John XXIII was in need of cash to carry on his war against King Ladislaus, the defender of Gregory XII, hence he promised indulgences to all who would help either in person or by contributions to promote the holy crusade. Tiem, the Dean of Passau, went to Prague to supervise the opening of the sale of indulgences; chests were placed in the larger churches; and soon the traffic was under full headway. Huss in 1392, when a poor student, had spent his last cent for an indulgence. He now denounced the religious war and denied the Pope's right to couple the sale of indulgences with it. In the Bethlehem Church he preached fiery sermons to large audiences against the whole system and theory of

[1] Workman, 51.
[2] Hus and Jerome of Prag., *Works*, Nürnb. edition, 1558, i, 135–9.

indu'gences. He declared that the remission of sins came through true repentance alone. The Pope had no right to wield the temporal sword. In his sermons and in a tract [1] he wrote he drew most of his arguments from Wiclif's books on the Church and on absolution. On 7th June, 1412, he held a public disputation against the Papal bull authorizing indulgences. Jerome of Prague took a part likewise and was more rabid than Huss. A great public uproar arose under Huss' radical leadership and, although public opinion was on the side of Huss, some of his former friends like Stanislaus and Palecz deserted him. The climax was reached when the two bulls of John XXIII were hung about the necks of two students dressed as harlots, drawn through the streets of the city amidst the jeers of the people and then publicly burned. [2] The whole incident reminds one of the action of Luther a century later.

The conservative party was aroused to action. The theological faculty of the University reasserted its orthodoxy by renewing the condemnation of the 45 articles of Wiclif, and included 6 more from Huss. The clergy of Prague appealed for protection from " the ravages of the wolf, the Wycliffist Huss, the despiser of the keys ". Huss was called before the Archbishop, and when asked whether he obeyed the apostolic authority, he replied " Yes ". The Papal legate then said : " In that case he should be ready to obey the commands of our Lord." Huss answered : " Understand me correctly. What I mean by apostolic commands are the doctrines of the Apostles of Jesus Christ. If the orders of the Pope coincide with these doctrines, then I obey them ; but if they do not, then I refuse obedience, even if the fire is kindled before my eyes to burn my body." [3] The Papal Curia pronounced the greater excommunication, ordering the heretic to be seized and handed over to the Archbishop ; and the destruction of the Bethlehem Church. The city was placed under the interdict. Three obscure followers were arrested ; Huss and 2,000 students begged the magistrates to set them free, but they were executed. Huss now became defiant. He declared that the Pope and even the Church could err ; hence he

---

[1] *De indulgentiis sive de cruciatu papae John XXIII fulminata contra Ladislaum Apuliae regem*, Nürnb., ed. ii, 213–35.
[2] Workman.   [3] Monnier, 177.

appealed from the Pope to God. He boasted that an unjust excommunication should be disregarded. He asserted that unless a Pope imitated Jesus, he was no true Pope—that an avaricious, greedy, immoral Pontiff was vicar of Judas Iscariot, not of Christ. He charged John XXIII with exercising prerogatives received from the devil. In an attack on the " power of the keys " he struck at the very foundations of the medieval Church and the whole Papal system. Great excitement prevailed throughout the city and there was much discontent because all religious rites and services were stopped in Prague.

Under the circumstances King Wenzel concluded that it was best to have Huss withdraw from the city for a while. So in 1412 Huss went into exile ; but he was not silent. He continued to preach in the churches, fields, and market places to large audiences for a period of two years. The lords in their strong castles protected him. Meanwhile he kept up a voluminous correspondence on the burning issues of the day. But the chief product of this period of his interesting career was his book *On the Church*,[1] written in view of the national synod to be held in 1413. It was sent to Prague and read in the Bethlehem Church on July 8. It was almost as famous as Wiclif's book on the same subject, or as Cyprian's work in the early days of the Church. At Constance D'Ailly declared that Huss' work combated the Catholic Church as much as the Koran did.[2] First he defined the Church as the congregation of the predestinate—the dead, living, and unborn.[3] The Church derived its unity from its unity in faith, grace, and charity. The Roman Pope and his cardinals did not constitute the Church because the Church existed for centuries without the college of cardinals, and could survive without a Pope. Christ did not intend to appoint Peter as the head of the Church.[4] In fact, the Roman Bishop was on an equality with all other bishops until Constantine made him Pope, and from that time on he began to usurp authority. Popes through ignorance and greed for money had erred, become depraved and heretical ; and to rebel against such a Pontiff was to obey Christ.[5] In the second part of the treatise, Huss declared, the

---

[1] *De ecclesia* is given in the Nürnb., ed. i, 244.
[2] Du Pin, *Opp. Gerson*, ii, 901.   [3] Nürnb., ed., i, 244.   [4] Ib., 257.
[5] Ib., 260, 284, 294.

bulls of Alexander V and John XXIII to be anti-Christian, and hence asserted that they should not be obeyed. He denied the Pope's right to go to war because contrary to Christ's will. The whole theory of indulgences was assailed because the Popes had no power to forgive sins. Indeed, many Popes themselves were among the damned. Confession of the truly penitent heart alone to God assured forgiveness and assured salvation. Thus Huss was brought to the point where he denied Papal infallibility, the divine origin of the visible Church, the sacerdotal absolutism of the priesthood. But these ideas were borrowed directly from the writings of Wiclif. Indeed the first three chapters of *On the Church* were based entirely upon extracts from Wiclif's book on the Church.[1] But one is conscious of the fact that Huss had made his teacher's ideas completely his own, because he does not mention Wiclif's name as he does the Church Fathers when he quotes them. Nothing is clearer than that Huss by 1413 had broken openly and irretrievably away from the fundamental teachings of the medieval Church. In 1414 he became through the Council of Constance an object of European interest.

The reform programme of the Italian party was shown in the tract of Archbishop Pileus Marini of Genoa written at Constance in 1415. He argued that the Pope was subject to a general council and that it could depose him. He held that two-thirds of the cardinals could call such a council. The pressing problems needing solution were : faith, the election of cardinals, translations, exemptions, tithes, and the arbitration of war. He suggested that the college of cardinals be restricted to twenty-four, and that not more than three be chosen from any one province. His object was not to destroy the college, but to strengthen it. The income of the cardinals should be restricted to not over 4,000 gulden, and no commendations were to be allowed them, but they could retain all their old privileges.[2]

Æneas Sylvius, who knew the whole of Christendom, cried out in 1453 : " Whether I look upon the deeds of princes or prelates, I find that all have sunk, all are worthless. There is no one who does right ; in no one is there pity or truth. There is no recognition of God on earth ; you are Christian in name, but you do the work of heathen. Execration and falsehood and slaughter and theft and adultery are spread among you,

[1] Loserth, 111.   [2] Souchon, ii, 169–70.

and you add blood to blood. What wonder if God, indignant at yoor acts, places on your neck Mahomet, the leader of the Turks, like another Nebuchadnezzar, for you are either swollen with pride, or rapacious with avarice, or cruel in wrath or livid with envy, or incestuous in lust, or unsparing in cruelty. There is no shame in crime, for you sin so openly and shamelessly that you seem to take delight in it." [1]

70. *Conclusions*

It has been conclusively shown that before the Council of Constance was called there had appeared a strong reform party in England, Germany, France, Italy, and Spain.[2] England was least interested in the problem of Papal reformation ; Germany was very bitter against the cardinals ; France was ready to repudiate both the Papacy and the college of cardinals ; and Italy alone was loyal to the Papacy and the curia.[3]

[1] Lea, *Hist. of the Inq.*, iii, 643.   [2] Souchon, ii, 145.   [3] Ib., 171.

CHAPTER XI

DISCUSSION OF A NEW CONSTITUTION FOR THE CHURCH

71. *General Character of the Literature*

THE great schism produced as one of its direct results a thorough-going discussion of the constitution of the Medieval Church, such as Western Europe had never known before. All Western Christendom from Naples to Scotland, and from Portugal to Poland, participated in it. Cardinals, bishops, abbots, civil and canon lawyers, universities, synods and councils, scholars, and princes all took a hand in the burning question of the day. Even the common people were profoundly stirred by the explanations, disputes, comments, suggestions, and demands that filled the air. The literature to which the period gave rise was voluminous, mostly in Latin of course, but some of it in the vernacular—a significant fact for it suggested the inclusion of the people in the problem. It appeared in the form of tracts, letters, sermons, dialogues, songs and poetry ; and it was historical, legal, argumentative, sarcastic, invective, and full of much coarse wit. The age was not blessed with the printing press, but by means of copies and oral communication a wide circulation was secured. Broadly speaking the literature fell into three classes:—

1. Treatises defending the orthodox view of the Papal constitution as interpreted by Innocent III and Boniface VIII and the Avignon Popes in upholding both the temporal and spiritual supremacy of the Bishop of Rome.

2. Works which in one form or another shifted the sovereign power in the Church from the Pope to a general council representing the whole ecclesiastical organization.

3. Writings attacking the very foundations on which the whole mighty Papal structure rested.

The leading thinkers of this period were not confessors, but were mostly university men and statesmen, although most of them were in one way or another drawn into the service of the Church. The supreme question before Europe was not one of faith, although that question was raised, but one of practical Church government. The very fact that one could think of the Papacy apart from religion was a sad commentary on the character of the Papacy, and seemed to demand some kind of a fundamental readjustment of the whole ecclesiastical constitution. During the Babylonian Captivity the dogma of Papal infallibility had been theoretically completed; but at the same time practically combated all over Europe. In sharp contrast to the claim of absolutism came the Great Schism with its disunion and clash of authority, first between a Pope and his cardinals; then between two rival Popes and their colleges of cardinals; and finally between two hostile groups of European nations. The schism seemed in itself to invalidate the idea of absolute supremacy under divine guidance, for how could divinely appointed Popes, cardinals, and bishops act in such a disgraceful and unchristian manner? What excuses and explanations could they offer Christendom for the perpetuation of a schism which worked for the destruction of the unity and solidarity of the medieval world?[1] The doctrine of Papal absolutism almost destroyed the Church during the prolonged schism. From first to last the Popes of both lines upheld that doctrine against their own cardinals, the secular princes, and the ablest men of the day.

72. *Rise of the Conciliar Theory of Church Government*

Another result significant and momentous for Christendom was the rise of the conciliar theory of Church government. The schism exposed the Papacy to criticism and attack from every quarter. The division of the Papacy for thirty years between two men each claiming to be Christ's vicar on earth, with two colleges of cardinals, two expensive Papal courts, two sets of legates travelling over Europe, two candidates for every vacant benefice, and two armies of tax-gatherers to squeeze the florins out of the people; and the still more disgraceful division for eight years among three Popes, produced an unprecedented and frightful scandal in Christendom. Such an intolerable condition, with a whole train of inevitable evil results, provoked a widespread discussion, not alone of the best means of speedily ending the schism, but likewise of the

---

[1] K. Müller, ii, 200.

very nature and justification of the office of the Papacy itself.
The selfish and querulous bickerings of the two Popes, each
claiming to represent God on earth, and the futile negotiations
of the two colleges of cardinals to heal the breach for the
origin of which they were responsible compelled the leading
minds in the Church to ask whether there might not be in
Christendom a power superior even to the Pope, which could
settle the uncertainty and bring peace and unity to the Church.
The logic of the situation led inevitably to the suggestion of the
conciliar theory of ecclesiastical government.   Of course,
the historical fact was known that from the Council of Nicea in
325 to the Council of Constantinople in 869 such bodies had
established the dogma of the Church and had acted for all
Christians, laymen, and clergy.   The difficulty was, however,
that since the first Lateran Council in 1123 all Western councils
had been regarded as merely convenient bodies ratifying
the wishes of the Popes who called them, dominated their
proceedings, and promulgated their decrees in the name of the
Bishop of Rome.

73. *Arguments Advanced by the Liberal Party*

The question of the supremacy of a general council over
the Pope had been raised in clear-cut academic terms by
Occam,[1] and Marsiglio [2] in their hostile attacks on the Avignon
Popes.[3] The Great Schism following on the heels of the Avignon
exile brought forth the proposition of conciliar sovereignty
as the only feasible solution of a most perplexing evil, which
apparently no other remedy could cure, and consequently
it was discussed as a practical necessity.   The man to whom
credit should be given for formulating the conciliar theory
of Church government in its completed form was Conrad of
Gelnhausen.   It is true that John of Paris had spoken of the
Pope as the head of a corporation ; and Marsiglio and Occam
had expressed the theory of popular sovereignty and had applied it to ecclesiastical polity.   These ideas were commonly
known among educated men and no doubt Conrad learned of
them at the University of Paris, where Marsiglio had taught
them.   Occam's writings were in Conrad's library.[3] With such

---

[1] Occam was quoted repeatedly by Conrad of Gelnhausen, Haller, 342.
[2] Marsiglio's *Defensor pacis* was translated into French in 1375, and had
been condemned by the Pope. Haller, 340.
[3] Wenck, *Hist. Zeitschrift*, lxxvi, 32 ff.

a foundation on which to build he sought to make a practical application of the theory to the solution of the perplexing problem of the schism. The Church, he defined, as consisting of, not the Pope and cardinals alone, but of all true believers. Hence the whole Church, represented in a general council, was sovereign and infallible. The Church had two heads : Christ the real head and source of all authority,[1] and a " secondary head " called the Pope, who was no more than the chief magistrate of the Church, and who governed the Church in all ordinary matters. The Pope was neither absolute nor infallible, but could err and blunder. He was subject to the Church, which could curtail his powers or even abolish the office altogether. A general council representing the whole Church derived its powers not from the Pope but from the primary head, Christ, and hence could convene without Papal authority. In clear logical terms he presented the infallibility of the universal Church acting in its sovereign capacity through a general council as against the doctrine of the superiority of the Pope.[2] In the evil days of the schism he put his trust in Christ as the soul-shepherd, and in his representatives the bishops. The Pope was not even a necessity. This position so clearly and so logically taken by Conrad formed the foundation on which the University of Paris, the secular princes, and the scholars of Europe stood in their endeavours to end the scandalous division. He richly merits, therefore, the title of father of the conciliar theory.[3]

Henry of Langenstein stood in the tracks of Gelnhausen, but swung his axe in a wider circle and cut deeper.[4] He went to the very foundation of the Papal constitution and ecclesiastical polity, and defined the Church as a sovereign, democratic organization of all faithful Christians. Christ was the founder of the Church, but did not specify how the Church should be organized or how the Pope should be elected. Hence the Church possessed the right to settle those questions. Now the Church had delegated to the cardinals the right to elect a Pope, but that power could be recalled and the college of

---

[1] Haller, 347.   [2] Bliemetzrieder, 97.

[3] Bliemetzrieder, *Konrad v. Gelnahusen u. d. Quellen d. Konziltheorie. Hist. Zeits.*, 76 ; and *Das General Konzil im grossen abendländischen Schisma.*; Kneer, *Die Entstehung der Konzilaren theorie zur Gesch. des Schismas*, Rome, 1893.

[4] He was greatly influenced by Occam, to whose *Dialogus* he referred, and by Professor Nicholas Oresmius and others. Wenck, *Hist. Zeitschr.*, lxxvi, 35 ; Kneer, 81 ; Scheuffgen, 91.

cardinals abolished if the Church so willed. A general council was simply the medium through which the whole Church expressed its sovereign will and consequently it could elect or depose a Pope. From 1379, therefore until his death he never ceased to champion the conciliar theory and urge the summoning of a general council to heal the schism.[1] He insisted that in case of a doubt about the rightful cccupant of the Papal throne, or a Papal vacancy, it was the duty of the whole Church to settle the matter through its representatives.[2] Christ belonged to the laity as well as the clergy. A genuine council represented all Christians and worked for the good of all. The cardinals could not decide which claimant was the true Pope because they would be virtually deciding their own case. He sang the praises of the earlier days of conciliar rule.[3]

D'Ailly and his distinguished pupil, Gerson, accepted the conciliar theory as defined by Gelnhausen and elaborated by Langenstein. They popularized it and caused it to be generally accepted ; and they helped to put it into practical operation in the councils of Constance and Pisa. D'Ailly started with the general premise that the Church was sovereign in reality but delegated that power to a representative general council. Hence in last resort neither the Pope nor the council was infallible—since that prerogative belonged to the universal Church. Priests and bishops held their authority from Christ, not from the Pope. The Pope was inferior to a general council and, like all Christians, was subject to its will, hence he could not even dissolve it. The Church had both a natural and a divine right to its unity and self-preservation, hence it could call a council without or even against the consent of the Pope. In short, he stripped the Pope of nearly every prerogative, made him a mere governmental convenience, and went so far as to assert that the French Church was not necessarily bound to Rome but could, in case the Roman bishop was heretical or schismatic, unite with some other bishop.[4] That certainly was revolutionary. D'Ailly called attention to the historical fact that the first four councils were not convened by the Pope. Hence the cardinals, princes, or members could call a council.[5] Priests as well as bishops should

---

[1] Scheuffgen, 58.   [2] Ib., 58.
[3] *Epistola concilii*, chap. 5, part 1.   See Pastor, i, 182.
[4] Gerson, *Opera*, i, 668, 691.   [5] *Opera*, ii, 299.

have a vote.[1] In fact no Christian should be excluded from participation.[2] His tendencies were very democratic.[3] He exalted the omnipotence of a council to excess.[4]

He asserted that the Pope was entrusted with the property of the Church only as its representative, and hence if the trust was misused or abused, the Church could take it away again.

Gerson argued for the unchangeable, monarchical government of the Church through Christ, its head. He took the ground that all Church offices existed for the good, peace, and unity of the Church. The Papal office was of divine origin however, and the bishops were not the equal of the Pope in authority. If the Pope should prove to be untrue to his high trust,the Church could separate itself from him and through its representative body, a general council, proceed against him even to the point of deposition for heresy and schism. Hence he put the council above the Pope in authority and declared that it was infallible when it acted for the whole Church.[5] He maintained that the whole body of Christians possessed the mind and immediate guidance of Christ, hence he confidently asserted that the judgment of Christendom, expressed through a council, was the infallible and absolute authority in all religious matters on earth. In his ecclesiastical science there was no room for the sovereignty of the individual conscience in faith and religion. The opinion of an individual no matter how learned in the Scriptures, could not stand before canon law and the authority of the Church expressed through a general council.[6] The Bible was a guide for the Church in behalf of the individual, and the Church alone could rightly interpret its contents to the individual.

Clemanges assisted in formulating the three methods of healing the schism—abdication, resignation, and a general council. He was an ardent advocate of the conciliar supremacy. He believed that the Church, under the guidance of the Holy Spirit, was infallible. The council derived its authority from " all the faithful " and from Christ who said : " Where two or three are gathered together in my name, there am I in their midst." But he expressed doubt as to whether general councils

---

[1] Gerson. ii, 299.　　　　[2] Ib., 205.　　　　[3] Salembier, 212, 219.
[4] Schwab, 507 ; Von der Hardt, ii, 265.
[5] Schwab, 520 ff. ; Valois, iv, 84 ; *Opera*, ii, 201.
[6] Schwab, 559, 601.

were always led by the Holy Ghost, and said that God alone knew where the true Church was.[1]

Zabarella attacked the whole theory of a monarchically governed Church. The Church he defined as an assembly of all true believers, sovereign and infallible, because guided by the Divine Spirit. To the individual he conceded the " right of revolution " against an heretical Pontiff. The Pope he called merely the supreme administrator who was subject to the will and laws of the Church. The general council acted in a sovereign capacity for the Church ; and it could be called by Pope, Emperor, or in case of schism by the cardinals. Should all refuse then the clergy could exercise the right. The council alone could adjust the schism and force the rival Popes to surrender their claims for settlement.[2]

Peter Leroy, another canon lawyer, asserted the supremacy of the council over the Pope. Every Catholic was duty bound to obey the council rather than the Pope.[3] The Pope was created to rule the Church, but he must obey the council. " The Pope is not the lord of the Church : Jesus Christ is its true lord. Care for My sheep, not thine, said He to Peter." [4] The Pope did not own the property of the Church, because the donors and founders of the wealth of the Church gave it to sustain the ministers of the Church.[5] The Pope needed no great political power since his duties were to teach, to convert unbelievers, to exhort the faithful to good works, and to manage the difficult administrative affairs of the Church. But alas ! the wealth of the Pope took so much of his time and attention that he could not oversee the Church properly.[6] Leroy advocated the restoration of local elections, the revival of episcopal power, and the rehabilitation of provincial synods.[7] He argued that the Church should return to its old freedom under the common law.[8] His criticism of the Papal government was scathing and his analysis of conditions in the Church keen. The logic of his argument led to a separation of the French national Church from Rome. In 1396 he spoke of the " original laws and ordinances of the Church, the Holy Fathers, and councils ". From 1396 to 1406 he repeated these ideas many

[1] Scheuffgen, 98.　　　　　　[2] Ib., 111.
[3] Haller, 359.　　　　　　　　[4] Bourg. du Chastenet, 172.
[5] Ib., 171.　　　　　　　　　　[6] Ib., 170.
[7] Haller, 359.　　　　　　　　[8] Bourg. du Chastenet, 166, 172, 176.

times.[1] To his mind a general council would be able to restore the Church to its original state.[2] Leroy in his fiery speeches showed that the supreme question before the Church was something more than the restoration of a single, universally recognized head. He demanded a completer readjustment of ecclesiastical foundations by returning to the original conditions.[3]

Simon Cramaud held that Christ was the true head of the Church and never failed it, hence it was heretical to claim that at the death of a Pope, or during a schism, the Church was headless. The schism had done nothing more than to vacate the Papal chair, but the Church had gone on without a Pope. He upheld the conciliar theory at every point.[4]

Bishop Bernard Allemand, of Condam, wrote six tracts against the schismatics and said: "If the Pope destroys the flock of Christ, or permits it to be destroyed, then Peter is not Peter but Satan; the shepherd is no shepherd but a thief and robber, not pontifex maximus but faex Romana." [5] These were plain words whose significance was not lost on the age.

The Archbishop of Tours, Amely du Breuil, declared: "The Pope is not God, but man. As the flock flees from the wolf that threatens to destroy them, so must man shun the obedience to that one who would kill the soul." [6] "Peter and his successors received their power to construct, not to destroy." [7] "My judgment fails, law is dethroned, and nature trembles" at the condition of the Church.[8]

John Courtecuisse, a young Paris theologian and an outspoken sceptic, denounced the Petrine theory as dangerous as it could not be traced back to Christ and said there was no Scriptural evidence to support it. The primacy of the Roman bishop came from the Emperor Constantine and it was not dangerous to recognize that historical fact. Consequently he denied the infallibility of the Pope on the ground that he derived all his prerogatives from the ecclesiastical constitution and had no powers beyond those definitely granted to him in that instrument. His power of compelling obedience came

---

[1] Bourg. du Chastenet, 47; Haller, 368–970.　　[2] Haller, 370–1.
[3] Haller, 166, 172, 176, 367, 370; Ehrle, *Archiv.*, vi, 221; Bulaeus, iv, 694.
[4] Bourg. du Chastenet, 218.　　[5] Valois, iii, 207.
[6] Ib., 159, n. 3; Haller, 144.　　[7] Haller, 355.
[8] Bourg. du Chastenet, 142.

not from Christ but from the Emperor, or from the community of believers, to whose will he was subject. He made fun of the doctrine of the trinity and of transubstantiation, and attacked the very corner-stone of the Medieval Church and its dogmas.[1]

Peter Plaoul, of the University of Paris, in the discussions of 1398 asked : "Whom shall we obey ? " and answered "God ".[2] In 1406 he said : " Of course the power of the Pope is the highest, but it is a serving power ; no one is lord of the Church except Jesus Christ—He is our real head."[3] " The Pope is only the lord over his servants and can punish them when they do not do their duty ; the Papacy has no other jurisdiction."[4] The king by inheritance ruled and was lord over his people ; the Pope was elected by the Church and was subject to it.[5] People obeyed the Pope in order to have peace and unity. If that obedience were more destructive than conducive to peace and unity, " should we not give up the arrangement, since it brings injury rather than help ?"[6] Plaoul urged the calling of a council and made a powerful address at Pisa in which he sought to prove that the authority of the council was superior to that of the Pope.

The Pope as a true Catholic must be subject to the Mother Church, just as Christ himself was subject to his mother.[7]

The Church of the fourteenth and fifteenth century was threatened with grave danger from two directions : first from Papal absolutism, and secondly from the destruction of Papal power altogether. The first danger was combated from all sides by clergy and laity ; the second danger was largely the outcome of Papal centralization and is apparent in most of the liberal literature of the age. In a letter to Clement VII in 1394 the University of Paris expressed the serious threat of the destruction of the Papal monarchy in these words : " Such is the state of affairs already that there are persons, who have no shame, who publicly say that it makes no difference how many Popes there are—two, three, or even ten or twelve—because then every land can have its own Pope."[8] The suggestion of independent national Churches

[1] Gerson, *Opera,* i, 872 ff. ; Haller, 336–7 ; Denifle, *Chartul.,* iii, 259, n. 9.
[2] Bourg. du Chastenet, 71.   [3] Ib., 186, 193.
[4] Ib., 186.   [5] Ib., 74, 120 ; Valois, iii, 433.
[6] Bourg. du Chastenet, 183.   [7] Bulaeus, iv, 689.
[8] Bulaeus, iv, 700 ; Denifle, *Chartul.,* iii, 633.

naturally grew out of the complete freedom with which the constitution of the Church was discussed on all sides. The testimony given in speeches, sermons, letters, and pamphlets from the leading minds of France, Spain, England, Germany, and Italy clearly proves the existence of a strong liberal party in the fifteenth century which was almost as pronounced as the progressive, reformatory party in the sixteenth century. The fundamental watchword that built up that party during the period of the schism was " union ".[1] The second plank of the party's platform was reformation. In order to secure and to preserve the unity of the Church against all decentralizing influences the party felt that it was necessary to form for the Church a new constitution in which :

1. Christ should be made the true head of the Church.

2. The sovereignty of the whole Church should be asserted under the leadership of Christ.

3. The supreme doctrinal, legislative, and judicial powers of the Church should be put in the hands of a general council representing the Church.

4. The Pope should be recognized as the supreme administrative and executive officer of the Church, elected by the college of cardinals acting for the whole Church.

5. The primative authority of the bishops and the local synods should be restored as supreme in all local affairs.

74. *Supporters of the Medieval Church Constitution*

It must not be taken for granted that the advocates of national Churches and the champions of a universal Church with a head shorn of all his medieval prerogatives monopolized the field of argument and discussion. On the contrary there were prominent men who stubbornly combated the attacks on Papal sovereignty and opposed the calling of a council without Papal authorization.

Cardinal Peter Flandrin, a university-trained man, a doctor of laws, who had seen service at Avignon, where he was made cardinal in 1371, during the exile and had gone back to Rome with Gregory XI in 1378, was himself a candidate for the Papacy.[2] He took part in the stormy election of Urban VI and at Anagni was a leader in opposition to that Pontiff.

---

[1] Haller, 350.   [2] Valois, i, 22.

He went to Fondi, helped to elect Clement VII as anti-Pope, and went with him to Avignon where he died in 1381. He wrote several tracts [1] to prove the legality of the election of Clement VII and to oppose the calling of a general council as suggested by the University of Paris. While he upheld the authority of the Pope, he believed the sovereign power of the Church was not in the council but in the college of cardinals. The cardinals were the supreme general judges of the whole Church just as the bishops were the judges in their dioceses. In case an intruder seized the Papal chair, it was the duty of the cardinals to excommunicate the guilty claimant. They alone had the right to pass judgment on the Pope. The cardinals had decided that Urban VI was not the true Pope, hence the whole Church had to accept that decision and recognize Clement VII. To prove his claims he cited the Old and New Testaments, the civil and canon law, famous commentators, Papal bulls, the Church Fathers, and the decrees of councils. His tracts were written in the scholastic method of question and answer, and his arguments formed the basis of other pamphlets by later writers.[2]

Cardinal Peter Amelius held that a council without the Pope would not constitute a true general council and that the argument of " necessity " was not sufficient ground for calling it.[3] He held that there could not be two Popes, for one of them must be a false one, but he denied the right of the general council to judge Papal affairs. He wrote from Avignon and opposed Gelnhausen at every point. He likewise asserted that the original college of cardinals could heal the schism and that all the faithful should trust its decision.

Cardinal Filastre was about the only conspicuous Papal defender in 1406.[4] He answered the points raised by Leroy and declared that they concerned reformation and not the schism.[5]

These writers who opposed the conciliar theory upheld either the absolute sovereignty of the Pope or the sovereignty of the college of cardinals. Their writings clearly show that

---

[1] The first tract was written in March or April, 1379, and consisted of two parts—the first with seven questions and answers, and the second of eight questions and answers. The second tract, the *Replik*, written in 1380, in Avignon, was very short.

[2] Bliemetzrieder, 37–8.   [3] Bliemetzrieder, 66.
[4] Haller, 350.   [5] Ib., 367.

there were two very different groups of theological and political thinkers in the fifteenth century.

These testimonials concerning reformation and a new constitution for the Church preserved in the tracts, sermons, speeches, and letters of the day reveal the fact that there were two distinct parties in the Church of the fourteenth and fifteenth centuries, differing in their theology, in their conception and interpretation of the ecclesiastical constitution, in their ideals of the priesthood's powers and duties, and in their attitude towards reformation. They were united in their acceptation of the monarchically organized Papacy, in the fundamental dogmas of the Church, in their desire to see the Church unified, and in their belief in the supreme mission of Christendom. There were holy men in both parties and on many points the differences were only on means and methods.

The conservatives accepted the theory of Papal absolutism as developed by Innocent III and Boniface VIII. They were not blind, but were indifferent to the terrible conditions of the Church. They did not possess the great spiritual vision needed for the age, and thought more of holding office and possessing power than they did of saving souls. They were opportunists, who thought their interests were best served by opposing a general council which might disturb them in their prerogatives and privileges. They honestly wanted the schism ended but by such methods as would least disturb their positions. They thought that things were not so bad as the alarmists painted them and seemed to be contented with conditions as they existed. They apparently did not realize, in their short-sighted, self-centred view of things, that the schism had undermined the spiritual position of the Church and brought such dire results as no other movement, rupture, contest, or period had up to that time produced. They were wholly unconscious of the significant fact that a great religious and intellectual change was at hand in Western Europe and, furthermore, were not aware that the forty years of discussion of ecclesiastical affairs prepared public opinion for a more penetrating reformation than the mere removal of two rival claimants to the chair of Peter. They gave little heed to the spiritual decay of the clergy, to their corruption and profligacy and sensuality, to the prostitution of the care of souls and religious services to the love of money, to pluralism, to concubinage, to illegitimacy, and to sinful exactions, abuses, exemptions, and to the excesses in indulgences and privileges.

The members of this party simply shut their eyes to such charges as these : " The priests frequent the brothels and taverns, and spend their time in drinking, revelling and gambling. They fight and brawl in their cups, and with their polluted lips blaspheme the name of God and the saints, and from the embraces of prostitute hurry to the altar." They seemed to ignore the patent fact that the friars were no better than the parish priests of the country, who were ignorant, poorly paid, neglected in their education by those above them, and the worst off of all the clergy. Ascetic enthusiasm had died out of the old orders. The monks' interest in culture, so valuable during the Middle Ages, had been taken over by the learned laity, hence they sank into self-indulgence, bestial vices, and stupidity.[1] Popular tracts in every land spoke of them in the coarsest terms. For the gravest offences monks and prelates could purchase freedom for gold. The chapters were largely in the hands of the nobles who looked upon their offices as sinecures. The canons lived openly with their wives and protected their children in their wills.

The members of this party could not and did not plead ignorance of the real conditions, simply because there was no lack of intelligent complaints, accurate lists of abuses, and bold demands for reforms from those whose loyalty and love for the Church could not be questioned. But this information was either underrated or ignored as coming from heretics, fanatics, idealists, and disappointed office seekers. The fact was well known that the Schism not only divided all Europe into two hostile camps, but also divided many localities. Breslau, Mainz, Liège, Basel, Lübeck, Constance, and other places had two rival bishops cursing each other, seeking to gain control of the clergy and laity, and attempting to lay hands on the revenues. In many cases worship was stopped altogether, since the quarrels between the rival groups of parishioners and the poverty of the priests made it impossible to keep the churches open. Under these conditions one does not wonder that the innumerable ecclesiastical abuses, known to all and pointed out in every corner of Europe, naturally grew greater

---

[1] The Carthusians were a conspicuous and noteworthy exception, but even among them the old spiritual vigour had largely disappeared.

during the Schism, since no effort was made by those in authority to correct them, and that the quarrelling between rival Popes led to a wider discussion of the Church with its fundamental claims and teachings.

The conservative party was led by the Popes of both lines, most of the cardinals, a majority of the two Papal courts, many of the bishops and abbots, the worst factions among the priests and monks, and large numbers of the laity who profited by the perpetuation of the old system. They were in complete control of the Church although divided in that supervision. They persistently upheld Papal absolutism, opposed the calling of a council to heal the schism and reform the Church, wrote pamphlets and preached sermons against the ideas advanced by the progressives, and deliberately shut their eyes to the real needs of the Church. They were destined to have a rude awakening in the reform council and their blindness and obstinacy almost wrecked the Church.

The liberals in the Church of the age of the Schism constituted a progressive party that stood for union, a complete reformation and purification of the Church, and a radical change in the ecclesiastical constitution in the direction of a government represented in a general council. The activity of the party was amply demonstrated by the numerous tracts and addresses of the leaders, which revealed a widespread awakened consciousness of the serious evils afflicting the Church and, in consequence, of the excellent opportunities for good, which the Church missed. The party included cardinals, bishops, university professors, princes, priests, and laymen. Had there been any way to count heads it could certainly have been shown that the liberals constituted a large majority. But organization was wanting, leadership was not of the most practical order and lacked co-operation, and it was impossible to obtain concerted action through any available ecclesiastical machinery, because the Papacy, the colleges of cardinals, and the curias were in the hands of the conservatives. On the other hand the liberals had to operate through local synods, universities like Prague, Heidelberg, Vienna, Oxford, and particularly Paris, and national parliaments such as the French and English. They were strongly in favour of the conciliar theory of Church government and urged the call of a general council to enable them to force their programme on the Church. Until that body was convened they had to content themselves with open attacks by pen and voice on the clergy in control of the Church, with denunciations of the flagrant evils in the Church, and with suggestions and demands for unification and reformation.

The forty years Schism in the great Church of the West, in breaking down the solidarity of the medieval world, supplied the liberal party with the occasion for insisting upon a constructive reorganization of the constitution on a democratic basis.[1] It opened the ears of Europe to listen to the daring voices of earnest men like Langenstein, D'Ailly, Gerson, Zabarella, Wiclif, and Huss. It permitted national states like Spain, France, and England to threaten the creation of national, independent churches,[2] a threat which after the Reformation resulted in the adoption of the principle of *cujus regio ejus religio*. It proved the impotence of the Papal machinery to meet a destructive crisis that demoralized the entire Church and shook its foundations to the bottom, and forced men to seek some adequate remedy. It stressed the unity of the body of the Church as never before and forced the college of cardinals to stand out in conspicuous relief. That body was subjected to such criticism as it had never before seen. Hence men openly and fearlessly expressed their opinions, which had only been mooted in violent conflicts with Popes, and these ideas struck their roots so deeply that they could never again be destroyed. It led men to point the finger significantly to the earlier and purer conditions of the Church and to propose new solutions of the pressing problems. It induced the universities to step forward as the leaders of the progressive policy in the Church, and to attain an influence formidable even to Popes.[3] It held up before the public gaze a comparison between the early Church and the later Church which gave rise to the expression of opinion unfavourable to the Papal monarchy. Indeed, some went so far as to say that the evils in the Church would only disappear with the destruction of the Papacy itself.[4]

The most dangerous part of the platform of the liberal party to the Church constitution was the attack on Papal absolutism.

---

[1] K. Müller, ii, 204.　　[2] Ib., 50.
[3] *Prima appelatio* to Benedict XIII in Bulaeus, iv, 806.
[4] *Epist. Univ. Paris* to Clement VII in 1396. Ib., 700.

A few bold spirits like John Guigneccurtius maintained that the Church could get along very well without a Pope.[1] Even the staunchest defenders of Papal prerogative acknowledged the unwarranted extension and exaggeration of Papal power,[2] and assigned Papal ambition for secular authority as the cause of the schismatic mischief.[3] The restoration of the days when emperors convoked synods, settled disputed elections, and cured evils in the Church was advocated.[4] Repeatedly the idea was expressed that the Papal oppressions of the Church could be removed only by limiting Papal jurisdiction.[5] Hitherto only royal foes of the Pope like Philip IV of France and his lawyers or Lewis of Bavaria and his followers had appealed to a general council as a power higher than the Pope, but during the Schism that belief became quite common among all classes,[6] and dominated the councils of Pisa and Constance so strongly that the Papal system of absolutism was threatened with a complete overthrow.

Everywhere individuals were forced to a decision on many vital questions raised by the crisis. The conviction quite generally prevailed that sovereignty in the Church was vested in all the faithful who must take the initiative in the exercise of its prerogatives. Great leaders like Gelnhausen and Langenstein made Christ the invisible supreme bishop and shepherd of souls. In the confusion over " obedience " Plaoul declared that God alone should be obeyed since the Pope existed only by the will of the Church as its servant, not its master. Out of these ideas gradually developed the conception of popular sovereignty in Church government, and the secession or " subtraction " of both men and property was openly preached in many quarters.[7]

75. Conclusions

It takes but little historical insight to see that these discussions of the nature of Papal authority, of the character of the dogmas of the Medieval Church, of the ecclesiastical

---

[1] *Catalogi Testium Veritatis Auctorium*, Cattopoli, 1667, p. 100.
[2] Du Pin, *Opera Tria*, ii, 69.
[3] John Peter of Ferrara, *Practica*, 1410.
[4] Niem, *Schismate*, iii, c. 7–11.
[5] Matthew of Cracovia, *De squaloribus*, c. 3.
[6] Ib. c. 21–2 ; Ullerton, *Petitions* (1408), Hardt i, 1127 ; Zabarella, *De schism*, Niem, 537 ; Du Pin, *Opp. Gerson* ; ii, 114.
[7] Krüger, ii, 200.

constitution in all its varied ramifications, and of the many reforms needed during this period of division and confusion, went far to prepare the minds of the people of Latin Christendom for the gigantic problems of the ages ahead. The platform of the liberal party led directly to the Protestant revolt of the sixteenth century, and to the Counter-Reformation within the Roman Catholic Church. The programme of the conservative party, after a conflict of five hundred years, ended in the Act of 18th July, 1870, when the Vatican Council decreed that the Roman Pope possesses a full, regular, and direct authority over all churches and all believers. " Who claims to the contrary, let him be accursed." [1]

Another result of the Schism was the increase of the power of the cardinals. The geographical distribution of the cardinals is suggestive. Of the 162 cardinals between 1378 and 1417, two were English, three Hungarian, seventeen Spanish, fifty French and ninety Italians divided as follows: twenty-nine Neapolitans, sixteen Upper Italians, sixteen from the Papal States, fifteen Romans, seven Florentines, and seven Venetians.

When the two colleges seceded and called the Council of Pisa, they virtually usurped Papal power and transformed the Papal monarchy into an oligarchy whose authority increased until in the pontificate of John XXIII the cardinals enjoyed more power than at any time in their history.[2] For the first time, likewise, they enjoyed a regular division with the Pope of the entire income of the Church.[3]

---

[1] Souchon, ii, 116.   [2] Ib., iii.   [3] *Consilii Vaticani*, Sessio iv, cap. iii.

SOURCES

These lists of sources for the various chapters are intended to be helpful for further study and not exhaustive. For additional works the specialist will consult :—

BRATKE, *Wegweiser zur Quellen- und Literaturkunde der Kirchengeschichte.* Gotha, 1890.

POTTHAST, *Bibliotheca historica medii aevi.* 2nd ed., 2 vols., Berlin, 1896.

CHEVALIER, *Répertoire des sources historique du moyen age.* 4 vols., Paris, 1877–86.

GROSS, *The Sources and Literature of English History.* 2nd ed., New York, 1915.

DAHLMANN-WAITZ, *Quellenkunde der deutschen Geschichte.* 8th ed., Leipzig, 1912.

PAETOW, *Guide to the Study of Medieval History*, Berkeley, Cal., 1917.

The works listed under particular chapters will be found useful also for subjects treated in other chapters. For convenience a few titles have been duplicated but most of the sources have been given a single entry.

CHAPTER I

A. PRIMARY.

I. ENGLISH :

1. GEE and HARDY, *Documents Illustrative of English Church History.* New York, 1896.
2. HENDERSON, *Historical Documents of the Middle Ages.* London and New York, 1892.
3. OGG, *Source Book of Medieval History.* New York, 1908.
4. ROBINSON, *Readings in European History.* New York, 1904; vol. ii, ch. xvi.
5. THATCHER and MCNEAL, *A Source Book for Medieval History.* New York, 1905.
6. VILLANI, *Chronicle* ; translated by Selfe and edited by Wicksteed. Westminster, 1897.

II. FOREIGN LANGUAGES :

1. Dante, *Inferno*, xix, 52, xxvii, 85 ; *Paradiso*, ix, 132, xxvii, 22, xxx, 147.
2. DENIFLE, *Die Denkschriften der Colonna gegen Bonifaz VIII*, in *Archiv. für Lit. und Kirchengeschichte des M.A.*, 1892 ; v, 493.
3. DIGARD, FAUÇON, and THOMAS, *Les Registres de Boniface VIII*, 7 sections. ⁾Paris, 1884–1918.
4. Döllinger, *Beiträge zur politischen, kirchlichen, und Culturgeschichte der letzen 6 Jahrhunderten.* Vienna, 1862–82. Vol. II gives the Chronicle of Orvieto and other documents.
5. FINKE, *Aus den Tagen Bonifaz VIII*, Münster, 1902 : contains many very important documents ; *Acta Aragonensia*, 2 vols., Berlin, 1908 : gives portions of the diplomatic correspondence of Jayme II (1291–1327).
6. HEFELE-HERGENRÖTHER, *Conciliengeschichte*, 9 vols. Freiburg, 1873–90.
7. HEMINGBURGH, *Chronicon*, 2 vols. London, 1848.
8. MANSI, *Sacrorum Conciliorum Nova et Amplissima Collectio*, 31 vols. Florence, 1759–98. New edition. 47 vols. Paris, 1900 ff.
9. MIRBT, *Quellen zur Geschichte des Papsttums.* 4th ed., 1924.

10. MURATORI, *Rerum Italicarum Scriptores.* Milan, 1723–51. Contains the writings of Bernardus Ptolemaeus, Amalricus, Ferretus, and Villani—all valuable sources for the period of Boniface VIII.

11. POTTHAST, *Regesta Pontificum.* 2 vols. Berlin, 1873. Gives the Regesta of Boniface VIII ; *Bibliotheca.* Berlin, 1896.

12. *Rolls Series,* 210 vols. London, 1858–96.

13. RYMER, *Foedera.* London, 1704–15.

14. ZECK, *De recuperatione Terrae Sanctae : Ein Tractat der P. Dubois.* Berlin, 1906.

B. SECONDARY.

I. *ENGLISH :*

1. CAMPBELL, " Causes of the Failure of the Papal Assumption or Boniface VIII." In *Presbyterian and Reformed Review,* July, 1893, 429.

2. CREIGHTON, *History of the Papacy,* 6 vols. London, 1897, Vol. I, ch. 1.

3. GREGOROVIUS, *History of the City of Rome in the Middle Ages.* 13 vols. London, 1894–1902, V.

4. GRISAR, *History of Rome and the Popes in the Middle Ages.* London, 1911 ff.

5. PASTOR, *History of the Popes.* Tr. 12 vols. London, 1908–32.

6. SCHAFF, D., *The Middle Ages,* part ii, of vol. v of Philip Schaff's *History of the Christian Church.* New York, 1910. Chap. i, § 2, is an excellent discussion of the period of Boniface VIII.

7. WISEMAN, " Pope Boniface VIII," in his *Essays,* iii, 161–222.

II. *FOREIGN LANGUAGES :*

1. BAILLET, *Histoire des désmelez du Pape Boniface VIII, avec Philip le Bel.* Paris, 1718.

2. BAUMGARTEN, *Untersuchungen und Urkunden über die Camera Collegii Cardinalium für die Zeit, 1295-1437.* Leipzig, 1898.

3. BOUTARIC, *La France sous Philip le Bel.* Paris, 1861.

4. CHRISTOPHE, *Histoire de la Papauté pendant le XIVᵉ siècle,* 3 vols. Paris 1853. Ger. tr.

5. CHANTREL, *Boniface VIII et son temps.* Paris, 1862.

6. DÖLLINGER, *Anagni* in *Akad. Vorträge,* iii, 223–244.

7. DÖLLINGER-FRIEDRICH, *Das Papsttum.* Munich, 1892.

8. DRUMANN, *Geschichte Bonifacius VIII,* 2 vols. Königsburg, 1852.

9. DUPUY, *Histoire du différend d'entre le Pape Boniface VIII et Philippe le Bel.* Paris, 1655.

10. FINKE, *Aus den Tagen Bonifaz VIII.* Münster, 1902 ; *Papsttum und Untergang des Templerordens,* 2 vols. Münster, 1907.

11. HALLER, *Papsttum und Kirchenreform.* Berlin, 1903.

12. HOLTZMANN, *Wilhelm von Nogaret.* Freiburg, 1898.

13. JORRY, *Histoire du pape Boniface VIII* (1217–1303). Plancy, 1850.

14. LOSERTH, *Geschichte des späteren Mittelalters.* Munich, 1903.

15. MOHLER, *Die Kardinäle Jacob und Peter Calonna.* Paderborn, 1914.

16. PICOT, Georges, *Histoire des Etats génèraux,* 2 ed. Paris, 1888.

17. RENAN, " Guilliam de Nogaret," in *Hist. Litt. de France,* xxvii, 233.

18. RUBEUS, *Boniface VIII e familia Cajetanorum.* Rome, 1651.

19. SCHOLZ, *Die Publizistik zur Zeit Philipps des Schönen und Bonifaz VIII.* Stuttgart, 1903.

20. SOUCHON, *Die Papstwahlen von Bonifaz VIII bis auf Urban VI und die Entstehung des Schismas, 1378.* Braunschweig, 1888.

21. TOSTI, *Storia di Bonif. VIII,* 2 vols. Rome, 1846.

22. WATTENBACH, *Geschichte des Römisches Papstthums.* Berlin, 1876, 211.

CHAPTER II

A. PRIMARY.

I. ENGLISH :

1. DANTE, *Divine Comedy*. Many translations ; the best by Cary, 1814 ; Pollock, 1854 ; Longfellow, 1867 ; Norton, 1891, and Tozer, 1904. *On Monarchy*. Several translations ; the best by Church and Wicksteed. *Vita Nuova* in good translations by Rossetti and Norton
2. *Dispute between a Priest and a Soldier*. London, 1540. Attributed by the translator to William Occam.
Note.—Translations of the other important tracts of this period have not yet appeared in English.

II. FOREIGN LANGUAGES :

1. *De jurisdictione, auctoritate et praeeminentia imperiali.* Basel, 1856. Gives anti-Papal tracts of Dante, Valla, and others.
2. GOLDAST, *Monarchia S. Romani imperii, sive tractatus de jurisdictione imperiali seu regia et pontificia seu sacerdotali,* etc. Hanover, 1610. Contains many of the pamphlets of these controversialists.

B. SECONDARY.

I. ENGLISH :

1. See Chapter I.
2. POOLE, *Illustrations of the History of Medieval Thought.* London, 1884.
3. SCHAFF, *History of the Christian Church*, V, ii, § 5, has the best account of this controversy in English.

II. FOREIGN LANGUAGES :

1. DENIFLE and CHATELAIN, *Chartularium Universitatis Parisiensis,* 4 vols. Paris, 1889–97. The statutes come down to 1452.
2. FINKE, *Aus den Tagen Bonifaz VIII* 159.
3. GRAUERT, "Aus der kirchenpolitischen Traktatenliteratur des 14. Jahrhundertes," in *Hist. Jahrbuch,* 29.
4. HALLER, *Papsttum und Kirchenreform,* Berlin, 1903.
5. HOEFLER, *Rückblicke an Papst Bonifacius VIII und die Litteratur seiner Geschichte.* Munich, 1843.
6. RENAN, " Pierre Dubois," in *Hist. Litt. de France,* xxvi, 471.
7. RIEZLER, *Die literarischen Widersacher der Päpste zur Zeit Ludwig des Baiers.* Leipzig, 1874, 131–55.
8. SCHOLZ, *Unbekannte kirchenpolitische Streitschriften aus der Zeit Ludwigs des Bayern.* Rome, 1912.

CHAPTER III

A. PRIMARY.

I. ENGLISH :

1. BLISS, *Calendar of Entries in the Papal Registries relating to Great Britain and Ireland,* i–iv.
2. FROISSART, *Chronicles.* Translations by Berners, 1525, and Johnes, 1805.
3. GEE and HARDY, *Documents Illustrative of English Church History.*
4. MARSIGLIUS OF PADUA, *The Defence of Peace.* Translated by Marshall. London, 1535.
5. OGG, *Source-Book of Medieval History.* Contains a few documents of the Babylonian period of indirect value.
6. ROBINSON, *Petrarch,* New York, 1898. Contains a number of typical letters. *Readings in European History,* i, 502, gives valuable documents on the Popes at Avignon.

7. SELFE and WICKSTEED, *Selections from Villani*, Westminster, 1897
8. THATCHER and McNEAL, *A Source Book for Medieval History*.
9. USK, *Chronicle*. Translated by Thompson, 2nd ed. London, 1904.

II. FOREIGN LANGUAGES :

1. COULON, *Lettres secrètes et curiales du pape Jean XXII relativ à la France*. Paris, 1900.
2. EHRLE, *Olivi : Sein Leben und seinen Schriften*, in *Archiv. für Lit. und Kirchengeschichte*, 1887, 409–540.
3. FIERUS, *Lettres de Benoit XII* (1334–42). Rome 1910.
4. FINKE, *Papsttum und Untergang des Templerordens*, vol. ii, contains unpublished Spanish documents.
5. GRANDJEAN, *Les Registres de Benoit XI*. *Paris*, 1883.
6. GUÉRARD, *Documents pontificeaux sur la Gascogne. Pontificat de Jean XXII*, 2 vols. Paris, 1897–1908.
7. MANSI, xxv, 368, 389.
8. MOLLAT, *Lettres communes de pape Jean XXII*, 3 vols. Paris, 1904–6.
9. RAYNALDUS, *Ad annum*, 1304 sq.
10. TANGL, *Die päpstlichen Regesta von Benedict XII–Gregor XI*. Innsbruck, 1898.

B. SECONDARY.

I. ENGLISH :

1. CAPES, *The English Church in the Fourteenth and Fifteenth Centuries*. London, 1900.
2. CREIGHTON, *History of the Papacy*, i, 33–61,
3. GREGOROVIUS, *History of the City of Rome in the Middle Ages*. VI.
4. JESSOPP, *The Coming of the Friars*, 5th ed. London, 1889.
5. KRUGER, *The Papacy*. N.Y., 1909.
6. LEA, *History of the Inquisition*, i, 242–304.
7. LOCKE, *Age of the Great Western Schism*. New York, 1896, 1–99.
8. PASTOR, *History of the Popes*.
9. SCHAFF, v, ii, 44–71.
10. STUBBS, *Constitutional History of England*.
11. SULLIVAN, *Marsiglius of Padua in Eng. Hist.*, Rev., 1905, 293.

II. FOREIGN LANGUAGES :

1. ASAL, *Die Wahl Johann XXII*. Berlin, 1909.
2. BALUZE, *Vitae paparum Avenoniensium*, 1305–94, 2 vols. Paris, 1693.
3. CHRISTOPHE, *Histoire de la Paupaté pendant le XIVe siècle*, 2 vols. Paris, 1853.
4. DÖLLINGER-FRIEDRICH, *Das Papsttum*. Munich, 1892.
5. EITEL, *Der Kirchenstaat unter Klemens V*. Berlin, 1906.
6. EHRLE, " Der Nachlass Clemens V " in *Archiv. für Lit. Kirchengh.*, v, 1–150.
7. FAUCON, *La libraire des papes d'Avignon*, 2 vols. Paris, 1786.
8. FUNKE, *Papst Benedict XI*. Münster, 1893.
9. HALLER, *Papsttum und Kirchenreform*. Berlin, 1903.
10. HILGERS, *Die päpstlichen Bibliothek in Avignon* (Stimmen aus M. Laach), 1900.
11. HÖFLER, *Die avignonesischen Päpste*. Vienna, 1871.
12. JACOB, *Studien über Papst Benedict XII* (1334–42). Berlin, 1910.
13. MOLLAT, *Jean XXII* (1316–34). Paris, 1910 ; *Les papes d'Avignon* (1305–78).
14. MÜLLER, *Der Kampf Ludwigs des Bayern mit der römischen Kurie*, 2 vols. Tübingen, 1879.
15. RIEZLER, *Die literarischen Widersacher der Päpste zur Zeit Ludwig des Bayers*. Leipzig, 1874.

16. SCHWAB, *J. Gerson*, Würzburg, 1858, 1–7.
17. SCHWALM, *Appellation der König Ludwigs des Baiern von 1324.* 1906.
18. VELARQUE, *Jean XXII sa vie et ses œuvres.* Paris, 1883.
19. WATTENBACH, *Röm. Papstthum*, 226–41.

CHAPTER IV

A. PRIMARY.

I. ENGLISH :

1. There are no sources of any value in English dealing with the financial system of the Avignon papacy.

II. FOREIGN LANGUAGES :

1. COULON, *Lettres secrètes et curiales du pape Jean XXII relativ à la France.* Paris, 1900.
2. *Flores Hist.*
3. GÖLLER, *Die Einnahmen der Apostolischen Kammer unter Johann XXII.* Paderborn, 1910. Part II contains the sources and part I, the explanations. This work is Vol. I of *Vatikanische Quellen zur Gesch. der Päpstlichen Hof- und Finanzverwaltung,* 1316–78 ; *Inventarium instrumentorum camerae apostolici* in *Röm. Quartalsch.*, 23.
4. HOFFMAN, *Der Geldhandel der deutschen Juden.* Leipzig, 1910.
5. MERIMUTH, ed. by Thompson (Rolls Ser.) 1899.
6. MÜNTZ, " L'argent et le luxe à la cour pontificale d'Avignon " in *Rev. des quest. hist.*, lxvi, 5–44, 378–406.
7. MURATORI, *Rerum Italicorum scriptores*, 25 vols. Milan, 1723–51. New ed. by Carducci, Cittá di Castello, 1900 ff.
8. TANGL, *Die päpstlichen Regesta von Benedict XII–Gregor XI,* Innsbruck, 1898.

B. SECONDARY.

I. ENGLISH :

1. CREIGHTON, *History of the Papacy*, i, ch. 2. Not much material on the financial system.
2. GASGUET, *Henry the Third and the Church.* London, 1905.
3. LEA, *History of the Inquisition.* Contains many isolated cases of financial practices and abuses scattered through the three volumes.
4. LUNT, " The Financial System of the Medieval Papacy " in *Jour. of Economics*, xxiii, 251 ; " The first Levy of Papal Annates," *Am. Hist. Rev.*, xviii, 48.
5. LYLE, *The Office of an English Bishop.* Philadelphia, 1903.
6. MILMAN, *History of Latin Christianity*, vi, bk. 12. A good general survey, but superceded by later studies, with comments here and there on fiscal matters.
7. PASTOR, *History of the Popes*, i, bk. 1. Gives some information on the methods of raising funds.
8. SCHAFF, *History of the Christian Church*, v, pt. 2, § 9. The best account in English of the Avignon financial policy. Gives an excellent bibliography.

II. FOREIGN LANGUAGES :

1. BAUMGARTEN, *Untersuchungen und Urkunden über die Camera Colegii Cardinalium 1295–1437.* Leipzig, 1898. *Aus Kanzlei und Kammer*, Freiburg, 1907
2. EHRLE, " Schatz Bibliothek und Archiv der Päpste im 14ten Jahrhundert," in *Archiv. für Lit. und Kirchengesch.*, i, 1–49, 228–365 ; "Der Nachlass Clemens V. und der in Betreff desselben von Johann XXII. geführte Process," in ib., v, 1–166.

3. GÖLLER, *Mittheilungen und Untersuchungen über das päpstl. Register und Kanzleiwesen im 14ten Jahrhunderte.* Stuttgart, 1903 ; *Das Liber Taxarun der päpstl. Kammer.* Rome, 1905, 105 ; *Zu Geschichte der päpstlichen Finanzverwaltung unter Johann XXII,* in *Röm. Quartelschr.,* 15 ; *Die päpstlichen Reservationen und ihre Bedeutung für die kirchle Rechtsentwicklung des ausgehend en M.A.,* in *Internat. Wochensch.,* 1910.

4. GOTTLOB, *Die päpstl. Kreuzzugssteuren des 13ten Jahrhunderts.* Heiligenstadt, 1892. *Die Servitientaxe im 13ten Jahrhunderte.* Stuttgart, 1903.

5. HALLER, *Papsttum und Kirchenreform,* Berlin, 1903. " Aufzeichnungen über den päpstl. Haushalt aus Avignoneischer Zeit" ; "Die Verteilung der Servitia minuta und die Obliogationen der Prelaten im 13ten und 14ten. Jahrhundert " ; " Die Ausfertigung der Provisionen," etc., all in *Quellen und Forschungen* edited by the Royal Prussian Institute in Rome, 1897, 1898, etc.

6. HENNIG, *Päpstliche Zehnten aus Deutschland in Zeitalter des avignon. Papsttums und während des grossen Schismas.* Halle, 1909. Thesis.

7. JORDAN, *De mercatoribus camerae apostolicae saecle XIII.* Rennes, 1909.

8. KIRSCH, *Die päpstlichen Kollektorien in Deutschland während des XIVten Jahrhunderts,* Paderborn, 1894 ; *Die Finanzverwaltung des Kardinalkollegiums im XIII und XIVten Jahrhundert,* Münster, 1896 ; *Die Rückkehr der Päpaste Urban V und Gregor XI,* Paderborn, 1898 ; *Die päpstlichen Annaten in Deutschland im XIV. Jahrhundert,* 1323–60, Paderborn, 1903 ; " L'administration des finances pontificales au XIVe siècle," in *Revue d'hist. eccl.,* i ; " Die Verwaltung der Annaten unter Clemens VI," in *Röm. Quartalsch,* 16

9. KÖNIG, *Die päpstlichen Kammer unter Clemens V und Johann XXII.* Wien, 1894.

10. KOTHE, *Kirchle Zustände Strassburgs im 14ten Jahrhunderts.* Freiburg, 1902.

11. LUX, *Constitutionum apostolicarum der generali beneficiorum reservatione, 1265–1378.* Wratislav, 1904 ; *Die Besetzung der Benefizien in der Breslauer Diözese durch die Päpste von Avignon, 1305–78.* Breslau, 1906.

12. MAYDORN, *Der Peterspfennig in Schliesen bis in Mitte des 15 Jahrhunderts (Z. d. f. G. u. Altert.* Schlesiens, 17).

13. " Prozess gegen Bischof und Domkapitel von Würxburg an der päpst-Kurie im 14 Jahrhundert," in *Röm. Quartalsch,* 21.

14. SAMARIN and MOLLAT, *La Fiscalité pontif. en France au XIVe siècle,* Paris, 1905.

15. SAUERLAND, *Vatikanische Urkunden und Regesten zur Geschichte Lothringens.* Bonn, 1902–7.

16. SCHNEIDER, *Die finanziellen Beziehungen der Blorentine Bankiers zur Kirche von 1285–1304.* Leipzig, 1899.

17. SCHOLZ, *Die Rückker.*

18. SCHULTE, *Geschichte des mittelalterlichen Handels,* 2 vols. Leipzig, 1900 ; *Die Fugger in Rome, 1495–1523,* 2 vols. Leipzig, 1904.

19. TANGL, *Das Taxenwesen der päpstlichen Kanzlei vom 13ten bis zur Mitte des 15ten Jahrhunderts,* Innsbruck, 1892.

20. THOMAN, *Le droit de propriété des laïques sur les églises et le patronat laïque au moyan âge.* Paris, 1906.

21. *Vatikanischen Quellen zur Geschichte der päpstlichen Hof- und Finanzwaltung, 1316–78,* Bd. III. Paderborn, 1912.

22. WOKER, *Das Kirchliche Finanzwesender Päpste.* Nördligen, 1878.

CHAPTERS V–VI

A. PRIMARY.

See Chapter IV.

SCHÄFER, *Die Ausgaben der Apostolischen Kammer unter Johann XXII, Nebst den Jahresbilanzen von* 1316–75, Paderborn, 1911. This work is vol. ii of *Vatikanische Quellen zur Geschichte der Papst, Hof- und Finanzwaltung,*1316–78, published by the Görrer Gesellschaft. This is incomparably the best account of the expenditures of the Avignon Papacy and is based entirely upon the documents preserved in the Vatican Library.

CHAPTER VII

A. PRIMARY.

I. ENGLISH :

1. MARSIGLIO of PADUA, *The Defence of Peace*. Translated by Marshall. London, 1535. Emerton's Translation. Cambridge, 1920.

II. FOREIGN LANGUAGES :

1. GOLDAST, *Monarchia romani imperii*. Hannover, 1611–13.
2. *Göttingische gelehrte Anzeigen*, 1883, 923–5, gives an unprinted last chapter of *Defensor Pacis*, by Müller.
3. KONRAD VON MEGENBERG, *Planctus ecclesie in Germania*, by Labbé Paris, 1653 ; *De translatione imperii*, in Höfler, *Aus Avignon*, 24.
4. LUPOLD VON BEBENBURG, *De jure et imperii Romani*, edited by Wimpheling, 1508, and Schardies, 1566. Other works edited by Böhmer, *Fontes*, i.
5. NICOLAUS MINORITA, " De controversia paupertatis Christi," in Baluze, *Miscellanea*, 3, and Böhmer, *Fontes*, 4.
6. OTTENTHAL, *Regulae calcellariae apostolicae*, Innsbruck, 1888.
7. SCHWALM, *Die Appellation König Ludwigs des Baiern von 1324*. Weimar, 1906.
8. WADDING, *Annales Minorum*, vols. 7 and 8. Rome, 1733.

B. SECONDARY.

I. ENGLISH :

1. CREIGHTON, i, 40–41.
2. GARDNER, *Saint Catherine of Siena*, London, 1907.
3. GREGOROVIUS, vi, pt. i, pp. 1–356.
4. KERR, *The History of the Popes from the Close of the Middle Ages*. St. Louis, 1898–1912.
5. LINDSAY, " Occam and his connection with the Reformation," in *Brit. Quart. Rev.*, July, 1872.
6. LITTLE, "Grey Friars ", *Eng. Hist. Rev.*, vi, 747.
7. LÜTZOW, *The Life and Time of Master John Huss*, London and New York, 1905–9, has an excellent summary of the *Defensor pacis*.
8. POOLE, *Wycliffe and Movements for Reform*, 22–42. London, 1896.
9. SCHAFF, v, pt. i, pp. 29–106.
10. SULLIVAN, *Am. Hist. Rev.*, 1896–7, ii, 409, 593 ; *Eng. Hist. Rev.*, Apr., 1905.

II. FOREIGN LANGUAGES :

1. GRAUERT, *Dante und die Idee des Weltfriedens*. Munchen, 1909.
2. JOURDAN, *Etude sur Marsile de Padoue*. Montauban, 1892.
3. LABANCA, *Marsilio da Padova*. Padova, 1882, 235.
4. RIEZLER, *Die literarischen Widersacher der Päpste zur Zeit Ludwig des Baiers*. Leipzig, 1874.

CHAPTER VIII

A. PRIMARY.

I. ENGLISH :

1. A few scattered sources are given in the source-books : Henderson, Ogg, Gee and Hardy, Thatcher and McNeal.

II. FOREIGN LANGUAGES :

1. BALLAGUET, *Chronique du religieux de St. Denys*, 6 vols. Paris, 1839–52. First series of *Col. de doc. inédit.*
2. BLIEMETZRIEDER, *Literarische Polemik zu Beginn des grossen abenländischen Schismas*, Wien and Leipzig, 1909. Gives the texts of Peter Flandrin and Peter Amelii, both cardinals.
3. BULAEUS, *Hist. Univ. Parisiensis*, 6 vols. Paris, 1665–73, vol. iv gives the documents for this period.
4. " Calendar of entries in the papal registers relating to Great Britain and Ireland," *Papal Letters*, i–iv (1198–1404), ed. by Bliss, London, 1893 ; *Petitions to Popes*, i (1342–1404), ed. by Bliss, London, 1896.
5. EHRLE, *Martin de Alpartils' chronica Actitatorum temporaribus domini Benedicti XIII.* Paderborn, 1906. An intimate account of Benedict's court. Many letters and documents—a rich mine of new material.
6. ERLER, *Der liber concilloriae apostolicae und der atilus palatii abbreviatus Dietrich von Nieheim.* Leipzig, 1888.
7. GEIGEL, " Gebrechen und Reformen in Frauenkloster Prediger Ordens zu Rothenburg o. d. Tauber, 1350–1406," in *Beiträge zur Bayerisch Kirchengeschichte*, xiii–xiv, 1907–8, 49–83, 205–26. Has many German sources printed for the first time.
8. MARTIN DE ALPARTILS, *Chronica actitatorum temporibus Domini Benedict XIII*, ed. by Ehrle. Paderborn, 1906, vol. i.
9. MURIMUTH, *Continuatio chronicarum*, ed. by Thompson (Rolls Series). London, 1889.
10. RAYNALDUS, *Annales eccles.*, give the original documents.
11. THEODORICK OF NIEM, *De Schismate inter papas et antipapas.* Basel, 1566, ed. by Erler, Leipzig, 1890. Held office under three Roman Popes and was papal secretary under Gregory XI.
12. USK, *Chronicle*, translated by Thompson. London, 1904.
13. VAN DER HARDT, *Magnum oecumenicum Constantiense Concilium de universali ecclesiae reformatione, unione et fide*, 6 vols. Frankfurt and Leipzig, 1696–1700. A monumental work with many documents and tracts.
14. WICLIF, *Works.* (Latin) 31 vols. London, 1884–1907. (English) *Three Treatises*, ed. by Todd, Dublin, 1851 ; *Select English Works* ed. Arnold, 3 vols. Oxford, 1869–71 ; *English Works Hitherto Unprinted*, ed. Matthew, London, 1880 ; *Bible*, ed. Forshall and Madden, 4 vols., Oxford, 1850 ; *New Testament.* ed. Skeat, Cambridge, 1879.

B. SECONDARY.

I. ENGLISH :

1. BRUCE, *The Age of Schism.* New York, 1907.
2. CREIGHTON, *History of the Papacy*, i, ch. i.
3. KITTS, *In the Days of the Councils.* London, 1908.
4. LOCKE, *Age of the Great Western Schism.* New York, 1896.
5. MANNING, *The People's Faith in the Time of Wicliffe*, Cambridge, 1919.
6. MILMAN, *History of Latin Christianity.*
7. PASTOR, *History of the Popes*, i.
8. SALEMBIER, *The Great Western Schism*, tr. London, 1907.

9. SCHAFF, v, pt. ii, § 12–15.
10. TAYLOR, *The Mediaeval Mind*, 2 vols., 1911.
11. VAN DYKE, *Age of the Renascence.* New York, 1897.
12. WORKMAN, *Christian Thoughts to the Reformation*, New York, 1916.

II. FOREIGN LANGUAGES :
1. BAYAT, " Un traité inconnu sur le grand Schisme " in *Rev. d'hist. eccles.* Oct. 1908.
2. DUPUY, *Histoire générale du schisme.* Paris, 1700. A general treatise without references to authorities.
3. EHLEN, *Das Schisma im Metzer Sprenge.* Leipzig, 1909
4. EHRLE, " Neue Materialen zur Geschichte Peters von Luna," 1892. in *Arch. für. Lit. und Kirchengesch.*, vi, 139–302 ; vii, 1–652, Gives many hitherto unprinted sources.
5. GAYET, *Le grand schisme d'Occident.* Florence and Berlin, 1889.
6. GÖLLER, *König Sigismund's Kirchenpolitik vom Tode Bonifaz IX bis zur Berufung der Konstanzer Concils.* Freiburg, 1902. " Zur Geschichte des Kirchlichen Benefizialwesens unter päpstlichen Kanzleiregeln unter Benedict XIII von Avignon," in *Archiv. für kath. Kirchengeschichte*, vol. 87, 1907, 203.
7. JANSEN, *Papst Boniface IX und sein Beziehungen zur deutsche Kirche.* Freiburg, 1904.
8. JEPP, *Gerson, Wiclefus, Hussus inter se et cum reformationibus comparati.* Göttingen, 1857. A work of 84 pages with ample references to sources.
9. KEHRMANN, *Frankreichs innere Kirchenpolitik von der Wahle Clemens VII und dem Beginn des grossen Schismas bis zum Pisaner Konzil und zur Wahl Alexanders V 1378–1409.* Jena, 1890. Doctor's thesis with rather doubtful conclusions.
10. KNEER, *Die Entstehung der Konzilien Theorie zur Geschichte des Schismas und der Kirchenpolitischen Schriftsteller Konrad von Gelnhausen* (d. 1390) *und Hinrich von Langenstein.* Rome, 1893. Contains two of Langenstein's tracts.
11. MAIMBOURG, *Histoire de grand schisme d'Occident.* Paris, 1678.
12. MIROT, *La politique pontificale et le retour du Saint-Siège à Rome en 1376.* Paris, 1899.
13. PFLEGER, "Ludolf von Sochren über die Kirchlichen Züstande des 14. Jahrhundert," in *Hist. Jahrb.*, 29.
14. RASTOUL, *L'unité religieuse pendant le grand schisme d'Occident.* Paris, 1904.
15. SCHEUFFGEN, *Beiträge zu der Geschichte des grosses Schismas*, Freiburg, 1889. Gives writings in German translation of Langenstein, Gelnhausen, Matthias of Cracow and Zabarella.
16. SOUCHON, *Die Papstwahlen in der Zeit des grossen Schismas*, 2 vols. Braunschweig, 1898–1899. Vol. I covers the period from 1378–1408, Vol. II, 1408–1418. Gives the election oaths.
17. THUDICHUM, *Papsttum und Reformation im Mittelalter*, 1143–1517.
18. TREVELYAN, *England in the Age of Wycliffe*, London, 1912.
19. VALOIS, *La France et le grand schisme d'Occident*, 4 vols. Paris, 1896–1901.

CHAPTERS IX–X

See Chapter VIII.

CHAPTER XI

A. PRIMARY.

II. FOREIGN LANGUAGES :
1. *Bibliothèque de l'école des chartes*, vol. lxv, 1904, 557–74. Sources on d'Ailly.

2. BLIEMETZRIEDER, *Literarische Polemik zu Beginn des grossen abenländischen Schismas.* Vienna, 1909.
3. *De difficultate reformationis,* and *Monits de necessitate,* in Du Pin, ii, 867, 960, credited to Ailly ; *De reformatione* and *De ecclesiae concil. generalis,* in Du Pin, ii, 903, 925, also ascribed to Ailly.
4. DENIFLE AND CHATELAIN, *Chatularium Universitatis Parisiensis.* Paris, 1894. Vol. III gives documents relating to Peter d'Ailly.
5. DU PIN, *Gersoniana,* 5 vols. Antwerp, 1706.
6. ELLIES DU PIN, published many of the writings of Ailly and Gerson at Antwerp, 1706.
7. GELNHAUSEN, " Epistola brevis " by Kaiser in *Hist. Vtjschr.,* **3** ; " Epistola concordiae, 1380 ", by Martène in *Thesaurus,* vol. iii.
8. LANGENSTEIN, *Consilium pacis,* in Hardt II, 1–60, and in Du Pin, ii, 809–39.
9. MATTHAEUS DE CRACOVIA, *De squaloribus Romanae curiae,* in Walsh, i.
10. NICHOLAS OF CLEMANGES, *De ruina ecclesiae,* given in Hardt, i, pt. 3, pp. 7–52.
11. PETER DE ALLIACO (AILLY), *De difficultate reformationis in concilio universali,* given in Hardt I, 6 ; *Canones reformationis ecclesiae in Constantiensis concilio suscipiendae,* ib., pt. 8.
12. SCHEUFFGEN, *Beiträge zur Geschichte des grossen Schismas,* 1889.
13. WATTENBACH, *Deutschlands Geschichtsquellen in Mittelalter.* 7th ed. Stuttgart, 1904.

B. SECONDARY.

I. ENGLISH :

1. BRUCE, *The Age of Schism,* 1304–1503. London, 1907.
2. CONNOLLY, *John Gerson,* 1927.
3. CREIGHTON.
4. KITTS, *In the Days of the Councils.* London, 1908.
5. L'ENFANT, *History of the Council of Pisa,* 2 vols. London, 1780.
6. PASTOR.
7. SCHAFF, v, ii, ch. 3–4.

II. FOREIGN LANGUAGES :

1. BLIEMETZRIEDER, *Konrad von Gelnhausen und Heinrich von Langenstein auf dem Konzile zu Pisa* 1409, *Hist. Jahresb.,* 25 ; *Das Generalkonzil im grossen abendländischen Schisma,* Paderborn, 1904 ; " Die wahre Bedeutung Konrads von Gelnhause," in *Stud. und Mitt. a. d. Bened. u. Cist.-Orden,* 28 ; " Über die Konzils bewegung," in ibid., 31.
2. ERLER, *Dietrich von Nieheim.* Leipzig, 1887.
3. FRANKE, *Matthäus von Krakau.* Griefswald, 1910.
4. FRIEDBERG, *Die mittelalterlichen Lehren über das Verhältnis von Staat und Kirche.* Leipzig, 1874.
5. HALLER, *Papsttum und Kirchenreform.* Berlin, 1903.
6. HARTWIG, *Henricus de Langenstein dictus Hassia.* Marburg, 1857.
7. KNEER, *Die Entstehung der Konzilaren Theorie zur Geschichte des Schismas.* Rome, 1893.
8. MULDER, *Dietrich von Nieheim,* 2 vols. Amsterdam, 1907.
9. SALEMBIER, *Petrus de Alliaco.* Lille, 1886.
10. SCHEUFFGEN, *Beiträge zur Geschichte des grossen Schismas.* Freiburg, 1887.
11. SCHMIDT, *Nicolaus Cusanus.* Coblenz, 1907.
12. SCHWAB, *Johannes Gerson.* Würzburg, 1858.
13. TSCHACKERT, *Peter von Ailli.* Gotha, 1877.
14. VALOIS, *La France et le grand schisme d'Occident,* 4 vols. Paris, 1896–1902 ; *La crise religieuse du XVe Siècle,* 2 vols. Paris, 1909.
15. WENCK, " Konrad von Gelnhausen und die Quellen der konziliaren Theorie," in *Hist. Zeitschr.,* 76.